London Churches

& Olde Celebrities

Vol. I: The City - A Compleat Guide and Perambulation

John Blythe Smart

Published by Blythe Smart Publications in 2012

A CIP catalogue record for this book is available from the British Library.

ISBN: 978 - 0 - 9545017 - 6 - 1

Cover, Type: Blythe Smart Publications
Printers: Berforts Group Ltd.

Blythe Smart Publications
Kingsbridge - England

Contents

London Environs (see Volume II)

About the Author

John Smart was born at Farnborough, Kent in 1960 and educated at Alleyn's School in South London and Nottingham University. His main academic interests were historical geography and the history of architecture.

In addition his forebears included E.G. Blythe and E.H. Niemann, 19th century artists, and Colin Blythe the famous cricketer leading to a further interest in matters historical. Consequently, he undertook genealogical study at home and abroad over many years, as well as indulging in local history research.

His family supported Millwall F.C. from the 1920s and it was this sporting experience which provided the initial inspiration for a writing career. After visiting most historic football grounds located in Britain, he determined to write about them and researched soccer history, and thus became interested in the lives and genealogies of the founders. The result was *The Wow Factor - How Soccer Evolved* with two editions in 2003-05, whilst as a diversion he wrote an historical allegory *The Wizards of Wight*.

More recently he published a seminal work on the first F.A. president, *Arthur Pember's Great Adventures*, a biography of the Victorian polymorph and undercover reporter over two continents. This was followed by a concise version *The Founders of Soccer* revealing the founders were connected to every aspect of British history.

His most recent work *The Real Colin Blythe* provided a detailed biography of the Kent and England spin-bowler, re-examining his origins and other related historical issues. The latter three books were published during the period 2007-09.

Introduction

The *Church-scape of London* exhibits multiple facets - social, political, economic and ecclesiastical being intricately entwined with the history of the burgeoning city. Only by understanding and exploring the development of the Metropolis can one appreciate how its churches came to be built, why they were located where positioned, and how the lottery of time selected some for survival whilst neglecting others.

But that was not all, since in the broader sense a church was not simply the fabric of the building but a communion of people in a social gathering, one that moulded the history of the city and ultimately the whole nation. The churches of London, Westminster and the Suburbs were not just cloistered in their own universes, but were breeding grounds for the most famous people connected to this Island's intellectual growth.

Initially the churches reflected the aspirations of leading individuals and religious men with God at the centre, but from the 17th century many were speculative with opulent stucco façades housing pew renting clients. Later developments were the politics of the Fifty Churches, great revivals under Wesley and Whitefield, and the Oxford Movement which took the Christian faith to the deprived of the city and beyond.

Forces such as these moulded the skyline and nations around the globe whilst fire and war were events which irrevocably altered mankind's best intentions. Indeed the decline of religion, juxtaposed with financial consumerism and profits, saw the Heaven aspiring vistas of Canaletto replaced by the grey, drab towers of modern times.

What factors, then, determined the evolution of the church horizon? In the period after the Great Fire much debate ensued regarding rebuilding with favouritism being muted. Then in the early 1700s ambitions of architects came to the fore, as locals clamoured for funds to build new churches on their patch. Despite this Hawksmoor complained that in every other country no expense was spared on *their* churches.

Some of the edifices by Wren and his contemporaries remain the finest architecture in the capital utilising materials, methods and aspirations of those times. Times that some would say had a greater purity and spirituality in society, as revealed by these religious icons built within such harsh environments. Elsewhere are links to the Freemasons and regarding our modern thinking, hidden symbols within the architecture.

These churches soared above London in glowing white stone with corporate buildings of equal merit, bringing forth the Classical and Gothic worlds of antiquity to the grimy city streets. However, in *Victorian Times* idiosyncratic restoration, demolition and other short-sighted objectives left just "a plaque on a wall." And today many are oppressed by futuristic office complexes jarring against their traditional merits.

Meanwhile, all is not negative or lost. On exploring the alleys and streets of London a hidden secret is soon revealed! Despite many changes, ones that have accelerated over the last sixty years, much of the old street pattern remains and hidden away are countless gems, protected by patrons and admirers working tirelessly for their cause. In addition listed status protects such heritage - always assuming it is not "re-classified."

Many books have been written about church architecture in London covering every buttress, quoin and cornice. Thus the aim here is to give a summary of the main points combined with a detailed analysis of famous celebrities patronising their halls.

In some cases there are many as seen in Marylebone. Men and women who forged a nation, painted grandiose art, scripted verbose literature and raised scientific vocation to a new level, whilst providing much theatrical amusement along the way.

Several surprises lay in store, as the book winds its way through the ancient streets to open the church doors, revealing a congregation of genius looking back at us through time. What would they make of the modern city landscape we can only wonder? What of the recent changes wiping out a millennium? Will the modern buildings be admired and cherished like those of old? But such questions apart, there is a fascinating heritage of parishioners who excelled in every field of endeavour - as shall be shown.

One self important successor to Whittington who twice held office stated, "London is the metropolis of England; England is the greatest country in the world, and I am the Lord Mayor of London." Such was the importance of the city that many travelled there hoping to achieve both fame and fortune. Meanwhile, the input of population from the countryside and war-divided Continent meant that growth was exponential, and although some resided in opulent mansions many remained in pestilent slums.

In fact as early as 1601, Stow talked of the sad loss of fields near the perimeter, "where inhabitants might recreate and refresh their dull spirits in the sweet and wholesome air." Regarding such inhabitants, "How did an innocent baptism bring forth a person now so acclaimed?" And in the style of Wren we must look around us for their monument.

John Stow's Survey

The most significant person regarding our knowledge of the main city is John Stow, the son of Thomas a tallow chandler, who was born at St. Michael's, Cornhill in c.1525. His father was quite poor paying just 6s 6d rent a year thus John fetched milk each morning from a farm in the Minories. However he improved himself as a merchant taylor in 1547 with some premises near to Aldgate between Leadenhall and Fenchurch Streets.

He first became involved in historical work in 1560 joining the Society of Antiquaries and received patronage from Archbishop Matthew Parker, but was also acquainted with William Camden and published the works of Chaucer the next year and *A Summarie of Englyshe Chronicles* in 1565. Many reprints followed, however he was involved in a bitter dispute with Richard Grafton about infringement of his work.

Indeed, all was not plain-seaming and his house was searched in 1568 since he was said to have many superstitious books on his shelves, including those in defence of papistry. Ultimately he was cleared of any charges although the issue never failed to leave him, and he moved house to nearby St. Andrew's parish in the 1570s.

Another valuable work by him was the *Annales or Chronicles of England* in 1580, again with reprints, but the most significant was his *Survey of London* with minute accounts of great detail and amusing anecdotes. Much of this provides the only trustworthy record of churches and other locations long since departed from us.

This Elizabethan classic was published in 1598 with a second edition in 1603 and was followed by several amended reprints by other authors, in particular Anthony Munday the playwright (1618, 33) and John Strype (in 1720). Stow transcribed many manuscripts and inscriptions for the survey and also wrote biographies of Matthew of Westminster, Matthew Paris and Thomas Walsingham to name but a few.

In later life he was on the verge of poverty and petitioned James I, noting that for 45 years he worked on the *Chronicles of England* and for 8 years on his *Survey of London and Westminster* and without other income asked for recompense regarding his services to the country. His prayer was granted by letters patent under the Great Seal stating that he had neglected his ordinary maintenance for the general good and compiled divers books, thus it was the Royal inclination "to allow him to collect gratuities from our subjects." However, the expected donations were not forthcoming and one parish gave just 7s 6d, whereas the period of collection had to be extended by a year.

Stow did not benefit from his labours but was venerated for his work and met with others such as Jonson, and has a grand monument at St. Andrew Undershaft erected by his wife Elizabeth in 1605. His meticulous survey of churches and other buildings was done from first hand knowledge, and portrayed a mediaeval London of stone and timber soon to be transformed beyond recognition by the Great Fire.

Pepys' Diary and Wren

An era of change was underway with the Stuarts on the throne, advances in science and literature, an expansion of trade under the East India Company and the influence of new Renaissance architecture. The classical styles of Palladio were in vogue and Inigo Jones and Wren utilized these in Britain in both civil and ecclesiastical architecture.

Christopher Wren was born at East Knoyle, Wiltshire in 1632 son of the vicar and was educated at Westminster and Wadham College, Oxford. He was appointed professor of astronomy at Gresham College in 1657 and helped initiate the Royal Society in 1660 with other members John Evelyn and Robert Hooke. After becoming Savilian professor of astronomy at Oxford he spent much of the 1660s amongst the dreaming spires.

Wren was skilled in mathematics and a gentleman architect thus his uncle the Bishop of Ely engaged him to design a new chapel for Pembroke, Cambridge and he worked on the Sheldonian Theatre, Oxford from 1663. On a visit to Paris he saw continental architecture and as the plague ravaged the city, he was employed to design a new St. Paul's.

There had been turbulent times under Oliver Cromwell but three months after Wren submitted plans for a new cathedral, London itself was destroyed by fire. This major conflagration was recorded in the diaries of John Evelyn of Deptford (who made money in gunpowder) and wrote from 1641-1706, and of Samuel Pepys of the Navy Office who recorded from Seething Lane in the years 1660-69:

2 September 1666 (The Lord's Day) - "So down, with my heart full of trouble, to the Lieutenant of the Tower, who tells me that it began this morning in the King's bakers house in Pudding Lane, and that it has burned down St. Magnes church and most part of Fish Street already. So I down to the waterside and there got a boat and went through the bridge, and there saw a lamentable fire."

3 September - "The servants were preparing a feast and called me down at three in the morning. My wife and I nor any others slept all this night and we rose again at 7, but then, and all this day, she and I and all my people are labouring to get away the rest of our things. Once loaded they were taken by lighter from Tower Dock and there I saw a poor crowd going over Tower Hill with all their possessions."

4 September - "The fire continued raging and I went with Sir William Penn to see the fire which had reached Trinity House, and saw the blowing up of houses in Tower Street to try and stop it. W. Hewer my clerk in the Navy Office went up to see his sick mother in Islington and said that Pye Corner was burned, and the fire reached the Old Bayly and went down to Flete Street. In addition Paul's is burned and all of Cheapside, and I wrote a letter for my father but the post house being likewise burned it could not go.

This afternoon sitting melancholy with Sir William Penn in our garden and discussed the almost certain burning of his office, so I wrote to Sir W. Coventry for the Duke of York's permission to pull down some houses rather than lose this office - which would much hinder the King's business." [Admiral Penn was father of the founder].

5 September - "At two in the morning there were cryes of 'fire,' it coming to Barkeing church at the bottom of our lane. But going to the fire I find that by the blowing up of houses, and the great help given by the workmen out of the King's Yard, sent by Sir William Penn, there is a good stop given to it and that in nearby Marke Lane.

It had only burned the dyall of Barkeing church and part of the porch, and was there quenched. So I up to the top of the steeple and there saw the saddest sight of desolation that I ever saw. But I became afeared to stay there long and therefore down again as fast as I would, the fire being spread as far as I could see it, and to Sir William Penn for a piece of cold meat - having eaten nothing since Sunday but remains.

Then walking in the city I observed Cheapside and Newgate markets were all burnt, whilst Fenchurch, Gracious and Lombard Streets are all in dust, and the poor wretches from there and all their belongings are camped out in Moorefields."

6 September - "There were new fires at Bishopsgate and amongst the clothworkers, some of which I feare were perhaps begun deliberately."

7 September - "I was up by 5 o'clock and blessed by God find all is well with us and went by water to Paul's Wharfe. I walked thence and saw that all the town was burned, and the miserable sight of Paul's Church with all the roofs fallen down and the body of the Quire fallen into St. Fayth's beneath it."

8 September - "Up and with Sir W. Batten and Sir William Penn by water down to Whitehall and they went on towards St. James's. I later saw Sir G. Carteret and Sir W. Coventry in the chambers at St. James's, while that day our goods previously removed to Deptford for safety were brought back to us."

In fact, the cause of the fire which began at the premises of Thomas Farynor the King's bakers in Pudding Lane remained unclear and theories included a Catholic plot, divine retribution for the burning of a Dutch town, and a Biblical act respecting gluttony within the city. Initially Pepys like many other Londoners was preoccupied with rebuilding his own life, and with this underway turned his attention to the causality of the fire:

24 February 1667 - "I asked Sir R. Viner about the cause of the fire. The baker, his son and daughter, all swear the oven was down by 10 o'clock at night. A candle was lit at 12 o'clock and no fire was seen in the bakehouse, not even enough of one to light a match, so they had to go elsewhere to light it.

At two in the morning they were choked with smoke, although the barns were not on fire in the yard. There is absolute ignorance as to the cause which is a strange thing, that so horrid an effect should have so mean and uncertain a beginning. By and by called in to the King and Cabinet and there had a few insipid words about money for Tangier, but to no purpose. Caught a boat at Whitehall and so home to supper, then talked with Hewer about business and so to my journal and to bed."

5 April - "Then home to the office and busy late, and then to Sir W. Batten where Mr. Young was talking about the building of the City again; and he told me that those few churches that are to be new-built are plainly not chosen with regard to the convenience of the City, they stand a great many in a cluster about Cornhill. All of them are either in the gift of the Lord Archbishop, Bishop of London, Lord Chancellor or the gift of the City! Thus all things, even to the building of churches, are done in this world." [1]

The former entry emphasises an apparent ignorance regarding the cause of the fire, although the baker may have just covered himself, and he was no doubt quite relieved when there was talk of a foreign plot or visitation. The plague itself had killed one-sixth of the population but fortunately the fire resulted in few deaths, yet whether there was any conspiracy is generally difficult to ascertain.

The disaster destroyed 13,000 houses, St. Paul's cathedral, 87 churches, the Bridewell and three western gates, burning out at Pye Corner, Smithfield; but in some ways was opportune as it rid the city of unsanitary housing and slums which harboured the plague. In addition it provided the basis for new ideas, new architecture and safer materials, albeit against a reticence to do away with the old alleys and byways.

In fact Wren was already on his way from Oxford with plans for a new cathedral and piazzas loaded up in his arms. He was then appointed surveyor of works to Charles II in 1669 and was involved in the rebuilding of 51 churches and the cathedral (1673-1711), although the construction of housing and livery halls was independent of him. Despite any higher aims, the old street pattern was retained, and the returning parishioners used temporary buildings until their new churches were completed.

Wren was knighted in 1673 and made an M.P. in the 1680s, while some of the most important architects of the day worked within his office. He married on two occasions and his son Christopher joined him as an architect, whereas he was employed on other major projects including Chelsea Hospital, Whitehall Palace, Hampton Court, Kensington Palace, Greenwich Hospital, Marlborough House and Westminster Abbey. However, he is best remembered for his prodigious ecclesiastical contributions to London.

Regarding the City there was a definitive history determined by its walls, but beyond was a more piecemeal picture with development over several centuries. The second area of growth was Thorney Island an area of marshland by rivulets of the Ty Bourne. Here Mellitus may have established the first abbey in the 7th century, whilst St. Dunstan and King Edgar installed Benedictine monks there in the later 10th century.

---

[1] In 1665 there were 109 churches - 84 were destroyed, 3 heavily damaged, and 2 partially. After lengthy debate 35 were suppressed in 1670 however of those not rebuilt Woolchurch, Querne and St. Gabriel's were required for street widening and market improvements, while many were minor establishments covering just a few acres. Thus Cornhill was not actually favoured.

This became the site for Westminster Abbey and the seat of Government while the Strand, linking the former to the City, was occupied by Lundenwic - a Saxon settlement with its "five churches." Indeed a large number of palaces, inns' of court, opulent houses and ecclesiastical institutions were developed, with the mansions of wealthy courtiers and bishoprics located between the Strand and river near to Whitehall Palace.

After the Great Fire there was a period of regeneration, "a boom economy," spreading from the centre to the outlying areas. This saw extensive development of sites that were virgin territory, development which dictated the city's layout up until the present day. It was the start of two hundred years of speculative growth with large fortunes to be made, swallowing up areas once familiar as fields, market gardens and country lanes.

For instance: To the north of Whitehall there was a Royal hunting park used by Henry VIII and named Soho Fields (from a hunting cry). Henry Jermyn, 1st Earl of St. Albans developed this in the 1660s and the land went to the Earl of Portland. Likewise Robert Sidney, 2nd Earl of Leicester built Leicester House by 1635, the area being developed in the 1670s with Leicester Fields (later Square) just to the south.

However by the early 18th century the gentry intended for this locale left and French immigrants and others occupied an ever-increasing density of housing. Bloomsbury was granted to Thomas Wriothesley, 1st Earl of Southampton by Henry VIII and the square was built by a descendant in the 1660s - but the area to the north arrived later.

Meanwhile, the parish of St. Margaret's, Westminster covered a large area reaching up as far as Marylebone and out of it emerged St. James, Piccadilly and St. John, Smith Square. The area of St. James's above The Mall was developed by Jermyn at this time and had a central square surrounded by aristocratic housing. To the north of Piccadilly a *may fair* took place in the area of Shepherd's Market which continued until about 1764.

Mayfair was developed in the mid-17th century and Berkeley House owned by Lord Berkeley, Lord Lieutenant of Ireland was one of three great mansions in Piccadilly at the time. It was replaced by Devonshire House to a design of William Kent with Berkeley Square behind in the early 18th century. To the north, Sir Richard Grosvenor son of Sir Thomas and Mary Davies appointed Thomas Barlow to develop "The Hundred Acres." This led to a grid of streets including Grosvenor and Hanover Squares by the 1730s, but regarding ecclesiastical London the main developments came under Queen Anne.

Commission for Building "50 New Churches"

The Declaration of Indulgence in 1672 aimed to give more rights to Nonconformists by lifting legal restraints, but it was only after the Act of Toleration in 1689 that they could worship more freely. The result was a spread of dissenters into the outer environs.

After a Tory victory in 1710, church-reform headed its agenda due to infidelity and bad press, and a Commission was set up by Parliament in 1711 to build Anglican churches for the growing city. But these "Queen Anne Churches" fell well short of their target.

And the reason for this deficiency was clear. It was relatively easy to build a meeting house and Nonconformists were estimated to have taken over a quarter of the suburbs, but the Anglican structure meant they only built new chapels for well-to-do pew renters, and Swift stated, "five in six could not hear divine service!" This was particularly true in London where one or two curates had the care of literally thousands of souls.

Immediately it was set up the hard pressed parishes and clergy clamoured for funds and the Commissioners were inundated with petitions. William Bromley the speaker and his High Anglican Tories did not know what they had started.

Initially Greenwich asked for money from the coal dues allocated to St. Paul's followed by a wave of petitions from metropolitan parishes - including Deptford with the steeple falling down, St. George's Southwark and Shoreditch in a ruinous state, and St. Alphage's and St. Botolph's Bishopsgate both "propped up." Defoe provided a rather poignant description in the 1720s detailing this rapid expansion of the city:

"All that vast mass from Blackwall over to Tothill and new buildings past Hanover Square and Hyde Park up to Marylebone and Acton Road, and how much farther it may spread who knows? Nothing in the world does or ever did equal it except for Trajan's Rome."

Parochial returns then exposed the serious nature of the situation: St. Giles Cripplegate included 4,600 houses, Holborn 3,785, St. Clement Danes 1,690, Shoreditch 2,278 and Clerkenwell 1,619 - many parishes without churches or inadequately supplied. Whereas Stepney had a particular problem, since Spitalfields had 20,000 inhabitants and Wapping 18,000. The best Government actuaries were put on the case and a bill was passed to impose an additional duty on coals brought into the Port of London.

Such a scheme had raised £265,000 for the Wren churches in 1667-88 and 3s per ton could provide £50,000 for the proposed churches, with the increased consumption since that time. Such a levy was then being used for St. Paul's, Westminster and Greenwich Hospital and the excess generated should have been sufficient for fifty churches.

But the remit was to provide architecture more costly than even for the Wren churches. All of this using stone, top materials, grand steeples and a whole host of Commissioners to decide on sites etc. with salaries to match - therefore the expenses spiralled!

Archbishop Tenison initially headed the Queen Anne Commission, but only went to one meeting and his role was taken by John Robinson, Bishop of Bristol. In fact, there were innumerable prominent members including many bishops, Henry Godolphin dean of St. Paul's, T. Sherlock master of the Temple and senior Tories including the Earl of Dartmouth secretary of state, W. Bromley the speaker and Robert Benson the chancellor. To these were added businessmen like Sir Gilbert Heathcote a Whig mayor, Sir Richard Hoare and Sir John Cass aldermen M.P.s, and from the Queen's Works: Sir Christopher Wren surveyor, John Vanbrugh comptroller and Christopher Wren jun. chief clerk.

Anyone in a committee will know how hard it is to reach common ground or even to understand other perplexing viewpoints, but there were further lawyers, M.P.s, various philanthropists, and additional architects such as Hawksmoor, Gibbs, William Dickinson and Thomas Archer the Tory courtier. So it seems the organisation was quite unwieldy from the very start and this may have hampered its ultimate achievements.

The early meetings were held at the Banqueting House, Whitehall with Thomas Rous as secretary and John Skeat as agent and solicitor (with Simon Beckley). There was also an official messenger and doorkeeper while the treasurer Henry Smith arrived a year later. At the outset the surveyors were Nicholas Hawksmoor and William Dickinson, but it was enlarged the next year and then included George Stanhope dean of Canterbury and vicar of Deptford and Lewisham, Lord Rochester a cousin of the Queen and the Royal physician John Arbuthnot to name but a few.

There were many inherent difficulties regarding the selection of sites and division of parishes before they even considered issues of design. In particular there were arguments over the Limehouse location and the parish of St. John's, Clerkenwell which saw great opposition, it being the Aylesbury Family Chapel. These debates often involved money and who would have to pay for the upkeep or otherwise issues of access.

Regarding design: Wren pointed to his church St. James's, Piccadilly as a good example of size, with room for a maximum of 2,000 catering for poorer residents. But Vanbrugh influenced by Hawksmoor had grander notions than this and postulated the posterity of Queen Anne - that they should be a monument to her munificence.

It was at this juncture that Hawksmoor, concerned about parsimony, noted, "In history most nations have put their churches first, no expense being thought too much. They should be features in the town and adorned with porticoes and towers." The Queen Anne Commission sat from 1711-15 and the nature of its progress was revealed in the minute books, whereas the initial aims were set down at Lambeth in the first year:

(1) To enquire which parishes needed a new church (2) What chapels can be converted (3) What limits should be set for the parishes (4) What sites should be selected (5) What land or property had to be purchased to achieve this - The answer to be placed in writing before Her Majesty and Parliament by the 24 December following.

The first meeting was duly held at the Banqueting House on 3 October 1711 and much time was spent deliberating. Initially it was decided that St. George's, Holborn should be a parish church, there should be five new churches in Stepney, the chapel of the E.I.C. at Poplar was to become a parish, and Deptford should also have a new church.

A map of London and Environs was provided by the secretary, discussions were begun with Lady Russell re Bloomsbury part of St. Giles, the Dean and Chapter of Westminster offered a site near the Abbey, and the inhabitants of St. Mary le Strand petitioned for a church. Wren, Vanbrugh and Archer were to view the sites which included Holborn (3), Aldgate (2), St. Sepulchre (2), St. Giles, St. James's and St. Martin's (all 4), Southwark (2), Shoreditch (2), Whitechapel (2), Westminster (2) and one in several other parishes.

Some more definite plans were made in November for Aldgate, Bow, Bethnal Green, Limehouse, Lower and Upper Wapping, and Spitalfields; and St. Giles in the Fields was to have a church at Lincoln's Inn Square but without churchyard or rings of bells. Other discussions involved the King Street Chapel in St. James's, the land of the Bishop of Ely at Holborn, Horsleydown, Rotherhithe, the Stockwell Liberty and St. Giles Cripplegate. At the end of the year a break was taken and they met again in June 1712 to discuss plans for Greenwich, whilst a public meeting was arranged at Somerset House.

Initially it was decided there would be one model for the churches and meetings took place at St. Clement Danes and Doctors' Commons, but they then had permanent offices at 6 Lincoln's Inn and at Old Palace Yard when Parliament sat. The sites at Old Street and Spitalfields were considered in 1713, and in November "Gibbs was elected surveyor in room of Dickinson," also ahead of the other applicant John James. [2]

---

[2] Gibbs was a pupil of Wren and travelled to Italy with patronage from Robert Harley and was surveyor to the Dean and Chapter of Westminster; while James was an assistant to Hawksmoor at Greenwich and the carpentry contractor on four of the churches.

There was to have been a statue of Queen Anne in every church but instead a pillar was scheduled west of the maypole in the Strand, and there was much discussion over which architect was to design each edifice - although most work eventually fell to Hawksmoor. Due to the rising costs it was determined in 1715 (last meeting on 1 September) that no church was to be commenced without "a plan, model and estimate."

The King George Commission

Queen Anne died on 1 August 1714 and was buried in Westminster Abbey which had a major impact on the work of the Commissioners, since it witnessed the end of the Stuart dynasty. George I of Hanover in the Holy Roman Empire was dubiously installed as the closest Protestant heir - despite several far better Jacobite claims to the throne.[3]

Britain was something of a renegade state failing to follow the rules of succession, and the Tories who opposed this went out of power - thus the Whigs came to dominance for the next fifty years. At the same time Walpole became First Lord of the Treasury and Chancellor in 1715, and took control of the purse strings to try and reduce the national debt (a rather familiar story). Indeed these were very different times and not the best of climates for funding large public projects such as church building.

Consequently, as the Queen Anne Commission closed its affairs just seven churches of the fifty were underway: Greenwich was almost finished, Deptford and Millbank were being roofed, the Strand had a lower storey, Spitalfields and Upper Wapping were being raised and Limehouse was just started. The cost of each church was about £15-20,000 and on that basis the outlay for fifty would come to twice the original budget.

The new Commission met with Hawksmoor and James as surveyors on 5 January 1716, but it was clear that 50-churches could never be completed and the search for sites was abandoned. There were stricter controls on planning and costing, and the coal tax was extended eight years. Indeed, after some strong objections to "church repairs," the only such funding went to St. Michael's Cornhill and St. Giles in the Fields.

The rebuilding of St. Martin's and several others was stopped, and by 1719 only two further churches were begun: St. Mary Woolnoth provided out of the St. Paul's money and Bloomsbury where the site was previously obtained. In a similar way they went ahead with St. George's Hanover Square (part of St. Martin's) in 1720, but this was a local initiative on donated land and to the designs of James their own surveyor.

---

[3] James II had daughters Mary and Anne by Anne Hyde, and a son James F.E. Stuart a Catholic heir at St. James's Palace by Mary of Modena from Italy. He abdicated and went to France in 1688 and Mary who married her cousin William of Orange a Protestant came to the throne, the matter being settled decisively at the Battle of the Boyne in 1690.

The Act of Settlement was passed in 1701 and prohibited Catholics from inheriting the throne while the son James Stuart was recognised by France, Spain, the Papal States and Modena. Anne became the Queen in 1702 and England and Scotland were joined by the Act of Union while she also held the spurious title, the Queen of France.

The Tories came to power in 1710 under Robert Harley, Earl of Oxford; while Robert Walpole a Whig on the council of the Lord High Admiral, H.R.H. Prince George of Denmark (husband of Queen Anne) was removed from his senior positions.

At the same time money from the coal tax was diverted elsewhere by the Government which forced the Commission to raise money from a loan. Several plans were put on hold including St. Olave's and St. Giles Cripplegate, the services of Archer at Deptford were dispensed with and Gibbs provided more economical estimates for the Strand.

Clearly these were difficult times and payments to contractors were often made a year in arrears. Such difficulties were exacerbated when the South Sea Company was formed, purportedly to trade in South America, although it mainly served as a repository for Government debt and in this way remunerated its investors with dividends.

However there was a general boom and bust in stocks promoted by its activities and when the bubble burst in 1720 many were ruined. It was up to Walpole to sort it out and estates of directors were confiscated, M.P.s like John Aislabie removed, and the stocks divided between the Bank of England and East India Company. The overriding aim was to restore confidence and Walpole became *de facto* Prime Minister by 1721.

Regarding the Commissioners they were also in a better position by the next year with their debts cleared, thus building continued apace. By 1726 they had worked on twelve churches however they had spent nearly £250,000 and only three were completed. As a result it looked likely not more than half could be built, but there were still many large parishes and in June 1727 they approved Old Street and Horsleydown - although these were to be constructed in a more economical fashion.

This was almost the last act and in 1732 with only £10,000 left in the building fund the officers salaries were cut in half. There was an allocation to rebuild Woolwich, Gravesend and St. George's Southwark in 1733, but with twelve churches finished the officers and surveyors were dismissed, and the next year the buildings at Lincoln's Inn and Old Palace Yard were given up. The Commissioners met occasionally until 1749 but the financial affairs of the project were wound up in 1758.

Churches Built by the Commissioners

Thomas Archer
St. Paul's Deptford 1713-30 and St. John Smith Square 1713-28

Nicholas Hawksmoor
Christchurch Spitalfields 1714-29, St George in the East 1714-29, St. Anne's Limehouse 1714-30, St Mary Woolnoth (rebuilt) 1716-24, St. George's Bloomsbury 1716-31

James Gibbs
St. Mary le Strand 1714-23

John James
St George's Hanover Square 1720-25

Hawksmoor and James
St. Alphege's Greenwich 1712-18, St. John Horsleydown 1727-33,
St. Luke's Old Street 1727-33

Also funded St. George's Gravesend, St. George's Southwark, St. Giles in the Fields, St. Mary's Woolwich and St. Michael's Cornhill (the tower only); whilst bought and altered St. George the Martyr at Holborn and purchased St. John's Clerkenwell.

The Freemasons: After the fire John Evelyn and Christopher Wren proposed plans to rebuild the City with wide avenues, although strictly speaking there was a grid dating back to Roman times. A cursory glance over Wren's outline suggests two compasses side by side and perhaps the influence of the Freemasons and their perfect forms?

Regarding this, John Aubrey a founder of the Royal Society published *A History of Wiltshire* with some handwritten notes about masonry in the margin. When B.G. Cramer their secretary prepared the book he included an entry agreed on by the two men and by Wren: "This day being Monday 18th May 1691 after Rogation Sunday there is a great convention at St. Paul's church of the fraternity of the Adopted Masons, where Sir Christopher Wren is to be adopted a brother with divers others."

At this time there were four lodges in London which joined to form the Grand Lodge with new premises at Great Queen Street in 1717 (see later). The fact that architects were masons does not seem improbable given their line of work, but it is strange how the fraternity developed as compared to other guilds and liveries in London. Both Nicholas Hawksmoor (at Ludgate) and John James (at Greenwich) were masons, but rather than anything more sinister this seems to have been strictly business related.

Hawksmoor trained under Wren and worked with him from 1684-1700 having several senior positions at Christ's Hospital, Kensington Palace and St. Paul's, and was surveyor for Greenwich Hospital where he worked with James. It was during his time assisting Sir John Vanbrugh at Blenheim and Castle Howard that he perhaps developed his grander ideas of design - his five churches clearly standing out from the others.

Sir James Thornhill a member of the ancient Painter Stainers guild decorated interiors with large scale compositions and worked on the painted hall at Greenwich Hospital, the St. Paul's cupola and the great hall at Blenheim. Indeed he was lodge master at Greenwich and Grand Master in the 1720s, whereas his son-in-law William Hogarth was introduced to the movement and lampooned them in print but was actually Grand Steward in 1735. So how did such factors eventually affect architectural design?

Hawksmoor's five churches are distinctive in the extreme and much has been written about their Masonic influences. In fact, both the much venerated St. Mary Woolnoth and St. George's Bloomsbury are based upon a perfect cube. All of those in the East End are monolithic in composition sporting grandiose towers, layer upon layer, with notable five tier arrangements and pyramids visible at several locations.

There are also suggestions they are laid out geographically, in geometric fashion, but given the number of people involved it seems unlikely there was any such intrigue. The aspirations of Hawksmoor may have come in part from the Freemasons ideals; but his Baroque theatrical statements are a testament to his ambition and training, architectural compositions of the classical school bringing Palladian style to the London scene.

Talman's Bronze: The Commission wanted to show their appreciation of Queen Anne by putting a statue in every church, but this proved financially unviable and by April 1714 they settled on a podium statue to the west of St. Mary le Strand instead.

At this time they contacted John Talman, the antiquary, in Italy and asked him to send one statue of the Queen in metal plus the price. For that purpose they furnished a medal of the Queen and a print. They then received a letter back in July saying he would provide the statue at £340, with the remittance to be forwarded to Leghorn.

This was all confirmed in March 1715 when £351 10s was advanced to Sir Edward Gould so he could send it to Florence for the brass statue. However in May it was noted "the Queen's statue at £800" and to remit the remainder at £50 per month.

The next development came in May 1717 when the secretary inquired about how much was remitted to Talman? The latter attended in person saying he spent £340 at Florence but further questions were asked of Smith and Gould, as to how a later sum of £460 was accounted for. The matter was apparently never resolved and whether there was any impropriety is unclear. Maps dating from that time show a statue in front of St. Paul's cathedral, but only a watch house in the Strand. [4]

John Strype and John Rocque

Winston Churchill stated, "The farther backward you can look, the farther forward you are likely to see." Such antithesis is clearly relevant here, as the sources for the book are an integral part of the story, not just a slightly tedious section at the rear.

With regard to this John Strype was born at Houndsditch on 1 November 1643 the son of John a Huguenot whose family came from Brabant. The father was a silk throwster and merchant at Petticoat Lane, whilst the son attended St. Paul's and Jesus, Cambridge then was curate of Theydon Bois by 1669. Soon afterwards he took on a similar position at Leyton and was a lecturer there and at Hackney from 1689.

He then corresponded with Sir William Hicks, Archbishop Wake and several bishops to obtain material to produce historical manuscripts regarding the Protestant Reformation. The outcome was the production of several biographies including Archbishop Thomas Cranmer, (Life of) the Learned Sir Thomas Smith, John Aylmer Bishop of London and ones to Archbishops Grindal, Parker and Whitgift during 1710-18.

His style was very reminiscent of Stow's writings and it was decidedly in that direction that he went. In fact, like Elijah's mantle there was no shortage of chroniclers to take on the work. The first of these Anthony Munday, "the City poet," was suspected of spying in Rome but produced volumes of poetry and plays, and claimed Stow had personally delivered manuscripts to him. He then published an updated survey in 1618, and a more sprawling edition in conjunction with Humphrey Dyson a playwright in 1633.

This was utilised by several hopeful amanuenses to supplement their own work, thus James Howell produced *Londinopolis* in 1657 and Thomas de Launes wrote *The Present State of London* in 1681. Richard Blome a prominent cartographer and bookseller began a new edition of Stow in 1694 with improvements and maps which never came to fruition. So he resurrected the project with one of its writers, namely John Strype, in 1702.

The latter was an accomplished editor and the new survey was ready in November 1707. But booksellers would not take it since Edward Hatton's *New View of London*, a slimmer more popular work, came out at the same time. However, the need for a revised work remained pressing and Strype set to work with his colleagues again in 1716. A second hugely expanded version therefore appeared in December 1720.

---

[4] The Queen Anne Statue in front of St. Paul's was sculpted by Francis Bird in 1712 but went to Holmhurst, Sussex and was replaced with a replica by R. Belt in 1886. There is another statue of the Royal personage also of stone secreted in a niche at Queen Anne's Gate.

A Survey of the Cities of London and Westminster

Written at first in the Year MDXCVIII
By JOHN STOW, citizen and native of London
Since Reprinted and Augmented by the AUTHOR
And afterwards by A.M. H.D. and others NOW LASTLY
Corrected, Improved, and very much enlarged: And the SURVEY & HISTORY brought down from the Year 1633 (being near Fourscore Years since it was last printed) to the present time: By JOHN STRYPE M.A. a Native also of the said CITY. - In SIX BOOKS

This was more scholarly than the work of Hatton with new research, maps and plates, and found its niche in the market. The volumes then depicted the late Stuart capital as it emerged into the Hanoverian era. Some 500-700 copies were printed for 271 subscribers but the price remained prohibitive at six guineas a copy.

Also, the book harboured some omissions. In the first instance there were no updates on "church beautifying" since the Munday editions and little was added after 1708, while some of the guilds and suburbs were skimmed over as were sports and pastimes.

Its overriding aim was to preserve Stow and in some cases the use of the original text was confusing, but Strype remains the main source in this period. Indeed, the publishers complained he was supplying late material and exceeded his limit by 80 sheets! He also produced *Ecclesiastical Memorials* in 1721 and the Oxford Press reissued his work, whilst he received the sinecure of West Tarring, Sussex from Archbishop Tenison. Later on he resided at Hackney with his granddaughter and was buried at Leyton in 1737.

As the reign of George I came to an end the King was courted by the all powerful Sir Robert Walpole, but greatly criticised by writers such as Lady Mary Wortley Montagu. He was thought too German by some but his son George II, the last monarch born outside of England, came to the throne in 1727. His coronation at Westminster included some new anthems which were on commission from the composer Handel.

The Georgian era, meanwhile, retained the architecture of the Renaissance but with a return to traditional values. At the outset this was dictated by the *Five Orders* of Vitruvius a 1st century Roman architect with strict rules of design, proportion, entablature, window spacing, and heights of storeys. The dictates had been found by chance in a monastic library during the 16th century, and were promoted by Andrea Palladio who produced a vital treatise on how to build in the Classical or Roman fashion.

Inigo Jones studied architecture in Italy and initiated the movement in Britain with the Queen's House at Greenwich, and the classical order then dominated British architecture for the next 250 years. This included the accentuated Baroque of Wren, Hawksmoor and their associates. It was a style utilised in many public buildings, churches, and Jacobean mansions of the time coupled with rococo designs for the interiors.

However, in the 18th century the taste was for purer forms therefore architects looked beyond Roman imperialistic design to ancient Greece, as exemplified by Robert Adam's work at Kenwood, Syon House and the Adelphi by the Strand. Other proponents were Roger Morris architect of Marble Hill, Twickenham and 3rd Earl of Burlington admired by [Horace] Walpole and given the epithet "A modern Vitruvius" by Defoe.

Indeed, the Palladian era was epitomised in the new squares of Bloomsbury, Mayfair and St. James's, and Frederick, Prince of Wales who held court at Leicester House was a patron of the arts, architecture and music. As such he was often seen at Spring Gardens that pleasure palace of firework theatricals in Lambeth by the Thames.

Meanwhile, London had greatly changed since Pepys' day when grand-houses clothed London Bridge and ubiquitous watermen plied their trade. The first new bridge was built at Fulham in 1729 after Walpole was delayed from reaching the Commons by an absent ferryman. Others were planned soon after with a petition for one at Westminster backed by several interested parties - despite any inherent costs to the boatmen.

The new landscape was documented by cartographers like John Speed who with help from Camden produced a *Historie of Great Britaine* and county maps in 1611, but it was his successor John Rocque who detailed changes in the capital. He came to England as a Huguenot refugee in 1704 (aged one) and then worked with his brother Bartholomew a landscape gardener - thereby being introduced to mapmaking and surveying.

Taking premises at Great Windmill Street and Hyde Park Row from 1736 he then did numerous estate plans: Claremont, Painshill, Wilton House, Kew, Syon and Chiswick as well as town plans of Bath, Exeter and Shrewsbury and the Royal houses. At the same time he began working on *A Map of London, Westminster and Southwark* in 1737 which appeared in 16 and 24 sheets in 1746. It was the most detailed of its time. The surveying was done principally from his own office, whilst the publishers included John Pine the engraver in Piccadilly and John Tinney in Fleet Street.

However, the extent of London remained limited as shown on his map. In the east it spread along the docks, up the Mile End Road, and out to Shoreditch and Spitalfields. To the north it ended just beyond Old Street, but included Clerkenwell and Holborn. Bedford and Montagu Houses lay beyond Bloomsbury Square below Lamb's Conduit Fields and the open road to Hampstead - likewise St. Giles was near to the countryside. The area of Drury Lane, the Strand and Soho was well built up down to St. James's, but there was little north of Oxford Street except for Cavendish Square. Marylebone also remained as a rural village surrounded by some pretty gardens.

To the west Grosvenor Square was developed however nearby Berkeley Square was still empty, and south of Hyde Park there were continuous fields with Buckingham House, a large inlet of water and an open road leading to Chelsea College. Westminster was also limited and went no further than Petty France, St. Margaret's chapel, Dacre almshouses and the Bluecoats. To the south were Tothill Fields (later Pimlico) and St. John's Smith Square, a horseferry to Lambeth, Grosvenor House on Millbank and little else besides. Nearby were St. Peter's Abbey, the Hall and the remains of Whitehall.

St. Martin in the Fields still had a churchyard adjacent (later part of Trafalgar Square and the National Gallery), while south of the river there was far less development mainly centred on Southwark due to the bridge. Property then continued down Borough High Street, Bermondsey Street and on past some docks towards Rotherhithe.

The area of Christchurch, Blackfriars Road was still loosely developed with housing and Lambeth Palace was by a small hamlet, as Westminster Bridge was under construction. The whole area was covered with fields and market gardens and Deptford, Greenwich and Camberwell (village) did not even appear on the map. However, this all changed quite dramatically as the century progressed.

Meanwhile, Rocque took premises at Charing Cross in 1750 but moved to the Strand after a fire and married Mary A. Bew the next year. He was cartographer to the Prince of Wales and produced county maps and an atlas with ten assistants by 1753, then after a time at Buckingham and Southampton Streets moved to the Old Round Court behind St. Martin's (on Agar Street). He also spent time in Ireland and made plans of Dublin, but died back in London in 1762 and his widow continued the business until 1770. [5]

Hardwicke's Marriage Act

There were considerable changes to both landscape and society in the later 18th century and Westminster Bridge was completed in 1750, whereas two major upheavals resulted in a lasting impact on our understanding of time and social interaction.

For many centuries the Julian calendar introduced by Caesar was applied in Europe but this required too many adjustments (to keep Holy Days within their requisite limits), thus Pope Gregory VIII replaced it with the Gregorian calendar in 1582. Spain, Portugal, Polish Lithuania and Italy adopted it immediately but other Protestant countries resisted this and some only conformed as late as 1700.

In the Roman world New Year was celebrated on 1 January and the Catholics followed this tradition, but elsewhere Lady Day the Feast of the Annunciation on 25 March was used. In Britain both timings were applied and the Government used the latter for civil and legal purposes. The reason, contracts between landowners and tenant farmers usually began at the Equinox when the day and night were equal in length.

However Britain and its American colonies found they were out of step with the rest of Europe and implemented the *Calendar Act* in 1752, adopting the Gregorian calendar and moving the New Year to 1 January. A correction of eleven days occurred thus Wednesday 2 September was followed by Thursday 14 September, and Hogarth satirised the event in his prints. Although suggestions of riots with "give us our eleven days" were exaggerated. The tax year retained the old system of 5 April but adjusted to 6 April in 1800.

With regard to historical research and parish records the main effect was that any event falling on 1 January to 24 March needs to be double-dated (prior to 1753), since without this there is much confusion as to which year the day actually falls in.

There was a lot for the public to adjust to at the time and only a year later came *Lord Hardwicke's Marriage Act*. There had been considerable abuse of 'the right to marry' and places such as the Fleet Prison, the Knightsbridge Chapel and Mayfair Chapel were the scene of many a clandestine union. Despite the presence of church requirements, these were just dictates and were not embodied in the law. [6]

---

[5] Mary Ann Rocque was topographer to H.R.H. Duke of Gloucester and in particular produced plans of 30 forts in North America in 1763/65 including New York with Castle Clinton, Albany the state capital, Montreal and Quebec.

[6] Philip Yorke, 1st Earl of Hardwicke (1690-1764) trained as a lawyer in the Middle Temple then became M.P. for Lewes in 1719, and under the Duke of Newcastle was made a lord in 1733. As Lord Chief Justice he entered the Privy Council and was appointed Lord Chancellor in 1737 thus entering the Walpole ministry; but stepped down with Newcastle in 1756. In part he made his name in an equity case concerning Walpole and later resided at Wimpole Hall.

The Act "for the better preventing of clandestine marriages" came into force on 25 March 1754, under the Whig ministry of Henry and Thomas Pelham who were protégés of Walpole. It required formal ceremonies (not common law) also the consent of parents for those under 21, while the male had to be 14 and female 12. In addition there were banns or a licence that had to be solemnized in an Anglican church, the only exceptions to this being the Jewish and the Quaker faiths.

All Catholic forms of worship were banned from the time of James I and from 1754 there were no marriages in Nonconformist chapels, although baptisms and burials were still permitted. In fact the main recourse was to Scotland resulting in the emergence of the famous blacksmith's at Gretna Green. A lesser known option was Temple Church in Cornwall, an archaic survivor from the days of the Knights Templar. [7]

In general a licence was required from the Bishop, but some had a dispensation from the Archbishop to marry elsewhere and Catholics might marry in an embassy, whilst the minimum age was increased to 16 in 1763. The monopoly was only gradually changed and the Papists Act (1778) provided the first relief to legal restrictions, and the Catholic Relief Act (1791) permitted the more open exercise of their religion.

Regarding political development, there was stability under George III and the Whigs dominated the arena until the arrival of Lord North in 1770. They supported Hanoverian succession, the aristocracy and nonconformism - although with Fox and Sheridan called for justice in America and supported the French revolution in principal.

In fact, Lord Chatham (the senior Pitt) a member of the Whigs collapsed in the Lords after a speech on America, complaining the Crown had exceeded its powers. George III then tried to put a brave face forward after losing his American colonies in 1778-83, and Britain promptly looked to its new acquisitions in the Southern Oceans.

There was further improvement in trade and industrial innovation, but also the fear of civil unrest or revolution as seen in the Gordon Riots of 1780. However, William Pitt the younger and the Tories came to power in 1783-1806 supporting the gentry and Church of England. They provided a degree of security against the increasingly rebellious beliefs of the Whigs as characterised by Lord Byron and Devonshire House.

This witnessed the arrival of the Regency period with its leisurely pastimes and opulent architecture of the Prince of Wales at Carlton House in Pall Mall and Brighton Pavilion. Likewise, Marylebone was developed by the Duke of Portland, Bloomsbury (manor of William de Blemond) was extended by the Duke of Bedford, and Sloane Square (named after Sir Hans Sloane) was postulated by Henry Holland.

In addition all the mediaeval gates were demolished and the houses on London Bridge removed for widening in 1762. A number of bridges followed including: Blackfriars in 1768, two speculative ventures Battersea a toll crossing by Earl Spencer in 1776 and also Vauxhall in 1816; succeeded by the triumvirate of Waterloo (1817), Southwark (1819) and the New London Bridge (west of the old one) finally finished in 1831.

---

[7] The chapel was built by the Templars on Bodmin Moor for the use of pilgrims from Ireland to the Holy Land in the 12th century - travellers landed at Padstow estuary on the north coast and thereby avoided a more dangerous route via Land's End. It was possible to marry there without banns or a licence from the 16th century however it came under the Episcopal system in 1774. It was then in the parish of Blisland and became a ruin, but was rebuilt in 1883.

The three were designed by the canal engineer John Rennie although London Bridge was completed by his son after his death. All of these brought great changes and caused the realignment of roads and the demolition of several Wren churches.

Another significant change occurred when the Prince Regent employed John Nash to develop Marylebone Park from 1818. The latter was a director of the Regent's Canal Co. and the scheme involved extending the Grand Union past Paddington Basin. The link to Camden was constructed first with wharves at Cumberland Hay Market and City Road Basin, and it was then extended to Limehouse with the Lea Extension.

However, the most important contribution was regarding architecture as Nash built the impressive classical terraces by Regent's Park, and a grand avenue south to open up the West End. Regent Street thus separated Soho from adjacent squares with All Souls at the top and Carlton House below, whilst Charing Cross was cleared to create Trafalgar Square - much of this work by James Pennethorne and Decimus Burton.

The Waterloo Churches

With cultural developments in the capital and industrial prowess in the provinces there was every reason for optimism; always tempered, though, by the threat from abroad and unrest at home due to the inherent pressures of industrialisation. The defeat of Napoleon created great heroes in Lord Nelson and the Duke of Wellington, and there was further reform with the abolition of the slave trade, religious tolerance through the Unitarian Relief Act (1813) and also greater enfranchisement of the populace.

A century had passed since the Commission for Fifty Churches and the capital had grown again. Not only was there a renewed expansion of Nonconformist chapels but some believed they were a breeding ground for radical beliefs. Less concern was attached to Wesley and Whitefield, but far greater to those such as Robert Wedderburn *the black preacher* who was openly involved with the Spencean philanthropists.

As a result a meeting took place at the Freemasons Hall on 6 February 1818 chaired by Charles Manners-Sutton, Archbishop of Canterbury. The Duke of Northumberland then proposed a plan which after lobbying resulted in the *Church Building Act (1818)*, and this gave £1 million to the Commissioners to build the "Waterloo" or "Million Act Churches" around the whole country - in thanks for the previous victory.

A further £500,000 was pledged in 1824 when Austria repaid a war loan, however the remit was entirely different from the days of Hawksmoor. In general the directive was for cheap, imposing structures of brick and stone housing the largest numbers, but at the lowest expense - clearly not a recipe for architectural splendour.

Despite this some impressive edifices were built in the 1820s and prominent architects attracted, resulting in All Saints Camden, St. Mary Bryanston Square, St. Paul's Shadwell and St. Anne's Wandsworth. However, the new Lambeth churches named after the four Gospels had criteria not to exceed £13,000 and incorporated 1,800-2,000 seats.

During this period Robert Peel and the Duke of Wellington were prominent Tories in Parliament and Daniel O'Connell was elected as a Catholic, but could not sit. This led to a staged duel between Lord Winchilsea and Wellington at Battersea Fields in 1829, and with honour restored the *Catholic Relief Act* was passed. This significant legislation gave them almost equal rights resulting in a further expansion in Catholic churches.

Hardwicke's Act was revoked by the *Marriage Act* in 1836 and civil registration started the next year. From that time registrars could issue licences and marriages were permitted in a registry office, Nonconformist chapel or Catholic church thus ending the Episcopal monopoly. In fact *the former* restricted freedom of religion by the State at a time when these rights were being embodied in the American constitution.

There were then other significant developments and Belgravia and Pimlico were begun by the 2nd Marquess and Thomas Cubitt, with similar schemes at St. John's Wood and Paddington. Further bridges appeared in the west of London and railway termini on the periphery, while the City was altered by King William Street, Gresham Street, Moorgate, Queen Victoria Street and other new routes. One of the greatest changes resulted from the building of Holborn Viaduct over Farringdon Street designed by William Heywood, the city surveyor, at a cost of £2 million from 1863-69.

The Chelsea and Albert Embankments were built in the 1850s but it was under Joseph Bazalgette that the sewage system and embankment from Westminster to Temple arrived in 1862. By then the population was over 2.8 million and further change occurred as new middle-class leaders Disraeli and Gladstone introduced more liberal policies.

In terms of architecture the Waterloo Churches were the last of a kind with St. Pancras a main cause of retrogression. The Tractarians then promoted High Church worship and a Gothic Revival led by Ruskin, its principal architects Barry and Pugin at the Houses of Parliament, William Butterfield and Sir George Gilbert Scott. This new movement then had a significant effect on the later development of several City churches.

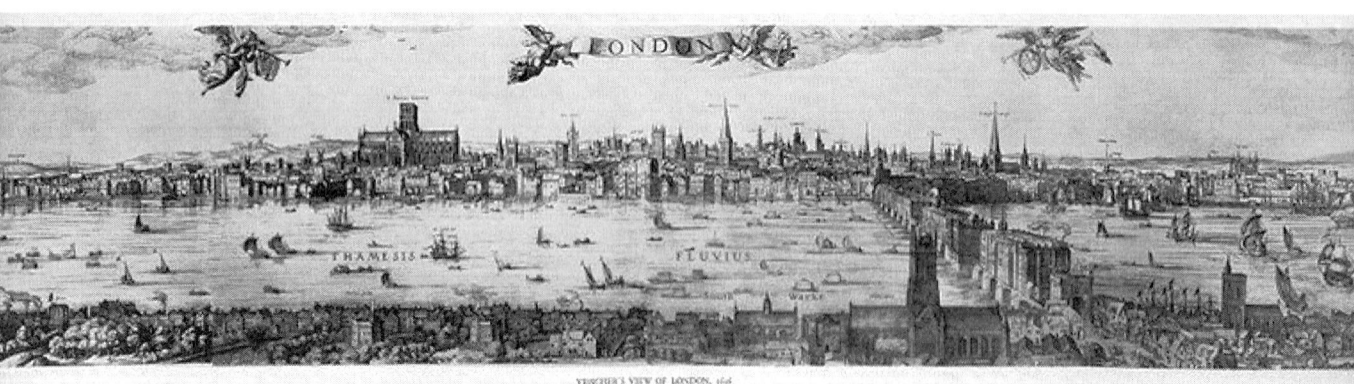

London Panorama (1616) showing the view from Southwark with St. Saviour's and St. Olave's either side of the bridge, then Old St. Paul's and the many City churches. In particular note the tall spires of St. Laurence Poultney and St. Dunstan in the East.

City North

A survey near to Gresham Street; being a perusal of the churches, streets, alleys and some prominent buildings in the area surrounding the Guildhall complex - taking in the ancient wards of Cripplegate, Bassishaw, Aldersgate and Coleman Street with an occasional detour into Cheap.

The section notes in particular the Compter, Blackwell Hall, where stood the Roman amphitheatre, the swampy regions about Moorfields, Dr. William's Library and the origins of the Barbican.

Notable persons recorded in the district are Shakespeare, Flamsteed, Milton, Frobisher, Wesley, Mrs. Beeton and Winston Churchill to name but a few. There is also a first meeting with the flamboyant "Olde Awdeley" as well as some prominent chemists and railway builders.

Today there are a whole cornucopia of church gardens in the area, while the truth of the "Large Feast in the Little Hall" and burning of the King's Jewels are *investigated* with mouth-watering aplomb.

The parish marker of St. Stephen Coleman depicts a cock in a hoop from a local hostelry. The owner was a church benefactor.

A second hall stood on Staining Lane from 1671-1940. It was designed by Edward Jerman who worked with Wren.

The Guildhall

So where does one start on a discussion of London's churches?

The answer is presumably at the beginning and for that purpose we look to the centre of the City, and then work around in an anti-clockwise fashion, and so on towards the outskirts. In ancient times the area was home to the Trinovantes but the Romans erected the first buildings some 2,000 years ago, however its etymology remains uncertain and theories include King Lud, Lund, Llyn or Llongdin relating to a ship town.

Stow started his survey with a detailed account of the capital noting it was comprised of four main parts namely The City, Westminster, East End and Southwark. The writer Fitzstephen declared that it was divided into wards just like Rome, with sheriffs standing in for consuls and aldermen sitting in dignity like the senators of old.

The installation of aldermen elected from wards dated back to Saxon times, whereas the Court of Aldermen at the Guildhall was replaced by the Court of Common Council. In addition, the sheriffs (or shire reeves) were also ancient and administered the law for the King - pre-dating the first mayor who was appointed in 1189. Later changes saw the Council decree that all mayors must have served as a sheriff after 1385.

Administration of the City was carried out using this system and initially there were 24 wards at the time of Henry III, with 13 to the east and 11 to the west. Each of these had one alderman. During the reign of Richard II in 1394 the western wards had grown larger thus Farringdon was split into two (intra and extra) with two aldermen, whereas the City also purchased Southwark in 1550 and this became Bridge Without.

Before the Great Fire there were 13,000 houses in the precincts which comprised of the 26 wards or aldermanries, whose boundaries were of historic design and not always in agreement with local topography. Stow delineated their division east-west along the Walbrook, and added, "The city is about 60 miles from the sea which is not so nigh as to be in danger of a Surprizal by the Fleets of a Foreign Enemy, nor to be annoyed by the boisterous Winds, and unwholesome Vapours arising from thence."

The modern day Guildhall, if transported back in time, would have provided a good vantage point from which to view the Roman amphitheatre. This was an extremely large arena, and on the present square there is a circle marked out on the pavement showing where it stood. Just opposite is the guild church of St. Lawrence Jewry, its location at the edge of the amphitheatre probably being of considerable significance.

The Guildhall, a centre of administrative life and guild activity, has parts dating back to the rebuilding by Sir Thomas Knollys in the early 15th century. On the east side is the chapel of St. Mary Magdalen founded c.1299 and renovated at the time of Henry VI in 1429, then used as the Court of Requests in Regency times. A new façade was added to the Great Hall with buildings to the left and right by George Dance in 1788, whilst it was restored by Sir Horace Jones in 1866 and again in more recent times.

Cripplegate ward, unlike the consolidated modern version, started in fields adjacent to St. Giles then wound its way down to Cheapside - taking in five other parishes en route. Three are discussed below whereas St. Alphage's and Milk Street are in later sections. St. Lawrence Jewry part of Cheap ward is included here due to its proximity.

The Guildhall with façade by George Dance the younger and chapel in 1805 (left), and the present building as restored by Sir Horace Jones in 1866 (right).

St. Alban's, Wood Street

This was an ancient church west of the Guildhall at the N.E. corner of Wood Street and Love Lane with Little Love Lane to the rear (now a police station). There is a tradition that Offa, King of Mercia (757-96) had a palace nearby and founded a chapel, since he also established the Benedictine monastery of St. Alban's, Herts. An excavation of 1962 revealed a possible 8th century foundation and it was documented as early as 1085.

Strype confirmed that this was "a church of great antiquity on three counts" - from the name, the nature of the arches and pillars, and the presence of Roman bricks. But he then went on to say it dated from the time of King Adelstane (Athelstane), the grandson of Alfred the Great, whose house was at the eastern end.

Of the memorials there were three mayors: John Woodcocke 1405, Thomas Chatworth grocer 1443 and Thomas Chalton mercer 1449 and to Sir Richard Illingworth a baron of the Exchequer d.1476. The name of the street may have come from Thomas Wood a sheriff 1491 who was a benefactor to nearby St. Peter's, or when Richard I decreed that houses should be built of stone against the risk of fire, but here remained of wood. The former also built some fine houses called Goldsmiths Row in Cheapside.

On the east side of Wood Street was the Compter a prison of the sheriffs built in 1555 whilst Love Lane was so-called of "wantons." Regarding the church there was a door located to the north leading out into Adel Street, whereas an ancient square of the tower of the King's House was situated at the corner of Love Lane.

The church was surveyed by Sir Henry Spiller, Enigo Jones Esq., Captains Leake and Williams but being too far decayed was likely to fall down before it could be dismantled. Therefore in the Easter of 1632 it was taken down and by July 1633 was a sad object in ruination, so the Bishop was petitioned for funds and it was rebuilt soon after.

St. Alban's church was of great antiquity, but the tower was built by Wren in 1682-88.

St. Lawrence Jewry whose structure was dictated by the adjacent buildings - now sits by the Guildhall Library.

However it was destroyed in the fire and rebuilt by Wren on the old foundations in 1682-85, with star-shaped lierne vaults and tracery in the aisles. A tower was appended to the northwest corner by 1688 - one of five constructed in the Gothic style.

More recent developments saw an apse added to the chancel in 1858-59 but it was badly damaged in the war, and was demolished except for the tower in 1955. The church was originally on the east side of Wood Street but is now in the centre. Its perpendicular lines are at odds with the diamond style offices to the west, whereas the view from Gresham Street sees the tower subjugated by the structure sitting astride London Wall.

St. Lawrence Jewry

The Old Jewry itself had two possible origins. Either where the Jews resided in the time of William I to Edward I until being expelled in 1290; or from the Roman *juris* relating to the city centre near the amphitheatre and road to the forum at Cornhill.

The church probably had Saxon origins but was first mentioned in 1136, and Balliol College were patrons from 1294. At the time of Stow it was *a fair parish church* and Sir Nicholas Bacon Lord Keeper to Elizabeth I, the father of Francis the philosopher, had a messuage nearby in King Edward's reign. Three mayors had memorials - Geoffrey Bollein 1457 of Hever in St. John's chapel, Sir Richard Gresham 1537 mercer father of Thomas and Sir Michael Dormer 1541. In addition William Grocyn scholar was rector in 1496 and the parishioner Sir John More a barrister was also buried there in 1530.

Regarding other early connections, Thomas Middleton was baptized at the church in 1580 and attended Oxford. He was a playwright and member of the Admiral's Men being popularly known for *The Wisdom of Solomon* dedicated to the Earl of Essex, *The Puritan Widow* and *A Game at Chess*. In later life he resided at Newington Butts.

Repairs were carried out with new windows, arms, pulpit and font in 1618/31, and Samuel Pepys attended in 1664, noting the structure was very fine. It was rebuilt by Wren in 1671-77 but was irregular due to adjacent properties - the walls varying in thickness to square the interior. A west tower faced Gresham Street with the nave offset, while two sides had Corinthian columns but the south remained plain. It was united with St. Mary Magdalen and the living was held jointly with the Dean and Chapter of St. Paul's.

The interior was a hall-type but stately in composition for the Corporation with a Lady Chapel to the north and two organs. Its benefactors included Sir John Langham M.P. £250 and Edward Reynolds, Bishop of Norwich and the incumbent £50 in 1657-59. It was re-opened with a Royal service in the presence of King Charles II in 1677.

Rev. John Mapletoft arrived as minister in 1686 and had several links (see p. 64) being involved with the S.P.C.K., Sion College and Greenwich Hospital. One of the lecturers was John Tillotson who married Elizabeth French niece of Oliver Cromwell, and went on to be Dean and Archbishop of Canterbury in 1691. He died at Lambeth in 1694 but was buried here and his alabaster memorial in Latin is to the north with plaque.

Other connections included John Flamsteed appointed first Astronomer Royal in 1675 at the time Wren and Hooke built the Greenwich Observatory. He detected Uranus in 1690 and was married at the church then had conflict with Newton president of the R.S. over his work. Being the vicar of Burstow, Surrey he was buried there in 1719, whilst his wife Margaret published his observations in *Historia Coelestis Britannica*.

Three children of Charles Young organist were baptised in 1713-17, including Hester an actress with her sisters. Benjamin and Elizabeth Mayson warehouseman of 24 Milk Street had three baptized in 1838-41, and Samuel and Eliza Beeton victualler of No. 39 two in 1839-40. The minister was Josiah Pratt j. of St. Stephen's and these were parents and in-laws of Mrs. Beeton. Likewise, Colin Blythe grandfather of the cricketer was a shirt warehouseman at 38 Gresham Street just west of the church from 1862-73.

St. Lawrence was united with St. Michael Bassishaw when it closed in 1892 and a font from Holy Trinity, Minories (dated 1620) came there. However it was badly damaged in 1940, and was restored by Cecil Brown as a guild church in 1954-57 with the parish going to St. Vedast's. The Wren vestry was lost but there were windows by Christopher Rahere Webb (the nephew of Sir Aston Webb) and a fine Commonwealth Chapel, hence several guilds hold services and it is the official church for New Zealand.

C. 18 April 1580 Thomas Middleton the sonn of William
17 February 1716/17 Hester d. of Charles & Elizabeth Young b. 14th Music Master

M. 23 Feb. 1663/64 John Tillotson of St. Andrew & Elizth French o.t.p. Dr. J. Wilkins
23 October 1692 John Flamsted of Greenwich and Margaret Lock of
St. Andrew's, Holborn were married by Dr. Mapletoft

B. 31 November 1694 Archbishop John Tillotson north chancel
29 Mch. 1705 Francis Levett knt. middle isle [partner R. Levett & Co.]
15 November 1721 John Mapletoft D.D. chancel aged 91

St. Lawrence - A view from the Guildhall with the north chapel and the restored east chancel.

St. Mary Aldermanbury

Returning to Love Lane this was the second of three churches in a row starting with St. Alban's. It was located on the west side of Aldermanbury above the Guildhall Library and a small churchyard was connected to it.

The first written record was in 1181, whilst Stow elucidated, "How Aldermanbury took that name many fables have been brited [sic], all of which I overpass as not worthy the accounting. But to be short and plain I say it took the name Alderman Bury of a court kept in the Bery or Court Hall, now the Guildhall, which of old stood on the east side of the street. This was not far from the west end of the one now used."

Richard Renery a sheriff gave lands in Aldermanbury to St. Mary at Osney, Oxford in 1157, and a new Hall was erected in 1411-31. Stow then added, "I myself have seen the ruins of the *old court hall* in that street which of late hath been employed as a carpenter's yard." There were many fair houses for merchants or men of worship; and Sir William Eastfield mayor 1437 at his charge conveyed water from the Ty Bourne, ran a lead pipe from Highbury to St. Giles, and erected a standard for water in Fleet Street.

Eastfield had a monument with coat of arms and paid for church repairs including a steeple, while other memorials were to Sir William Browne mayor 1507 and Dame Mary Gresham d.1538. Her husband John a mayor trained under John Middleton mercer. She left a bequest of £3 p.a. for the poor via the Mercers Company (see below).

This was a fair parish church with churchyard and cloister still attached being repaired with a steeple, battlements, walls, two fair galleries and many new pews in 1594. Strype noted that it was repaired by the parishioners in 1633, and had some famous links since Shakespeare worshipped there and John Milton was married in 1656. Wren rebuilt it of Portland stone using a mediaeval plan in 1667-87, including a nave of five bays and a barrel vault, whilst the middle bay had barrel-vaulted transepts.

Regarding preachers, James Janeway a Puritan minister was one of the many ejected by the Act of Uniformity in 1662. Forced to build a meeting house at Rotherhithe he was very popular however remained at odds with the Official Church. He published *A Token for Children* re conversions which became as popular as John Bunyan's *Pilgrim's Progress*, and was an influence on Spurgeon during the 19th century.

Another minister connected with the church was William Jowett, a relative of Josiah Pratt jun. (mentioned above). Jowett was a member of an extensive family of clergy and was secretary of the Church Missionary Society in 1832-41 with links to the reforming Venn family of Clapham. His roots emanated from Newington and he is discussed later, but was a lecturer at St. Mary Aldermanbury and other city churches.

The building was damaged in 1914-18 and destroyed in 1940 but then had an unusual and unlikely history. Churchill visited America in 1946 and General Vaughan part of the Truman administration arranged for the former to speak at Westminster College his alma mater in Fulton, Missouri. At this time Churchill became wary of Russia and anticipated the nascent Soviet Bloc, thus in the gymnasium gave his acclaimed "iron curtain speech" which heralded the advent of the notorious Cold War.

In honour of this event the old church was rebuilt in the grounds of the college from 1965-69, and stands there little changed from Wren's time, its position on a rise showing it off to better effect than in the City. Remaining central to the Churchill Memorial it is located by a museum and eight sections of the Berlin Wall. In fact the pediments above the door of the church came from St. Dionis Backchurch demolished in 1878.

Meanwhile, back in London the 15th-century foundations remain in a pleasant garden with the base of the piers protruding through the grass, and Westminster College placed a plaque there. The old parish was united with St. Vedast's, whereas that of St. Alphage's which was demolished in 1923 transferred to St. Giles Cripplegate.

Within the garden there is a bust of Shakespeare commemorating the work of Henry Condell and John Hemminges actors in the King's Men, and whose troupe the former wrote for. The two were residents in the parish and produced the first folio of the bard's plays in 1623 then were buried there. It remains a grade II listed "pile of stones" but of leafy interest and presumably this excludes any Time Team excavations.

M. 12 November 1656 The agreement and intention of marriage: John Milton Esq. of Margaretts, Westminster & Mrs. Katherine Woodcock o.t.p. publ. on 3 market days and no exceptions made they were maryed by Sir John Dethicke alderman J.P. [2nd wife]

B. 29 December 1627 Mr. [Henry] Condall
12 October 1630 John Hemmings a player
18 March 1673/74 [Rev.] Mr. Janaway minister
18 February 1677/78 Dame Lady Jeffreys wife of Sir George [1st wife] *

> * Also 5 Jeffreys children bapt. 1680-84 "Recorder of the City and Chief Justice"

St. Mary Aldermanbury

The elegant church dated c.1760 and the remaining foundations today.

A bust, "Mr. William Shakespeare's comedies histories and tragedies 1623," was donated by Charles Clement Walker of Lilleshall, Shropshire, in 1896.

St. Michael's, Wood Street

The next church to consider was first mentioned in 1225 and lay north of Huggin Lane and west of Wood Street. Just opposite was Lad Lane leading over to Cateaton Street and the Guildhall. Robert Lucas a goldsmith by his will of 1381 left £40 to the fabric and £20 to Westminster for his burial there. It was also improved by the receipt of two messuages and shops with solars, cellars &c. which were donated by John Jue the parson, John Forster a goldsmith and Peter Fikelden a tailor in 1383.

The most important family connected to the edifice were the Harveys who had several links to the prominent Audleys (or Awdeleys). John Audley a mercer married Margaret Hare from St. Mary le Bow and 11 children were baptized at St. Michael's in 1562-79, the most important being Hugh their tenth child. The latter became a lawyer and property owner who held the "Hundred Acres" in the west of London, and bequeathed them to the rather fortunate heiress Mary Davies (see St. Clement Danes).

John Audley died in the parish in 1577 and his widow Margaret then married William Harvey a grocer on 2 February 1581/82. Further to this Sarah a sister of Hugh married a cousin Robert Harvey and had three sons and three daughters including William who had sons Robert, Hugh and Benjamin. Hugh Audley in his will of 1662 left money and trusts to his half-brother William Harvey and godson Robert Harvey.

With regard to this Stow recorded a comely monument at the east of the north quire denoted thus: "William Harvie grocer deputy to the aldermen of Cripplegate 20 March 1597, 58 and Maudlin his first wife issue 4 sons and 1 daughter 16 November 1581, and Margaret his second wife 1 son 14 January 1593 and Joane his third wife survived him. A son Robert Harvey of Old Jewry comptroller of the Customs House, warden of the grocers died 9 November 1608, 47 and married Sarah Audley" - near Queen Elizabeth's monument. Strype also added, "Since the fire there are monuments to William Harvey the son of Robert died 1677 and his brother Hugh died 1679."

The church itself was repaired in 1620 and a new door was inserted through the north aisle beside the chancel, into Wood Street, in 1627. Prior to this the only entrance was located in the middle of the south aisle and led out into Huggin Lane.

After the fire Wren rebuilt the structure with a grand pediment and pilasters (or half columns) at the east end from 1670-75. A new organ was installed by Thomas Elliot in the 1800s, but the church suffered from a declining population in the mid-19th century. Several old lanes wound their way along just north of the building and these were then straightened and widened to form the current layout of Gresham Street. Consequently both the church and Huggin Lane were demolished in 1897.

At this time the parish passed to St. Alban's and then St. Vedast's while several items moved to other churches. A painting of Moses and Aaron (dated 1700) went to nearby St. Anne's, a Wren period pulpit was transferred to St. Mark's Kennington, and the Royal Stuart arms once part of the reredos were removed to St. George's Southwark.

C. 13 January 1576/77 was bapt. Hugh Awdley [s. of John and Margaret Hare]

B. 12 October 1577 was buried John Awdley
14 January 1593/94 Margarett wife of Mr. William Harvey

Bassishaw Ward

The small ward of Basinghall or Bassishaw covered basically just one street although it is enlarged to the west today. It was unique in the City in having a single parish church and nearby were livery halls of the Girdlers, Coopers, Weavers and Masons.

At the south end of Basinghall Street on the west side was a mediaeval house built by the Bassing family. It passed to Thomas Bakewell in the 36th of Edward III (1348) and thence to the Crown. The derivative Blackwell Hall an ancient market for woollen cloth with factors attached to it was built in 1558 and again in 1672 after the fire. However the Bankruptcy Court was built on the site by William Fowler (architect of Covent Garden and Hungerford) in 1820 - its business formerly conducted at the Guildhall.

St. Michael Bassishaw

This was the third of the three churches above the Guildhall and could be reached down a small alleyway from Aldermanbury, but the east end faced on to Basinghall Street. In fact it abutted the rear of the Guildhall, and prominent buildings on the street were the adjacent Coopers Hall, Blackwell Hall and Weavers Hall to the east.

The earliest reference, in common with others, was of a rectory dated c.1140 while the name originates from the Bassing family and a haw or yard. Originally it belonged to the priory of St. Bartholomew's, but from the 1400s the patron was St. Paul's. Despite such longevity there were several problems, and the north wall built on a Roman rubbish tip required buttressing. Likewise, some "rustic work" covered over the corners.

A new ceiling was provided by the will of John Burton mercer d.1460 and Agnes his wife consequently his mark appeared on the roof of the quire and middle aisle. In return for this he asked that prayers be said for members of his family, Henry IV, Queen Joan and Thomas Langley who was the late Bishop of Durham.

There were also memorials to Sir James Yarforde mercer mayor d.1527 of Blackwell Hall and Elizabeth in the chancel; and Sir John Gresham mercer mayor d.1556 husband to Mary and Katherine and the uncle of Thomas in the south aisle with marble tomb. The church was repaired and beautified at the cost and charges of the parish in 1630.

Like most buildings it was lost in the fire which should have given an opportunity to improve both the fabric and foundation - but it did not. This was one of Wren's poorer efforts carried out from 1676-79. In fact, the contractor John Fitch had to pile the east end, the walls were atypically faced with brick, and the Corinthian columns of the nave had a plaster surface "hiding an assortment of materials underneath."

The east end had a large round-headed window but the parish complained to Wren to repair their crumbling edifice, which Strype noted was done using rubbed-brick in 1697. Meanwhile, the upper walls were rebuilt and a tower added to the west with octagonal drum, lantern, turrets and a small spire in 1712-14. The work was undertaken by Robert Hooke and the weather vane is now located at St. Andrew by the Wardrobe.

Despite such problems the church outlasted many, but the foundations continued to cause concern and it was shut down in 1892 and the parish joined to St. Vedast's. It was finally demolished in 1900. The land was sold to the City for £36,000 and some of the proceeds went towards a church of the same name in Edmonton, whereas a coat of arms once decorating the wall can be observed in the Guildhall.

The site of the church is now a paved area adjoining the Barbican development, and a blue plaque records it; then opposite is a tablet to the Coopers Hall (1547-1940). Three such halls stood on the site but the guild is now in Devonshire Square, and next door there is a modern hall of the Insurers Guild. In olden times the Girdlers Hall was north of the church down an alley. But today they have a new building on Basinghall Avenue with parish markers on the wall to St. Michael's (1815) and St. Stephen's (1886).

Thomas Wharton was one of the most prominent with connections to the church. His family had links to Fountains Abbey, but he was a physician at St. Thomas's Hospital from 1659-73 staying there throughout the plague. He provided accounts of anatomy and Izaak Walton talked of their friendship in *The Compleat Angler*, while he joined with Elias Ashmole to work on the catalogue of the Tradescant Museum in Lambeth meeting with John Tradescant the younger. Wharton resided in nearby Aldersgate Street and he was buried at the church before it was rebuilt.

B. 20 November 1673 Doctor Thomas Wharton was bur.

Cripplegate Ward

A Roman fort stood near the site of Cripplegate from about 120 A.D. and may have been replaced by the palace of Ethelbert founder of St. Paul's. The name itself derives from crepel a covered way and Aldermanbury from a fortified site of the aldermen. The gate which had two castellated towers was rebuilt in 1491 and nearby fortifications gave rise to the name of the *Barbican*. Cripplegate and the others were all unhinged and their portcullises wedged so they could no longer be used in defence in 1660, and the former was demolished in 1760. A plaque and information board now marks the site.

It is hard to imagine the earlier appearance of the area between Aldersgate and London Wall, since it was so greatly transformed in the post-war era. In particular the Barbican designed in the "brutalist" style by the partners Chamberlin, Powell & Bon.

At the time of Stanford's Map in 1862, London Wall was a narrow street running west from Moorgate and ended where Monkwell Street turned south - following the line of the old Roman wall. At this apex was St. Giles Cripplegate with a large debtors' prison opposite, now the site of the City of London Girls' School and a lake. There were a network of alleyways and Redcross Street went north to the short Barbican Lane, whilst Whitecross Street went up to Chiswell Street and Whitbread's brewery.

This area was greatly devastated during the war and much of the old street pattern was removed. Geoffry Powell won the contract for the Golden Lane Estate in 1951 and as a result the partners were chosen to design the Barbican, one of the main influences being the work of Le Corbusier especially his Unité D'Habitation (in Marseilles). The estate with its futuristic flats was built from 1965 to 76 and included the Barbican Centre, the Museum of London, the Girls School and St. Giles in its remit. The result left divided opinion as to its success although in recent times it became listed.

CRIPPLE-GATE.

Beyond the gate Fore Street ran along the wall to Moor Lane End, the town ditch, a pot maker's house and cow house near to Finsbury Court.

For many years the Moore Fields were, "a Moorish rotten ground," un-passable except for causeways. Stow noted they were improved by the mayor &c. and "John Speed, my especial kind friend had a map of these improvements" - which he hoped to include in his next edition of the survey.

As stated the ward consisted of six parish churches, two detailed below, three near the Guildhall, and one in Milk Street near to Cheapside. Today the section by the latter road is part of Cheap and the modern ward is mainly situated to the north.

Lamb's Chapel

A mediaeval traveller going south down Redcross Street would initially have come to St. Giles with the churchyard, city walls and round tower just behind. They then turned the corner and entered via Cripplegate to see Wood Street before them. However a detour to the right took them down Hart Street to the junction with Monkwell Street and there in the angled recess of the old walls sat "Lamb's Chapel."

The foundation took place as early as 1289 in the days of that Welsh castle-builder Edward I. At the outset there was a small hermitage housing two Cistercian monks and this was dedicated to St. James. It was held by the influential Monastery of Garendon patronised by the Earl of Leicester and for a time the Abbot had a seat in Parliament.

At the Dissolution, the monastery was demolished under the instructions of Thomas Cromwell and the chapel passed to William Lambe, a wealthy clothworker, in 1543. He presented the chapel, his house and any rents appertaining to the Clothworkers in 1577, and they appointed Arthur Jackson rector of St. Michael's, Wood Street as minister of the edifice on 8 July 1625. In fact the baptism records date back to 1629. The latter also transcribed earlier entries, and a brass to the daughters of Nicholas Bestney J.P. was moved to the north aisle of St. Olave's, Hart Street in the late 19th century.

The chapel and related almshouses were rebuilt in 1825, at which time there was some evidence of a Norman crypt. It then became known as *St. James by the Wall* chapel in the parish of St. Olave, Silver Street. But it was demolished in 1872 and the 12th century crypt was removed to All Hallows Staining by the Clothworkers Co. Just to the south was the Barber Surgeons Hall now in Monkwell Square, one member being John Harrison philanthropic founder of the London Hospital (see St. Paul's, Deptford).

M. 18 August 1586 Nicholas Bestney Esq. of Gray's Inn and Bridget Mitchel daughter and heir of John Mitchel of Warham, Sussex
28 July 1608 Henry Hudson gentleman of the Inner Temple and Sibyll Bestney

B. 22 March 1632 Bridget Bestney widow of Mr. Nicholas Bestney

St. Alphage's

London Wall originally ran just north of its present location where St. Alphage's Gardens sit today, and the top end of Aldermanbury viz. Gayspur (or Jasper) Street intersected it. In mediaeval times the parish church was beside the Roman wall in the churchyard, but was then removed to a new location a short distance to the south.

Stow recorded that on the west side of Gayspur Street where it met with London Wall was a house of nuns which being in decay passed to William Elsing a mercer in 1329. He then gave the nunnery and two houses as the foundation for a hospital called the priory of St. Mary the Virgin in 1331. It was also known as Elsing Spital and had a chapel with 14th century tower - however major changes took place at the Reformation.

The main north aisle of the chapel was pulled down and a frame of four houses set up in its place, whilst the chancel and tower were converted into a new parish church. The hospital, priory, canon's house and lodgings became a substantial dwelling with its garden in the churchyard and a fair gallery adorning the cloister. Likewise, lodgings for the poor were transmuted into stabling for horses. The old parish church near to Cripplegate was then demolished and became a carpenter's yard and saw pits.

In the year 1541 Sir John Williams, Master of the King's Jewels resided there and on Christmas Eve a great fire began in the gallery at 7 pm, "which burned so sore that the flames were seen all the city over and was hardly quenched." In fact, many of the King's jewels were thereby destroyed and others were *imbezelled* [sic] "as was said."

Regarding the church the eastern parts consisted of smooth flint stones which seem to have come from the ruins of Elsing Spital. There were memorials to Lord Williams of Thame and his family, while John Brown merchant adventurer of St. Bartholomew by the Exchange gave £30 for church repairs. Due to its great age it was under constant renovation - firstly at a cost of £500 in 1624-28 and then again in 1701 and 1775.

The mansion just west of the church was replaced by Sion College and Almshouses, an institution for the clergy of London and its Liberties with accommodation for 20 men and women. It was established by the will of Rev. Thomas White vicar of St. Dunstan in the West who provided £3,000 for a college and almshouses in 1624.

St. Alphage's - beside the walls and the tower of Elsing Spital.

Sion College was nearby in 1630-1884, and a centre for religious discussion.

This became a meeting place for discussion, often associated with Presbyterians, and was criticised by Rev. John Goodwin of St. Stephen's. Indeed, John Sedgwick rector of St. Alphage's took up the Parliamentarian cause there during the Civil War. [1]

The church itself became redundant and was demolished in 1923 but the remains of the 14th century tower with flint still stands on London Wall, and parts of the Roman Wall and old churchyard are found in St. Alphage's Gardens off Wood Street. There are two modern guild halls - the Salters in Fore Street with gates from 1887 and salt crystals at the entrance, and the Brewers on an ancient site opposite the church tower.

St. Giles without Cripplegate

Some of the churches had a plethora of more minor celebrities however St. Giles was connected with persons famous throughout the Kingdom. The most significant aspect was its location near the site of an extensive Roman fort erected in about 61 A.D. after the incursions by Queen Boudica, and therefore near to Cripplegate.

Of all the gates into the City this was in fact the most obscure and was accessed from Redcross Street which came down from Aldersgate. Today this is the only gateway that is not a major thoroughfare. Beyond the church there was a labyrinth of alleys and before the building of St. Luke's, the parish extended right out into the fields.

Above Redcross Street was anciently the Barbican or Burgh Kenning located on a small elevation. It was one of several towers positioned to provide a vantage point beyond the city, but all were pulled down when the Barons were reconciled with Henry III in 1267. Nearby, Sir Thomas Wriothesley of the Garter and uncle of the Chancellor constructed Garters House or Place which had a chapel secreted in its upper rooms.

St. Giles was almost certainly a Saxon foundation by the walls, and the first record is of a shrine built by Alfune in 1090. He was an almoner to the priory of St. Bartholomew and friend of the founder Rahere. Walbrook Stream ran under London Wall near to the church which resulted in silting and made the adjacent ground extremely swampy. As a result there were several re-buildings the first in the perpendicular style in 1394, whilst it was burnt to the ground despite "all of that dampness" in 1545.

There were further repairs in 1623 when the chancel roof was replaced although on the inside it was "very curiously clouded." In the next three years, some spacious galleries were added on each side. Likewise the steeple and four corner spires were repaired with additional turrets in 1629 - the work done at great cost to the parishioners.

Only a few memorials survived the early fire, whilst a slightly later one on the chancel wall was to John Foxe or Johanni Foxo born at Boston in c.1517. His mother married a yeoman at Coningsby, Lincolnshire and John Hawarden of Brasenose, Oxford was vicar of the adjacent parish; thus he attended that college and became a fellow of Magdalen. He was acquainted with Robert Crowley the printer and both left the Church over their beliefs, while his most famous work *Acts and Monuments* (or *Book of Martyrs*) was based on Crowley's work. After ordination he lived with the Duke of Norfolk, a former pupil, at Aldgate but died at Grub Street north of Fore Street on 18 April 1587.

---

[1] The almshouses closed in 1884 and Sion College moved to Victoria Embankment, but the latter buildings were sold in 1996 and the charity is now administered from Fleet Street.

Rev. Robert Crowley "a stationer of St. Andrew, Holborn" was ordained in 1551, but like Foxe spent time abroad during the reign of Mary I. He became the vicar of St. Giles in c.1565 and Foxe probably assisted him in his duties, while he died on 18 June 1588 and his memorial was on the chancel floor. Lancelot Andrewes succeeded him then gave published sermons on the *Temptation in the Wilderness* and *Lord's Prayer* and advocated the doctrines of the Reformation. He was appointed a prebend of St. Paul's, master of Pembroke and chaplain to Whitgift and the Queen through patronage, and was vicar for seventeen years until he became a bishop in 1605 (see St. Saviour's).

The exact reason is unclear however Strype failed to record some famous people who had links to the church, with memorials there. One of these was the seaman Sir Martin Frobisher who travelled to the New World looking for the North West Passage on three occasions. In later life he commanded under Sir Walter Raleigh and was wounded during a siege at Brest in November 1594, his residence just nearby at Beech Lane.

Regarding exploration, John Speed was born at Farndon, Cheshire in 1542 and joined his father's business, being a merchant taylor with rooms in the Moorfields area. He only produced maps in later life after Sir Fulke Greville became his benefactor and these included *County Maps*, a *World Atlas* and *Genealogies of the Sacred Scriptures* in 1611. He died on 28 July 1629 and his memorial in Latin was placed in the south chancel.

The church was greatly influenced by Parliamentarian connections and Oliver Cromwell was born in 1599, a relative of the Tudor statesman. He was educated at Sidney Sussex which had Puritan leanings and possibly attended Lincoln's Inn, then married Elizabeth daughter of Sir James Bourchier in 1620 - which resulted in many political associations and nine children. He was M.P. for Huntingdon and for Cambridge then leader of the Commonwealth, and his statue (of 1899) sponsored by Rosebery is at Westminster.

Following on from this, John Milton was born at Bread Street in 1608 (see later) and after a good education and continental travel wrote articles criticising Archbishop Laud. He was appointed to the Council of State under Cromwell in 1649 but went into hiding for a time at the Restoration. Of independent means, he had four children from his first marriage to Mary Powell (d.1652) and his epic poem *Paradise Lost* appeared in 1667. He resided at Aldersgate Street and like his father was buried at the church.

St. Giles, Cripplegate once sat beside the Roman walls…

…and perhaps Milton's paradise lost?

Rev. Samuel Annesley became a Presbyterian whilst at Oxford and was the chaplain to Robert Rich, 2nd Earl of Warwick. He was then appointed Puritan minister at the church by son Richard Cromwell in 1658, but was ejected under the Act of Uniformity in 1662. After this he preached privately and John and Charles Wesley were his grandsons.

St. Giles itself covered an extensive parish and the church was large, whilst an offset tower was raised up with brick and old material in 1682-84, and pews and a vestry were added in 1704. The ground plan then tapered to the east. By the year 1746 the housing in the parish outside the City jurisdictions reached as far as Old Street, although beyond this there remained agrarian fields leading up to Islington.

One of the later events at the church was the baptism of William Holman Hunt in 1827 the son of a warehouseman in Cheapside. However, his family came from Deptford and Rotherhithe and William Hobman his uncle owned a large farm at Ewell where he often visited. After several attempts he was admitted to the Royal Academy Schools and in this way met with other artists, thus helping to form the Pre-Raphaelites in 1848.

Regarding the church there was a Victorian restoration in the Tudor perpendicular style in 1897, but most was destroyed except for the walls and tower in 1940. It was renovated with mediaeval plan and a cast of bells arrived from Mears & Co. in 1954. The altar and organ came from St. Luke's in 1964 - the latter including a Renatus Harris case from St. Andrew's, Holborn. The building is prominent in the Barbican but is incongruous in its ultra-modern surroundings, and its cathedral-like arcade leads to the chancel arch.

At the rear are busts to Bunyan, Defoe, Cromwell and Milton presented by J. Passmore Edwards newspaper owner and philanthropist in 1888 (the first two being parishioners). To the north are modern windows to Edward Alleyn a benefactor, the Fortune Theatre in Golden Lane, and St. Luke's created from the parish. To the south is a memorial to Milton (and his statue), bust to John Speed (restored by the Merchant Taylors in 1971), plaque to Frobisher and tablet to Sir Thomas Lucy 1600 who employed Foxe as a tutor. The west window also contains coats of arms to the Archbishop and Bishop.

A Cast of Local Players - With this thespian theme in mind Edward Alleyn and Philip Henslowe established the Fortune Theatre just north of the church in 1600. Henslowe already owned the Rose Theatre in Southwark which was a rival to Shakespeare's Globe, and in fact the bard attended his nephew's baptism at St. Giles in 1607.

The new arena was situated in an area of tightly packed alleys and courtyards between Golden Lane and Whitecross Street, with the aptly named Cupid's Alley opposite. The Admiral's Men performed there but it was destroyed by fire in 1621 then closed down by the Puritans and demolished in 1661. The site was initially Playhouse Yard but was then renamed as Fortune Street, whilst a plaque records its location.

A short distance down Whitecross Street is Chiswell Street, and on the south side is the old Whitbread Brewery complex with its large chimney. Samuel Whitbread came from a strict Nonconformist family but joined the brewery at Chiswell Street and was eventually the owner, it being the largest in the country by the end of the 18th century.

He approached Boulton and Watt in 1784 but did not travel up to the Soho Works at Handsworth, instead he went to see Goodwyn's pioneering 4-h.p. engine at East Smithfield (see Aldgate). An order was promptly placed for a far larger 10-h.p. engine and John Smeaton helped to design some Georgian buildings with engine house in 1785.

St. Giles, Cripplegate showing the 17th century tower - also its elegant perpendicular interior, restored in Victorian times and after the war.

Being of great renown, King George and Queen Charlotte visited two years later, while the company stayed in the family and Edgar Lubbock a director was a brother of Baron Avebury and Director of the Bank (see St. Peter's, Eaton Square). A tablet was erected to record the Royal visit and recently it was renovated as a conference centre.

Meanwhile, at the other end of the spectrum were the Glasites who were established in Scotland, as part of the Great Awakening, in the 1730s. The movement was spread by Robert Sandemann son-in-law of the founder, who started a Sandemanian chapel at Glovers Hall below Beech Lane, Cripplegate in 1761. This was moved to Paul's Alley by Redcross Street above the church in 1785. Michael Faraday was born in Newington but his family were adherents thus he attended in his youth, and later became an elder of the meeting house - which removed to Barnsbury Grove in 1862.

Immediately opposite to Paul's Alley was the Dr. William's Library. Daniel Williams was born in Wrexham but preached as a Presbyterian in Ireland from 1664-87, and then came to Hoxton. At this time he provided a sermon for John Shorter former mayor and also advised William III. He left a legacy of £50,000 plus 7,600 books in 1716, and directed that they be used to start a library, although his trustees had to raise more funds before this opened in Redcross Street in 1729. In fact the foundation remained at this address until the Metropolitan Railway purchased the site in 1865.

C. 10 June 1827 William Holman s. of William and Sarah Hunt of Love Lane

M. 22 August 1620 Oliver Cromwell and Elizabeth Bouress [sic] by licence

B. 20 April 1587 John Ffox house holder [sic] preacher
14 January 1594/95 Sir Martyn Ffairbrosher baronet d. 15 November
31 July 1629 Mr. John Speed a merchant taylor
12 November 1674 John Milton gentleman of consumption, chancel

Aldersgate

The Aldersgate ward included St. Botolph's, five other parish churches and the collegiate establishment of St. Martin le Grand. Four of these churches are considered in the next section whereas St. Leonard's is treated separately under Foster Lane.

Historically this was the location of an important gate into the city. To the north of St. Martin le Grand was the grand vista of Aldersgate and a structure with statues was built in 1617. This was engraved by Hollar then rebuilt after the fire but demolished in 1761 and a plaque marks the site. To the south were the French Protestant Church, the Bull & Mouth Inn and Northumberland House on the west side, all of which were demolished for a new Post Office building in 1888 (each having a plaque).

According to Stow in the parish of St. Anne's there was a great house commonly called Northumberland House which belonged to Henry Percy the earl. Henry IV in the 7th of his reign (1406) gave this (with tenements appertaining) to Queen Jane his wife and it was called her wardrobe, but was eventually used as a printing house.

Beyond the gate on the west side was the church St. Botolph's and opposite was the Cooks Hall, "which cooks or pastelers were admitted a company with masters and wardens in 1464." A little further was Barbican Street or Houndsditch with many fair houses. The hall was originally built in c.1500 but was lost during a fire in 1771. Just to the north on the west side was London House home to the Bishops of London from the 18th century, when not at Fulham Palace. There was a convenient chapel attached but the house was likewise destroyed by fire in 1766 and both locations are now marked by a plaque.

St. Botolph's, Aldersgate

St. Botolph was the patron saint of travellers and four churches thus dedicated were at the gates of the City. Traditionally they were on the outside so that travellers could pray upon arriving or leaving, and as a result the parishes were usually larger than those lying within the city walls. This was true of the Aldersgate parish which was long and narrow and stretched north from the walls up as far as Charterhouse.

The first church was built on the site in c.1050 and was possibly a Cluniac priory and hospital established by Edward the Confessor, while the patronage passed to the Dean and Prior of St. Martin le Grand soon after. A new church was built in 1350 at the corner of Briton Street (Little Britain) - named for the Dukes of Brittany lodging there.

It ceased to be monastic after Henry V created St. Botolph's parish, and Stow noted three brotherhoods or fraternities being founded there - one to St. Fabian & Sebastian in 1377, one to Holy Trinity with a chapel in 1446 and one to St. Katherine but these were suppressed in the reign of Edward VI. All the land of the church and hospital were then granted to William Harris alias Somers(et) a herald at arms in 1548.

There were early memorials to John Hartshorn the King's servant 1400, John Michael sergeant at arms 1415, Robert Cawood clerk of the pipe 1466 and Dame Ann Packington widow of Sir John who founded almshouses at White Friars, Fleet Street administered by the Clothworkers d.1563. In her will she left further lands at Islington to that guild the rents for the poor of St. Botolph's - their brass and niche is south of the chancel.

St. Botolph's, Aldersgate

The church survived the Great Fire thus the hand of Wren is absent from its design. Nathaniel Wright designed a new building in 1788-91 - but the east end was added in 1831. Its interior was inspired by All Hallows, London Wall.

The steeple was much decayed and perished but was rebuilt with Portland stone and a new pulpit installed in 1624, while the pews and clock were replaced at a cost of £415 in 1627. There was a tablet to Sir Henry Beaumont and extensive family in the middle aisle, and a memorial to Mr. Richard Chiswell bookseller of St. Paul's Churchyard, also to his parents and family in the north aisle: born 1639, died 1711. The latter was a proprietor of John Strype's book and the memorial is still present today. A second one to Chiswell who was "a constant benefactor to the parish" is by the entrance door.

Meanwhile the mediaeval church survived the fire due to the city walls and there was a partial repair in 1754, but this was all swept away in 1788-91. Nathaniel Wright designed a simple brick oblong with western tower, wooden turret and gilded vane, with an interior by Nathaniel Evans who was influenced by George Dance the younger at All Hallows, London Wall. The most obvious similarities are the dull exterior and clerestory windows which contrast with the far more striking internal ensemble.

Such an assessment certainly holds true since there is a delicate stairway juxtaposed with a fine column in the vestibule. Then on entering the sanctuary there are three elements to be observed - Corinthian columns supporting galleries of dark wood, a white plaster ceiling heavily decorated and suffused with light, and beyond an apse and half-dome with exquisite recessed lines. However, the two real gems dating back to 1788 are the organ by Samuel Green and the east window transparency, a painting on glass by James Pearson. Both of these are the only ones to be found in any City churches.

At the same time the visitor is perplexed as to why there is an apse inside - but a flat wall outside? During 1831 the east end was moved eight feet when a new General Post Office was developed on St. Martin le Grand, and a stucco façade was added with Ionic columns and pediment - a concept that certainly ameliorates the design. There was a Victorian restoration in 1873-74 followed by some dedicated round-headed windows in 1886, and those on the northern aisle-wall depict various Biblical scenes.

On the south side there are four more: James I entering through Aldersgate, one of the Ironmongers whose hall is just to the north in the Barbican, a third showing Henry Compton giving refuge to Queen Anne at London House in 1688, and the last has John Wesley preaching in Moorfields with a panoramic of London. These provide quite an interesting and colourful addition to the interior although not to everyone's taste.

George Frederic Watts the painter and sculptor moved in an extensive circle and went to stay with Henry Prinsep and his wife Sarah (Pattle) at Little Holland House "for a few days" in 1850 but stayed for 30 years! Her sister was pioneer photographer Julia Margaret Cameron and their son Val Prinsep a Pre-Raphaelite whilst there were links to Thackeray, Tennyson, Leslie Stephen and Virginia Woolf (see St. Pancras).

Regarding Aldersgate, the churchyard was closed in the mid-19th century and joined to that of Christchurch which was adjacent, to form Postman's Park. Watts had the idea of creating a memorial to those who carried out heroic acts and this remains just behind the church today. The parish was closed in 1954 and divided between St. Bartholomew the Great and St. Giles Cripplegate then became a guild church. More recently it was used for lunchtime services under St. Helen's and by the Presbyterians on a Sunday.

Wollaston Family - There are a number of notable residents connected with the church who are now considered separately. William Wollaston was a student of Sidney Sussex, Cambridge and inherited the noble estate of Shenton near Leicester in 1688, the family motto being "Ne Quid Falsi." Then with considerable expectations he married Catharine the daughter of Nicholas Charlton a London draper and merchant.

The couple settled in Charterhouse Square and William never spent a night away from home until his death! He was a moral philosopher with many learned papers in particular *The Religion of Nature Delineated* which sold 10,000 copies and he died in 1724. His son Francis with wife Mary Fauquier remained in Charterhouse Square and a grandson also called Francis was baptized at St. Botolph's on 24 November 1731.

Francis Wollaston j. graduated with a LLB but "had some moral hesitance in regard to an advocate's duties," and became a priest in 1754 preaching at St. Anne's, Soho in 1758. He married Althea Hyde daughter of a resident of the Square at St. Botolph's and had connections to East Dereham, Norfolk and Chislehurst, Kent. But his bill to reduce the "39 Articles" to a simple declaration of faith was firmly rejected by Parliament. [2]

Francis and Althea Wollaston had no less than 16 children several of them baptized at the church. In fact the father became rector of nearby St. Vedast's in 1779 and he held all three parishes until his death in 1815 (being buried at Chislehurst).

---

[2] The first ten articles were introduced by Cranmer in 1536 and the expanded version came out under Elizabeth I in 1571. They set out the position of the Church with regard to God, Roman Catholicism, and Calvinist Doctrine while a Royal declaration appeared in the *Book of Common Prayer*. The Test Act of 1672 made adherence a requirement for public office but was repealed by the Catholic Relief Act in 1829. Cardinal Newman wanted them interpreted in a way that was less hostile to the Catholic doctrine.

Two of his sons appear in the National Biography. Francis John Hyde Wollaston was born at Charterhouse Square on 13 April 1762 and became a prebend of St. Paul's, but lectured on chemistry and experimental philosophy performing over 300 experiments. His brother William Hyde Wollaston was born at East Dereham in 1766 and was educated at Charterhouse and Caius, Cambridge gaining an M.D. and was elected fellow of the Royal Society in 1793 - his membership being confirmed by his father Francis, uncle William Heberden, the Hon. Henry Cavendish and Sir William Herschel.

St. Botolph's Vestibule - An elegant staircase with column, a classical style repeated in the interior.

William Hyde Wollaston (1766-1828)

He was a brilliant chemist who made a fortune from his work on platinum, being just one spark behind Davy and Faraday.

However his family came from Charterhouse Square, and were connected to St. Botolph's for several generations.

He failed to obtain an appointment at St. George's but probably gave up medicine due to his sensitivity about his patients, stating, "Allow me to decline the mental flagellation called anxiety, compared with which the loss of thousands of pounds is as a fleabite." After receiving a legacy he engaged in chemical research at 14 Buckingham Street just west of Fitzroy Square (now Greenfield St.), and his work on platinum earned him about £30,000. Indeed his research was extensive and he produced 56 papers on every branch of science while declaring, "My predominant principal is to avoid error."

He patented the Camera Lucida in 1807 which led to the discoveries of Fox Talbot, adopted the wave theory of light, gave evidence on the Imperial gallon in the Commons, and served on the Board of Longitude. His most interesting work was on electricity and he made a wire revolve next to a current in the laboratory of Sir Humphrey Davy in 1821 but it was Faraday who was credited with the electric motor. After the death of Joseph Banks he was acting president of the Royal Society but stepped aside for his friend Davy who had greater ambition in that regard.

In later life he established the Wollaston Fund at the Geological Society and left money to the Astronomical and Royal Societies, then died at 1 Dorset Street, Marylebone on 22 December 1828 (home of Charles Babbage mathematician 1829-71). His brother Henry was born in 1776 and became a merchant in Clapton, Exeter and Bristol and had a son Rev. Charles Buchanan Wollaston who is discussed further under Hackney.

John and Charles Wesley - The Wollastons may have tried to change moral attitudes from the parish church of St. Botolph's, but the Wesleys nigh on produced a convulsion in society. There was a degree of religious fervour in the area and John and his brother Charles were born at Epworth, Lincoln where their father was rector, but were educated at Charterhouse and Westminster Schools respectively.

After travelling to Georgia in 1735 they received inspiration from the Moravians while back in England John assisted Rev. John Heylyn at St. Mary le Strand. His conversion took place at a Moravian meeting house probably at 28 Aldersgate Street on 24 May 1738 after listening to a reading of Martin Luther's *Preface to the Epistle to the Romans*. A few weeks later he preached on personal salvation by faith through God's grace, and brother Charles had a similar conversion at 12 Little Britain near St. Barts. A plaque was erected outside the church by the Intl. Methodist Historical Union on 24 May 1926.

Thereafter the two brothers helped to establish the Methodist faith and John preached outside St. Botolph's, although was at odds with the Church having no licence to preach. Their particular version was known as Arminian, and although John Wesley was a friend of Whitefield from his days at University and preached in his Bristol Tabernacle, there was disagreement on doctrine since the latter followed Calvinistic beliefs.

John and Charles Wesley

A window showing the former preaching in Moorfields, and a tablet located south of the church in St. Martin le Grand.

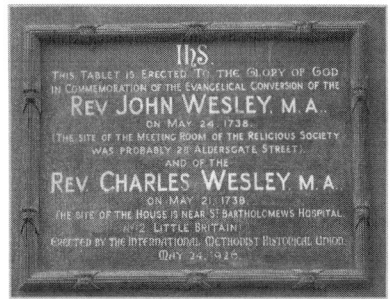

Thomas Hood - The next celebrity with local links was born in Cheapside in 1799 his family being in the book trade, but after his father died they moved to Islington where he was duly educated. Initially he tried his hand at finance and engraving then moved for his health to relatives in Scotland and came back to London in 1818.

By then he submitted humorous and poetical articles to magazines and became sub-editor of the *London Magazine*, thus he met the literary elite including John Hamilton Reynolds (s. of George and Charlotte) a playwright and close friend of Keats.

Hood married his sister and wrote one of his first pieces of work, *Odes and Addresses* with help from his brother-in-law J.H. Reynolds, and Coleridge averred to Charles Lamb that it must in fact be written by the latter. Meanwhile there was one other resident who had no time at all for any poetical deliberations.

Samuel Morton Peto - His family emanated from Kirdford, Sussex but moved to East Horsley in Surrey and Henry Peto was born there in 1774. The latter was a "gentleman builder" at 31 Little Britain, whereas his brother William married Sophia Alloway at St. Vedast's and resided at "Whitmore House," Sutton, Woking. Their famous son Samuel M. Peto was born there on 4 August 1809 and after a good education went to work for his uncle Henry, and supervised construction of Raymond's Buildings, Gray's Inn. These offices are still present today and have the date "1825" above the doors.

Meanwhile, Thomas de la Garde Grissell was born at Shoreditch in 1778 and married Ann Peto (sister of the above) at Stoke D'Abernon in 1801. A son Thomas was baptized at Shoreditch later that year and also went to work for his uncle Henry thus his own son was baptized at St. Botolph's. When Henry died in 1830 the cousins Samuel and Thomas formed the partnership of "Peto and Grissell" which proved extremely lucrative. These relations were cemented when Samuel Morton Peto married the sister Mary de la Garde Grissell at St. Mary's, Lambeth on 18 May 1831.

At the same time the partners secured the contract to rebuild Hungerford Market sited between Craven and Villiers Streets (later Charing Cross Station). This was designed by the architect William Fowler and the foundation was laid on 18 June that year, but as a general market it failed to compete with Billingsgate or Covent Garden. This was only the beginning and they developed railways with Brunel, built several clubs in London, and constructed Nelson's Column designed by William Railton in 1838.

The partnership was dissolved in 1846 and the former joined with Edward Ladd Betts a prominent railway contractor as "Peto and Betts" (see St. Pancras), and thereby worked on other major projects throughout Britain and around the world.

Peto retained a large country estate at Somerleyton near Lowestoft and properties at Russell Square and 12 Kensington Palace Gardens, and was a leading Baptist being the benefactor of Bloomsbury and Regent's Park Chapels. As an M.P. he introduced *Peto's Act* in 1850 which rationalised the holding of property by religious bodies.

The partners Peto and Betts also worked with Thomas Brassey on numerous projects including a vital rail link in the Crimea, and with Thomas Crampton on the London, Chatham & Dover Railway from 1860. The Metropolitan Extension ended at Holborn Viaduct but there were problems over capital during a severe banking crisis in 1866 and all pressure left the boiler. Thus the two were declared bankrupt in 1868 (see Dulwich) and the railway became a remnant but the Baptist chapels still remain.

Samuel Morton Peto (1809-89): A Victorian railway magnate, builder and philanthropist; but it all started at Little Britain.

Aldersgate (1650), as drawn by W. Hollar, was just nearby.

St. Botolph's, Aldersgate (parish records)

C. 24 November 1731 Francis s. of Francis & Mary Woollastone Charterhouse Yard
5 February 1738/39 Althea the daughter of John and Mary Hyde
29 April 1776 Henry Septimus Hyde s. of Rev. Francis and Althea Wollaston b. 14 Apr
14 August 1808 Ellen d. of Thomas and Mary Orchart b. 30 July [married S. Beeton]
14 August 1826 Thomas de la Garde s. of Thomas & Sarah Grissell, Little Britain bldr.

M. 11 May 1758 Francis Wollaston clerk, bach of law, and Althea Hyde spin b.o.t.p. a minor, consent of parents by Thom. Moore min wit. John Hyde, George Wollaston
5 May 1825 Thomas Hood of St. Mary's Islington and Jane Reynolds o.t.p. by licence by Edward Rice officiating minister; witnessed by George Reynolds, John H. Reynolds, James Rice junior and Charlotte Reynolds

B. -- December 1773 Mary Wollaston of Charter House Square
2 January 1775 Francis Wollaston Esq.

St. Martin le Grand (Collegiate)

According to Stow, "In St. Martin's Lane of old time a fair and large college (le grand) with a dean and secular canon of priests was founded in 1056." The college included a monastery with entrance solar and became well-known as a sanctuary for those who had fallen foul of the law. This situation persisted to the benefit of numerous felons for many years. But in 1442 the sheriffs broke down the doors of the church to remove a fugitive and thereafter confirmed rather emphatically, "There is no Immunity."

The college and its buildings were surrendered to Edward VI in 1548 and the church was pulled down. Secular houses were then built there and the east part became a tavern whilst Northumberland House was next door. For some years a plaque marked the site in St. Martin le Grand but during rebuilding was inexplicably removed to Foster Lane.

Gresham Street (west)

Following on from the above exuberant section of note-worthies there is now a complete dearth of famous Londoners - but not of history relating to the area. All of the following four churches fell within the historic Aldersgate ward.

St. Anne and St. Agnes

The church was located just inside Aldersgate on the east side and south of the Roman wall. Its double dedication was unique within the City, but Stow was perplexed by the matter and stated, "The exact reason for this appellation I so far know not."

However it was first mentioned in 1291 and in the Norman records was referred to as both St. Anne and St. Agnes which suggests clerical error was the reason. It is interesting to note that both Rocque and Stanford recorded it on their maps simply as *St. Ann's*, suggesting the later appendage of St. Agnes related to this discrepancy.

What he did know, however, was that the church sat on the north side of Pope Lane named for one Pope who was the owner thereof. This was renamed St. Anne's Lane and was south of the present Gresham Street the church being reached via St. Anne's Alley. The churchyard itself was found on the plot of land situated in-between.

At one time it was known as St. Anne in the Willows although by Elizabethan times any such trees had long gone, whereas at a latter date it was by some distinctive lime trees. The church was destroyed by a fire except the tower in 1548 and was "newly repaired," and it was restored again on three occasions including the steeple in the 1620s. Two fair arched doors were made in the walls of the two churchyards with one to the south, and a paved passage led from St. Anne's Lane across to Noble Street.

Lightening then struck twice and in the Great Fire it was all destroyed except for the base of the tower, and it was then joined to the defunct St. John Zachary parish and was rebuilt by Wren in 1676-87. The church was square in plan and the exterior of red brick included a single round-headed window and extended pediment above, while there was a small tower situated in the northwest corner.

The interior was like St. Mary at Hill and St. Martin's Ludgate with a *cross in a square* and low Corinthian columns supported heavily decorated dipping arches at each corner. Arms of Charles II were above the door on the western side. There was a memorial in the chancel to Peter Heywood d. 2 November 1701 son of Peter a counsellor of Jamaica and Grace d. of Sir John Muddeford - also great grandson of Peter Heywood magistrate who helped apprehend Guy Fawkes and took the dark lantern from his hands. [3]

The church received a stucco exterior in 1821 and later additions were: a reredos from St. Michael's, Wood Street in 1897, a pulpit from St. Augustine's, and a font from St. Mildred's, Bread Street both in 1940. However there was much damage in the war and it was restored without the stucco, receiving a re-creation of the 14th century tower with cupola, and a weather vane sporting an "A" on the top. The restoration was carried out so that the Lutheran Church could take over the building in 1966.

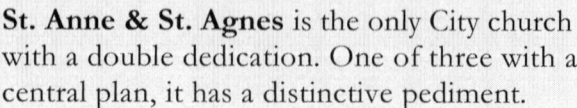

St. Anne & St. Agnes is the only City church with a double dedication. One of three with a central plan, it has a distinctive pediment.

---

[3] Another branch of this family lived on the Isle of Man and Peter Heywood (1772-1831) was a young naval officer on *H.M.S Bounty* with Captain William Bligh.

St. John Zachary

The church was on the north side of Maiden (Engain) Lane where it met Noble Street and was "a fair parish church" with its monuments well preserved. Of these there were ones to Thomas Lichfield who founded a chantry in the 14th of Edward II, Sir Nicholas Twiford goldsmith mayor 1388 and Dame Margery his wife by whom the church was made whole and new built, and also several other goldsmiths.

One of these, Drugo Barentine lord mayor in 1398 donated lands to the Goldsmiths Co. for their hall just opposite (to the south) and dwelt next door. Further to the east was the Wax Chandlers Hall opposite Staining Lane and both halls are present today.

Regarding the incumbents, William Byngham was installed on 25 May 1424 and with the rectors of St. Andrew's Holborn, St. Mary Magdalen Old Fish St. and St. Peter's Cornhill petitioned the Aldermen and King to restore grammar schools. This led to the formation of God's House, Cambridge in 1437 which became Christ's College in 1505.

Another notable resident was Bartholomew Reade a goldsmith who was mayor in 1502 and gave the parish £100. He was reputed to have arranged a sumptuous feast at the Goldsmith's Hall for no less than one hundred persons, but the smallness of the hall meant "this was by far incredible," and Westminster Hall would have barely sufficed for such an astonishing number. Reade was then buried at Charterhouse Chapel.

The church was destroyed in the Great Fire and the parish joined to nearby St. Anne in 1670, while today there is a garden with several trees and a plaque marks the site. To the east across Staining Lane was the large Haberdashers Hall and three halls occupied that site from 1461, just beside an independent chapel. However, the former was moved to an impressive new location at West Smithfield in 1996.

Haberdashers Hall Chapel - C. 5 January 1815 Edward Lear s. of Jeremiah and Ann Clarke born 13 May 1812 [father a stockbroker of Holloway] - see Marylebone

St. Mary Staining

Moving east from John Zachary the traveller sees the edifice of St. Lawrence Jewry in the distance, its asymmetrical tower providing a fine sight. Then, by dodging the proliferation of taxis in the area whose cabbies line up nearby for a chat and a coffee, one comes to the ancient Staining Lane running northwards. City workers hurry everywhere like their contemporaries of old but not a top hat or cap to be seen; while the streets are spotless and clean with no vestige of horses, sewage and sweet aromas long departed.

A quiet oasis - St. John Zachary …

… St. Mary Staining …

... and St. Olave, Silver Street. This small churchyard is by remains of the Roman wall and the Plaisterers Hall.

At the end of Staining Lane located between the Pewterers Hall and offices near St. Alban's, is a small garden with tree of an ancient church. It was listed as a religious foundation *Ecclesia de Stainingehage* in 1189, the likely origin of the name being a family with property in Staines who also owned the land.

St. Mary's is the most popular appellation for a church in the City with no less than fifteen being dedicated to the virgin mother, followed by eight to All Hallows and seven to St. Michael. There are also a number to St. Martin and St. Peter, although this version of the designation was a very small church located beside Oat Lane.

Strype's report had little to say on the matter except that King Edward II owned a tenement in this minor parish whose boundary went to London Wall in the west, and the church was repaired and beautified in 1630. There were few monuments worth noting except those to George Smithes goldsmith alderman on the south chancel wall d.1615, and armorial inscription to Sir A. Savage knighted at Cadiz and general of H.M. Forces at the Siege of Amiens, France in the 39th of Elizabeth d.1632.

The church was destroyed in the fire and it is marked by a small boundary wall, whilst a house replaced the parsonage at a lease of 20s ground rent and the glebe was worth £8 10s per annum. The parish was then joined to St. Michael's, Wood Street.

On an 18th century map the churchyard is shown between the Coach Makers Hall and Frying Pan and Sheers Alleys, which former site was taken by the Pewterers as late as 1960. However their previous hall at Lime Street, an ancient property, had a Charles II parlour with oak panels and moulded ceiling (temporarily in storage).

In more recent times the parish was transferred to St. Alban's in 1897 and then finally to St. Vedast's in 1954. The design of some offices to the west incorporated a curve to protect a listed London Plane tree growing in the churchyard.

St. Olave, Silver Street

Continuing on down Oat Lane there are remains of the Roman wall in front (more of anon), then we turn up Noble Street and come to another small garden secreted among the towering office blocks. A modern information plaque explains that this was originally listed as St. Olave de Mukewelle Strate reference King Olaf in the 12th century.

Stow made little comment except to say that, "it was a small thing with few noteworthy monuments." Due to the presence of the old wall which had tenements up against it, Noble Street then turned eastwards into Silver Street and the church was on this corner. But today Silver Street has been replaced by the highway called London Wall.

The church was greatly decayed being rebuilt and increased in width in 1609 and 1619 then enriched with a fair gallery in 1632 with inscription *Deo Patri Filio Spiritui Sancto.*

The only monuments were to John Darcy son of John Lord Darcy of Ehie d.1593 and to Griffeilde daughter of Henry Lord Windsore and Lady Anne d.1600. There were two small charities, whereas the parish boundary continued north along the wall taking in Lamb's Chapel - then reached across to St. Alphage's and St. Alban's.

It was not rebuilt after the Great Fire and remained there as a garden. The parsonage house was replaced and leased out, and the parish was combined with St. Alban's but is now one of the many under St. Vedast's. Today this is a small sanctuary by the road and there are some 17th century grave stones amongst the attractive lawns.

With reference to the Roman wall there are some good remains just to the west that were uncovered during the blitz. These continue south down to St. Anne's and include the cellars of Victorian properties, whilst opposite is a view into the opulent hall with its chandeliers of the Plaisterers now ensconced at 1 London Wall.

Old Jewry

As stated this was probably denoted regarding its Jewish residents and just opposite St. Olave's Court in Old Jewry is a plaque stating, "The Great Synagogue stood near this site until 1272." In earlier times Lothbury continued west as far as Old Jewry and just to the south was the synagogue, but it was defaced at roughly this date and the Jews after much persecution were then expelled by Edward I in 1291.

To the north of St. Olave's church their houses were replaced by a large stone building which was "a principal palace" under Henry VI in 1438 and thereafter a Royal wardrobe. But by the time of Stow it was built on with several fair houses. The area came within the Coleman Street ward which went beyond the walls and had three churches at the south end (as below), while St. Martin Pomary in Cheap is included for convenience.

St. Margaret's, Lothbury

Lothbury was described by Stow as a street well built and was inhabited by founders who made candlesticks, small bells and like wares from brass and copper. The appellation was possibly derived from Albert Lotheringi a local landowner, or from *lode* a culvert which ran into the Walbrook, since the latter stream ran under the building.

The church itself which now sits just north of the Bank of England was first mentioned in 1181 and a chantry was established in "the chapel" at the time of Edward II (1322). But, it was Robert Large mayor and master of the Mercers who rebuilt it in 1440 giving £120 for ornaments and 200 marks to vault the building over the stream. Regarding this link Caxton had served his initial apprenticeship as a mercer under Large.

Meanwhile, one can imagine these mediaeval city churches appearing like those seen in the countryside or in the provinces at Canterbury, Winchester and York. Here there were several early memorials including ones to Reginald Coleman d.1383 son of Robert the builder of St. Stephen's and Coleman Street, Sir Hugh Witch mercer mayor d.1466, Hugh Clopton mercer mayor d.1496 the builder of New Place in Stratford later home to Shakespeare, and Sir Brian Tuke treasurer of the chamber to Henry VIII d.1536.

St. Margaret's - with external view, famous rood screen designed by Wren, and font and reredos transferred from St. Olave's.

Regarding parish bequests: John Merchaunt common clerk of the City buried at Holy Trinity convent left by his will of 1419 five marks per annum to the rector; and John Benet the parson left from his residue in 1497: one third to the provost of Eaton [sic], one third to King's College, Cambridge and the final third to needy parishioners - Sir William Peacock a chantry priest of St. Peter's Cornhill being his executor. In addition, Henry VIII left a small sum of £3 6s 8d, Anthony Bedingfield a mercer donated £100, and the Mercers Company gave alms of bread to the value of £2 12s.

The ward boundary between Broad and Coleman ran down the middle of the church and to the east was Tokenhouse Yard. The latter was built at the time of Charles I on the site of the Earl of Arundel's House, when it moved to The Strand. On the western side was a water conduit built at the charge of Martin Bowes mayor in 1545, which had water taken from springs between Hoxton and Islington. Next was an alley with the Founders Court and Hall, and in Lothbury itself there were many wealthy merchants.

Some general repairs took place in 1622 but the church burnt down and Wren rebuilt it during 1686-90. The new structure was of Portland stone and the nave had three plain round-headed windows to the south, with a solid balustrade above, while the tower and small spire added during 1698-1700 dominated the concept. Just below the tower was the main entrance consisting of Corinthian columns and a pediment.

Everything about the church was dictated by the restricted site and the interior had a nave, no chancel and a south aisle. Over the years the building became "beautified" with much 17th-century furniture from other churches, ones that succumbed to the ravages of time, and these beautifications now comprise its principal glory viz.

1781	**St. Christopher le Stocks**	paintings Moses & Aaron by the altar c.1700
1892	**St. Olave's, Old Jewry**	altar rails, reredos and font (maybe by Gibbons)
1894	**All Hallows the Great**	the pulpit and the impressive Wren screen

(The screen is only one of two by Wren to survive - the other at St. Peter's, Cornhill).

In addition a bust to Sir Peter le Maire (1593-1631) was placed on the north wall and came from St. Christopher's, as did a list of that church's benefactors for 1601-1717. Le Maire left £1,500 in his will to establish a charitable foundation, and his brother-in-law Sir Francis Crane assigned this to the Poor Knights of Windsor which were associated with St. George's Chapel there (the bust was restored in 1973).

Other memorials were to Nicholas Style an alderman born Langley, Beckenham son of Humphrey and Bridget who married Gertrude daughter of Thomas Bright ironmonger d.1615, and to the incumbent Christopher Flower rector for 46 years d.1698. The organ to the rear was built by George P. England in 1801, and a memorial and bust to Boydell designed by Thomas Banks also came there from St. Olave Jewry (see below). [4]

The parish combined with several others namely St. Stephen Coleman, St. Christopher, St. Bartholomew, St Olave Jewry, St. Martin Pomary, St. Mildred Poultry and St. Mary Colechurch from 1954. In addition there are plaques: "Charles Brooking 1723-59 marine painter lived near this site" Tokenhouse Yard and "Here stood Founders Hall 1531-1845 rebuilt 1666" just beside the church. One of the principal factors benefiting the edifice is the sympathetic re-building on either side, quite unlike that seen elsewhere.

C. 17 April 1662 William sonn of William Docwra by Rebecka his wife
15 March 1662/63 Mary Docwra daughter of Wm. and Rebecka was baptized
(Docwra senior had some important connections and his baptism is below.)

St. Martin Pomary

Just beyond the Mercers Chapel was Ironmonger Lane home to the ironmongers since Edward I. In this lane was the small parish church of St. Martin called Pomary but Stow added "upon what occasion I certainly know not" - although generally it was thought to be derived from the growing of apples there in olden times. The street was just west of Old Jewry and the church was once quite large, being built in place of Jewish properties, and was held by St. Bartholomew's Priory but became a separate parish in 1547.

Further to the west was the narrow St. Lawrence Lane which had no antiquities but fair houses and Blossoms or Bosoms Inn with the sign of St. Lawrence the deacon in flowers above the door. In between were some dwellings and tenements since King Street which went down to Cheapside and on to Queen Street was built at a future date.

---

[4] Ralph Langley was the last to hold the Langley Estate in 1452 and it passed to Sir John Style an alderman of All Hallows Barking, London d.1500. His son Humphrey sheriff was an esquire to Henry VIII and died at Beckenham in 1557 and had three children - Edmund who succeeded him, Oliver who became a sheriff, and Sir Nicholas (as treated above).

Another Humphrey descendant of Edmund was gentleman of the privy chamber to James I while the line was extinct in 1650 and passed to the Elwills. The mansion was destroyed by fire in 1913 then became Langley Park Golf Club, and Langley Farm home to the Colviles (see later) was rebuilt in 1884 and became Boroughs Wellcome research laboratories.

Nearby was Eden Park a classical mansion home to William Eden, 1st Lord Auckland. The Style family have memorials at Beckenham Church where they were benefactors and Styles Way is located on the Langley Park estate with other relevant eponyms.

The old church in Ironmonger Lane was beside St. Olave's and its churchyard was only separated from the latter by the ward boundary of Cheap and Coleman. There were no memorials worth mentioning in Stow's time, but later on there was one to Eleanor wife of Hamlet Clarke fishmonger, one of four clerks to the Lord Mayor, d.1626. Mr. Stodder also left 40s for a sermon on St. James's Day to commemorate the deliverance of 1588, and the Ironmongers donated 50s per annum to the poor.

The north wall was rebuilt by John and Humphrey Slany whose arms appeared on the improvement in 1627, while further repairs were carried out in 1629 - in particular a fair screen at the entrance. All of the church and parsonage burnt down in 1666 and it was united with St. Olave's in 1673. The old parsonage toft was then let by Dr. Hibbert vicar of the latter as a dwelling to raise money for the parishioners.

Rocque's map of 1746 showed the old Pomary churchyard directly west of St. Olave's but today it forms an integral part of the latter on St. Olave's Court. The entry below is to the wife of John Boydell and suggests that the records became intertwined.

B. February 4th 1781 in the doctors vault Mrs. Elizabeth Boydell aged 63

St. Olave Jewry

The earliest record of the church was in c.1130 but excavations in 1985-86 revealed the remains of a 9/11th century Saxon church with recycled Roman bricks and ragstone in the southwest corner. The edifice was also designated as St. Olave Upwell in about 1320 since at the eastern end there was a pump connected to a well.

John Brian the parson founded a chantry there in 1323 and there were monuments to John Forrest vicar and of St. Stephen's chapel d.1399, and Thomas Morested chirurgeon to Henry IV-VI and sheriff 1436 who built the new north aisle d.1450. Amongst the other memorials were ones to: Robert Large mercer mayor 1439 who donated £200, Giles Dewes the clerk of the library to Henry VII/VIII and schoolmaster in French to Arthur and Mary d.1535, and Richard Chamberlain ironmonger sheriff 1562 a merchant adventurer and freeman of Russia d.1566.

On the north wall of the chancel was a picture of Elizabeth I in her stately monument flanked by columns of porphyry and opposite was one of Charles I at devotions, both of these being very large. Within the altar rails there was an ascent on three sides up to the communion table the floor consisting of black and white marble.

The building was repaired in 1608/28, at which time a gallery was added at the lower end but it was without pillars and had a plain ceiling. After the fire it was rebuilt by Wren at a cost of £5,580 in 1671-79 and had a regular plan with central west tower and curved walls joining it to the nave. Arches dating to the 14th and 15th centuries were built into the tower, and at the east end on Old Jewry was a large Venetian window; whilst there was a shared churchyard with St. Martin's from that time.

On the south wall of the chancel were memorials to Sir Nathaniel Hearne sheriff and alderman, governor of the H.E.I.C. who gave to seamen and education d.1679, 50 also Ephraim Skinner merchant consul at Livorno of Islington d.1678, 41. The Clothworkers and Ironmongers also donated money, but the vicarage burnt down and the land was let by Dr. Hibbert to Sir John Frederic who built a house there.

The most notable person connected with this small parish was John Boydell the son of a land steward in Shropshire. After coming to London he was apprenticed to W.H. Toms an engraver at Union Court, Holborn and attended St. Martin's Lane Academy. He then set up business at The Unicorn, Queen Street, Cheapside in 1750 and was said to douse his head with water from the well by the church to awaken himself.

His business expanded from 1770-90 especially after he produced his fine *Collection* of Shakespeare prints. These were displayed at the Shakespeare Gallery at 52 Pall Mall in 1789, the text being edited by George Steevens who specialised in the bard.

Through such success he entered civil life and was master of the Stationers in 1783, an alderman of Cheap, a sheriff and finally the mayor in 1790. He worked with his nephew Josiah and his niece Mary ran his home at Cheapside, whilst his engravings were a great success. But like many of these famous artistes he died almost bankrupt in 1804.

Meanwhile, the church came under the Union of Benefices Act and was demolished in 1888-91 the proceeds of £22,400 going to St. Olave's, Manor Park. The Wren tower, west wall, and part of the north were incorporated in a new building, some of which was the rectory for St. Margaret's Lothbury. The tower was wider at the bottom and had a Doric doorcase with columns and obelisks above, while its sailing ship weather vane came from St. Mildred Poultry. Today the building and gardens are a business premises.

C. 26 April 1635 William sonne of John Dockrey armourer and Margaret his wife (Associated with the Grosvenors and founder of the Penny Post - see page 197.)

B. 10 December 1755 Maurice Greene Esq. aged 60 [master of the King's musick]
19 December 1804 John Boydell died 12th

St. Olave Jewry which could be annotated as "In the Trees."

John Boydell (1720-1804) pictured as the Lord Mayor in 1791.

St. Stephen's, Coleman Street

There is some debate about this church as to whether it was a chapel, a parish, or even a synagogue! It was located at the south end of Coleman Street opposite King's Arms Yard and just to the rear of the north churchyard was the Masons Hall, accessed down a small alley - today a plaque marks the site of the ecclesiastical edifice.

In fact the church was infested with chroniclers of debate and Stow believed it was at one time a synagogue since it had the appellation in the Jewry, and was first mentioned in the reign of King John. Likewise, he considered it to be a chapel of St. Olave's since the vicar Rev. Forrest was also "of the chapel annexed" in 1399. But Strype disputed this and found a record of tenement rents at St. Margaret's for a chantry "in the parish church of St. Stephen's" in 1321. However it is generally agreed that it was initially a chapel of St. Olave's and only acquired parochial status in Edward IV's reign (c.1468).

The Old Jewry, a very fine open street, was graced with good buildings inhabited by merchants and persons of repute; whilst the church to the north was carefully repaired and beautified at the charge of the parishioners in 1622, and further enriched with a very fair gallery in the south aisle in 1629. Regarding its memorials there were ones to Thomas Bradbury mercer mayor 1509, Sir William Glover alderman in the chancel d.1601, and of warring chroniclers that to Elizabeth "I have fought a good fight &c." also one:

"To the memory of that antient servant to the City with his pen, in divers employments, especially, the Survey of London, Master Anthony Munday, citizen and draper of London (long verse) obit aet 80 domini 1633 Augusti 10." [sic]

During the early 17th century the church became known for its Puritan associations and John Davenport whose father was Mayor of Coventry was minister. He left the Church and went to Holland then was part-founder of New Haven colony and died in Boston. The next incumbent Rev. John Goodwin was installed on 18 December 1633 and was in trouble for breaching canons and preached justification by faith. He came into conflict with Rev. Walker of St. John's, Friday Street, a champion of the English Church as the true Catholic religion, and was ejected from his position in 1645 for failing to administer both the rites of baptism and the Lord's Supper.

These were fiery times and Strype bemoaned that, "The church was consumed by the late dreadful fire." It was rebuilt under Wren in 1674-77 and consisted of brick covered in stucco, a northwest tower and tapering at the east end. The latter was of Portland stone with a round window and curved pediment between two pineapples. Inside were two great vaults at the west end, and the gallery on three sides was erected chiefly under the procurement of Mr. William Fazackerly of the Common Council in 1691.

Regarding later memorials Sir Thomas Vernon lived in the parish and was an M.P. for London who was knighted by James II for his loyalty, and on the south wall there was a monument to his son Henry Vernon Esq. who died at Aleppo, Syria in 1684.

In the 19th century the church became associated with *Evangelical Christianity* and Rev. Josiah Pratt (1768-1844) was born in Birmingham the son of a manufacturer. He was an assistant at the reforming St. John's Chapel, Bedford Row in 1795 and married Elizabeth

Jowett on 7 September 1797 residing at 22 Doughty Street just to the north. She was the elder sister of Rev. William Jowett and from a pioneering religious family.

Pratt attended meetings of the Eclectic Society a discussion group that met fortnightly at St. John's. Other notables at the meetings were John Newton of St. Mary Woolnoth, John Venn from Clapham and Thomas Scott who wrote the influential *A Commentary on the Whole Bible*. In the first instance Rev. Pratt posed the vexing question, "How far may a periodical publication be made subservient to the interests of religion," and this gave rise to the *Christian Observer* which he briefly edited.

However the most significant act was to create the Church Missionary Society on 12 April 1799 with Rev. Scott as the first secretary but replaced by Rev. Pratt from 1802-23 who promoted it around the country. The founders included members of the Clapham Sect - Thornton, Wilberforce and John Jowett the father of Elizabeth. Josiah was also a lecturer at St. Mary Woolnoth where he assisted Rev. Newton and he became incumbent of the Sir George Wheler Chapel at Spital Square from 1810-26.

He was then appointed the vicar of St. Stephen's and published a collection of psalms and hymns that sold 52,000 copies and died there in 1844. His son also Rev. Josiah Pratt became his curate and took over the position of vicar from 1844-79, as did his grandson Rev. James Weston Pratt who held the post from 1879-1911. Thus the three ministered to the parish for a total of 85 years consecutively.

Their job was clearly demanding since the church was at the far southwest corner and the parish extended up Moorgate and across to the area of Moorfields (Finsbury Square). Further up Coleman Street was the Armourers Hall and opposite there is a plaque on a modern building in London Wall - "Near this spot at 62 Fore Street on 29 January 1850 was born Sir Ebenezer Howard founder of the Garden City Movement." He is discussed in considerable detail under St. Saviour's, Ruskin Park.

St. Stephen's was one of five churches completely destroyed during the blitz of 1940 and the parish is now part of St. Margaret's, Lothbury.

B. 9 August 1633 Anthony Munday haberdasher was bur.

17 October 1844 Rev. Josiah Pratt B.D. the late vicar of this parish of 15 Finsbury Green aged 75 in vicars vault north aisle by H. Brandrang [sic] rector of Beckenham [5]

---

[5] Rev. Andrew Brandram M.A. born 1790 attended Oriel, Oxford and was curate of Beckenham from 1816-27 then rector from 1838-50. During the intervening years he was minister of the Savoy Chapel from 1825-38 and from 1823 a secretary of the British and Foreign Bible Society. At one time he lived at Elm Cottage, Village Place in Beckenham and died at Brighton in 1850 but has a memorial at Beckenham where he spent so much time.

St. Mary le Bow

Built by Wren
from 1670-80.

"12 Bell Court" was
just to the south.

City Central

A survey of the area around Cheapside showing how the ravages of time meant a large number of churches are now gone - to wit, fifteen in total. Of these only St. Vedast, St. Mary le Bow and St. Mary Aldermary remain with the latter's parish markers exposed during our sojourn.

Particular items of interest include three crosses in Cheapside, the conduits, a prominent school, several Cockneys and the Bow Bells, the mystery of the counterfeit bust and the real truth about Gerard the Giant?

Notable personages in the locale were Mr. & Mrs. Beeton, Admiral Phillip, the Rev. Venn, the poet Shelley, Milton and Leland, Hugh Myddelton of New River fame, and several dissident ministers - whilst the connection between Dr. Mapletoft and Eliot's Little Gidding is duly explained.

Cheapside

Foster Lane ran south from Noble Street but being near to St. Paul's is discussed later, so we leave the backstreets west of the Guildhall and emerge into the main thoroughfare of Cheapside, which formed the old main "High Street" of the City.

This was part of the processional route from Westminster to the Tower and before her coronation Elizabeth I passed this way and a pageant was held. Cheapside or Westcheap was a principal market locality the word cheap or "ceapan" being a mediaeval term for that function, as witnessed by the neighbouring (produce) streets including Milk, Bread, Friday (fish), Honey and the stretch known as Poultry.

Cheapside was a broad expanse even in earlier times but was restricted to the west by the presence of St. Michael le Querne church, a warren of alleyways and the area of the shambles. Also in this location at the northeast corner of the cathedral was Paul's Cross, a meeting place for both exultant preachers and congregation alike. In addition one of the twelve *Eleanor Crosses* was erected nearby in Cheapside by Edward I to the memory of his wife Eleanor of Castile in 1291-94.

This had a symbolic association to the Stations of the Cross in Jerusalem and under the direction of Sir Robert Harley it was demolished in May 1643 - as representing the idolatry and superstition of Catholicism, and providing a visible sign of the changed base from Royal power to autocratic Government. [1]

Also situated here was the Great Conduit which basically followed the processional route. In 1237, Henry III granted rights to take water from the Ty Bourne and a water head appears to have existed in the locality of Oxford Street.

Wood and lead pipes were then run past the Royal Mews at Charing Cross, along the Strand towards Ludgate and joined with a conduit in Cheapside. Another watercourse the Little Conduit was built east of St. Michael le Querne in 1389-90 utilising the same supply, and midway between them was a monument the Standard where the four wards of Bread Street, Cheap, Cordwainer and Cripplegate all intersected.

Cheapside was patently of major significance at that time, consequently a number of important churches were situated there - although only St. Mary le Bow remains today. It also had two schools of considerable repute, the City of London School discussed below and St. Paul's School which is detailed in the next section.

All Hallows, Honey Lane

Opposite to St. Mary le Bow in an area now completely modern was Honey Lane and a small church stood on the east side. This appears to have been a private chapel in the late 12th century being termed Helias presbyter de Hunilane, then Omnium Sanctorum, and even St. Elfigi but was designated All Hallows in Hunilane by 1279.

The parish covered one acre of ground and was a market for cloth while the advowson was held by the Grocers who generally appointed graduates as the rector. At the end of Honey Lane where it met with Cheapside was the Standard cross.

In Stow's report the church only received a few lines so little is known of it although he described the Honey Lane area thus, "So called, not of sweetness thereof, being narrow, somewhat dark, but rather of often washing and sweeping, to keep it clean." He added that there were few monuments except one to John Norman draper mayor 1453, who gave to the Drapers some tenements on the north side of the said church.

Norman represented the City in Parliament in 1449 and being an alderman and sheriff was then elected Lord Mayor. The normal procedure after taking oath at the Guildhall was to ride or walk to Westminster, but he had some infirmity and was the first to go by boat. The watermen are reputed to have adapted an old folk song in honour of the great event, "Rowe the boat Norman, Rowe to thy lemman" (*archaic* for mistress).

In the 16th century it had Lutheran leanings under the Rev. Robert Forman who was rector from 1525-28 and president of Queens', Cambridge. He had a number of books

---

[1] The crosses were erected on the processional route from Lincoln to Grantham, Stamford, St. Alban's, Waltham and the final destination in London after 1291. The last two were situated at Cheapside and at Charing Cross between the hamlet of Charing and the Royal Mews - a replica by T. Earp recently restored sits outside the station. The latter name was possibly derived from this and may refer to chère reine (dear queen) or from cerring a bend in the river.

Cheapside - A view of the busy main City thoroughfare in the 1830s. St. Mary le Bow is seen in a familiar position on the south side.

pertaining to Luther's work and preached accordingly, while his curate Thomas Gerrard became rector in 1537 and contravened the Six Articles. This led to further accusations of heretical associations within the parish in 1543.

The church was repaired in 1625 however as Stow noted it had no bequests or charities for the poor, "nor to any publick use." Consequently it was not rebuilt after the fire and the land on which it stood was purchased by the City, as were some houses and the Milk Street church adjoining it to the west. This then became the Honey Lane Market, and the parish passed to St. Mary le Bow who held the glebe valued at £13 p.a.

The only later event regarding the locality was when the City of London School was built on the site of the market in 1835. John Carpenter the town clerk left a bequest for a school in 1442, and initially this was in the Guildhall Chapel, but the Chantries Act of 1547 closed it down and the funds were then applied more generally.

In the 1820s a number of people including Richard Taylor who helped found University College suggested the need for a permanent school and this was opened at Honey Lane in 1837. There was a Gothic façade on Milk Street reminiscent of a college entrance and during construction remains were found of an Anglo-Norman church - which was either All Hallows or possibly St. Mary Magdalen. As stated the area is now very modern and a plaque in Milk Street records the school site from 1835-82. [2]

St. Mary le Bow

Meanwhile across the road just past the Standard there was a whole different story. The origins of the word Cockney are believed a derogatory term given to the inhabitants by country dwellers viz. a nestle cock from a child that suckled long, or from Cockayne a land of idleness and luxury. By the early 17th century a resident of London was deemed to be "born within the sound of Bow Bells." Cockney was later applied to the whole of the East End although there was never any connection to Stratford le Bow.

Perhaps this interest in bells related to their ringing for curfew and war and Whittington may have heard the great bells at Bow from Highgate Hill (at least in panto land). In fact some milestones have a bow and four bells on them, to indicate the distance measured to the church rather than London Stone or the Standard in Cornhill. But whatever the case there was far more to this historic edifice than simply its bells.

---

[2] Herbert H. Asquith the P.M. attended during 1863-70 and it moved to an imposing building at Victoria Embankment, Blackfriars in 1883. A tablet on the wall records the original bequest, the establishment at Honey Lane and later relocation. It then transferred to a new building on Queen Victoria Street next to St. Benet's church in 1987 and remains there today.

Stow rather perversely talked of the stone arches on top of the steeple but these were built later, then confirmed the word Bow came from the arches of stone in the crypt that it was erected on. This was at a time when other churches were of wood and strangely Stratford le Bow had the same etymology. It was situated in the Cordwainer ward and he believed it was more famous than any other in the city or suburbs.

There is evidence of a Saxon building on the site whilst in the Norman era it was St. Mary de Arcubus (arches) or New Marychurch. In addition to being one of the oldest parochial buildings in the city, the parish was principal peculiar of the Archbishop of Canterbury and home to the *Court of Arches* from the 13th century. Its main jurisdiction was over this parish and twelve others (most of them being adjacent) but in practice it decided more wide ranging ecclesiastical issues and judgements.

In 1090 the 3rd year of William Rufus the roof blew down and the timbers were strewn in the High Street. Then in 1271 there was a disaster when most of the steeple fell down on those within. John Rotham donated some land at Hosier Lane to the church in 1465 and the steeple was gradually repaired, such that a decree was passed to ring the bell there for curfew at 9 p.m. each day in 1469. John Dunne mercer gave tenements also at Hosier Lane to maintain the Bow Bells, while the apprentices whose day ended when it was rung and others in the parish complained that it was being rung far too late!

Regarding curfew, notice was given for it to be rung there and at three other churches some distance away viz. Berkin [sic], St. Bride's and St. Giles, but if any other parish clerk rung after that time - then he was to be called forth to the Ward-Mote. The new steeple was completed in 1512 with the arches thereon and lanterns, five in number to light the way for travellers, all of this being in Caen Stone from Normandy.

William Copland, tailor, the King's merchant was a churchwarden at this time and gave the *Great Bell* which made the fifth in the ring, and a sixth was added later. Apart from these developments there was a redundant grammar school in a house in the churchyard and this was let out with a cellar of the parsonage and part of the vaults.

Stow recorded only a few early monuments to survive viz. John Coventry mercer mayor 1425, and Richard Lambert grocer, alderman and sheriff a merchant adventurer and free man of Muscovia and Russia who died in 1567.

St. Mary le Bow - The tower, linking vestibule and nave - with statue of Capt. John Smith to the west.

The church had a tradition in lectures and five parishioners left a total of £210 which generated some £30 for fees, thus the first lecture took place in January 1621/22. Rev. Smalwood preached this regular discourse and continued it after the fire until his death when it stopped, although it was reinstated a few years later.

The bells continued to be a major feature and the Society of Cheapside Scholars were started there in 1603, and Fabian Stedman "father of change-ringing" was a member but it disbanded shortly before the fire. In addition the bells were rung out to celebrate the demolition of the Eleanor Cross as a blow to Popery in 1643.

Just prior to the fire Samuel Pepys had to visit the church regarding his uncle Thomas and a libel case. This uncle came from St. Alphage's parish and quarrelled with Pepys about a family will then in later life resided at Sion College. On this occasion the diarist noted, "Away thence and to Bow Church, to the Court of Arches, where a judge sits and his proctors about him in their habits, and their pleadings are all in Latin."

Wren's Edifice - Most of the church was destroyed in the fire although some of the tower survived, and Wren came there at an early date establishing an office on the site. The church was rebuilt from 1670-80 by master mason Thomas Cartwright, not to be confused with the Rev. T. Cartwright. A decision was made to remove the old tower and erect a new one nearer to the road - using a portion of the old materials.

For that purpose buildings were removed on Cheapside and a linking vestibule was built to join the nave to the new tower. This was an expensive construction and the resulting steeple was 223 feet high. It was comprised of rising stages of Ionic pilasters then a spire with a circular colonnade of columns and flying buttresses, a square of 12 columns, and an obelisk of granite. Indeed it is considered to be one of Wren's finest creations.

The exterior of the main church was of red brick with white quoins at the corners, and a set of three round-headed windows - the larger one reaching up to a pediment. Inside there was an impressive square nave with Corinthian columns rising to a cornice, barrel roof with clerestory, small aisles, and round-headed windows in an almost imperceptible chancel. During building work the Norman crypt was found and its columns were used to support the structure - and there was also a Roman tessellated pavement.

But what happened to the bells? These were destroyed and the immense new tower was designed to take twelve, but Christopher Hodson of Crayford cast just eight in 1677 then Thomas Lester of Whitechapel Bell Foundry recast the tenor bell in 1738. There is a bit of a mystery since the Bodleian has a document suggesting there were ten bells rung and two tolled before the fire. And on Rocque's map of 1746 "12 Bell Court" is just south of the church off Bow Lane, but perhaps these alley-dwellers were just hopeful!

The other seven which were inferior were recast by Lester in 1762 and two more were added, thus "the ten" were first rung on the 25th birthday of George III. They finally became twelve in 1881 but for several years could not be used, and were restored at the expense of H.G. Selfridge the American retail magnate before the war. [3]

---

[3] Trinity Church in Broadway, New York was established by William III in 1697 and had similar privileges to St. Mary le Bow thus they became sister churches. A new Gothic edifice was built there by Richard Upjohn in 1846 with soaring spire, not out of place in London, and to honour such connections a stone from the Bow crypt was removed there in 1914.

However they were not used for long since the church was completely destroyed in 1941 and the reconstruction was not completed until 11 June 1964. The architect of the refurbishment was Laurence King and it was rededicated by R.R. Robert the Bishop of London. Wren's decision to use the Norman arches caused problems when rebuilding, but the old design was kept with modern furnishings, and the steeple which had survived was taken down and rebuilt. Salvaged metal from the bells was used to recast them at Whitechapel and the twelve were replaced, although using a lighter design.

Present Day - The church is a sole survivor in the area incorporating the parishes of All Hallows Honey Lane, St. Pancras Sopars Lane, All Hallows and St. Mildred Bread Street, St. John Friday Street, St. Margaret Moses, St. Augustine's and St. Faith's.

It is situated on the narrow Bow Lane with the churchyard a pleasing open space and here stands the statue of Captain John Smith (1580-1631). He was a citizen, cordwainer, noted author and parishioner of St. Mary's, also the first settler of Jamestown, Virginia leading to other colonies and the husband of the famous Pocahontas.

Regarding Wren's creation one can use the football parlance "a tale of two churches." His aim to make the steeple clearly visible from Cheapside and the use of materials has resulted in an incongruous design. The towering spire of white stone stands alone against the road distanced from the main church by the vestibule, the latter with its red brick and curving windows at odds with the soaring classical lines of the spire.

It is like the mismatched parts in that children's game where pages are flicked over to create a gir-rhino. However if Cheapside could have been moved south rather than the steeple north it might have worked better and created a more convincing whole. Despite this it remains impressive and the separated nave adds an archaic atmosphere, but the modern building at the northeast corner (now O2) is a planners' disaster. Not something to be built right besides a much loved ancient building.

Upon entering the main doors, since there are two under the tower, one looks up to see a dome. Then there is a procession into the vestibule with its rich wood and carved semi-circular pediments, "church" and "vestry." Just in case the wayfarer loses their way. The interior arrangement works better, and one is promptly presented with King's inspiring design with its recreation of the nave and sanctuary (**see opposite**).

The sheer white of the columns, the gold leaf highlighting the capitals, the dark stained glass above the reredos, the chandeliers and other furnishings, all capped by a Royal blue ceiling cannot fail to inspire. Its restoration is only matched by St. Mary Woolnoth and St. Stephen Walbrook - a fact witnessed by all the tour groups that regularly visit.

One last item of interest is the bronze bust to Admiral Arthur Phillip at the rear of the church on the south side. But is it real? Phillip was baptized at All Hallows, Bread Street in 1738 and entered the Navy in 1755 becoming the first Governor of Australia (d.1814). The stylish bust to him was erected at St. Mildred's by Charles Cheers, Baron Wakefield of Hythe an alderman (1915) on 7 December 1932.

After this church was destroyed in the war it was recovered with two bronze plaques depicting the settlement of Australia, and moved to a plinth in Watling Street with stone inscription underneath. These were eventually brought to St. Mary's for safe-keeping and the plaques stored, while the bust &c. were replaced by a fibreglass reproduction near to No. 25 Cannon Street - see later.

St. Mary le Bow - The opulent chancel as restored by the architect Laurence King in 1964.

With the present day in mind Robert Boyle, who as well as research wrote on religious philosophy, left in his will (of 1691) funds to establish a series of lectures directed at the atheist and unbeliever. The first took place in 1692 and were delivered by Richard Bentley, pupil of Newton and master of Trinity, some of them at the church.

This set up a tradition and Rev. Samuel Bradford rector in 1693-1720 delivered lectures from 1699 on *The Credibility of Christian Religion* - later becoming Dean of Westminster. Another rector William Van Mildert was appointed lecturer there in 1812, although by that time the tradition had declined. The Boyle Lectures were revived at St. Mary's on an annual basis in 2004, the presentation by an eminent theologian or leading scientist; their aim to explore the relationship of Christianity towards the natural world.

C. 9 July 1542 Margrett Hare the daughter of John (an early baptism record) [4]

St. Mary Magdalen, Milk Street

We now return to the north side of Cheapside and to the area of Honey Lane Market and the City of London School. The derivation or origin of Milk Street clearly requires little explanation from Stow since milk was explicitly sold there, whereas the church was a short distance up this narrow street on the east side.

The earliest mention of the building was in the late 12th century, and the locality had many fair houses for wealthy merchants. Gregory de Rokesley who was master of the King's Mint and mayor from 1274 lived in a house there, held by the Priory of Lewes, at 20s per year without being bound to repairs (such were the rents in those times).

A number of mayors were buried: John Browne 1480, William Browne 1513, Thomas Exmew 1517 and Thomas Skinner clothworker 1596 a benefactor to Emmanuel, whilst Henry Cantlow mercer merchant of the staple built a chapel d.1495. Sir Thomas More was born at Milk Street and preached at St. Lawrence's, while a memorial in the south aisle quire to Mary wife of John Collet citizen salter d.1613 may have links below.

Stow records several repairs in 1619 and Benjamin Henshaw a merchant taylor paid for a chancel window at £60. Others took place in 1633 and a new communion table arrived but there was no vicarage, bequests or legacies - thus its days were numbered.

Thomas Cartwright was a preacher there and became rector of St. Thomas the Apostle. Later on he was chaplain to the King, Dean of Ripon and Bishop of Chester and tried to obtain an Act of Toleration for Catholics from the King - going to Ireland in 1688. He

---

[4] The father was a wealthy Cheapside mercer and she married John Audley of St. Michael's, Wood Street. Their son Hugh owned the land that created Belgravia and Mayfair.

was also officiating minister at the marriage of Sir Thomas Whetstone. The latter was a nephew of Oliver Cromwell by his mother Catharine and served in the Commonwealth Navy, but under Charles II became a privateer in the West Indies. [5]

The church itself was not rebuilt after the fire and its parish was joined to St. Lawrence Jewry, whereas the land passed over to Honey Lane Market. Rev. John Mapletoft who became incumbent of St. Lawrence preached a Friday lecture in the parish.

The latter was born in 1631 his father Joshua being vicar of Margaretting, Essex while his grandparents were John and Susanna Collet. As a result he was brought up by the Rev. Nicholas Ferrar his godfather and brother of Susanna at nearby Little Gidding. This was a Christian community involved with the London Virginia Co. and the writings of Ferrar inspired T.S. Eliot to use that name in his *Four Quartets*. However the Puritans denounced this informal gathering as a "Protestant Nunnery."

Mapletoft attended Westminster and Trinity, Cambridge and earned an M.D. then met with many eminent notables such as John Locke, Thomas Sydenham, John Tillotson and later Robert Nelson. Indeed, he became professor of physic at Gresham College in 1675 and vicar of St. Lawrence Jewry in 1686 where he preached until he was eighty. He also joined the Society for Promoting Christian Knowledge and Propagation of the Gospel at the outset and died at Westminster in 1721 (also see St. Lawrence).

Mrs. Beeton - However there was an even more interesting connection in the parish. Had history been different Milk Street might have become a place of pilgrimage for all those budding Jamie Olivers and Delia Smiths. Yet in reality there is very little to mark the momentous events that took place - just some rather soulless buildings.

One Benjamin Mayson was born at Thursby, Cumberland in 1801 but had moved to London by 1831 and was a linen-factor or Manchester warehouseman. He lived in the Marylebone area but also had premises in Clement's Court at the top end of Milk Street on the west side. This backed onto the Compter prison not far from St. Lawrence. He married Elizabeth Jerrom at St. Mary's Bryanston Square in 1835, her father Isaac being a stableman at Wyndham Mews on the Portman Estate.

Their daughter Isabella Mary Mayson was born the next year and generally this is said to have been at 24 Milk Street, although her baptism states of 40 Upper Baker Street. But whichever the case the small family moved to No. 24 soon afterwards. This was a poor area of stalls and shops surrounded by alleys, and the district to the north near Gresham Street was occupied by numerous warehousemen trading in fabrics.

At the same time Samuel Beeton who came from Hadleigh, Suffolk moved to No. 39 the "Dolphin" in 1808 and was a victualler there. On his death his widow Lucy returned to Hadleigh, whilst their son Samuel Powell Beeton was a pattenmaker and worked as a Manchester warehouseman in Watling Street. He then married Helen Orchart daughter of a baker from Wood Street and their son Samuel Orchart was born at Watling Street in 1831, but was sent to his grandmother's in Hadleigh. The father took over the Dolphin and through such connections knew the Maysons for several years.

---

[5] Pepys refers to Thomas Whetstone in his dairy dated 8 March 1662/63 - noting he brought some important papers from King Charles II. However he played a game of subterfuge with those they were intended for "due to his coxcombly humour."

Isabella Beeton cooked up a storm at Milk Street with her *Household Management*.

The City of London School replaced Honey Lane Market in 1835-82 - on the site of two churches viz. All Hallows and St. Mary Magdalen.

Benjamin Mayson died in 1840 being buried at St. Botolph's, Bishopsgate thus Isabella was sent to her grandfather Rev. John Mayson vicar of Great Orton in Cumberland. His widow Elizabeth through her father's connections then married Henry Dorling clerk of the course at Epsom. As a result Isabella spent her teenage years in the grandstand and at Ormond House next to the racecourse kitchens, while helping to look after the twenty children from the three marriages (Dorling was also a widower).

Meanwhile, Samuel Beeton junior became acquainted with printing through advertising associated with licensing and went to the States for that purpose in 1852. The next year he was in business with Charles Clarke a printer at 148 Fleet Street. All of these families appear to be simply tradesmen, but their "trade" was most lucrative and the children of Beeton, Dorling and Mayson were all educated with Madame Heidel in Heidelberg. In addition Isabella had piano lessons from German composer Julius Benedict who resided at 2 Manchester Square in Marylebone (where there is a plaque).

Samuel and Isabella knew one another from their childhood in Milk Street and kept up a romantic correspondence, although this led to a family dispute, and were married at St. Martin's, Epsom on 10 July 1856. Beeton had considerable success publishing books and magazines and they moved to 2 Chandos Villas, Hatch End near to Harrow, an Italianate property of distinction. From there, his wife wrote articles for magazines and with his encouragement they published *The Book of Household Management* in 1861.

The couple had four children although only Orchart and Mayson survived; while Mrs. Beeton's cookery book became the standard guide for running a Victorian household, with instruction on all levels of the social order and all aspects of life. The family moved to Mount Pleasant, Swanscombe in Kent and she died there in 1865. Today there is a memorial to the couple at West Norwood Cemetery (a modern replacement), but their *recipe for success* all began in the aptly named Milk Street.

M. 12 Dec 1661 Sir Thomas Whetstone knight and Anne Dehuberland widow both of St. Clement Danes were married by licence from his grace William, Lord Bishop of Canterbury by me Tho: Cartwright

Poultry

Stow remarked that Cheapside was not solely in Cheap ward which was certainly a very accurate assessment. In fact the ward was mostly at the eastern end and covered seven parishes including the two below, Honey Lane and St. Martin Pomary discussed above, and St. Pancras and St. Sithe's following. However the most inexplicable inclusion was St. Lawrence Jewry to the north whose large parish reached almost to Cheapside.

The modern ward of Cheap runs most of the length of that thoroughfare and does not go far to the north, certainly not as far as the Guildhall. Such an archaic, idiosyncratic arrangement might be contrasted with the Commissioners' Plan for New York in 1811 of road grids and uniform wards (the latter being abolished there in 1938).

Regarding Poultry there are two matters of great contention - one ancient and one modern. In the first instance Stow is uncertain if the old Standard was in the same place as that beside St. Mary le Bow. He contends that it may have been elsewhere or perhaps moveable, since at the time of Edward III there were joustings and horse racing from Sopars Lane to the Great (Eleanor) Cross and it would have stood in the way.

Such problems of location then re-emerged in modern times. The area south of Poultry was already much changed due to Queen Victoria Street in the 1860s, but by 1985 it was proposed to build an 18-storey structure there - opposite the Bank of England, Mansion House and the Royal Exchange. Peter Palumbo a property developer owned the site and several years earlier consulted with modernist architect Mies van de Rohe for the design. Its construction was to involve the removal of eight listed buildings, Mappin & Webb silversmiths to the Royal family, and most of Bucklersbury besides.

A fiercely contested planning dispute took place and Prince Charles termed it "a glass stump" thereby falling out with his former friend Lord Palumbo, and the plan was finally rejected. However, as is common in these matters the issue didn't go away and consent was eventually given, using planning criteria apparently out of line with the location.

James Stirling and Michael Wilford then conceived a building which the Royal Prince soon dubbed "a 1930s wireless set" and No. 1 Poultry was born during 1994-98. With its bands of pink and white stone incongruous to its surroundings, it remains a monument to planning law which states, "We can do it so we will."

One benefit of construction was the discovery of a Roman road and artefacts, dating to 47 A.D. and the founding of London. But as shall be shown this was an extremely sensitive area not unfamiliar to contentious issues of design.

St. Mildred's on Poultry by Wren was located near the Mansion House - but was demolished for its valuable site in 1872.

St. Mildred Poultry

Two ecclesiastical buildings sat on the northern side of Poultry and one was located just west of the Walbrook stream. St. Mildred's was first recorded in 1175 the name possibly derived from the daughter of Ethelbert, King of Kent and founder of St. Paul's.

This was a limited site squeezed between Scalding Alley immediately to the east named for work of the Poulterers, and Compter Alley to the west where there was latterly a prison the Poultry Compter. Due to such restrictions Thomas Morested sheriff, alderman and chirurgeon to Henry IV-VI provided some extra land in 1420 reaching some 45 feet from the Walbrook. In addition a religious body built a parsonage (or mansion) on posts and pillars with a cloister below and four priests' chambers to the east.

At this time the church had become very old and was rebuilt about 1456 with a number of benefactors: John Saxton rector gave £32 for a new choir by the Walbrook, Richard Bowyer parson gave £6 15s for the great east window which displayed arms, and Thomas Ashehill d.1455 a churchwarden gave a great sum towards a south chapel his arms in the roof. Confirming its Catholic associations at the time Christopher Suliok gave 5 marks towards a tabernacle or the Corpus Christi chapel in 1500.

Later benefactions came from Richard Shore draper sheriff 1505 who provided a porch and Thomas Lane scrivener of London Wall near Bishopsgate who gave his tenement to the church for relief of the poor in 1594. At the latter date there was also a successful legal challenge in the Guildhall to stop "an evil doer" from selling the church, so that the parson would have to pay rent to live in his own house!

The most interesting person connected with the parish was Thomas Tusser who came from a farming family in Essex but entered St. Paul's choir, went to Eton and then up to Cambridge where he obtained property. As an Elizabethan writer his most famous work was *A Hundredth Goode Pointes of Husbandrie* in 1557, a rhyming couplet depicting the country cycle; whilst he penned some now popular proverbs: "A fool and his money are soon parted," "Xmas comes but once a year" &c. He died in 1580 and his memorial at the church alluded to such points of husbandry and elements of faith in his work.

The church was repaired at £183 in 1626 then rebuilt after the fire by Wren at public charge in 1671-76. Further repairs took place in 1701 but Strype noted, "It hath no pillars and the ceiling is plain, only adorned with a large garland of fretwork, but a capacious gallery at the west end." The priests' chambers were removed and a tenement shadowed the church, while a map alone recorded the site of the parsonage and cloisters.

There was a later memorial to Dr. William Croone physician, a founder and fellow of the Royal Society d.1684 and to his widow Mary d.1706 who married Sir Edwin Sadleir. Croone had worked on respiration and muscular motion and by her will she left property in Little Knightrider Street to the College of Physicians. She also instigated the Croonian Lecture and Sermon - the latter being revived at St. Mary le Bow in 1970.

The church had many bequests including money for coal and £130 to send a child to Christ's Hospital, but was demolished in 1872 the parish going to St. Olave (with its ship weather vane) and then to St. Margaret Lothbury. There is a plaque to the church next to St. Mildred's Court erected on the Midland Bank designed by Lutyens (1924-39).

C. 2 June 1559 Benedict sonne of Ffrancis Barnham (see St. Clement ref. F. Bacon)

The Local Area - To the east of the church was Broad Street ward and Princes Street which at that time was not straight, having "a turning passage." Indeed it ran across the current site of the Bank of England to come out at St. Margaret's, Lothbury.

Adjacent were four houses followed by the Compter and in olden days a chapel and fraternity of *Corpus Christi and St. Mary's* erected under Edward III. However this was purchased by Thomas Hobson haberdasher (buried in the church 1581) and thus became a warehouse-building and shops with some lodgings above.

Next was Coney Hope Lane due to a sign of three conies (rabbit or fur shop) hanging over a poulterer's stall and this became Grocers Hall Court - or Alley. At the end of the alley was the company of Grocers (formerly Pepperers) who were incorporated in 1345. They bought a mansion and St. Edmund's chapel from Lord Robert Fitzwaters for 320 marks in 1426 and built a Common Hall, later used by the Bank of England. [6]

In terms of prestige the grocers came second only to the mercers and spent 500 marks to buy some adjacent land for seven almshouses in 1429. Further to this Thomas Knollys a grocer mayor gave a tenement in St. Antholin's churchyard for poor brethren, while Henry Keble grocer mayor gave the seven almoners 6 pence per week for ever which was later raised to 2s. Likewise, Henry Ady gave 1,000 marks in 1563 and Sir Henry Pechy gave £500 and built almshouses at Lullingstone, Kent - being buried there.

Beyond Coney Hope Lane was Old Jewry and its shops once occupied by poulterers were then taken by grocers, haberdashers and upholders (upholsterers). The conduit in Westcheap came from Paddington and was castellated with stone and cisterned in lead by the mayor Henry Walleis in 1283, being rebuilt in 1479. The ward of Cheap itself ended at Bow Lane which was originally denoted as Cordwainer Street.

Bank of England - Now where did the Grocers put their money? In the Stuart period there was still a reliance on goldsmith bankers and poor management led to a deficit of public money. At the suggestion of William Paterson a Bank of England was established by Royal Charter on 27 July 1694, and despite the risks individuals put up £1.2 million which was then owed by the Government. Initially the Bank was in the Mercers Hall but later that year transferred to the Grocers Hall where it remained until 1734. In fact at the outset there were just seventeen clerks and two gatekeepers. [7]

The undertaking was not without criticism and Nathaniel Tench the third governor in 1699-1701 wrote a defence of the Bank in 1707. He eulogised that it was of good service to the Government without crime: "They never bought one foot of land, monopolized any commodity or obstructed trade, and by the discounting of bills had lent money upon notes to very great sums at low interest thus lowering the latter; whilst never concerning themselves in the election of MPs."

---

[6] The first hall was replaced after the Great Fire and in 1802 and 1893. However the latter was also lost in a fire and rebuilt in Grocers Hall Gardens off Princes Street in 1970.

[7] Early governors included Sir John Houblon (1694-97) and Sir Gilbert Heathcote (1709-11) and it moved to Threadneedle Street then acquired adjacent premises such as St. Christopher's. "The Old Lady" was rebuilt by Soane the bank's surveyor from 1788-1830 and his statue is there while the rebuild by Sir Herbert Baker in 1925-39 was dismissed by Pevsner as vandalism but is listed. Houblon grandson of a Huguenot appeared on the reverse of the £50 note in 1994.

"**Mrs. E. Fry** (1780-1845) prison reformer lived here 1800-09." Elizabeth Gurney part of the Quaker banking family of Gurney and Barclay married Joseph Fry a tea dealer whose uncle started W.S. Fry chocolates. The marriage was at the Norwich Meeting House on 10 August 1800 but they then lived over a shop in St. Mildred's Court where the plaque is found. On the decease of her father, John Gurney they moved with their children to Plashet House, East Ham and daughter Katherine wrote a history of that area. Fry was a minister in the Society of Friends and first visited Newgate in 1813.

"In a house on this site **Thomas Hood** was born 23 May 1799." A short distance along Poultry on the north side is a plaque to the poet who was discussed under Aldersgate. He later resided at 28 Finchley Road, St. John's Wood where there is also a plaque and his memorial is at Kensal Green Cemetery.

"**Disraeli** worked here 1821-24." There is a plaque to the Prime Minister at 6 Fredericks Place significantly off of Old Jewry at the southern end. He was born in 1804 and during his time there was articled as a solicitor.

Mercers Hall - the frontage on Cheapside was built in 1676, but restored in 1877.

St. Mary Colechurch

The significant factor about the second church near Poultry was its connection to the powerful Mercers Company. In terms of precedence the latter received first place from 1551 followed by the grocers, drapers, fishmongers, goldsmiths and merchant taylors. All of these still have halls commanding an imposing presence in the City.

At the south end of Old Jewry was the parish church of St. Mary's named for one Cole who built it (similar to Coleman). It was situated next to the Great Conduit and erected on a vault such that parishioners had to ascend some stairs to reach it. There were no monuments in the edifice; however it is recorded that William Marshall &c. were given permission to found a brotherhood of *St. Katharine* by Henry IV in 1400 - the reason being that Thomas à Becket and St. Edmond Rex were baptized there.

The living was just a curacy under the Mercers before the fire but they gave it over to the incumbent, although the church did not own the site. The above fraternity or guild was confirmed by Henry VI in 1447 but little else took place there and the church was repaired in 1623. It was not rebuilt after the fire despite objections that the area was over-crowded and it joined with St. Mildred's who gained a gift sermon. There was one 'parish' baptism of note presumably at the latter and today the church has a plaque.

C. 23 July 1757 Thomas son of William and Mary Rowlandson b. 13 July [a satirist]

The Mercers Company - On the north side of Cheap Street west of St. Mary Colechurch was the Mercers Chapel and Hospital. Thomas Fitz Theobald de Helles and his wife Agnes, daughter of Thomas à Becket, founded a hospital just west of Ironmonger Lane in 1190 on the site where her father was born. He was the son of Gilbert a mercer and reputed Crusader who married a Saracen woman who released him from prison. She being from Acre the hospital was dedicated to St. Thomas of Acon (or Acars).

Henry III provided additional land confiscated from the Jews such that the Mercers who held the hospital occupied the site between Ironmonger Lane and Old Jewry. They were officially incorporated in 1393 and in the time of Whittington became trustees of his college near to St. Michael's. Initially they dealt mainly in woollens competing with the Lombards but by Henry VI's reign traded in fine silks and velvets.

A number of prominent mayors were connected with the Mercers and the company were closely linked to the hospital as a fraternity. The associated church of St. Thomas's was very grand and lay back from Cheapside in what were monastic grounds of the Augustine order with cloisters and gardens. In addition, Sir John Allen built a separate chapel for the company beneath their hall in front and was buried there.

However at the Dissolution the hospital and church of St. Thomas's were taken by the Crown, and purchased mainly due to the efforts of Sir Richard Gresham. It then became the official Mercers Chapel and contained many monuments including ones to:

Stephen Cavendish draper 1362 ancestor of Cavendish and Devonshire, Thomas Butler Earl of Ormond 1515, Sir W. Locke sheriff 1548 and several mayors: Sir Edmund Shaa goldsmith 1482, John Allen 1525, Thomas Leigh 1558, Richard Malory 1564 all of them mercers and George Bond haberdasher 1587. Allen's chapel was converted to shops and an Italian convert the Archbishop of Spalatro and Dalmatia provided sermons.

An image of Becket on the hospital gate was destroyed in the time of Elizabeth I but the whole site was rebuilt after 1666. A free grammar school connected to the company (since 1542) occupied the location of St. Mary Colechurch, whilst the Mercers Hall was rebuilt just beside Ironmonger Lane with a new chapel to the east. [8]

The second hall was destroyed in the war and the Mercers are now on the same site just off Cheapside. A recessed area has the motto *Honor Deo*, several banners and stained glass windows with stylish entrance beyond; although not as impressive as Barclays next door. Inside, there appear to be parish markers, one of St. Mary Colechurch and two of St. Martin in the Fields where the company owns land, while a brass and a blue plaque record the birth of Thomas à Becket in c.1120. In addition the *Mercers Maiden* an old sculpture (dated 1669) can be found in Corbet Court off Gracechurch Street.

Mercers Chapel M. …. April 1707 Thomas Arne senior and Anne Wheeler

---

[8] The Mercers School remained in Cheapside until 1787 then after some temporary sites went to College Hill next to St. Michael's in 1808 - but was finally closed in 1939.

Budge Row

At the east end of Watling Street was Budge Row with Sise Lane to the north leading up to Pancras Lane. This locality was considerably altered by Queen Street, the Cannon Street extension and Queen Victoria Street which went right through the site.

The area near to Sopars or Pancras Lane was associated with curriers, leather workers and shoemakers in the time of Henry VI, whereas Cordwainer Street (Bow Lane) gave rise to the Cordwainer ward which had three churches: St. Mary le Bow treated above, St. Mary Aldermary and St. Antholin's. Also included in this section are St. Benet and St. Pancras on Sopars Lane which came under Cheap ward but were nearby.

St. Antholin's

This was a substantial church with an interesting history however since the war the area became tarnished by office blocks, grey and drab in the extreme, and Budge Row where it sat was generally underneath them. Today the location is to be redeveloped across to Walbrook Street, with the only ancient survivor the Mithras Temple ruins to the north, which was situated quite close to the original site of the church.

There is not a great deal known of the mediaeval building and Stow called it "the fair parish church of St. Anthonine's in Budge Row on the north side thereof." In fact, the first records were during the 12th century, and it was initially rebuilt and re-edified by Thomas Knollys grocer mayor 1399 and his son Thomas grocer mayor 1410.

It was repaired by Sir William Craven alderman and others in 1616, which combined with a gallery added in 1623-24 cost upwards of £900. Indeed the gallery was very rich and beautiful, every pane or division being filled with the arms of Kings, Queens and Princes of the Kingdom. These included Edward the Confessor right down to Frederick who was Count Palatine of the Rhine, Duke of Bavare and Prince Elector.

There were memorials to Thomas Knollys and to Henry Colet mercer mayor 1495, a great benefactor who was buried at Stebunhithe (Stepney) and had a window. Whereas another fine tomb located in the chancel was to William Dauntsey mercer, alderman and merchant of the staple died 1543.

St. Antholin's, Budge Row - Wren's church with its impressive lead-covered spire, as seen from Watling Street. The tablet was first erected in Budge Row in 1880, but is now by the wall of St. Mary Aldermary.

After the fire it was rebuilt by Wren being one of his most original creations. It had a central plan with an elongated octagon of columns, and oval dome in an irregular space tapering to the west. There was an oval window and the spire was an elongated octagon as at St. Swithin's and Margaret Pattens (still present). Strype noted that there was a large comely cupola and the church and gallery were pewed at this time.

The new structure was completed in 1678-82, and during the work a strange discovery was made. Above a small door in the south quire was a curious ancient figure clothed in scarlet with hands open, which was reputed to be of John Wells whose executors built the Standard in Westcheap. Meanwhile, there was a lecture every day of the week divided among three preachers and the mercers, merchant taylors and skinners donated money to the poor, and the ground of the parsonage was leased out.

Regarding this, Mr. Hotchkis, incumbent with St. John, reported to a parochial visitation in 1693. There were encroachments on the unbuilt church &c. and the parish underhand had consented to them, as had the mayor and court of aldermen without the consent of the Archbishop and Bishop of London. Rents were received by the Chamberlain while part of the ground of the parsonage house had been taken into a nearby property.

In latter years the most significant link was Rev. Richard Venn who began a dynasty of reforming preachers with multifarious connections. The family had been clergy since the Reformation and his father Dennis was rector of the remote parish of Holbeton, Devon and he was born there on 7 January 1690/91. He attended Sidney Sussex, Cambridge and married Mary Ann Isabella Margaretta Beatrix Ashton in November 1716, who was the goddaughter of Mary of Modena which accounted for her lengthy name.

Venn became a priest at St. Giles, Cripplegate the next year and rector of St. Antholin's in 1725-39, whilst several children were born at their home in Barnes. He was a preacher at Paul's Cross, an intimate friend of Henry Temple 1st Lord Palmerston and opposed Rundel's appointment to the see of Gloucester - a most inflammatory affair.

His son Henry Venn was born in 1725 and was the rector of Huddersfield and Yelling, whereas grandson John Venn (1759) became rector of Clapham. Both were prominent in promoting the evangelical revival, and with Jowett and Wilberforce were involved in the Clapham Sect and the Church Missionary Society (see Clapham &c.).

Regarding St. Antholin's there was a strange development. The top part of the spire had to be rebuilt in 1829 and the original with its weather-vane was sold to Robert Harrild a printer who erected it on his property Round Hill House near Sydenham. The house was later demolished, but this unusual artefact and survivor now stands in Round Hill among modern houses off Dartmouth Road - being quite a surprise to see.

The Union of Benefices Act put "redundant" churches in the City under pressure and St. Antholin's was demolished in 1874, despite its architectural importance. The money thus released went to the repair of St. Mary Aldermary and a new church St. Antholin's at Nunhead. The doorcase with its fluted Corinthian pilasters, fruit and flowers also went to St. Mary's. A tablet relief of the church was erected in Budge Row in 1880 but by the nineties was placed in storage, and was re-sited outside St. Mary's in memory of Douglas Alfred Barber the church warden from 1989-2000.

B. 20 February 1738/39 The Revd. Mr. Richard Venn buried - two others that month (His grandson John was rector of Clapham and led an evangelical revival)

St. Benet Sherehog

At the east end of St. Antholin's was Sise or Sithe's Lane which ran northwards up to two small churches located on Pancras Lane next to Bucklersbury. Today three plaques are to be found in Pancras Lane just off Queen Victoria Street namely St. Pancras 1666, St. Benet Sherehog 1666 and the Institute of Taxation formed in 1930.

The latter church started as a single cell in Saxon or Norman times and was recorded in c.1111. Stow then remarked, "On the north side of the High Street in Budge Row by the east end of St. Anthony's have ye St. Sithe's Lane, so called of St. Sithe's which standeth against the north end of that lane, and near to Soper's Lane."

This was a modest building and the name was amended with Benet Shrog or Shorne after one Benedict Shorne a fishmonger who built and repaired it in Edward II's reign. In addition John Fresh bequeathed rents from his property in Do Little Lane by his will of 1397 and the memorials included three mercer mayors viz. John Froysh 1394, Henry Froweke 1435 and Sir Ralph Warren 1536 merchant of the staple in Callis.

Other monuments there were to Sir John Lion grocer mayor 1554 and Edward Hall of Gray's Inn the under-sheriff d.1547 who wrote some important *Chronicles* from the time of Richard II to Henry VIII, in particular on the Houses of Lancaster and York. These writings were then used by Shakespeare when producing his historical plays.

The church being very much decayed and perished was amply repaired and beautified by the parishioners in 1628. But it was destroyed in the fire and not rebuilt - the parish and churchyard going to St. Stephen's, Walbrook. According to Strype the plate, bells and other ornaments had long ago been embezzled by the churchwardens, while after the fire the only funds were £5 p.a. from Mr. Davison for keeping a vault in repair.

St. Mary Aldermary

In this instance Stow noted, "At the west corner of Budge Row on the south side and to the east of Cordwainer Street [Bow Lane] is another fair church called Aldermarie, being old, and older than any church of St. Mary in the city." With fifteen others of that name this was hard to confirm, and the appendage probably signified it was older than nearby Le Bow, or it was dedicated to the elder Mary rather than Mary Magdalene.

The first mention came in 1080 but it was rebuilt by Sir Henry Keble grocer mayor in 1510, whereas a new tower was begun in 1530 and the upper part was completed in 1629. This latter work was made possible by bequests from William Rodway who was born there but lived at St. Michael Bassishaw and Richard Pierson who gave about £300 each. Indeed the result was one of the finest churches anywhere in the city.

Of the memorials these included Thomas Romane mayor 1309 who had a chantry, Richard Chawcer vintner who gave a tenement in Royal Street d.1348, and Sir William Laxton grocer mayor founder of Oundle School d.1556. Regarding Keble his daughter Alice was second wife of Sir William Browne, and wife of William Blount Lord Mountjoy who erected Keble's memorial - which stated he spent £2,000 on the church. [9]

---

[9] Stow believed that Richard was the father of Geoffrey Chaucer but it is generally stated that he was named John. However the Chaucer family were indeed employed as vintners.

St. Mary Aldermary - showing the fan-vaulted Gothic ceiling and restricted site on Queen Victoria Street.

After the fire the church was rebuilt by Wren mainly in the Gothic style from 1679-92. This was at the expense of Ann Rogers, a niece and executor to the will of Henry Rogers a wealthy Somerset squire, who stipulated that it should be "a faithful copy of the old." Indeed, the tower built at great expense by Keble partially survived the fire and Wren rebuilt the top and faced the rest with Portland stone. The chief glory was its fan-vaulted ceiling the only such example in the City, whilst an organ by G. England was added to the west in 1781 and later restored and moved to the north aisle.

One significant marriage was of Edmund Creswell to Susannah Drawbridge in 1802. They resided in the parish of Kingston near Lewes where he was a corn merchant and yeoman. In fact the old post office which remains was once a grain store. Edmund then moved with his wife and children to nearby Falmer, but was appointed Agent for the Packets in Gibraltar in 1822 - basically the postmaster under another name.

Three generations of the family carried on this duty in Main Street, with son Edmund taking over from 1831 and becoming Surveyor of all Post Offices in the Mediterranean in 1867. A granddaughter Margaret Susan was the postmistress from 1877 to c.1907 and was awarded the I.S.O. The original Post Office at 104 Main Street was the family home until 1890 and they had connections to many prominent families, including the Carvers who emanated from Ingarsby - a deserted village in Leicester (see All Souls).

Closer to home James Braidwood was interested in fire fighting after surviving a fire in Edinburgh in 1824, and moved to Watling Street and established a London Fire Engine utilising a scientific approach. His company fought fires at Bank 1834, Royal Exchange 1838 and the Tower 1841 however he died during the notorious Tooley Street fire on 22 June 1861 - being buried at Abney Park Cemetery. He is considered to be "The Father of the Fire Brigade" and there is information on him in the north aisle of the church, while Mr. Brian Henham has written a book about this real life hero.

The area was greatly changed with the building of Queen Victoria Street in 1871 which in one sense opened up the aspect of the church, but offices erected on the south side still obscured it. The result was that the tower and one aisle protruded leaving the best view from the east - whereas a parish marker is located opposite.

An extensive Victorian restoration took place in 1876-77 the money coming from the sale of St. Antholin's (a tablet on the south side of St. Mary's records this). Pevsner stated this was one of the most important late 17th-century Gothic churches with perpendicular interior, stunning fan vault, and slant on the east wall due to the shape of the site. In fact the door-case at the west end was transferred from St. Antholin's.

To the rear there is a tablet recording the history regarding the rebuilding by *Kebble* in 1510 and by Wren at the expense of Henry Rogers (when it joined with St. Thomas); also the addition of St. Antholin's and St. John the Baptist in 1873. The building remained intact during the blitz and became a guild church in 1954 the parish going to St. Mary le Bow. There was also a major restoration in 2005 in particular the ceiling.

M. 24 February 1662/63 John Millton of St. Gyles Cripplegate and Elizabeth Minshall of St. Andrewe Holborne married by licence [3rd wife]

16 January 1802 Edmund Creswell o.t.p. of Funtington in co Sussex batch and Susannah Drawbridge o.t.p. spin by licence by me John Frith Am both signed pres John Balcock, Phillis White, Richard White [only five others that year]

14 November 1838 James Braidwood supt. fire establishment of 68 Watling Street son Francis cabinet maker to Mary Ann Jane Jackson wid. of 69 Watling St. daughter Samuel Sibery a gent by licence by H.B. Wilson rector witness Margaret and M.J. Jackson

St. Pancras, Sopars Lane

Now who ate all those pies? In Henry VI's reign the lane was occupied by cordwainers and curriers thus the grocers and pepperers moved to a more open site in Bucklersbury. With such spices freely available the locality was famous for its pies and they were placed out for sale during the time of that prodigious feaster Henry VIII.

Meanwhile, at the upper end of the lane in Cheapside was found the common place for standing to watch great cavalcades and shows. During these Kings, Queens, Princes and Foreign Ambassadors passed by on their way from Westminster to the Tower &c.

There is little known of the early church history although given the dedication it seems likely it went back well into the Middle Ages. It was probably quite similar to St. Benet's in style and was just a short distance to the west of the latter, whilst a small apse was added to the original Saxon church during Norman times.

Stow stated in 1598, "Then in Needlers Lane have ye the parish church a proper small church but divers rich parishioners therein and of old times many liberal benefactors." It appears that Needlers Lane ran west into Sopars Lane, being interchangeable with it, and then went north up to Cheapside. The latter section was replaced by New Queen Street after the fire and the rest of Sopars Lane became Pancras Lane.

However, these liberal benefactors departed "and of late the bell was broken and sold for half the value rather than recasting it, while many memorials were in bad repair." But despite this the church was restored in 1621 and the main benefactors were Sir Thomas Bennet alderman, Dame Anne Soame and Mr. Thomas Chapman.

The principal memorials *all gone* were to four mayors: John Barnes mercer 1370, John Hadley grocer 1379, John Stockton mercer 1470 and Sir Richard Gardener mercer 1478. Stow also recorded Thomas Knollys mayor and son Thomas twice mayor, although they were listed at St. Antholin's and the mayoral records show only 1399 and 1410. Likewise there was one to Elizabeth I "in thanks for her restoration of the true faith." [10]

The primary benefactor was Thomas Chapman whose will dated 1615 requested three sermons (which transferred to Bow Church) one for the deliverance of 88, one reference the Gunpowder Plot, and one for the accession of the Queen. This was to be paid for out of his annuity to the church of £3 10s. In addition, he provided an expensive table for the church bearing the figure of Queen Elizabeth in 1617.

His son Thomas Chapman junior paid for the building of a fair porch in 1624 and left a further legacy of £11 3s in 1626. Part of this was to supplement his father's sermons and part for another sermon to be preached on St. James's Day, 25 July (his birthday). The money also provided dinner for the parson, churchwardens and relations who were in town on that day, the poor of Barly Hertford and Bursted Essex, sweeping of the pulpit at Paul's Cross, and two lanthorns [sic] with candles to be hung in the parish - the funds for this to come from the rents on a tenement at Whitecross Street. [11]

After the fire the parish went to St. Mary le Bow with the sermons but the churchyard remained on Rocque's map in 1746 next to that of St. Benet. Today, this is still present in the form of a small garden with an ancient wall and plaque beside it.

Bread Street

Stow described Watling Street just south of Cheapside as, "A street of great thoroughfare, with good buildings, which are very inhabited by great dealers, chiefly by wholesalers." This was the middle road of the City starting south of St. Paul's at Old Change then ran across Bow Lane and into Budge Row - which bent southwards to reach Cannon Street. It remains today as a narrow, mostly paved area but is shortened at each end.

Running north to south was Bread Street inhabited by rich merchants and divers fair inns for the receipt of carriers and travellers to the city, also Buckingham House. One of these the Mermaid was frequented by those famous writers Donne, Fletcher, Jonson and Shakespeare. Bread Street (Hill) continued down to Thames Street, and the ward of that name reached from Cheapside through to Old Fish Street and Trinity Lane.

The latter had four parish churches All Hallows and St. Mildred in Bread Street and St. John and St. Margaret in Friday Street, whereas the modern ward has an extension up to Paternoster Square (which was formerly part of Farringdon Within).

---

[10] The Mercers and Grocers Halls were just to the north and have already been discussed.

[11] The term "lanthorn" referred to lant a type of cow which produced horn with a translucent quality. From this derivation came the modern word of lantern.

All Hallows with St. Mildred's behind.

One of its most notable neighbourhoods was The Mercery at the top end of Bread Street an area inhabited by mercers. When Edward III began his reign in 1327 he decreed that no foreigner should bring in gold or silver coin, and Old Change where the King's coin was exchanged lay nearby. The mercers then moved east to be replaced by goldsmiths, while no plate could be sold except at the Exchange or by the goldsmiths in Cheap.

Thomas Wood a goldsmith and sheriff then built the opulent Goldsmiths Row at the upper end of Bread Street in 1491. This was a single frame structure with ten four-storey dwellings and fourteen shops situated on Cheapside, near to the cross at Cheap. It was adorned with coats of arms and woodmen on beasts, all cast in lead with rich paintwork and gilding. The properties were then given to young goldsmiths and Sir Richard Martin who was mayor in 1594 dwelt there during his mayoralty.

All Hallows, Bread Street

The church was situated at the southeast corner of Watling Street whilst behind was Red Lyon Court and opposite was 3 Cups Inn (an alleyway). The first written record was in the early 13th century and the principal monuments were to John Walpole a goldsmith 1349, Thomas Beaumont sheriff 1442 and three salter mayors: Robert Basset 1475, Sir Richard Chaury 1494 and Sir Thomas Pargiter 1530.

In fact several salt merchants settled in Bread Street by 1394 generally meeting at the church. Thus Thomas Beaumont a salter, sheriff and alderman gave land for a hall and six almshouses for decayed brethren on the east side in 1454. Several fires occurred at the site and each time the hall was rebuilt - but they moved away in 1641. [12]

In the reign of Henry VIII in 1532 there was a serious fight between two of the priests. This resulted in the closure of the church and no service sung for a month. In addition they went to prison and as penance walked the streets barefooted and bareheaded with beads and books in their hands. Laurence Saunders was minister at the time of Mary I and preached against the Popish religion and became a martyr, while George Marsh his curate then returned to Lancashire suffering a similar fate.

On 5 September 1559 "a great tempest struck London" causing lightening and a terrible clap of thunder which struck the stone spire (as judgement maybe) - it was taken down to spare any costs. With the church in disarray Richard Stock came there as priest in 1611 having lectured at St. Augustine's and been a private tutor. He spent 32 years working for the Church with piety and wisdom and died there on 20 April 1626, while his loving parishioners erected a memorial to him on 28 January 1628/29.

At this time one John Milton senior was disinherited by his Catholic father and came to London setting up as a scrivener in Bread Street. He married Sarah Jeffery and their son John was born there in 1608 (a plaque marks the site). Due to some financial success the

---

[12] A new hall was built at London Stone after the fire, and in 1827, but was destroyed in 1941. Their modern hall at Fore Street was built to the design of Sir Basil Spence in 1976.

latter was educated by a private tutor Thomas Young possibly through links to the rector Rev. Stock and then at nearby St. Paul's School. After a university education he went on to become an acclaimed author, poet and promoter of the Commonwealth.

Tablet (at St. Mary le Bow) - "John Milton was born in Bread Street, Friday 9th day of December 1608 and was baptized in the parish church of All Hallows on Tuesday 20th." Erected at All Hallows in the 19th century and moved when pulled down in 1876.

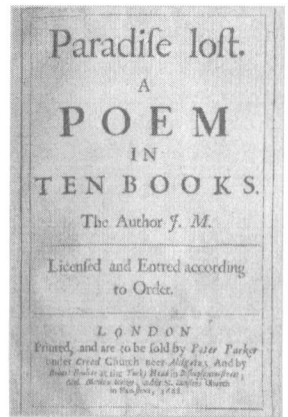

John Milton (1608-74) - his epic discourse on life, the universe and everything; with **a parish marker** located in Watling Street.

Meanwhile, the church was well repaired at the parishioners' expense in 1625; and in the Salters Chapel on the south side built by Thomas Beaumont a new window was erected in 1629. This depicted the aforementioned philanthropist in an unusual pose.

After the fire the parish was joined to that of St. John the Evangelist and Wren rebuilt the structure in 1681-84. The tower was boarded up due to the large amount of work being undertaken at other churches, and after a petition was finished by Hawksmoor in 1698 - the total cost £4,881. Strype described the completed edifice as being, "Without any pillars, but it is very decent and a lightsome church."

The side of the building along Watling Street displayed round-headed windows and a balustrade above, whereas the detailing suggests it was designed by Hooke. The steeple in Bread Street had a bell-stage completed in 1684, whilst its main features were distinctive triple openings and four corner obelisks added later by Hawksmoor.

During the next one hundred years two notable families were resident in the parish. The first of these was Admiral Arthur Phillip who was born there in 1738, and is discussed under St. Mildred's (where he was commemorated). The second connection is to Samuel Powell Beeton who married Helen Orchart at All Hallows in 1830. As stated he was a local warehouseman and his son Samuel O. was born at 81 Watling Street and baptized there in 1831. The latter spent his early years at Hadleigh and was educated at Pilgrim Hall Academy in Brentwood before entering the printing business.

However the population of this vibrant area declined and the parish passed to St. Mary le Bow in 1876, and the church was demolished the next year. Money from the sale then helped to build All Hallows, East India Dock Road. The richly-carved pulpit went to St. Vedast's, the font cover to St. Andrew by the Wardrobe, and the organ case replaced the one lost at St. Mary Abchurch (in 1940). Bread Street now covers just the northern end and is wholly modern; the only indication of its past being a plaque to John Milton. This is located on the eastern side near to the top of the road.

C. The XXth daye of December 1608 was also baptized John ye sonne of John Mylton a scrivener - the other baptism being Thomas son of Thomas Goodies draper

A type written note adds: *John Mylton author of "Paradise Lost" born 9 December*

11 November 1738 Arthur son of Jacob and Elizabeth Phillip was baptized: b. 11 Oct
3 April 1831 Samuel Orchart son of Samuel Powell and Helen Beeton of Watling Street warehouseman by Gerrard Thos. Andrewes

M. 21 April 1830 Samuel Powell Beeton o.t.p. and Helen Orchart of St. Alban's Wood Street by licence by Gerrard Thos. Andrewes rector witness Thos. Orchart, M. Cooper

St. Mildred's, Bread Street

This was situated below All Hallows south of Basing Lane (now Cannon Street) and was also on the east side. It was dedicated to St. Mildred the Virgin by 1252 and its memorials recorded its history viz. Lord Trenchant of St. Alban's the builder and benefactor c.1300, John Shadworth mayor 1401 who gave a parsonage, vestry and yard in 1428 (monument pulled down) and Sir John Hawlen who built a further parsonage d.1485.

Shadworth left several endowments by his will in 1429 including to Nicholas Overton the rector one *placca terrae* to the south for the rectory, a tenement in St. Bartholomew the Less for the abbess and convent of St. Clare Aldgate, and tenements in Basing Lane for the rector of St. Alban's, Wood Street. Later memorials were to Christopher Turner chirurgeon to Henry VIII and Sir Ambrose Nicholas salter mayor 1575.

Nearby were some interesting oddities one being the Compter prison on the west side which was owned by Richard Husband the gate-keeper. Sir Rowland Hill mayor in 1549 found him guilty of ill-using the prisoners and of charging thieves and strumpets a nights lodging at 4d per night "to avoid searches abroad." For these indiscretions he was sent to Newgate while the prison was closed and replaced by that in Wood Street.

Such problems were long lasting and the reporter Arthur Pember, who went to New York, arranged to be arrested on a trumped-up debt in 1871. He then spent several days and nights as "a poor prisoner" in Ludlow Street Gaol near Avenue A. During his stay he became ill on slops and bad ventilation, but prisoners with money spent their days in comfortable cells and received entertainments (see Brixton). Indeed, these were perfect situations for Dickens' *Mark Tapley* who revelled in such misfortune!

Returning to 16th-century London, which clearly mirrored New York's vagaries, it was noted that the Compter was located between divers fair houses and inns for passengers. Just north of the church was Basing Lane. In this lane was a hostelry called Gerard's Hall - and in that hall a 40 foot long pole said to be "the staff of a giant."

Stow, wishing to be further illuminated on the matter, visited the premises and spoke to the hostler who confirmed its length and said *"It was so described in the Great Chronicles as belonging to one Gerard a giant."* However further investigation revealed the hall belonged to John Gisors and his heirs, mayors in 1246/1311 constables of the Tower, the name a corruption. In fact the pole, as was the fashion in old times, was set up outside the hall in summer as a Maypole and decked out with holly and ivy at Xmas time.

Returning to the church interior there was a memorial to John Ireland d.1614 deputy of the ward and first master of the Salters who resided there some 60 years. It was on the south side of the chancel and erected by his grandson Capt. Nicholas Crispe.

In addition there were windows either side of the chancel given by Hester wife of Ellis Crispe and her son Samuel, and at the upper end a fair window paid for by son Nicholas. The latter was in five parts viz. the Armada in 1588, Queen Elizabeth's monument, the gunpowder plot 1605, the plague 1625 and the Crispe family. Lastly Nicholas gave a sum of £75 and Samuel £25 towards the repairing of the building in 1628.

The church was rebuilt by Wren utilising an elongated central plan in 1677-83 and this included a plain parallelogram, saucer dome and short barrel-vaulted bays to the east and west - with Gerard's Hall Alley just behind. Strype then noted, "It hath no pillars but a very fine cupola and ceiling curiously fretted; the pulpit is extremely good work being inlaid and richly carved [perhaps by Gibbons]." However it was destroyed in 1940 and the parish went to St. Mary Aldermary then St. Mary le Bow in 1954, while the carvings and font cover were removed to St. Anne and St. Agnes.

M. 30 December 1816: Percy Bysshe Shelley o.t.p. a widower and Mary Wollstonecraft Godwin of Bath, spinster a minor by licence with consent of her father William Godwin, married by William Heydon curate, witnessed by William Godwin, M.J. Godwin

Percy Bysshe Shelley - Regarding this celebrity he was born near to Horsham in 1792 the son of Sir Timothy a Whig M.P. However his grandfather Bysshe Shelley came from New Jersey but through a profitable marriage had built up Castle Goring in Sussex. The aspiring poet was educated at Eton although he despised its tyranny and was sent down from Oxford in 1811 for his pamphlet, *The Necessity of Atheism*.

He then eloped to Scotland with Harriet Westbrook a 16 year-old schoolgirl and spent time in Ireland carrying out radical propaganda, but often left his wife and daughter alone visiting William Godwin's house and bookshop at 41 Skinner Street, Holborn (near to Newgate). Godwin was a journalist and political philosopher however Shelley fell in love with his daughter which resulted in a two and a half year estrangement.

During this time the lovers had addresses at St. Pancras, Blackfriars Road and Pimlico and there were two journeys to Switzerland. In the first instance they travelled with her step-sister Claire Clairmont; then the three with John Polidori, Lord Byron and a young son at which time they rented two residences including the Villa Diodati. It was here that some famous writing and nascent creativity took place (see St. Pancras).

On their return the couple went to Bath although the Godwins were still living in their Holborn house-cum-bookshop. After the death of Harriet in 1816 they married just a few months later at St. Mildred's, by which time her father gave his consent; whilst the choice of church is hard to explain but was probably due to its legal proclivities.

Regarding the details of the wedding it was carried out by the curate, and the witnesses are the father and his second wife Mary Jane Vial Clairmont. The couple then spent time in Italy and in addition to the classic poem *Ozymandias* the writer delivered *The Mask of Anarchy* reflecting events in Britain at the time. He also produced *The Liberal* newspaper with Leigh Hunt and Lord Byron as a rebuke to more conservative magazines, from Italy to avoid prosecution, but was sadly lost at sea off Leghorn in 1822.

And perhaps this poet is reflected in the demise of Wren's churches with their many years of labouring, architectural aspiration and inscriptions to notables, once grand and majestic, but now paved with tarmac as vehicles hasten heedlessly above them:

"And on the pedestal these words appear: 'My name is Ozymandias, King of Kings; Look on my works, ye Mighty, and despair!' Nothing beside remains - Round the decay Of that colossal wreck, boundless and bare - The lone and level sands stretch far away."

St. Mildred's (interior) - showing the barrel-vaulted bay at the west end.

Percy Bysshe Shelley

Admiral Arthur Phillip - One other significant piece of history relates to this famous pioneer who was baptized at All Hallows, Bread Street on 11 November 1738. His father Jacob was a language teacher from Frankfurt and the son attended Greenwich Hospital School and joined the Navy during the Seven Years War, then after several positions was put in charge of the fleet to Botany Bay in 1787. Among the eleven ships in the flotilla were *H.M.S. Supply* under Capt. Ball and *H.M.S. Sirius* under Capt. Hunter.

On arrival he found it unsuitable and moved the convicts in his charge to Port Jackson naming it Sydney Cove, and was Governor of the colony and settlement (a few huts) until 1792, being replaced by John Hunter three years later (see Hackney). On leaving the Navy he retired to Bath and was buried at Bathampton in 1814, but for many years his role in this pioneering colonisation was largely forgotten.

As a result Charles Cheers, Baron Wakefield of Hythe alderman of Bread Street ward and mayor 1915-16 presented a bust of Admiral Arthur Phillip, citizen, founder and first Governor of Australia born in Bread Street. Its rousing motto noted, "The success of the first settlement at Sydney on Saturday 26 January 1788 was due to him." [13]

Next to the bust were two brass plaques depicting the historic event: The first shows a rowing boat leaving *H.M.S. Supply* on the Saturday with crew Capt. Arthur Phillip, Lieut. P. Gidley King and Lieut. George Johnston marines. The second depicts five men on the shoreline, being the discovery and fixing of the site on Wednesday 23rd - surg J. White, Capt. Arthur Phillip RN founder (with hat), Lieut. George Johnston marine ADC, Capt. John Hunter RN and Capt. David Collins marine (kneeling).

The bust and plaques were unveiled at St. Mildred's by His R.H. Prince George on 7 December 1932 - also a memorial at Bath Abbey in 1937. However after the church was destroyed in the war they were erected outside; but were rededicated at St. Mary le Bow by Archbishop F. Everard before Hon. Sir Alex Downer High Commissioner in 1968. In fact the versions in the garden west of Watling Street are fibreglass duplicates.

Admiral Arthur Phillip (1738-1814) - replacement bust and plaque depicting the founding of Australia in 1788, situated near the site of Friday Street.

---

[13] The Rev. Phillip "Tubby" Clayton established Talbot House (Toc H) as a soldiers club and rest home for all ranks behind the Ypres salient at Poperinge in 1915. After the war the movement grew and received a Royal charter in 1922, while Baron Wakefield purchased the property and donated it to the Talbot House Association in 1929.

Friday Street

In the lottery of time Friday Street did not fare well and only 70-yards remains between Cannon and Queen Victoria Streets. It originally ran north-south from Cheapside to Old Fish Street between Old Change and Bread Street, whereas Stow noted, "Now in Friday Street so called of fishmongers dwelling there who served Friday's Market." Its significance becomes apparent when one considers there were once three churches present.

St. John the Evangelist

However all of these churches served very small parishes and St. John's (the middle one) was on the east side below the junction with Watling Street from the 14th century. Stow made few remarks about it, but noted monuments to John Dogget merchant taylor and sheriff 1509 and Sir Christopher Agnew draper mayor 1533.

During its brief history the most significant events were in the early 17th century when Christopher Foster held the rectory. He had tutored one George Walker a graduate of St. John's, Cambridge and resigned the benefice in his favour on 29 April 1614. At the time it was "the smallest parish in London." Walker, a man of holy unction and humble heart, then turned down any prospective improvements and remained there all his life.

Being of strict Puritan persuasion one of his first acts was to accuse Anthony Wotton the lecturer at All Hallows, Barking of the crime of Socinianism and deviation from the *Trinity*. The latter was ultimately acquitted although the debate continued for many years and during this period there were numerous "conferences on religion."

Walker became chaplain to Nicholas Felton, Bishop of Ely in 1619 and as a respected theologian he entered into disputes with Papists at the church and nearby viz. Sylvester Norris and John Fisher a Jesuit convert. The church itself was repaired in 1626 including a gallery at the cost of Thomas Goodyeare a parishioner and draper.

However the rector then preached against the Bishop of Ely regarding the Lord's Day and published *A Doctrine of the Sabbath* in 1638, thus Archbishop Laud had him sent to prison. This was declared unlawful by the Commons and from 1641 he concentrated on preaching and writing, including a treatise "God made visible in his works, an account of a debate with a Jesuit, and a rejection of Socinianism." The latter recorded some conflicts with Rev. John Goodwin of St. Stephen's who breached canons and again with Wotton, whereas Walker remained a champion of the English Church.

He joined the Westminster *Assembly of Divines* in 1643 at the start of the Civil War and preached a sermon before the House of Commons with published epistle in 1645 which recorded his imprisonment. Walker died in 1651 and was buried at the church. This was the main item of interest and after the fire it was not rebuilt, while the parish was joined to All Hallows, Bread Street and the small churchyard appeared on Rocque's map.

A plaque at No. 25 Cannon Street at the west end of Watling Street near to St. Paul's marks the site, and records the fact the church was "destroyed in the Great Fire." The adjacent garden has the reproduction bust to Admiral Arthur Phillip on the original base with its inscription and two plaques (as shown opposite).

St. Margaret Moses

This was another small church and parish just south of St. John's at the corner with Little Friday Street. It was also on the east side and in the part of Friday Street which survives today. Like others it was first recorded in the 12th century, and Stow stated that it was named for one Mr. Moyses who was the founder or new-builder of the church.

Nicholas Bray and Nicholas Stanes both founded chantries, whereas John Rogers held this living and St. Sepulchre from the Crown from 1550. The principal monuments were to Sir Richard Dobbes skinner mayor 1551, William Dane ironmonger sheriff 1569 and Sir John Allet fishmonger mayor 1590. Unlike its neighbour there were a couple of small legacies but there was no parsonage and it was repaired by the parishioners in 1627. Not surprisingly it disappeared after the fire and was joined to St. Mildred's, Bread Street in 1670 thereby passing to St. Mary le Bow in 1954.

Situated opposite the church in Distaff Lane was the Cordwainers Hall and Stow noted they were a fraternity in 1410 with a Royal charter in 1439. With regard to this Richard II married Anne of Bohemia in 1382 bringing the fashion of piked boots, tied to the knee with silken laces or chains of silver and gilt. However, Edward IV made a decree in 1464 stating the beak should not pass above two inches on pain of a fine of 20s, whereas any cordwainer who shod a person on a Sunday would forfeit 30s a pair!

The location of the hall is now covered by Cannon Street at the modern junction with New Change. It is marked by a plaque stating: "On this site stood six successive livery halls of the Cordwainers Co. from 1440 until the destruction of the sixth in 1941."

St. Matthew's, Friday Street

This was the most significant church in Friday Street and in the days of Stow the top end was adjacent to the Eleanor Cross. St. Matthew's was a short way down on the west side and unlike the others had an entrance at the east end. A small alley called Fountain Court abutted the northern side and it fell within Farringdon Infra ward, whilst it was first recorded in the 13th century and sometimes given the postscript of Cheap.

In the parish were three abodes standing together all pertaining to religious houses. The one in the west belonged to the Dean and Chapter of St. Paul's, the middlemost was a tenement of Robert Harding goldsmith and sheriff let for 30 years by the prioress and convent of St. Helen's in 1470, and that to the east belonged to St. Mary Overie.

A number of goldsmiths had monuments in the church from the 14th century, and of its benefactions Sir Nicholas Twiford mayor gave a house nearby called the Griffon on the Hope with its appurtenances. But the two most significant people connected with the church were Rev. Henry Burton and Sir Hugh Myddelton.

Burton like his neighbour was educated at St. John's and was a Puritan involved in the debate between Walker and Fisher, whereas he criticised Archbishop Laud for Catholic tendencies. After the accession of Charles I he was appointed to the parish in 1625, but continued to protest and was cited at Doctors' Commons in 1636. The Star Chamber sent him to the Fleet Prison and he was later removed from London then after a change of policy he was released in 1641. Upon returning to the church he lectured at St. Mary Aldermanbury, whilst Laud was then charged with treason.

Hugh Myddelton the son of the governor of Denbigh Castle became a goldsmith in London and was M.P. for Denbigh from 1603-28. As a wealthy merchant he had mines in Wales and undertook major engineering projects including a harbour at Brading, Isle of Wight, and significantly built the New River to bring water from Ware to Clerkenwell. He was a parishioner and churchwarden and has a memorial at Islington Green near to the end of the aqueduct. In fact Myddelton Square is nearby (see Vol. II).

The church was repaired in 1632-33 however dissent continued and Pepys noted a very worrying disturbance in August 1662. Several of the churchgoers cried out "porridge" a retort against the *Book of Common Prayer* and some were even seen to tear it apart. The diarist added, "…which appears to me very ominous, I pray God will avert it." [14]

During the Great Fire the building was 'torn down' and Wren rebuilt it in 1682-85 and some extra land was provided. The parish was then combined with St. Peter's. This was one of Wren's cheapest designs being an irregular rectangle built of rough materials, but the visible east end was faced with stone. The latter had a row of five round-headed windows, with cherubs above, and the tower in the southwest corner was very plain with just one bell. Perhaps this lack of funds pertained to the recusants.

The parsonage house was not rebuilt after the fire and the ground was leased out. As compensation for the extra land taken up during rebuilding, the parish was to have £240 per annum from the "coal money" received by the Chamber of London. Henry Venn was influenced by *A Serious Call to a Devout and Holy Life* (William Law, 1728) as were Wesley and Whitefield and came to the parish as curate in 1750. He left for Clapham in 1754 but remained a lecturer at St. Alban's and St. Swithin's in London.

Notwithstanding all these links the united benefices kicked in and being of restricted merit the church was demolished in 1886. As with other churches the pulpit and font went to St. Andrew by the Wardrobe while the parish, monuments and altar table were transferred to St. Vedast's. A sum of £22,000 was then raised from the sale of the land and this was used to build St. Thomas's at Finsbury Park.

However, the most significant event was when Mrs. Margaret Greville purchased the reredos after her husband obtained Polseden Lacey, Surrey in 1906. The house had a very interesting history being discussed elsewhere, and the reredos was erected in the main hall with other major changes at the time. The hostess then entertained Edward VII and it became a honeymoon retreat for George VI and Queen Elizabeth. Indeed, this feature with its Corinthian columns, large pediment, and recess for the Ten Commandments can still be seen at the National Trust property today.

In the 18th century the north end of Friday Street had several alleyways including Blue Boar Court, Saracens Head Inn, Angel Court and Bell Inn near the church, but by 1862 only Mitre Court still survived. This section of Friday Street was destroyed in the war and built over by New Change Buildings later the Bank of England Offices, and recently has been redeveloped once again in the ultra-modern style.

B. 10 December 1631 Sir Hugh Middleton [sic] knight

---

[14] The Act of Uniformity proscribed the rites of the church in 1662 as laid down in the *Book of Common Prayer* and "porridge" was a Puritan term for the said Book. It reintroduced Episcopal ordination abolished under Cromwell and 2,000 clergy then left the Church.

Foster Lane

The ward of Farringdon Within (or Infra) was always quite complex and covered the area to the west of Cheapside, taking in St. Paul's Cathedral and part of Newgate Market, then down past Ludgate to Blackfriars and the river. In addition a narrow section extended right up to Lamb's Chapel and the wall at Cripplegate. Today, it has lost the area to the east and instead incorporates some land above St. Bartholomew's.

The ancient ward which also included the area beyond the walls was named after one William Farendon [sic] a goldsmith, sheriff and alderman who purchased the aldermanry in the 9th of Edward I (1281). His son Nicholas, four times mayor 1308-23, was buried at St. Peter's in 1361 - apparently some 53 years after first being elected.

There was a whole list of parishes covered by the ward including three of those below but excluding St. Leonard's which was just in Aldersgate. Six more churches and St. Paul's which were also in the ward are considered in the next two sections, whereas St. Matthew in Friday Street has already been treated. There were two religious brotherhoods in the locale ministering to the townsfolk but at the same time depending on their charity, the first the Franciscans or Greyfriars established in 1209 and the Dominicans or Blackfriars founded in 1215. As mendicants they took a vow of poverty but their houses in London appear to have become collectively, extremely wealthy (see later). [15]

St. Leonard's Foster

The church of St. Leonard's was on the west side of Foster Lane above St. Vedast's just opposite to Rose and Crown Court and was first recorded during the 13th century. The small parish served those who lived in the precincts of St. Martin le Grand College, and could also be accessed along alleyways to the west such as Round Court.

A number of tenements were built in place of the collegiate church and as a result the residents living there were "mightily increased" in number. Outside the church the name of John Broke was engraved in stone, he being the new builder thereof. A fair window was inserted at the upper end of the chancel in 1533, and the structure was repaired in 1631 at a considerable cost of £500.

There were few monuments while the church and vicarage (partly over an alley) were not rebuilt after the fire. The parish was then combined with Christchurch to the west and the site became the main Post Office in 1829. A plaque to the church is now located in St. Martin le Grand.

St. Leonard's ruins - with St. Vedast's behind.

---

[15] These were distinct from the Benedictine order first established in the 6th century and its later offshoots the Cistercians and Cluniacs, which were both self-sufficient and withdrawn.

St. Michael le Querne

This parish dated to the 11th century and the name was a corruption of *At the Corn*, since a corn market occupied land west of the church stretching over to the shambles. It was also called St. Michael ad Bladum. John Mundham established a chantry there in 1311, and it was rebuilt in stone in the reign of Edward III. This was confirmed by the fact that Thomas Newton the (first) parson was buried in the quire in 1361.

To the east of the building was the start of Cheapside and the Old Cross but the latter was taken down in 1390. The church was then rebuilt in 1430 and William Eastfield *the Mayor and Corporation* gave ground to the north and east for enlarging it. Both of these were just beside Paul's Gate at the northern end of Old Exchange, and in place of the cross the Little Conduit was installed at a cost of 1,000 marks in 1431.

The church, however, was in a restricted location and blocked access from Cheapside to Newgate causing a considerable problem. Just to the west was Blowbladders Street and then came Lovels or Lovets Court. This was once a large house belonging to the Earls of Brittany, later owned by John Lovel and called Lovel's Inn in 1422. Beyond there was the edifice of St. Nicholas at the top end of Ivy Lane (above Paternoster Square).

Regarding matters of antiquity, John Leland was born in London in c.1506 and was one of the early pupils at St. Paul's School. He had a university education and became a tutor while Henry VIII appointed him a chaplain near Calais and his official library keeper. As a result he approached Thomas Cromwell to try and preserve all of the records of the dissolved monasteries. In addition he received the rectory of Great Haseley, Oxfordshire in 1542, a canonry at Oxford (city), and a prebend at Sarum (Salisbury).

These appointments were generally a sinecure and with ample funds he set forth over six years. He then stated, "I have traviled your dominions booth by the se costes and middle partes sparing nether labor nor costes;" and using material from ancient buildings, cathedral libraries and monuments published the first local history: *A New Year's Gift* (or) *Itinerary* in 1549. Suitably exhausted he retired to St. Michael's parish hoping to do a history of the shires, but is thought to have "lost his wits" and died there in 1552.

Stow followed in his footsteps and recorded his memorial located in the church. The latter was repaired in 1617 and again in 1638-40, with some classical advice from Inigo Jones that was not welcomed. It was destroyed in the Great Fire and with the parsonage was laid into the street to improve access, although the little conduit still remained. The parish itself was then combined with nearby St. Vedast's.

Strype noted a small passage Panyer Alley to the west, joining Paternoster Row with St. Martin's Lane. In this alley was the figure of a boy on a pannier with grapes in token perhaps of plenty, with inscription below: "When ye have sought the Citty round, yet still this is the highest ground, August 27, 1688." This is still present, and there is also a rusty parish marker on St. Paul's Choir School of 1855, sporting an armorial crest.

B. 18 April 1552 John Leyland [sic]

The famous antiquary as pictured and the relief in Panyer Alley.

St. Peter's, Westcheap

The church of St. Peter the Apostle was at the southwest corner of Wood Street and was just opposite the Eleanor Cross erected by Edward I. There were few records until the 15th century and Thomas Wood goldsmith and sheriff 1491 was believed to be one of the principal benefactors due to some images of woodmen on the roof.

According to Stow it was a proper church newly built and John Shaa goldsmith mayor d.1503 left money to rebuild it with both a flat roof and steeple. In fact Queen Elizabeth was presented with a Bible when she passed by the church doors in 1559.

It was repaired at a cost of £314 in 1616-17 and had coats of arms displayed. There were also memorials to three mayors: Nicholas Farringdon goldsmith (four times) the son of William d.1361; Sir John Mundy goldsmith 1522 whose wife descended from William and John Browne and Edmund Shaa; and thirdly Sir Alexander Aventon 1569.

There was no parsonage before the fire; whilst the narrow strip of land in front of the church was occupied by a long shop which encroached on the road and was let for £3 per annum. Nearby in the parish was Goderon (Guthurun) Lane whose inhabitants had long been goldbeaters although their Easter money was generally made of silver. In this lane (later Gutter Lane) was the Embroiderers Hall - discussed under St. Vedast's.

The Rebuilding Act of 1670 did not include St. Peter's but Wordsworth wrote of the locality in his poem *The Reverie of Poor Susan*. Today it is a small garden overshadowed by offices with a tree and gravestones, and the shops recorded above still remain.

St. Vedast alias Foster

St. Vedast was a Gallo-Roman saint, Foster being the English equivalent, and the only other such dedication is at Tathwell in Lincolnshire. The church was first recorded in the 12th century and was listed as St. Faster in 1315-16, Saints Vedast and Amandus in 1352, and as "St. Fauster's, a fair church lately new built" at the time of Stow.

Today this is a significant building but of little fame in its earlier years. Henry Coote a goldsmith and sheriff built St. Dunstan's chapel there d.1509, and other memorials were to William Trist cellarer to the King 1425, John Browne sergeant painter and alderman a benefactor 1532, and John Lonyson master of the mint and goldsmith 1583.

However there were two connections of note. Nicholas Hilliard son of a goldsmith was born in Exeter in 1547 and travelled overseas with John Bodley, then was apprenticed to Robert Brandon Royal jeweller and married his daughter. He lived at Gutter Lane and St. Martin's and was a miniature painter of renown in particular for Elizabeth I.

Likewise, Robert Herrick also son of a goldsmith was born in Cheapside in 1591 and went to the Merchant Taylors, then was apprenticed to his uncle Sir William Herrick a jeweller to the King. He attended St. John's, Cambridge writing poetry as an aficionado of "The Ben Jonson School" and became vicar of Dean Prior in Devon.

During the Civil War he was deprived of his position for Royalist leanings and moved to Westminster depending on the charity of relatives. At this time he published his most famous work *Hesperides* which included a poem with the line "Gather ye rosebuds while ye may" pertaining to virgins. Charles II reinstated him to Dean Prior in 1662, especially as his poems had venerated the King and he died there in 1674.

The church received some major repairs in 1614 including the re-laying of stones, some new pews and an enlarged window in the north aisle. It was only partially destroyed in the fire and initially it was patched up in 1670-73, while some extra land was obtained by seconding "a fair court" from the Saddlers Hall to the east.

Wren then took charge of matters and rebuilt the church on remains of the walls from 1695-97, the pewing and ornaments being carried out the next year. The interior was a plain rectangle with a south aisle and an arcade of Tuscan columns, although the door to the west was 17th century and pre-fire. The famous steeple may have been started at this time with stone from Greenwich, but was finished as funds became available, and in terms of architecture was disproportionate to the main body of the church.

The latter upon examination appears to have been designed in two stages and the lower section is square and plain. The upper part displays two-tiers of moulded columns with openings topped by an obelisk - clearly exhibiting shades of Hawksmoor.

There were a couple of memorials from that time: William Fuller D.D. vicar of nearby St. Giles and Dean of Durham d.1659 *"loyal in times of rebellion"* and William Hall deputy of the ward and goldsmith d.1680, 75. In addition the organ by Renatus Harris who built one of those tried at Temple Church was installed there in 1731. This was followed by a number of beautifications which arrived from other churches:

The altar piece came from Christopher le Stocks in 1781, the organ-casing came from St. Bartholomew by the Exchange in 1841, the pulpit from All Hallows Bread Street in 1875, and the communion table from St. Matthew's Friday Street in 1884. The tower and spire both survived the war, but much restoration was needed and Sir Hugh Casson initially suggested the steeple be left there as a war memorial.

St. Vedast's, Foster Lane
Showing the two elements of the tower with Hawksmoor's double lantern - and the interior towards the east end.

Nicholas Hilliard (1547-1619)
He was a renowned miniature painter to the courts of Elizabeth I and James I.

This rather quaint idea was ignored and instead it was fully restored by Stephen Dykes Bower who worked on Westminster Abbey. The result was a stunning interior ensemble in collegiate style with pews on each side facing the font, leading down to the altar and reredos with three round-headed windows at the east end. The floor detail, capitals and ceiling are extremely intricate and the south aisle is separated by a wooden partition to form a chapel - the whole composition being completed in 1962.

Externally the main feature is the baroque steeple which contains six bells and recent redevelopment has been "restrained," so this is still visible from Cheapside and St. Paul's. Regarding the nave, the curved mediaeval stone and brickwork is displayed on the south and east sides. The church is full of interest and the modern glass doors make the interior clearly visible to pedestrians in Foster Lane, just beyond the vestibule.

There are few memorials but the information board notes that the church is connected to eight livery companies and the churchwardens included Lt Col Sir John Laurie mayor 1941 and the poet laureate John Betjeman. The organ was restored by Noel Mandor and the church now covers 13 united parishes being the sole survivor of them viz.

Michael le Querne, Matthew, Peter Cheap, Alban, Olave Silver Street, Michael Wood, Mary Staining, Mary Magdalen, Michael Bassishaw, John Zachary, and Aldermanbury; as well as St. Anne and St. Lawrence which are no longer parish churches.

To the north of the church there is a small doorway and just inside is Fountain Court. This is of compelling design with a cloister garden and covered colonnade, as well as the rectory and a bust of Epstein in a niche. All of this reminds one of most ancient times and in the southern wall are Roman tesserae from a pavement found beneath the site of St. Matthew's, Friday Street in 1886.

Continuing up Foster Lane one comes to Priest's Court and walking along it there is a good view of the rear of St. Vedast's, also the gardens of the Saddlers Hall with a classical porch - although such a façade seems un-necessary. Just to the left is a plaque recording the site of the Broderers Hall 1515-1940 (Embroiderers) and soon after is Gutter Lane. On the right is the front entrance of the modern Saddlers Hall with noted pilasters and scrolls and a coat of arms with motto "Hold fast, Sit sure." [16]

C. The 14th day of Auguste 1591 Robert Herricke sonne to Nicholas was baptized

M. XVth July 1576 Nicholas Hilliard and Alice Brandon were married
29 October 1808 William Peto bachelor and Sophia Alloway spinster b.o.t.p. by banns by Wm. Parker minister witness Henry Peto, Caroline Hassell (see p.44)

Rector: Rev. Francis Wollaston 1779-1815 - with East Dereham and Chislehurst

---

[16] The Saddlers Hall stood on Cheapside beside St. Vedast's since 1395 but the building dates from 1958, while further up Foster Lane is the Goldsmiths Hall located there since 1339. The latter structure with its monolithic columns, grand doors, and gilt at the entrance was designed by Philip Hardwick (see later) during 1829-35.

City West

The third precinct of the City covers the western area within the old walls, all of the churches noted being within a stone's throw of great St. Paul's. In addition it takes in the ward of Farringdon Extra centred on Fleet Street, the extent of its jurisdiction once delineated by the Temple Bar.

Not a place for the common man but one of Kings, Lords, Noblemen and Knights with a plethora of Friars to keep things bubbling along. Here were found some Royal Palaces in abundance cheek by jowl with religious houses and "at His Majesty's displeasure" - a few prisons besides.

Amongst the note-worthies are acclaimed military, naval and artistic heroes with memorials at the Cathedral whilst the nearby churches record Hogarth, Jones, Bushnell, Hazlitt, Brunel, Richardson and Pepys to name but a few. In addition this was the haunt of that loveable old rogue Dr. Johnson, also the birthplace of two aspiring Prime Ministers.

Wren's cathedral as completed - and St. Faith's parish pump of 1819 by the Chapter House.

St. Paul's (area)

All of the churches in this section came within the ward of Farringdon Infra except for St. Gregory at the southwest corner of the cathedral. Today, however, the boundaries are re-aligned and this area is generally located within the Castle Baynard ward.

To the east of the great church was Paul's Cross built in the late 12th century, and site of political assembly. Henry III commanded one in 1259 and in person told the mayor to have every boy of twelve and upwards pledge allegiance to their King. Likewise in 1262 he read a bull there from Pope Urban IV of his absolution, whilst all who were sworn had to maintain the articles agreed in Parliament at Oxford.

Then in 1299 the Dean cursed all those who had searched for a hoard of gold at St. Martin in the Fields, and the cross was hit by lightening and rebuilt by Thomas Kempe the Bishop of London in the year 1449. Money was provided to pay for preachers at the cross and nearby was The Shrowds an area of communal shelter.

The Lord Mayor in 1607, to encourage those from the universities to preach, said they would be entertained with sweet and convenient lodging for five days thereafter! The site had a pulpit-cross of timber mounted on stone steps and covered with lead, however it was demolished by the Long Parliament in 1643 (a tablet and memorial mark the site), and all the preachers then retreated inside to less inclement surroundings.

Nearby was the bell-house belonging to Jesus Chapel, consisting of a large stone and timber frame, a great spire covered in lead and four bells within. It is believed that at the Dissolution, Sir Miles Partridge won the clochier by gambling £100 on the roll of a dice against the King. Thereafter he pulled the whole of the edifice down. A structure of like appearance or at least function can be observed at Chichester today.

Also in this area, between the cathedral and Old Change, John Colet D.D. the Dean of St. Paul's and chaplain to Henry VIII founded St. Paul's School in the year 1512. This learned gentleman was the son of Sir Henry Colet a mercer and twice mayor, thus it was overseen by the Mercers Company and he left land worth £120 p.a. for its upkeep. The foundation initially provided for 153 children regarding John ch.21 v.11, and such were the workings of Dean Colet's mind to provide for so many students. [1]

The school abounded with inscriptions and mottos suggested by the Dean, who provided an *Introduction to Latin* for their elucidation and a catechism with the articles of faith. Being well endowed it was one of the largest in the country and Colet, who was a critic of many aspects of church life, associated with both Erasmus and Sir Thomas More.

St. Paul's School (1827) situated in Old Change.

---

[1] Simon Peter was unable to catch any fish, but Jesus appeared and told him where to cast his net; the resulting haul being 153 fish precisely.

After the fire it was rebuilt with a library in the same location and many of its pupils appear in this book, but the most significant was surely John Strype the chronicler. The school moved to a building there with grand classical façade in 1822, but as people left the area it relocated to Hammersmith in 1884 and later to Barnes.

The Choir or Cathedral School which had similar origins to the grammar school had a reputation for acting as well as singing, and moved to premises in Carter Lane in 1874. However a modernist building was erected on the site of the old school in New Change in 1967, just beside the ruins of St. Augustine's. A plaque there records "Near this spot from 1512 until 1884 stood St. Paul's School founded by Dean Colet."

Moving anti-clockwise around the cathedral below Paternoster Row (now Square), one came to the Bishop's Palace situated on the northwest side. This had a great hall and inside the bishop would entertain the Kings of England therefore a great household was kept for that purpose. For instance Edward V stayed there before taking possession of the Crown, the French Ambassador was lodged in rooms there during 1546, and soon after this Edward VI entertained the Scottish Queen in the said palace.

This grand building was all destroyed in the Great Fire and as Strype noted, "Long since converted into tenements - the rents going to the bishop." It was then shown on maps as London House Yard. To the east of this site were Mitre Court and Paul's Alley while next to them Wren designed a functional rectangular Chapter House (still present today), which replaced the mediaeval complex discussed in fuller detail below.

The Dean's lodging was situated directly beside the palace and was a fair old house but like those of various prebends nearby became decayed and was converted to tenements. In this location was the Stationers guild formed by Royal charter in 1403 to include both booksellers who copied manuscripts and limners who illustrated them. They purchased Peter College from the cathedral after the Dissolution, clearly a convenient location, but moved to nearby Amen Corner in Ave Maria Lane in 1603.

Their hall was rebuilt after the fire in 1673 and for the most part remains there today. A plaque records: "Wynkyn de Worde father of Fleet Street first set up his press by Shoe Lane near this hall circa 1500." He was the assistant to Caxton (see later).

To the south of the cathedral just above Carter Lane there was a large mansion and this was rebuilt after the fire by Sir Joseph Sheldon mayor 1675. The property then became Deans Court and was the principal seat of the Deans of St. Paul's.

The Cathedral

Much has been written about St. Paul's so the aim here is to explore the more salient points and the characters associated with it. The main difference between the pre-fire cathedral and that built by Wren were the clean-cut lines and space around it, since the mediaeval edifice had a proliferation of ecclesiastical structures in close proximity.

The Old Cathedral - It is generally believed that five buildings have stood on the site and according to Stow the first church/yard was established by Ethelbert, King of Kent in c.610 with Mellitus as first Bishop of London. A wooden structure was erected when the Saxon Lundenwic was established in 886, but burnt down and was replaced in 962, while the fourth edifice arrived after a fire destroyed most of the city in 1087.

A great cathedral was gradually erected over the next two hundred years after a charter was laid down by William the Conqueror - with the steeple finished in 1222 and the east end above the choir in 1251. This was a strictly mediaeval building in complete contrast with Wren's design and its squared-off Gothic lines came from the *English School*, being something like Salisbury Cathedral today. The church measured 690 x 130 feet and had two small transepts but the spire - its principal glory, soared to 520 feet.

The latter was repaired in 1462 but was struck by lightening in 1561 and the ensuing fire burnt down to the battlements and subsequently consumed most of the roof. Meanwhile within the church there were numerous chapels including the Jesus Chapel and St. Faith's (see below). To the north of the building was the great cloister with a library above built by Walter Sherington the Chancellor of Lancaster in the time of Henry VI. Also in this area was the Pardon churchyard with a chapel built by Gilbert Becket.

One of its main attractions was on the south side this being the two-storey cloister with chapter house, "a beautiful piece of work built in Edward III." However by the time of Stow this was utterly defaced and replaced by low sheds then by high houses, which hid the church except for the top of it and the south gate. The same fate be-fell the cloister to the north which was laid out as a garden for the priests and most of the vellum books from its library "were departed."

At the west end of the cathedral were two bell towers flanking the façade the southern one known as the Lollards Tower encompassing a prison. In 1632 it was decided by the Commissioners to rebuild this and the work was undertaken by the appointed surveyor Inigo Jones at the expense of Charles I. The result was a striking portico with Corinthian pillars the total expenditure £100,000 by 1643, and on the restoration of Charles II the work continued but this was all in vain as it burnt down in 1666.

Wren's Cathedral - Strype happily recorded - "Yet this did not discourage his Majesty who by an Act of Parliament, appointed a certain duty upon every chaldron of coals, for the carrying on and perfecting the work of St. Paul's." Explosive charges were laid to bring down the remains of the old walls in 1673 and Sir Christopher Wren provided the model for a grandiose, expensive work started in 1678. Thus the chronicler added, "According to which model, with some alterations, it hath since been erecting."

Henry Compton the Bishop of London then sent forth a letter promoting the scheme with much wordy argument regarding the necessity and rightness of a contribution. Work continued under Wren's Office for three decades to produce today's building, although a fire in the north aisle of the choir in 1699 nearly put an end to matters.

The result was a Baroque masterpiece with stunning west façade, the greatest dome in Christendom using a concealed cone for support, and an exterior of choir and transepts with round-headed windows, niche pediments and balustrade adornment. It was slightly shorter than the mediaeval cathedral but used its ground plan and cost £800,000.

Wren's magnum opus then dominated the skyline of the City of London from 1710 up until the modern era, the main attributes being its simplicity of design combined with the grandeur of the Classical order. Many important State events took place there including funerals of Nelson and Wellington, whilst it witnessed the Diamond Jubilee celebrations of Victoria, the marriage of Prince Charles to Diana Spencer and commemoration service for the victims of 9/11.

Old St. Paul's

Note the towering spire, the flying buttresses rising from the walls of the aisle, and the chapter house and cloister next to the south transept. St. Gregory's is located at the west end.

Virtual Tour of St. Paul's Cathedral

The Exterior - The western front of St. Paul's provides a grand vista looking up from Ludgate Hill with Queen Anne's statue to the fore, also Temple Bar to the left as part of the successful new development at Paternoster Square.

Two Baroque bell towers flank the entrance which consists of a grand flight of stairs for tourists to relax on, six sets of double Corinthian columns with entablature, supporting a further set of four double columns with pediment, frieze and statues above. Its delicate composition might be compared to St. Peter's in Rome which suffers from an elongated façade focused on just a single level - although the interiors are comparative.

On the south side is a small garden behind the walls and in the marble pavement is a diagrammatical plan showing the new cathedral superimposed upon the old. The main feature is the chapter house which was nearby just below the ground, and its footprint is delineated in concrete running under the nave wall.

At the west end is an information plaque explaining that the garden was established in 1878 from three churches (viz. Augustine, Faith and Gregory), but the cast iron railings around it are original, dating from 1714.

The Nave - Entering the narthex and emerging out into the nave one is struck by the openness of the design, with its Romanesque arcade of monumental piers leading to the dome space. Its main feature is the contrast of the nave's simplicity and whiteness with ample room for the funerary sculptor to blossom, compared to the elaborate choir set between the walls like some Greek temple of old. The aisles are continued around the nave, transepts and chancel as part of a Latin cross favoured by the clergy.

Looking back at the west entrance it has the appearance of a triumphal arch with giant pilasters and imposing marble font. The nave includes Corinthian columns and pilasters with shallow domes above and the Romanesque arches are detailed with flowers.

In the north aisle is a black marble effigy to Frederic Lord Leighton d.1896 president of the Royal Academy on a mottled plinth with muses holding a brush and sculpture. A short distance along is a memorial to Maj. Gen. Charles Gordon - "*Who at all times and everywhere gave his strength to the weak - he saved an Empire by his warlike genius.*" He died while trying to save the garrison at Khartoum and it was erected by his brother Sir Henry W. Gordon d.1887 - John ch.15 v.13 "*Greater love hath no man.*" Nearby is one to the latter's son a midshipman lost on *H.M.S. Captain* off Cape Finisterre.

Commemorations came at the highest level and in the north wall are doors to William Viscount Melbourne who was P.M. under William and Victoria, and to Frederick his younger brother Ambassador to Vienna. Beneath the adjacent arch is a monument to the Duke of Wellington which fills the full height of the space, and has a black effigy under a canopy the names of numerous battles adorning its pedestal.

Moving towards the centre there is an exhaustive list of the Deans of St. Paul's since 1066 including: Wulfstan 1090, John Colet 1505-19 and John Donne 1621-31.

Emerging at the crossing there are two paintings on either side of the nave adjacent to the dome, both of them by the artist G.F. Watts. Each of them is oil on canvas the one to the north of *time, death and judgement* displayed since 1897. The southern space was meant to be occupied by a new piece *love triumphant* but Watts died before its completion in 1904, and his widow Mary donated *peace and goodwill* in February 1907 at the request of Canon Scott-Holland. These two pieces of artwork are according to taste.

In the south aisle are three sculptures more familiar for the artist than the recipient and are as follows: Richard Rundel Burges commander of the *Ardent* at Camperhorne 1797 with a ship relief and canon by Thomas Banks; Thomas Fanshaw Middleton first Bishop of India in preaching pose 1822 by J.G. Lough; and George Blaydon Westcott captain of the *Majestic* off Aboukir against the French 1798 also by Thomas Banks.

The Dome - As with St. Peter's this is the crowning glory both within and without and the main body and short transepts are framed by four triumphal arches. Above the piers at each corner is an apse with double Corinthian columns on either side, surmounted by a gilded half-dome depicting Biblical scenes. Considerable gold was used in this area to make an impressive display while statues of saints adorned the clerestory level, and angel paintings were inserted in the spandrel between the gallery and arches.

Looking upwards with some discomfort to the whispering gallery and dome one sees a muted composition by Sir James Thornhill depicting eight heavenly scenes in arches. The whole effect upwards towards the cupola is surreal, producing an enticing play of light that floods down onto the crossing below. And the reason is depicted on the floor. A compass star marks out the space with the famous Wren inscription around it.

There is no screen as found at Westminster and the organ is on each side with the main pulpit to the right, then a view past the choir to the altar (see below). The light coming from the east end with its stained glass window illuminates down towards the dome.

The Transepts - These are of plain Portland stone and to the north are memorials to Capt. Robert Faulkner of the *Blanche* against the superior *La Pique* erected by Parliament in 1795, and to Maj. Gen. Thomas Dundas in the West Indies with Roman themes and wreaths sculpted by John Bacon junior 1794.

In the ambulatory around the north transept is a statue to Samuel Johnson in thoughtful pose with document leaning on a small plinth (N.E. side); and one to Joshua Reynolds (1723-92) dressed in robes holding a book by a small column with a relief-face inscribed "*M. Angelo,*" all on a plinth (N.W. side). This impressive piece is by Flaxman.

Within the south transept on the west side is a monumental piece to Vice Admiral Horatio Viscount Nelson. It comprises his statue on a column with coat casually draped whilst holding a rope and anchor. The battle names Copenhagen, Nile and Trafalgar are inscribed on it and at the base is a Roman goddess, two boys and a lion. Above is George N. Hardinge who died on pursuing a French vessel in the Indian Ocean in 1808.

On the east side are memorials to Charles Marquis Cornwallis, the Governor General of Bengal, who died at Gahzeepore while progressing to the front of his army in 1805. This has a large fluted column with a person holding a parchment and Biblical figures below. Just above is a relief to Capt. R. Willett Miller of St. Vincent and the Nile erected by his companions in victory with palm tree and Roman figures by Flaxman.

In the ambulatory around the south transept on the west side is Lt. Gen Sir Ralph Abercromby with two sphinxes, a horse and figures supporting another by R. Westmacott ARA, a most impressive design. On the east side is a statue of J.M.W. Turner with pallet and brush d.1851 by P. MacDowell ARA and nearby ones to Cuthbert L. Collingwood a vice admiral who served with Nelson d.1810 and Admiral Earl Howe who fought in both the American and French wars d.1799.

The Chancel (Choir) - A white rimmed arcade on each side has columns and pilasters topped by gold leaf, whilst arched vaults separate three highly gilded domes. The latter with its Byzantine influences contrasts markedly with the plainness of the nave.

Within the choir are the bishops' stalls carved exquisitely by Grinling Gibbons and the altar sits under a temple arch of dark wood, gilt, fluted and spiral columns, crowned by a cupola and figurines. Chandeliers combined with natural lighting add a mystical quality to the altar composition; and at the front is located "a mediaeval style" picture of St. Paul with halo, holding a model of the cathedral on a Bible.

In the ambulatory behind the choir are found dark wooden partitions with double half columns and smaller gilded domes above, all ending in a small apse. On the south side is a statue in shroud to John Donne preacher, poet and dean d.1631 with Latin inscription and Carolus Jacobus Blomfield (1786-1857) in repose, the Bishop of London.

St. Paul's from the south, with **St. Augustine's** to the right   Mediaeval plan with Chapter House

The Refectory - On entering the crypt from the northwest corner one enters the modern cafeteria and at the west end are four major sculptures. Beside the west wall is one to Maj. Gen Sir W. Ponsonby who fought in the Peninsular War d.1815 with the statue of a horse; and a joint-memorial to Capt. James Robert Mosse who served under Lord Howe and Capt. Edward Rion who guided his ship the *Guardian* to safety over ten weeks - both then fought at Copenhagen under Nelson in 1801.

On the north side of the cafeteria is a statue to Henry Hallam (1771-1859) "*Historian of the Middle Ages.*" Affiliated to the intelligentsia of the Whig Party he produced two major works *Europe during the Middle Ages* in 1818 and *Constitutional History of England* in 1827 and was a fellow of the Royal Society, a trustee of the British Museum and won a gold medal for his writing from George IV. However his son Arthur Henry a great friend of Lord Tennyson died in 1833 and was commemorated by "*In Memoriam.*"

Opposite on the south side is a sculpture to John Jervis, Earl of St. Vincent (1735-1823) the First Lord of the Admiralty at the time of the Napoleonic Wars. Who, in the guise of David Farragut and his "damn the torpedoes" told the House of Lords, "I do not say the French will not come, I say only they will not come by sea!"

Near to the entrance is a list of memorials destroyed in the Great Fire of 1666 which included ones to Ethelred King of the Saxons 1016, Sir John Poultney 1349, John of Gaunt Duke of Lancaster 1399 and Sir John Warde mayor 1501. Stow also recorded a memorial to Erkenwalde, Bishop of London d.700 re-sited behind the altar.

Central Crypt - On leaving the cafeteria there is a kiosk at which to pay for entry, the amount considerably reduced if the dome is excluded. Just beyond on the north side is a model of the old cathedral with annotations which shows the Galilee porch at the west end, the cloisters, the bell towers, and two adjacent churches. This area is now the New Zealand corner - and has a floor brass and bust to Sir George Grey twice governor of that country; and marble to Richard John Seddon otherwise "King Dick."

Seddon, a latter day Mr. Micawber, was born in St. Helen's, Lancashire but became a gold-miner in Hokitika on the west coast of New Zealand then its longest serving Prime Minister from 1893-1901. It was under his Liberal rule that women received the vote (the first country in the world) although he opposed this, whilst he fell out with William Pember Reeves his radical High Commissioner in London (see Brixton).

On the south side there are wall memorials to Sir William Alexander Smith (1854-1914) the founder of the Boys Brigade; and the apparently unrelated George M. Smith (1824-1901) "*To whom English literature owes the Dictionary of National Biography,*" a colleague of both Thackeray and Leslie Stephen who collaborated with him on the work.

Around the corner is a wall memento and floor marble to George Cruikshank born Duke Street, Bloomsbury in 1792. Then in the walkway there are statues to Charles James Napier general and commander in India (ref. NZ) also to his brother William F.P. writer, and Thomas Heneage (1595) Elizabethan courtier - one of the few that survived the fire.

> **Henry Hallam R.S.** - "Historian of the Middle Ages."

"*Lector, Si Monumentum Requirus, Circumspice!*"

C. Wren Esq.
(1632-1723)

The central area has two of the most important memorials firstly to Horatio Viscount Nelson with a black and gold marble bier on stone plinth. Here also there is a mosaic floor of anchors, motto *England Expects*, and a display of his call to national prayer from his diary dated 21 October 1805. The ensemble is set in a circular vaulted chamber with eight columns and a walkway very reminiscent of a mediaeval building.

On the south wall is a relief in white marble with mottled brown pillar and pediment to Florence Nightingale (1820-1910); then to the east in a separate area, a mottled red-black bier on grey plinth with four sleeping lions to Arthur the Duke of Wellington.

Jesus Chapel - This was established as the Chapel of the Order of the British Empire by George V in 1917 and has by far the largest number of commemorative tablets. In the northeast corner are artistic memorials to Sir Arthur Sullivan, Sir Edward J. Poynter and John Constable erected by the Leighton fund. Also located in this area are memorials to the artists Millais and Reynolds and the famous sculptor Henry Moore.

On the south side near the entrance are Henry Venn B.D. prebend and secretary of the C.M.S. (1796-1873), John Rennie a floor marble "*His works are the true monument of his public merit*," Sir Edwin Landseer marble relief with reposing setter, Wm. C.E. Newbolt canon in repose by the wall and a tablet to Sir Edwin L. Lutyens the architect.

In the southeast are those to William Blake "*artist poet and mystic*," Anthony Van Dyck the Flemish master whose original memorial perished d.1641, and in Latin *Maria conjut Christophori Wren* (junior) d.1712 daughter of Philip and Constance Musard. Next to the south wall is the most important of all, a raised marble to Wren the builder of this church d.1723 "*Lector, Si Monumentum Requirus, Circumspice.*" Above this is a modern tablet to Robert Hooke of the Royal Society both a friend and colleague.

(From) St. Paul's burial register

9 January 1806 - Lord Horatio Nelson, Viscount Nelson and Duke of Bronte
16 October 1821 - John Rennie civil engineer of Stamford Street, Blackfriars
22 January 1825 - George Dance Esq. of Gower Street, 5th son of George senior
30 December 1851 - J.M.W. Turner of "Cremorne," New Road, Chelsea
18 November 1852 - Field Marshall, Arthur Duke of Wellington of Walmer Castle
11 October 1873 - Edwin John Landseer RA of 18 St. John's Wood Road
29 November 1878 - George Cruikshank of 263 Hampstead Road, son of Isaac
21 January 1890 - Robert Cornelius Napier, Baron of Magdala of 63 Eaton Square [2]
3 February 1896 - Frederic Lord Leighton of 2 Holland Park Road, president RA
20 August 1896 - John Everett Millais of 2 Palace Gate, president of the RA, married Euphemia the daughter of George Gray [previously wife of John Ruskin]
26 September 1898 - George Grey K.C.B. of Norfolk House, Harrington Road

St. Augustine's

Only the tower survives of this church which was originally located on the northeast corner of Old Change and Watling Street. Above it were a number of alleys and opposite was St. Paul's School (which as stated had the Mercers Co. as patrons), however the later realignment of New Change meant the church is now on the opposite side.

It was formerly just beyond the east gate of the cathedral precincts and across the road to the south was the King's Exchange for the receipt of bullion. The Exchange's function was to receive old stamps and iron for coining, which was then made new and delivered to all the mints around the country. Henry III decreed a prohibition sent to the Scabines [jurymen] and Men of Ipre [Ypres] in 1222, that none should change plate or any mass of silver, but only in his Exchanges at London and Canterbury. Whilst in the reign of Edward I the mayor Gregory de Rokesley became the keeper.

The church itself was first mentioned in c.1148 and a fraternity of St. Austin's was set up in 1387. All of its members would meet in the vault of St. Paul's usually at St. Faith's then bring torches and tapers to the church, hold a mass, and after paying a penny would engage in a feast and revel - all in the honour of God and the saint. In the church there were just a few early monuments and it was renovated and leaded in 1630-31.

After the fire it was rebuilt by Wren's office one of fifty-one such rebuilds undertaken. The work on the nave took place in 1680-84 and the result was plain and modest with a barrel vault on Ionic columns and six groin-vaulted aisles. There was a fine altar piece inserted framed with Corinthian columns and a carved oak pulpit, the cost of engraving being £200. The spire by Hawksmoor was added in 1695 and like that at St. Martin's to the west was designed as a foil to the dome of St. Paul's.

Thomas Holbech D.D. late rector of the church and Dame Margaret Ayloff gave £100 a piece for pewing, and the parish was combined to St. Faith's which brought a further £700 in benefactions. A later memorial in the south aisle displayed a particular flourish of Armenian character, pertaining to foreign merchants who were common in Old Change. Indeed it contained an inscription to Tavakoll de David d.1696/97.

---

[2] R.C. Napier was a field marshall, commander in India and governor of Gibraltar (see p.98).

There was some restoration of the tower in 1830 and Arthur Blomfield modernised the pulpit in 1878, but the church was destroyed in the blitz of 1941. One heart warming story connected with this was Faith the church cat, who hid in the basement to protect her kittens and was rescued from the ruins by the vicar. This was done at considerable risk due to the instability and the cat itself received a medal from the P.D.S.A.

The church tower was restored and attached by concrete to the modernist choir school complex in 1967, and perhaps provides the defiant memorial that was proposed by Sir Hugh Casson at St. Vedast's. During the excavations to build the school the remains of the north aisle dating back to the mid-13th century was uncovered.

St. Faith's under St. Paul's

When first reading about City churches this seems a strange concept but grows on one after some pertinent explanations. In the 37th of Henry VI (1459) a chapel to Jesus was built under the choir and William Say the dean became rector. Richard Ford and Henry Burnis purchased land to pay an annuity of £40 for its support which continued under Henry VII/VIII, and Deans Dr. Colet, Richard Pace &c. were also the rectors.

At the west end of the Jesus Chapel was a parish church of St. Faith's for the stationers and dwellers in the Churchyard, Paternoster Row and adjacent localities. Strype recorded that his own printer and distributor operated in this location, and in general the residents were Puritan adherents or sympathisers - being strictly anti-Royalist.

The Jesus Chapel was suppressed under Edward VI and the parish of St. Faith's moved there, "To a place more sufficient for largeness and lightsomeness in the year 1551 and so it remaineth." In fact Evelyn in his diaries talked of the crypt under the choir.

Being so closely linked with the cathedral it operated like a chantry with several wealthy benefactors, an early memorial being to Elizabeth wife of Lord Shandoys 1559 who was brought there from Knightrider Street with priests singing, heralds of arms and banners. Others were to Thomas Dockwray stationer and notary proctor of the arches 1559 and in the chancel George Whitgift d.1611 the brother of Archbishop John.

St. Augustine's with choir school and St. Martin's at Ludgate with its volutes. Their spires were a skilful device, providing a foil to the dome of St. Paul's.

Amongst the benefactors were John Law proctor of the arches who gave £10 in 1614 and John Speed merchant taylor who gave £5 in 1629. Three years after this the parish purchased a vestry room at the lower end of the south aisle and bestowed much cost and beauty upon it. Of course in general the edifice needed very little maintenance and it was stated, "This church needs no repair at all; for Faith's is defended by St. Paul."

However, after the fire it was not reinstated and was united with St. Augustine's. Today there are parish markers: "St. F.P. 1828" in New Change and "St. F.P. 1880" north of the crypt near to Nelson, also a water pump just north of the cathedral dated 1819.

M. 5 March 1623 Paul D'Ewes wid. married Lady Elizabeth Denton
4 December 1626 Thomas Bowes of Much Bromley, Essex married Mary D'Ewes [3]

St. Gregory by St. Paul's

This church at the southwest corner of the cathedral was held by the petty canons and first noted in the 11th century. Adjoining it was the Lollards tower, or bell tower, which housed the Bishop's prison "for those of contrary opinions in religion." One of the last inmates was Peter Burchet, gent of the Middle Temple (1573), who convinced them he had committed no heresy but was then sent to the Tower for another felony.

In the church there was a chantry supported by a messuage or tenement called Holmes College, which was obtained especially for its maintenance but Edward VI alienated it to John Hulson. And with regards to its monuments there were only a few remaining.

The building was repaired within and without, in every part richly and very worthily, at the cost of William Weston merchant taylor and John Hart proctor of the arches in 1631/32, which sumptuous repair cost £2,000 and upwards. There was also a petition to Inigo Jones for further renovations when the west front was restored.

After being destroyed in the fire the church was not rebuilt and the parish was initially joined to St. Mary Magdalen, Old Fish Street and later to St. Martin's and St. Sepulchre's. The ground where it stood is on the pavement in front of the present cathedral.

C. 3 June 1679 Christian s. of Christian Risen taxman by Isabell b. 31 May [engraver]

B. 4 June 1698 Dr. Thomas White the late Bishop of Peterburgh [sic] - he was also rector of All Hallows Barking and chaplain to Queen Anne

St. Gregory ruins (in 1666) - It was in an unusual location by the cathedral, like St. Margaret's, Westminster.

[3] Sir Simonds D'Ewes (1602-50) of Stow Hall and Milden, Suffolk was diarist for the Long Parliament until 1649, and wrote *Journals of all the Parliaments during the Reign of Queen Elizabeth* which came out posthumously in 1682. His parents were Paul D'Ewes and Cecilia Simonds - but his father remarried (above) whereas Mary was his younger sister.

St. Martin within Ludgate

A mariner sailing into Fleet Ditch in the 1740s would see the Bridewell on the left and had to moor at Fleet Bridge, since beyond was a covered stream and the Fleet Market. The church of St. Martin's was up the hill on the right past Ludgate, and immediately behind were the Stationers Hall at Amen Corner, St Paul's Almshouses and the Oxford Arms Yard. Just opposite the edifice was the entrance to Blackfriars Lane.

This was named for St. Martin of Tours patron saint of travellers and unusually for gate churches was on the inside. A tradition dates it to the 7th century since Cadwallo, King of the Britons was reputedly buried in 677 however it was recorded as *by the wall* in 1174. John Michell mayor gave to the parson William Downes land for a steeple and money to rebuild it in 1437, but the spire was damaged by lightening with St. Paul's in 1561.

Westminster held the living up until the Reformation when it passed to St. Paul's, and adjacent was the Ludgate Jail. After a dispute with the minister over incomes in 1560, it was directed that the prison should pay all tithes, clerks' wages and church duties.

The jail housed merchants driven to want by losses at sea who went there to escape creditors, as a form of voluntary prison. Phillip II of Spain during his brief sojourn with Mary arrived in London in August 1554 and was petitioned by 30 inmates owing £10,000. They addressed him in Latin of their miseries and by his Royal generosity he freed them, since, "They were not villains but went there in hope of a better fortune."

The whole matter was recorded by Roger Ascham tutor to Elizabeth I, while a scale of fees applied to the prison: 1s at the coming in of every prisoner to the turnkey, 2d to an officer to take them abroad and 8d for a clean sheet per month. Clearly reminiscent of the arrangement pertaining to that other Lud - Ludlow Street Gaol in New York.

Sir Roger Cholmeley, John Went and Roger Paine had chantries in the church but there were only a few memorials although these included two mayors: William Sevenoake 1418 and Stephen Peacocke 1532. The pioneering travel writer Samuel Purchas became the minister in 1614 and published his *Pilgrimages* - from which Coleridge received inspiration for *Kubla Khan* and its pleasure domes in a dream when staying on Exmoor.

The church was repaired in 1623 and consumed in the fire but Strype noted few other details. In fact, it was rebuilt by Wren in 1677-87 incorporating part of the old walls with its south façade facing onto Ludgate Hill - squeezed in like a sandwich filling.

Having the appearance of an Italian city-church with scrolls beside the tower and three round-headed windows, its principal glory was the lead-clad cupola, lantern and obelisk at 158 feet - finished after the main church to match St. Augustine's. The interior design was a Greek cross similar to St. Anne's and Mary at Hill, while it had work by Grinling Gibbons and was furnished with a Bernard Schmidt organ in 1684.

An inner vestry and vestibule at the entrance distanced the sanctuary from the traffic; while Lud Gate was removed in 1760 and a plaque marks the site. The pulpit board came from St. Mary Magdalen - destroyed in a fire in 1886, and the church itself was restored at this time. After surviving the war it became a guild church in 1954 and the parish with St. Gregory and St. Mary Magdalen passed over to St. Sepulchre's.

C. 3 October 1619 Nathanyell Hardye sonne of Anthony and Ann [Dean of Rochester]

M. 6 June 1643 [Adm.] William Penne and Margaret Vander Shuren wid. by banns

Newgate Street

The Greyfriars or Friars Minor founded by St. Francis first arrived in Dover in 1224 and of the original nine missionaries, four established cells at Cornhill. But as their numbers increased they removed to a place by St. Nicholas's, since John Ewin mercer purchased an empty piece of ground there and became a lay brother in 1225.

This developed as a substantial institution on the north side of Newgate Street and can perhaps be observed in the depiction of Old St. Paul's (p. 95). Not only was it large with many monastic structures but received great patronage and "divers other citizens erected a beautiful building." Of these, William Joyner mayor 1239 built the quire, Henry Walleis mayor 1273/98 constructed the main church, and Gregory de Rokesley mayor built the dorters and chambers - plus a refectory, infirmary, chapter house and vestry.

However the first church was pulled down soon afterwards and Margaret second wife of Edward I began a new quire in 1306, and John Britaine Earl of Richmond and other Royal patrons rebuilt the nave. Eventually it was 300 x 89 feet and consecrated in 1325 but the building was surrendered at the Dissolution on 12 November 1538.

Initially it was used as a store house and was stashed with prizes taken from the French however the Bishop of Rochester preached on the matter at Paul's Cross. An agreement was then made between Henry VIII, the mayor Sir Martin Bowes and the City that all the edifice of Greyfriars with its grounds, buildings and cloisters should form a new church of Christchurch, and for that purpose the nearby parishes of St. Ewin and St. Nicholas were abandoned. It opened again for worship on 3 January 1547/48.

Christchurch

The new parish church was also grand on two levels. It occupied the former monastic friary with its many monuments to the rich and famous, and covered an area stretching up to the walls at Newgate - encompassing the two historic parishes.

There was then a significant development. Dr. Ridley the Bishop of London went and preached a sermon before the King at Westminster, exhorting those who were rich to help the poor. As a result the Greyfriars House was made into the foundation of Christ's Hospital for fatherless children in 1552. Shortly afterwards, on Xmas Day, 340 boys in their pristine blue uniforms lined the pavements at Cheapside.

But that was not all. Edward VI in his youthful wisdom established a second tier of relief at St. Bartholomew's, Smithfield and St. Thomas's, Southwark. These were not only hospitals but fed and nourished the inmates. In addition, the old Bridewell Palace was given over to vagabonds and strumpets such that they may be put to useful labour. At this time the Regent's Council was led by John Dudley, 1st Duke of Northumberland but it is likely that Edward was led into such philanthropy by Cranmer. In this way the father was responsible for the pulling down and the son for the building up. [4]

---

[4] Archbishop Thomas Cranmer established the original *Book of Common Prayer* in 1549 which had one volume with all the services and prayers in English. It was updated in 1559 and there was a major revision after the Restoration in 1662.

Lastly, money was provided "to help the honest decayed householder in his home" and Sir William Chester alderman and Sir John Calthrop draper paid to improve access from St. Bart's to Christ's Hospital. They also vaulted the town ditch from Aldersgate to Newgate - "since it was noisome and contagious to these places of refuge."

The church itself was repaired in 1605, while a fair and spacious gallery was erected in the north aisle in 1628 at a cost of £149. But this grand historic pile with its labyrinthine myriad of altars, chapels and passageways was all destroyed in the Great Fire.

It was the burial place of Queens, lords and baronets from the Plantagenet era and beyond, all sitting stately in the Quire, All Hallows, Apostles and Lady Chapels, Chapter House, east wing and walls. A full list appears in Strype including John Gisors 1311, Sir Nicholas Brembar 1377, John Philpot 1378 and Stephen Jennings 1508 (all mayors), John Duke of Bourbon of Agincourt 1433, and Walter Blunt Lord Mountjoy 1474.

Then, in keeping with its eminent and sumptuous heritage, it was rebuilt by Wren on the foundations of the Franciscan friary in 1677-91. The walls were raised up after a colossal expenditure of £11,000 and it became his most expensive church. The result was a complete transformation from Mediaeval Gothic to English Baroque, whilst the tower was added from 1701-04 **(see picture of ruins and interior below).**

There was a steeple with three tiers of squared open columns and pediments rising high above the western façade. The nave consisted of rows of five columns, with capitals of elaborate design, and at each end there were pilasters and round-arched windows.

Large galleries rose up above the pews, and the ceiling had a ridge vault with arches harking back to the purity of the Romanesque. A Renatus Harris organ was installed to the west in 1690. Outside was a churchyard, Christ's Hospital on a square, and the open spaces of the town ditch. Just to the east was Butcher Hall Lane turning across into Bull and Mouth Street, the former being renamed as King Edward Street.

Later memorials were to Richard Royston bookseller to three kings 1686, his daughter Mary wife of Richard Chiswell bookseller 1698 (see St. Botolph's, Aldersgate), Thomas Hollier chirurgeon of St. Thomas's 1690, Capt. Valentine Pyne of Devon and India 1691 and Thomas Firmin a governor of Christ's Hospital and St. Thomas's 1697.

The church with its grand surroundings became a centre for music and Samuel Wesley organist, nephew of John, performed there. Samuel Coleridge, Leigh Hunt and Charles Lamb were all pupils at Christ's Hospital in the later 18th century, and when the latter wrote of begging in *Essays of Elia*, perhaps he remembered the charitable status of his former school?

Christchurch replaced a monastery and two parish churches.

For many years this was a substantial church with large congregation but its future was uncertain after the school went to Horsham in 1902. This was decided on 29 December 1940 when a firebomb destroyed it along with seven other Wren churches that night. Yet the steeple and walls being of sound construction survived and were restored as a garden in 1960, and the churchyard to the north was combined with St. Botolph's.

The church remains a great landmark but the only record of the earlier foundations are two blue plaques: "Greyfriars Monastery 1225-1538" and "Christ's Hospital 1552-1902." Just to the north is another plaque to the short lived "Poulters Hall 1630-66" which was the last one belonging to that company. The Post Office also occupied sites on either side of King Edward Street, thus there is a statue to Sir Rowland Hill.

On the east side at the junction with Newgate Street opposite the church is a modern plaque stating, "From this site Guglielmo Marconi made the first public transmission of wireless signals on 27 July 1896." This took place due to the support of William Preece chief electrical engineer of the British Post Office. It had taken a millennium to progress from sending messages by beacon, pigeon and semaphore to telegraph and wireless, yet just another hundred years for the worldwide internet to be fully operational.

B. 14 February 1317/18 Lady Margaret d. Phillip III of France, 2nd w. Edward I
22 August 1358 Queen Isabella d. Phillip IV of France w. Edward II (in alabaster)
7 September 1362 Joan Plantagenet d. Edward II (born in the Tower) m. David II
5 October 1382 Isabel Plantagenet d. Edward III m. de Courcy, Earl of Bedford [5]

25 July 1291 (by) Gregory de Rokesley, Kent goldsmith/merchant, mayor 1274-80/1284
14 March 1470/71 Thomas Mallory of Monks Kirby, Warks wrote *Le Morte D'Arthur*

St. Ewin's

There were two ancient parish churches on Newgate Street and like Christchurch both came under the ward of Farringdon Within. St. Ewin's was just west of St. Nicholas's at the top of Eldenese Lane, whilst the Earl of Warwick had an ancient house or inn there thus it was re-titled Warwick Lane. Nearby was Newgate Market which initially sold corn and meal and later other victuals then just beyond was Paternoster Row.

According to Stow the small church was not named after Edwin the first Christian King of Northumberland, but emanated from a saint called Owen or Audoen. However, one can't help noticing that there was one John Ewin, a Franciscan brother, who purchased the land on which the adjacent Greyfriars establishment was constructed.

It was first mentioned in c.1220 and later termed as Sti. Audoeni juxta Fraters Minores or Infra Newgate and had a fraternity of *St. Anne* there, but was pulled down under the orders of Henry VIII in 1547 for the erecting of Christchurch (one of four churches lost before the Great Fire). In its place, "A fair storing frame of timber was erected wherein dwelt men of divers trades."

---

[5] Henry II, Count of Anjou succeeded the Normans as King in 1154 but a favourite castle and residence was at Chinon in the Loire valley. As a result he and his wife Eleanor of Aquitaine and his son Richard I were buried at Fontevraud Abbey nearby. The latter has a statue at Westminster but spent little time in England and the links to France were of more significance.

On the west side of the lane was a building of some considerable note. The (Royal) College of Physicians was established by Thomas Linacre in 1518 and initially they met at his home in Knightrider Street, but then took rooms at Amen Corner in 1614-66. They were established with a Royal charter in Warwick Lane after the fire, and remained there until 1825, at which time the buildings were converted into a foundry.

The Cutlers Co. was originally at Cloak Lane next to a tenement once owned by Dick Whittington from 1451, but after a long legal battle they were ousted by the Metropolitan and District Railway Co. in 1882 (see St. John the Baptist).

They then built a new hall on the site of the Physicians in Warwick Lane, and moved there in 1888, while the terracotta frieze outside is by Benjamin Creswick a pupil of the art critic John Ruskin. Internally there is some Jacobean oak and a hammer-beam ceiling, also a banner dating back to the Lord Mayor's parade of 1763. Today, an information tablet placed outside records the various uses of the site.

St. Nicholas (Shambles)

The area west of Cheapside included some narrow alleys and the district known as the Shambles, then beyond was Newgate Street south of the Greyfriars church. A small lane ran from St. Vedast's to Great St. Martin and the church, but was "stopped up" under Edward II and a legal dispute ensued since this proved to be quite an annoyance.

To the north of Paternoster Row were the ivy-clad houses of prebends on Ivy Lane, and the offices of the church including the Pregorative Court of Canterbury which later moved to Warwick Lane. It was here that wills were proven and probate given.

St. Nicholas's was on the west side of Ivy Lane where it emerged into Newgate Street and was situated between St. Michael's to the east and St. Ewin's to the west. The site is now located south of King Edward Street. This was described as a proper parish church by the chronicler Stow but that was all he had to say on the matter.

Therefore the building was pulled down by the orders of Henry VIII in 1547 and some fair houses in a court were built upon the site. A strong frame of timber covered in lead was set up just west of here under Sir John Gresham mayor at the charge of the city in the 1st of Edward VI. This then enabled meal to be weighed and retailed.

Smithfield

The appellation was derived from Smooth Field a large marshy area in mediaeval times, rather like Moor Field, which suggests the outskirts of London were a boggy place. This fell within the ward of Farringdon Without or Extra which encompassed land beyond the walls west of the city. It included the three churches below, those in the next section, and also the Bishop of Ely's land, the Liberty of the Rolls and the Whitefriars.

Today, this open area with its Victorian market built by Sir Horace Jones remains little changed from olden times, although the site of the market-house was formerly occupied by sheep pens. On the west side is the new Haberdashers Hall, and to the east in Cloth Street and Bartholomew Close are the halls of a miscellany of companies, viz. Farmers & Fletchers, Founders, Information Technologists and Butchers.

St. Bartholomew the Great

This grandiose church was founded by Rahere as an Augustinian priory with hospital on Little Britain, east of Smithfield, in about 1103. Stow noted that he was a pleasant witted gentleman who also served time as the King's minstrel.

The chancel of the priory originally ended in an apse but was squared-off in 1330 and a lady chapel was added (which can be seen next to the Founders Hall today). This was an extensive building at 349 feet, one of three in the area with the Greyfriars and St. Paul's, and was in fact larger than the cathedrals at Bristol, Chester and Rochester.

Henry II granted a fair for clothiers and drapers in the vicinity and they had stalls in the grounds, hence Cloth Fair with its wooden framed buildings. Meanwhile the structure was repaired in the Gothic style in 1410, and the last overseer was Prior William Bolton who added the famous oriel window to the chancel gallery in the 16th century.

Bolton carried out many repairs and built the manor of Canonbury at Islington which belonged to the canons. He also owned the parsonage of Harrow and reputedly built a house there against the fear of flooding in 1524 - as forewarned by an eclipse, but there was little more than a dove-house ever to be seen in that locality.

The nave was pulled down after the Dissolution in 1543, but the chancel and tower were retained and the 13th century west entrance was made into a gateway. Sir Richard Rich the Lord Chancellor under Edward VI lived there, and one morning at the King's request several nobles arrived to demand the Great Seal from him. In the time of Mary the church was conveyed to the Blackfriars, but under Elizabeth they were expelled and it passed to Sir Walter Mildmay the Chancellor of the Exchequer.

From 1558 it became a parish church for the inhabitants of Bartholomew Close, while the old tower of rotten timber was about to fall down and was replaced by the present brick structure during 1622-28. There was also a new gallery and porch, and there were repairs to the east aisle and other areas at a cost of £698 in 1633.

St. Bartholomew the Great - tower dated 1628 and Tudor gatehouse of the priory.

William Hogarth (1697-1764), painter and satirist was born at Bartholomew Close.

The principal monuments were to Rahere 1144 on the north side of the chancel with friars in habits (restored in 1405), Roger Walden the Bishop of London 1406, Sir Walter Mildmay 1589 founder of Emmanuel College and the Chancellor, and Thomas Roycroft 1677 the King's printer of oriental languages and of the *Polyglot Bible*. It was erected by his son Samuel and is now in a side chapel retained for private prayer.

In May 1695, the church, under pressure from a higher authority, instituted a separate parish register for Nonconformist parishioners who formed a majority in the vicinity of nearby Bartholomew Close. This practice mainly pertained to baptisms though some still appeared in the main register, and the most famous entry recorded was William Hogarth in 1697. However, this idiosyncratic custom was dispensed with in 1710.

The mediaeval Lady Chapel housed a printing shop and Benjamin Franklin worked there in 1724, whilst an organ was erected in the church by Richard Bridge in 1731. This was lost during repairs, and one by G. England was brought from St. Stephen Walbrook in 1886. The Tudor gateway and main church were then renovated by Sir Aston Webb, Edward Alfred Webb and Frederick C. Dove over a period of some forty years. A tablet beside the gatehouse which was restored in 1932 commemorates this fact.

Today, the church is a significant Norman edifice and the west door opens onto the south ambulatory of the chancel. Inside are remains of the cloisters, a fine example of Romanesque arches on three tiers, and the famous oriel window. It was used in a number of films in particular *Four Weddings and a Funeral*, and just opposite was No. 43 Cloth Fair home to Sir John Betjeman (with plaque). However, St. Bartholomew's became the only parish church in Britain to charge admission to tourists (currently £4) in 2007.

C. 28 November 1697 William Hogarth son of Richard and Anne born in Bartholomew Close next door to Mr. Downinges the printers on 10 November

St. Bartholomew the Less

The original hospital of St. Bartholomew's was established by Rahere beside Smithfield in 1123 and a chapel was attached to it by around 1184. However the earliest surviving part of the church is the tower dating back to the 15th century.

Alfune who built a shrine at St. Giles, Cripplegate was first overseer of the hospital and went to the nearby markets to beg charity for the poor inmates from devout people. The foundation was confirmed by Edward III in 1353 with a master and eight brethren who also served the chapel; and Whittington's executors repaired the hospital in 1423. It was valued at the sum of £35 6s 7d when suppressed in 1539.

The Bishop of Rochester preached at Paul's Cross in 1546 stating that the King had given the Greyfriars, St. Bartholomew's, the Hospital, and appurtenances in the City and at Stepney for relief of the poor. Local residents were then called to their parish churches and Sir Richard Dobbes mayor, several aldermen and *other grave citizens*, using eloquent oration, persuaded the people to give liberally to the hospital according to ability.

All agreed, and the poor or sickly were to be removed there and some were to receive weekly support at home. In July 1552, the Greyfriars was set up for fatherless children and the hospital was repaired and endowed by the citizens. A hole was also made in the city wall from Christchurch to the Governor's House adjacent to the Smithfield Hospital (the latter also known as The House for Work).

The chapel of Holy Cross was then designated a parish church for the tenants dwelling within the hospital precincts. This was situated on the northwest side of the institution near to the Tudor gate of the priory at what might be termed Smithfield corner. Of the memorials there was a brass with *Latin inscription* to William Markeby gent and Alice his wife dated 1439, a copy of which is found just inside the church door.

Another one with flat stone and brass was to John Shirley Esq. and Margaret in the habit of pilgrims - he died in 1456 aged 90 and had twelve children. Shirley was a great traveller in divers countries and collected the works of Chaucer, John Lidgate and other learned writers and produced sundry volumes for posterity. Stow proudly added, "I have seen them and partly do possess them."

Inigo Jones (1573-1652)

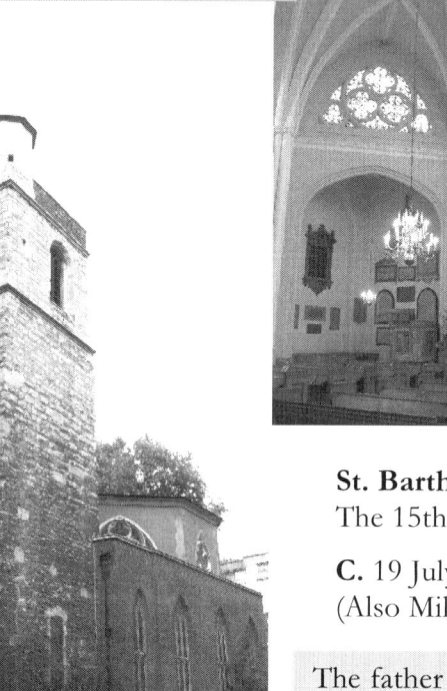

St. Bartholomew the Less
The 15th century tower - and interior by Dance and Hardwick

C. 19 July 1573 Enego Jones the son of Enego Jones
(Also Milicent, Philip and Anne Jones baptised from 1570-78)

The father was a Catholic cloth-worker, but Jones rose up and was one of the first architects to go to Italy. His most prominent work was the Queen's House Greenwich, Banqueting Hall at Whitehall and Covent Garden piazza - all in the early 17th century.

George Dance the younger rebuilt much of the church in 1789, some twenty years after working on All Hallows, London Wall. His design involved placing an octagonal nave in the mediaeval walls with Gothic ribbed-vaulting and triangular chapels in the resultant spaces. In addition some high windows in the raised ceiling brought in extra light. At this time the hospital had just a few buildings and there were also courts and alleys.

The church was repaired by Thomas Hardwick using this blueprint in 1823-25, but an iron frame replaced the plaster/wooden roof. The hospital was rebuilt by the Hardwicks in 1842/61 under William Cubitt mayor and its president - as per a tablet outside.

St. Sepulchre, Newgate

Today this is the largest parish church in the City and sits just opposite the Old Bailey, but the area was once very different. In ancient times a traveller along Newgate Street would have passed Physicians Court on the left and Christ's Hospital on the right then arrived at Newgate with its attached prison. Passing through the gate, Old Bailey Street was to the south and Giltspur Street to the north then St. Sepulchre's. [6]

The whole area was a warren of courts and alleys and the main thoroughfare wound its way on down Snow Hill to Holborn Bridge over the Fleet River. It was only in the 19th century that Holborn Viaduct, Farringdon Railway and Smithfield transformed it forever. The church also marked the extent of the fire, but first regarding its origins.

This was a large parish outside the walls stretching up to Clerkenwell and Smithfield, its origins being traced to Saxon times and a dedication to St. Edmund the Martyr the King of East Anglia. It served the Knights of the Holy Sepulchre of Jerusalem, an Augustinian order, in the Crusades from 1103-73 resulting in a joint dedication, which was contracted to the Holy Sepulchre or St. Sepulchre. But of course there was no such saint.

Sir Hugh Popham treasurer to Henry VI rebuilt the church, tower, south chapel and porch in 1450, whilst there was a fraternity of St. Katherine. Next door was an inn for travellers, the Saracens Head, and the conduit at Oldbourn Cross (1498) near Turnagain Lane was replaced by William Lambe gentleman to the chapel of Henry VIII.

Regarding incumbents, John Rogers was raised at Deritend, Birmingham but attended Pembroke, Cambridge and was minister of Holy Trinity the Less in 1532-34. He went to Antwerp as chaplain to the Merchant Adventurers, meeting Tyndale, and published the *Matthew Bible* (a pseudonym) on the Continent. This English version came out just after that of Coverdale and Cranmer gave licence for it to be distributed.

He then spent time at Wittenberg University, but returned to England and in 1550 was granted the livings of St. Margaret Moses and St. Sepulchre, also being a prebend of St. Paul's. On the accession of Mary I he preached "the true faith" of Edward VI, and was imprisoned at Newgate and died at Smithfield in 1555. He is commemorated there with several others next to a tablet to William Wallace the Scottish hero.

Stow described it as, "A fair parish church in the Bailey, not so large as of old due to the letting out of buildings." One resident was William Harvey of the College of Physicians who married (in 1604) the daughter of Lancelot Browne a doctor. The former was physician at St. Bartholomew's from 1609 and ministered to two Kings whilst working on circulatory laws.

St. Sepulchre's - with its 15th century porch and tower.

---

[6] Newgate Prison was present from the 12th century and still remained when the gate was demolished in 1777, while plaques record the gate and Giltspur Compter opposite. The former was replaced by the Old Bailey in 1904, whereas a prison of the same name was located in Greenwich, New York from 1797-1828.

There were numerous repairs to the church in the 1620s and 1630s and at one time the pinnacles were replaced for £139. On the south side of the quire was a brass in memory of Capt. John Smith governor of Virginia and admiral of New England d.1631.

Another notable connection was Thomas Gouge son of William the rector of St. Anne's Blackfriars. The former was born at Bow and attended Eton and King's, Cambridge then was appointed vicar in 1638. He supported the Puritan movement and as a philanthropist wrote *Riches Increased by Giving to the Poor* but was ejected from St. Sepulchre under the Act of Uniformity in 1662. His daughter Elizabeth married Sir Edward Clark mayor 1696 and the latter were buried at St. Matthew's, Friday Street.

The church was mostly destroyed during the fire although it burned out nearby at Pye Corner in Giltspur Street - a tablet records this fact on the site of an old hostelry and details the probable cause of gluttony. It was renovated by Wren from the 1670s utilizing Portland stone and had classical arches in the aisles and impressive flat ceiling.

Of its parishioners Henry Jowett was born in London in 1719 the son of Henry of Manningham, Bradford and was a skinner residing in Cow Lane and West Smithfield in 1744-56. However he moved to Leeds in 1757 and as a result his children met the Venn family through school and church connections. His sons included John a founder of the C.M.S. and Revs. Joseph and Henry of Cambridge (see London South East).

The exterior was remodelled in 1790 in the prevailing fashion, but the perpendicular Gothic style was reinstated with battlements and windows in 1873-79. The tower was not completely refaced giving the appearance of top heavy pinnacles, whilst the fan-vaulted porch dating to the 15th century is its most impressive mediaeval feature. There was no extensive damage to the exterior during the war.

C. 30 May 1744 John, 9 Nov. 1751 Joseph, 30 Dec. 1756 Henry - the sons of Henry and Sarah Jowett were baptized (also five others during 1744-56)

M. 24 November 1604 William Harvey married Elizabeth Browne
29 May 1742 Henry Jowett married Sarah Woodman by licence

B. 23 December 1568 Roger Ascham - tutor to Elizabeth I and writer of *Toxophilus* on the skills of archery and *The Schoolmaster* or the right way of teaching
21 June 1631 Captain John Smith of Virginia [explorer and writer]

St. Sepulchre (detail): 15th century fan-vaulted porch and font dated 1670.

Virtual Tour - The porch has a notable three tier entrance and inside is a font given by the parish dated 1670 - the second font at the west end is from the ruined Christchurch as are the tiles (whose parish joined). There is an arcade of Tuscan columns with arches and panelled ceiling bordered by two spacious aisles with groin vaults, the whole of this creating a monumental space that some compare to a small cathedral.

In the south aisle there is a plaque and window to John Smith showing his three ships which formed part of the fleet that sailed to Virginia, while a tablet marks the site of his burial. Beyond the north aisle is the Lady Chapel previously that of St. Stephen Harding and now re-dedicated as the Musicians' Chapel.

Holborn Viaduct, showing the opening of the new bridge in 1869 (at the same time as the Suez Canal). This witnessed the removal of some extensive slum housing, dramatically altering the geography of the area.

"The Musicians Church" has the largest interior in the City.

The organ in the northeast corner was by Renatus Harris dated 1670 and for 200 years was located in the west gallery below the tower. Amongst those who played there were Handel, Mendelssohn and both Samuel Wesleys while Sir Henry Wood took early lessons and there are windows to Wood, Dame Nellie Melba, John Ireland and Walter Carroll. This was rebuilt by Harrisons in 1932 and the case dates to Charles II.

There are several ancient wall memorials and a spacious chancel with side aisles, while a fine copy of a Raphael painting from the 19th century hangs by the organ, portraying a traditional Renaissance setting. There is a window from the Cordwainers Hall which was kept in storage during the war and installed in the building in 1973.

Outside the church at the east end is a notable bust to the essayist Charles Lamb. This was proposed by the Elian Society on his anniversary in 1934, the main proponents Sir James Barrie, E.V. Lucas and E. Blunden - Lamb being a pupil at the nearby bluecoats. It was designed the next year by Sir William Reynolds-Stephens president of the R.S. of Sculptors based on a Hazlitt painting and was placed on the west wall of Christchurch. After the war it was removed to St. Sepulchre with a plaque in 1962.

Fleet Street

St. Andrew's, Holborn

This was first recorded in a charter of Westminster Abbey in 951 and Roman pottery was found nearby, whilst in the early mediaeval period it was *St Andrew Holbourne Strate*. The parish was significant as it included both Lincoln's and Gray's Inn who rented pews and a new stone edifice was built in the 15th century.

The church was all about its connections and prominence in High Holborn thus Henry Wriothesley, Earl of Southampton was baptized there on 24 April 1545 with Henry VIII as his godfather. His own son Henry (1573) was a patron of Shakespeare.

There were many altars and a fraternity of St. Sithe's, while in 1632 the church was very decayed and in need of rebuilding, rather than reparation. It survived the fire but due to its poor repair Wren rebuilt the crypt and nave from the foundations, re-clad the tower, and used Purbeck marble for the interior. The large edifice was completed in 1704 and its new organ by Renatus Harris included materials tried out at Temple church.

St. Andrew's, Holborn
baptized two Prime Ministers:

Henry Addington in 1801-04 later Viscount Sidmouth and…

Benjamin Disraeli in 1868 and 1874-80 who was the only Jewish leader (later Lord Beaconsfield).

In addition eight of the rectors became bishops and the incumbent from 1713-24 was Henry Sacheverell. He was previously at St. Saviour's, Southwark and preached political sermons in favour of the Tories thus helping them to power.

However in 1710 he was suspended for three years and his printed sermons burnt, and this was followed by unrest and heavy taxes leading to the Riot Act in 1714. Immediately the suspension ended the new Tory ministry provided him with the valuable living of St. Andrew's, but his High Church sermons and political stance meant many parishioners left and established St. John's Chapel, Bedford Row. A chapel of ease, St. George's, was also built nearby in 1707 and was soon taken over by the Church Commissioners.

Beneath the church tower there is a memorial to Thomas Coram (1668-1751) mariner and adventurer in the American colonies. Dismayed at the sight of so many abandoned children in London, he established the Foundling Hospital by Royal charter in Hatton Garden on 20 November 1739. This rapidly outgrew the premises and moved to a new building at Lamb's Conduit Fields to the north in 1742 - the west wing appears on the map by Rocque although the chapel and east wing are still being built.

This soon became a major charity with numerous admissions and was just south of the burial ground of St. George's (see Volume II). It had many prominent benefactors and William Hogarth who was one of the first governors painted a portrait of Coram.

Handel supported the hospital through musical performances and Dr. Charles Burney attempted to set up an Italian-style music school there, while Coram was buried in the chapel with memorial bust by Roubiliac. The latter was moved to St. Andrew's when the school left in 1926 and today there is a museum at Coram's Fields near to Russell Square and Gray's Inn Road. Coram's portrait sits inside and his statue is outside.

To continue this musical connection there were two notable organists at St. Andrew's viz. Daniel Purcell the younger brother of Henry from 1713, and John Stanley a friend of Handel. The latter was the Governor of the Foundling Hospital and there were regular performances of the Messiah there, while Stanley succeeded Handel as governor and the pulpit, font and organ-case from the hospital chapel were moved to St. Andrew's.

There were several significant baptisms at the church, in particular of the sculptor John Bushnell, singer Cecilia Young daughter of Charles an organist, two Prime Ministers who are discussed below, and Edward Stanford of mapmaking fame.

In terms of politics, Henry Addington was the son of the physician to William Pitt and formed a Tory ministry but was removed by Pitt's son. During his tenure he was given an honorary position at the Foundling Hospital and was also created the 1st Lord Sidmouth. Indeed he was the Home Secretary in the turbulent early 19th century.

The baptism of Disraeli took place at the church after his father a writer fell out with the leaders of Bevis Marks synagogue. He was then apprenticed in the law but turned to politics and writing producing significant works such as *Vivien Grey, Sybil* and *Coningsby* as well as an anti-Whig pamphlet for Croker during the Reform Bill. He was elected to Parliament for Maidstone in 1837, twenty years before the Jewish Disabilities Bill was passed, this being possible solely through his baptism at St. Andrew's.

St. Andrew's - after the blitz and today.

Regarding the marriages: Joseph Banks voyaged with Cook then took a house at Soho Square and was president of the R.S. from 1778; Marc Brunel was educated at Rouen in France and met his wife a governess there, but was an engineer in New York in 1793 and worked for the Admiralty from 1799; William Hazlitt the literary critic and philosopher had a circle including William Godwin, S.T. Coleridge and Charles Lamb.

A second local resident was Dr. William Marsden (1797-1867) who trained at St. Barts and resided at 65 Lincoln's Inn Fields where there is a plaque. He established the Royal Free Hospital at Gray's Inn Road in 1828, after he found a sickly woman on the steps of St. Andrew's (moved to Hampstead in 1974), and also founded the Royal Marsden with its roots at 1 Cannon Row, Westminster in 1851. He is commemorated on the south side of the church tower opposite to the Thomas Coram memorial.

Meanwhile, there were great changes nearby with the building of Holborn Viaduct in 1863-69. This removed a large portion of the north churchyard and neighbouring slums which featured as Fagin's Den in *Oliver Twist* (see St. Alban's, Holborn). As part of these changes the rectory and a court house were built on the south side by Samuel Teulon in the Gothic style, contrasting with the simple classical lines of the church.

Just beyond here was Farringdon Market, while across Farringdon Street was the Fleet Prison famous for clandestine marriages and whose inmates included John Donne and *Samuel Pickwick* 'to whom Sam Weller performed such loyal duties.' The church, except for the walls and tower, was completely destroyed in the blitz on 7 May 1941 and after some deliberation was restored and re-opened as a guild church in 1961.

C. 22 April 1636 John Bushnell s. of Richard and Mary plomer above Gray's Inn Gate
7 February 1711/12 Cecilia d. of Charles Young and Elizabeth in East Street
30 June 1757 Henry son of Anthony Addington and Mary his wife of Bedford Row
16 April 1800 Henry Revell s. of Henry R. Reynolds and Ann, James St. (see All Souls)
31 July 1817 Benjamin son of Isaac and Maria Disraeli, King's Road gent aged c.12
9 May 1830 Edward s. of William and Ann Stanford tailor born 31 May 1827 [7]

M. 24 Feb. 1679/80 John Evelyn j. of Deptford and Martha Spencer of Cov Garden lic
23 March 1779 Joseph Banks Esq. of St. Ann Westminster and Dorothea Hugessen o.t.p. minor lic consent Francis Filmer surviving guardian by will of William Western Hugessen father dec. by Edmund Filmer minister presence F. Filmer, S.S. Banks
1 November 1799 Marc Isambard Brunel o.t.p. married Sophia Kingdom of the same by licence by J. Pyne curate, witnessed E. Kingdom and Triv. Dalton
1 May 1808 William Hazlitt o.t.p. and Sarah Stoddart of Winterslow, Wilts by licence by Charles Pryce curate, witnessed John Stoddart and Mary Ann Lamb [8]

B. 30 July 1550 Thomas Wriothesley, Earl of Southampton [father of Henry]
12 June 1724 Dr. Henry Sacheverell the rector of St. Andrew's
26 April 1823 James Sayers of St. George's Hanover Square, 75 [caricaturist]

---

[7] Isaac Disraeli and Maria (née Basevi) had sons Raphael and James baptized there on 11 July 1817 who were born in 1809 and 1813 respectively. William Stanford married Ann Thompson at Ringmer, Sussex on 17 March 1825 and five other children were baptized from 1825-35.

[8] Charles Lamb was best man at the wedding and his sister Mary Ann was bridesmaid.

St. Bride's by Wren with its classic "wedding cake" spire. There were seven churches erected on the site and some important local connections, in particular with printing at Shoe Lane and Fleet Street.

St. Bride's

This is one of the oldest religious establishments in London with seven churches on the site, and was possibly founded by St. Bridget or the Celts during the 6th century. It was similar to one of that date in Kildare, and has Saxon remains from the next century. A Norman church was built in the 11th century and King John held Parliament nearby, but it was replaced by a larger building in the 15th century as described by Stow:

"The parish church of St. Bridges was of old time just a small thing," but this part then became solely the choir; and it was increased in size with a large nave to the west and side aisles at the charges of William Venor Esq. Warden of the Fleet in c.1480. A screen from the Duke of Somerset's House purchased for £160 and placed between the 'old and new' churches was broken in 1596 hence they were forced to restore it.

Nearby was Bride Lane and just beyond was the Bridewell owned by the King and until the 9th of Henry III courts were kept there. Henry VIII replaced it with a stately house to receive the Emperor Charles V who was at Blackfriars in 1522, and stayed there with Queen Catherine whilst the question of their marriage was debated by the friars in 1529. But Edward VI converted it into a house of correction and workhouse for the poor in 1553, with an east chapel and burial ground to the rear. The Savoy Hospital was briefly closed and its furniture was transferred there and to St. Thomas's, Southwark. [9]

To the west was Salisbury Court home to the Bishops of Salisbury and Earls of Dorset and just beyond the Whitefriars from 1241-1539. The area became Dorset Street after the fire and had three theatres being an infamous liberty for creditors &c. (see Vol. II). [10]

St. Bride's mediaeval church was also lost in the fire and replaced by one of Wren's most expensive creations in 1670-84, wedged between the alleyways of Salisbury Square. Its "wedding cake" spire was designed in 1701-03 with four diminishing octagonal stages capped by an obelisk, although eight feet were lost due to lightening in 1764. It is believed to be the inspiration for the tiered wedding cake of local baker William Rich.

The area nearby beside Fleet Street had a long association with the printing industry and an equally lengthy listing of literary residents. Wynkyn de Worde a pupil of William Caxton moved his printing press beside the church in 1500 (buried there 1535), and was followed by Richard Pynson, Thomas Barthelet printer to the King and Richard Grafton who produced the first *English Bible* in 1539. Their customers were bookbinders, clergy and lawyers many of whom lived just across the road in Shoe Lane.

---

[9] A gateway dated 1802 became part of 14 New Bridge Street when the prison was demolished in 1863 (and has a tablet), whilst King Edward's School, Witley had its foundation there.

[10] Other buildings there were the City Gasworks 1814, Sion College 1884, City of London Boys in 1883-1987 and City of London Girls at Carmelite Street from 1894-1969 (with plaque).

118

.... **Detail of St. Bride's** with view from Bride's Passage, and restored classical arches with carved reredos beyond. Note the aisles separated by wooden partitions.

The first newspaper the *Daily Courant* was printed at Fleet Bridge in 1702 followed by many others; whilst Dr. Samuel Johnson lived at Gough Square to the north, and was an essayist and critic known to many leading celebrities such as James Boswell. He published his famous *Dictionary of the English Language* in 1755, and his house remains just beyond Bolt and Hind Courts with a plaque and statue of his cat "Hodge."

As a result many literary people came to visit and a panel in Wine Office Court records this while Pepys was baptized, John Milton lived in the precincts and Samuel Richardson wrote *Pamela* and *Clarissa Harlowe* at Salisbury Square. Others with links were Dickens, Dryden, Evelyn and Thomas Tompion the father of clock-making (with plaque). It was therefore no surprise that St. Bride's was dubbed "The Printers' Cathedral."

Other services followed and Joseph Bonsor was a stationer at 132 Salisbury Square in the late 18th century. This was most lucrative and when Sheridan succumbed to financial problems he purchased his "run-down abode" Polesden Lacey in 1818, building a large Regency villa there. His brother-in-law Musgrave Lamb ran a sailcloth factory at Reading and produced so much material it was said the Battle of Trafalgar was won there!

The stationery business, however, remained at Salisbury Square and a son Joseph was educated at Eton and Oxford then married an heiress Eliza Denne Orme at St. Pancras. The husband was also very eligible and inherited Polesden Lacey then purchased homes in Belgravia, and disposed of the former in 1853, investing the money in the Combe & Co. brewery at Long Acre near to Covent Garden (see Vol. II). [11]

Due to the size of the parish Rev. Thomas Dale found the church inadequate and John Shaw jun. built Holy Trinity above Gough Square in 1838-39. The land was given by the Goldsmiths Co. and it had a Gothic tower at one end but was demolished in 1906.

St. Bride's was badly damaged in the war and restored under the inspiration of Cyril Moxon Armitage rector in 1951-62. The result was impressive and below the tower is a dome and welcome *Enter into Praise*, a floor reminiscent of St. Vedast's, raised wooden pews in the aisles, triumphal-arches, and a columned altar and painted apse. There is also a wooden memorial to Robert and Harold Harmsworth the journalists.

---

[11] Salisbury Square was numbered 1-19, 46-49 and 132-140 and to the south were St. Bride's and Dorset Wharves. Henry and Thomas Lamb took over the business as Henry Lamb & Co. from 1851 and it continued until 1906, but was incorporated with Venables Tyler in 1911.

One of the principal attractions is the Saxon crypt with its fine displays of church and local history, leading to a raised Roman pavement secreted at one end - all of which were revealed during excavations after the bombing. It was rededicated in 1957 and claims to have witnessed the marriage of the parents of Virginia Dare, but that marriage was in fact found to be recorded at St. Clement Danes (see that church).

C. 3 March 1632/33 Samuell son to John Peap's from Margaret his wife
28 May 1675 Grinling the son of Grinling Gibbons and Elizabeth his wife
8 October 1807 Joseph s. of Joseph and Jane Bonsor, 132 Salisbury Sq. b. 15 Aug
4 April 1825 Sarah d. of Henry and Sarah Lamb, Fleet St. stationer born 7 March [12]

M. 5 October 1697 Thomas Savory batch. and Martha Davis spinster by ye Arch Bishop
(An engineer, inventor, mine/colliery owner, and partner of Thomas Newcomen)

B. 1555 Thomas Barthelet citizen and stationer in the Lady Chapel - as per his will
1 December 1623 Thomas Weelkes [organist Winchester Coll. and Chichester Cath.]
10 July 1761 Samuel Richardson aged 70 - only three others that year

The Bridewell (and Chapel) - it was united with the church in 1864

B. 1657/58 Richard Lovelace [poet of *To Althea* "walls do not a prison make"] [13]
20 January 1782 Dr. Robert Levett aged 90 [lived in Dr. Johnson's house & eulogised]

Pepys - a plaque in Salisbury Court, and **Samuel Johnson** with house in Gough Square.

[12] Samuel Pepys was born at Salisbury Court on 23 February 1632/33 and died in 1703, whereas Grinling Gibbons was born in Rotterdam in 1648 and moved to Deptford in 1667 where he was discovered by John Evelyn. Jane Bonsor the sister of Joseph was also baptized there in 1805 and married Malcolm Orme a proctor of Doctors' Commons at Great Bookham in 1829.

[13] Richard Lovelace son of Sir William of Kent and g-grandson of Sir George Barne mayor went to Charterhouse and was a *cavalier poet* like Jonson and Herrick, but as a Royalist was imprisoned at Westminster. He became ill in the country and came to London where he died. Wood tried to find details for the *Oxford Alumni* and his sister Joan wife of Robert Caesar said she went to St. Bride's for his funeral. There is no record of this so it was possibly at the nearby chapel.

St. Dunstan in the West

This was one of five churches of Lundenwic a Saxon trading settlement on the Strand viz. St. Martin, St. Mary, St. Clement, St. Dunstan and St. Bride. It was founded in 988 to 1070 and like the others predated most of the churches within the City walls.

St. Dunstan or his priests were the probable founders and it was first recorded in 1185 whereas Henry III held it from Westminster Abbey in 1237 and donated it to converted Jews. However it was neglected and their residence became the Court of the Rolls. Here were kept the rolls or parchments of chancery and like Lincoln's Inn nearby and Gray's Inn at Holborn these were liberties outside of the parochial system. [14]

In addition there were Clifford's and Serjeant's Inns the former being given to Robert Clifford by a grant of Edward II. Another local institution the Cordwainers or Curriers was formalised in 1415 and based at the Carmelite Friary south of Fleet Street, hence they were associated with the church from that time. Later on they removed to Cannon Street and now share the Tallow Chandlers Hall at Dowgate (see City South).

A chapel of St. Katherine was added to the church in 1421 and there were memorials to Ralph Bane the Bishop of Coventry and Lichfield 1559 and Sir Roger Cholmeley knight to Henry VIII d.1538. Two famous incumbents followed, the first Rev. Thomas White from Bristol was a student at Magdalen Hall, Oxford with an M.A. in 1573.

He was briefly the rector of St. Gregory's and was appointed vicar at St. Dunstan's on 23 November 1575, then was a canon of Oxford and Windsor preaching at Paul's Cross. By his will he left a large bequest of £3,000 in 1624 which established the charity of Sion College (see St. Alphage's) and was buried in the chancel. The second minister of note followed him immediately afterwards, and John Donne the poet and preacher was vicar from 1624-31 at the same time as he was the Dean of St. Paul's.

Pepys recorded the church in his diary and one morning (14 July 1664) arose early to see Sir Edward Montagu - "And thence hearing a psalm sung I went into St. Dunstan's, and there heard prayers read, which it seems is done every morning at 6 o'clock."

The mediaeval church survived the fire but only after the Dean summonsed scholars of Westminster School to its aid. They formed a voluntary fire brigade and passed down buckets which quenched the conflagration which was burning just three doors away. In memory of this miraculous escape a new clock was erected with moving figures, chimes and a minute hand in 1671, being quite an attraction. It is referred to in various literatures including *Tom Brown*, *The Vicar of Wakefield* and a Cowper poem. A later memorial on the south wall was to Edward Marshal Esq. master mason of England d.1675.

However the church's days were numbered with the increase in traffic on this important thoroughfare and it was demolished in 1828, the clock being stored at the Marquess of Hertford's house in Regent's Park. Fleet Street was then widened and a new church was built on the churchyard behind - close up to Clifford's Inn.

John Shaw senior was the architect having worked on offices in Fleet Street and his son took over when he died in 1833, the design based on St. Helen's Pavement in York. The new church was quite distinctive with octagonal nave, tall tower with lantern, and various

---

[14] The Liberty of the Rolls to the east of Chancery Lane dealt with chancery cases from 1286. It had its own ancient chapel and the Public Record Office was established there in 1838.

St. Dunstan in the West is at *the heart of the press*. With its tower dated 1833, famous 17th century clock, and altar-screen brought over from Romania.

other adornments. The clock was returned by Lord Rothermere in 1935 and below is a bust to his brother Lord Northcliffe designed by Lutyens - both newspaper magnates of the Harmsworth family. Above the vestry door is a statue of Elizabeth I (date 1586) which once sat on Ludgate Hill and later outside the parochial school.

Internally there is a communion rail carved by Grinling Gibbons and a memorial to Sir Richard Hoare mayor of 1712, a founder of the banking firm - just opposite at 37 Fleet Street is a plaque to the Mitre Tavern and to Messrs. Hoare bankers (established 1672). In addition there are four stained glass windows donated by the Hoare family, and Izaak Walton a parishioner has a plaque and window by C.E. Kempe (1895).

Considerable restoration was carried out during 1950 then it became a guild church and home to the Romanian Orthodox Church and its religion. Their influence is revealed by an iconostasis or altar screen brought from a cathedral near Bucharest. On Fetter Lane is part of the old churchyard, and by Breams Buildings a statue to John Wilkes (1727-97) M.P. and Lord Mayor - that eloquent champion of English freedom (see Vol. II).

C. 18 August 1799 Isabella d. of John and Isabella Wilkie of White's Alley b. 31 March [15]

B. 11 March 1623/24 [Rev.] Thomas White doctor of divinity and vicarre of the parish church of St. Dunstan's was buryed [formerly rector of St. Gregory]
16 April 1632 The R.H. George, Baron Baltimore was buried d. 15 April [16]

---

[15] White's Alley was situated between Chancery Lane and St. Dunstan's churchyard in the Liberty of the Rolls. John Cotter married Isabella Wilkie at St. Martin in 1821 and their son John fought in the Crimea being raised to an officer. A grandson Edmond William Cotter R.E. played in the first Cup Final (1872) and received medals for his part in the Ashanti War under Wolseley.

[16] George Calvert (1579-1632) established Avalon, Newfoundland but found it uncongenial and removed it to Maryland named for Henrietta Maria consort of Charles I in 1629. He was made Baron Baltimore after his estate in Ireland and son Cecilius was named after Robert Cecil then married Anne Arundel (ref. co. of Annapolis). Baltimore was another of their eponyms.

St. Benet, Paul's Wharf, or the Welsh Church, has sermons in the two languages. It is situated on an ancient site near the River Thames.

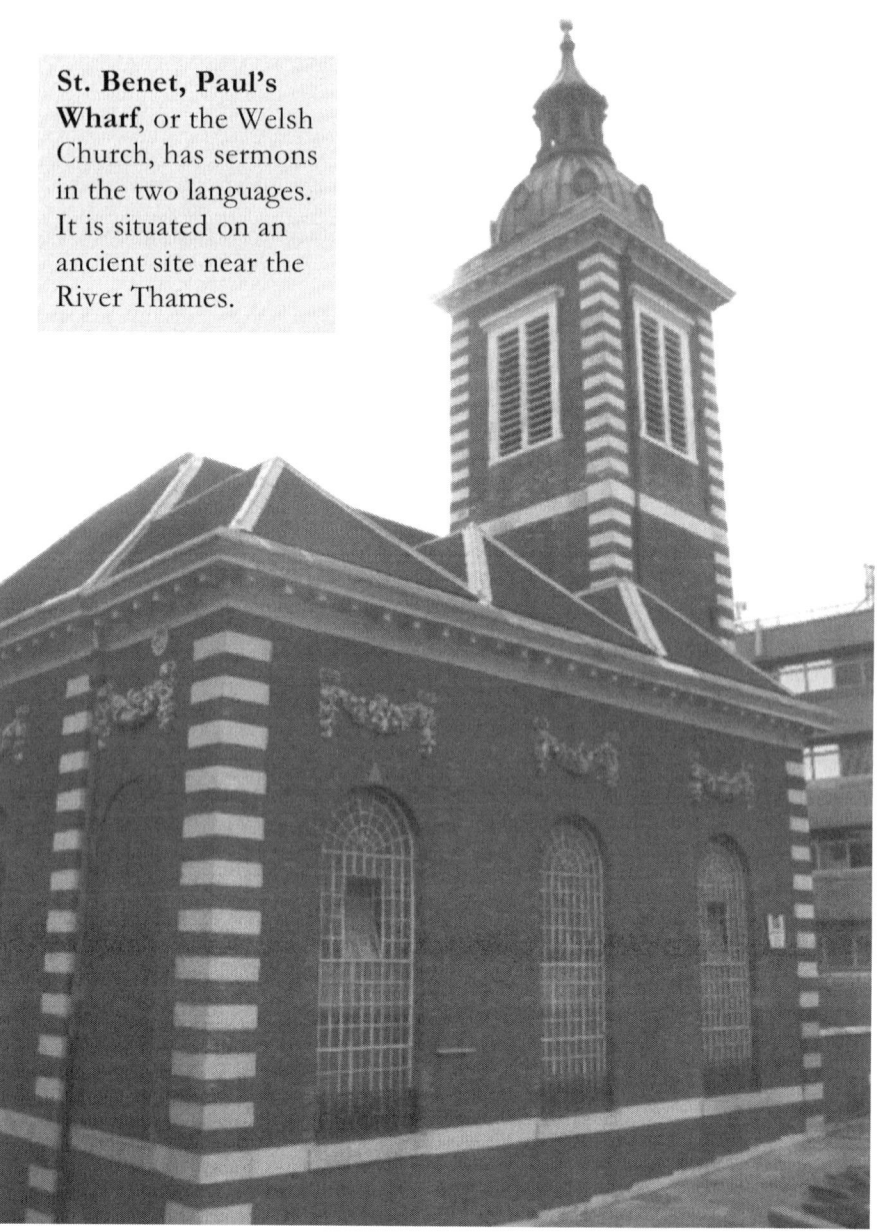

City
South West

Having considered the wealthy churches near Fleet Street we now look at several more humble abodes, albeit punctuated with the occasional abbey, castle and Royal residence. With many lanes, wharves and wardrobes in the locale there was undoubtedly a great chronicle to be told.

Amongst such famed sagas was the story of the King's Printing House and His Royal Highness's wardrobe resplendent with coats of many colours. Also in the vicinity was that profanity of Charles Dickens the Doctors' Commons adjacent to that source of "gules a bend or" the Royal College of Arms. And where did the knights go on emerging from the Tower Royal?

Regarding the rich and famous this was the manor of Whittington who on turning again saw Wren's Lantern close behind him. Other notables in the area were Charles Young, Theophilus Cibber and Inigo Jones while Fielding began a merry romp to boot and John Rocque left his imprint. And for a change there was a female of note with a memorable name to recall.

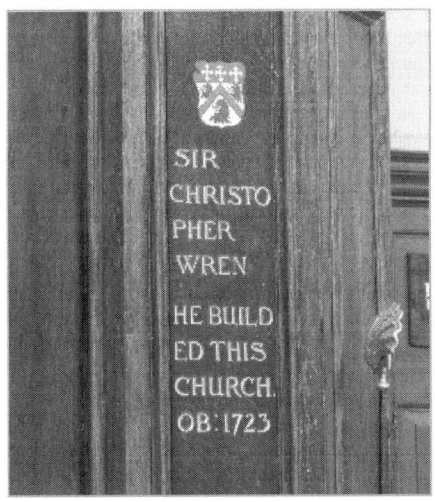

SIR CHRISTO PHER WREN

HE BUILD ED THIS CHURCH. OB: 1723

St. James, Garlickhythe

A pithy inscription situated in the nave and parish markers just west of the church (another dated 1862 is on the tower).

Castle Baynard

The ward of Castle Baynard included St. Gregory (already discussed), St. Andrew's and St. Benet's treated below and on its eastern border St. Mary Magdalen, Old Fish Street (see later). For convenience this section includes St. Anne's in Farringdon adjacent to St. Andrew's and St. Peter's in Queenhithe allied by name to St. Benet's. The modern ward is far more extensive taking in St. Paul's and reaches past Fleet Street to Holborn.

Baynard's Castle was seated on the banks of the Thames and had its origins at the time of the Norman Conquest being built by Baynard a nobleman. It passed to his kinsmen but after a felony was forfeited and went to Robert FitzRichard from Little Dunmow, and then to Robert Fitzwalter who also had an interest in Hertford Castle. The latter family relinquished it by 1428 when there was a great fire and it was rebuilt by Humphrey the Duke of Gloucester; then at his decease passed to Henry VI and thence to Richard Plantagenet, 3rd Duke of York who was lodging there in 1457.

On 28 February 1460/61 the Earls of March and Warwick "with a great power of men" entered the city and questioned whether the unstable King Henry was fit to reign? The Earl of March took up residence in Baynard's Castle (his father's home) and after a form of "election" was exhorted by the Archbishop, Bishop of Exeter and some noblemen to take up the throne. The next day he went on procession to St. Paul's and *Te Deum* was sung, then he was crowned Edward IV in the Great Hall at Westminster.

The castle was briefly in the hands of Richard III and also passed to Henry VII who repaired it, not as a castle but as a place to entertain princes and noblemen in 1487. He was resident there in 1492 and worshipped at St. Paul's. Subsequently it was owned by the Earls of Pembroke and from there a council confirmed Mary I as Queen.

When Henry VIII came to the throne he inherited Greenwich and Richmond and soon built modern palaces that are well documented, thus by the end of the 16th century the castle was pulled down and only a single tower remained. The latter was converted into a tenement and today the castle is commemorated by an obscure street name.

St. Andrew by the Wardrobe

The bastion was situated between Castle Street and Puddle Dock south of the church, while along Thames Street were the abodes of noblemen. Amongst them were Beaumont Inn which passed to the Earls of Huntingdon, Scrope's Inn, and Burley House home of Sir Simon Burley a knight of the garter. But generally these became breweries, dye-houses and wharfs. In addition, the Templars had a mill on Castle Lane using waters from the Fleet but this was closed in 1307 since it stopped vessels sailing up the stream.

Today the area is dominated "historically" by St. Andrew's although it seems to have had less significance in the past. The first mention was in about 1170 and it was designated as *St. Andrew juxta Baynard's Castle* - having connections to the latter.

Stow called it "a proper church" and John Wenlock relative of the Earls of Shrewsbury was buried and established a chantry there by his will in 1477. There were few memorials but they included William Nicolson of Walton, Bucks draper died 1531 whose daughter

Helen married Sir John Branch mayor 1580. A print displayed in the church shows the adjacent Dominican Priory, the Bridewell Palace with its watergate, St. Andrew's Steps, the Puddle Dock and finally Baynard's Castle just to the east (dated 1530).

However, these illustrious surrounds were soon transformed - firstly by the Dissolution and secondly after the Great Fire. The rector provided services for St. Anne's from 1540 with the two parishes closely linked, whilst the church was repaired and beautified at the cost of the parishioners in 1627 and there was a fair window on the south side.

Wren rebuilt the church after the fire using a simple, cost effective design and Strype noted it was quite handsome. It had a plain red-brick tower, white quoins, an entrance vestibule and north and south galleries. Puddle Dock Hill was just to the west and it was hidden from Thames Street (and the old site of the castle) to the south.

Considerable restoration took place in Victorian times and the view was opened up by Queen Victoria Street, but it was gutted in the blitz and restored to Wren's blueprint then re-dedicated in 1961. The weather vane came from St. Michael Bassishaw, the arms from St. Olave Jewry and pulpit and font from St. Matthew's, Friday Street. Other features are a memorial to Shakespeare who lived at Ireland Yard carved in oak in the west gallery, a figure of St. Andrew dated circa 1600 and a stylish stucco barrel vault.

Indeed, despite being a more minor church it took over St. Nicholas Cole Abbey and Olave, St. Mary Mounthaw and Somerset, and St. Benet and St. Peter in 1954 then was joined in a plurality with St. James Garlickhythe from 1986.

The Wardrobe - But what explains this unusual name? Sir John Beauchamp knight of the garter, constable of Dover and warden of the Cinque Ports (d.1359 St. Paul's) built a house north of the church and sold it to Edward III in 1361. His wardrobe was moved there from the Tower thus it became the Crown's storehouse with ceremonial robes - and was known as the Great Wardrobe to distinguish it from other lesser ones.

At this time the parson of St. Andrew's complained that Beauchamp had pulled down many houses to build it, depriving the church of tithes paid by the tenants, and he was granted 40s from that house in perpetuity. Richard III was lodged there in 1484 and it was later home to Sir John Fortescue master of the wardrobe, chancellor, member of the Privy Council and under treasurer of the Exchequer. Thus the secret letters and writings of state departments were lodged there rather than in the Chancery Office.

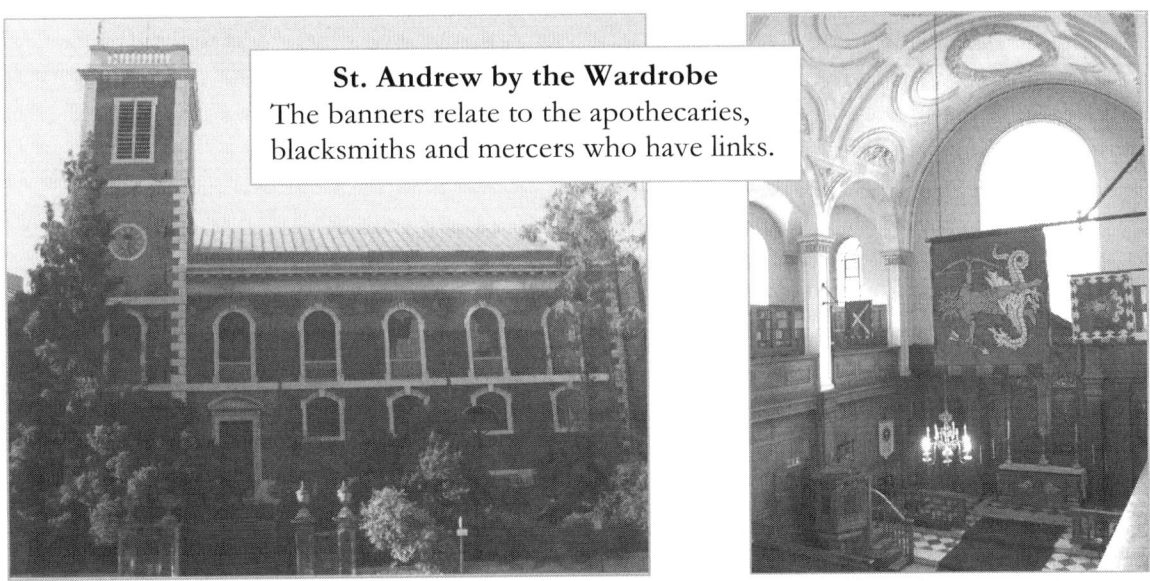

St. Andrew by the Wardrobe
The banners relate to the apothecaries, blacksmiths and mercers who have links.

This was all burnt down in the fire of 1666 but a fine courtyard was built on the site just north of the church and off of Great Carter Lane. This remains there today, and in fact a plaque at 5 Wardrobe Place demarcates the original site of the wardrobe.

St. Anne's, Blackfriars

This was an unusual kind of parish lacking a church in the normal sense but covering a large area from New Bridge Street across to St. Andrew's. Its origins were in a castle built by William Mountfichit at the time of Henry I - between the Fleet Ditch and Baynard's Castle. However, after a dispute it transferred to King John who rebuilt it.

There was then a decree from Robert Kilwarby, Archbishop of Canterbury, in 1276 to pull it down and give it to the Blackfriars or Dominicans who for the last fifty years had been in Oldbourne. The grant to the church was agreed by Gregory de Rokesley mayor and the barons of the City with two adjacent lanes for the friars to erect a church. In fact Edward I and his wife Eleanor became the principal benefactors.

The priory of the Blackfriars which was just south of Ludgate was large in extent and richly furnished with ornaments, including the images of Erasmus and Thomas Aquinas. There were gates and walls around its precincts whilst its connections were notable and multifarious - with ancient Kings using it as a repository for their records:

1450 The Parliament of Henry VI commenced at Westminster then was adjourned to the Blackfriars before removing to the shires at Leicester.

1522 Emperor Charles V of Spain and the Holy Roman Empire was lodged there.

1524 A tax was agreed there by parliament on goods and lands "at 2s in the pound" ref. property worth £20, but adjourned to Westminster Palace amongst the black monks.

1529 Legate Cardinal Campeius sat there with Wolsey to debate the King's marriage.

However, this all ended at the Dissolution and the Blackfriars house was valued at £104 5s 5d then surrendered on 12 November 1539. The land was granted to Sir Thomas Cawarden with its tenements, whereas the *Hall and Prior's Lodgings* went to Sir Francis Brian at the start of Edward VI's reign. Being a place of comfort and spaciousness it was then inhabited by noblemen and gentlemen until the time of Elizabeth I.

During 1586 there was a serious dispute between the City and the then owners of the precincts of the Black and White Friars. Of old, these areas claimed many privileges and were exempt from musters, supplied inferior goods without remedy, refused to pay taxes, gave refuge to villains and harmed traders beyond their walls. The matter passed to the Lord Chief Justice at this time - the aim to overthrow these injurious claims [rights].

The ancient church of the Blackfriars was one of the most spacious and fair churches in London, but after the friars were removed it was "utterly demolished." This was carried out by Sir Thomas Cawarden and it then became the parish of St. Anne's. Under Queen Mary he was forced to find the inhabitants a local *church* and gave a lodging-chamber above some stairs measuring 50' x 30'. The parishioners fitted this room out for a place of worship, but the roof fell down in 1597 leaving them in disarray.

St. Ann's Vestry Hall in Church Entry - houses the *Ancient Monuments Society* and the *Friends of Friendless Churches*.

Apothecaries Hall at Blackfriars Lane - dates from the time of Wren.

Upon arranging to repair it, they obtained extra ground from Sir George Moore for a west aisle of 15 feet and leased the warehouse below to Sir Jerome Bows, the total cost being about £300. Rev. William Gouge (1575-1653) who was born at Bow and educated at St. Paul's was ordained there in 1607 and remained in the parish the rest of his life. He gave midweek lectures which attracted large crowds and was Father of the London Divines being hailed as a great oracle of the age.

Under his ministry there were further improvements and in 1607 the parishioners paid £120 to Moore to purchase the freehold of the church, porch, churchyard and preacher's house; then in 1613 they bought housing to the south so they could enlarge the premises with additional rooms. Likewise, they obtained a new pulpit and inserted modern pews making the total cumulative expenditure £1,546 at that point.

Meanwhile, in 1632 the parish purchased the rooms below the church and repaired the decayed walls for £500, thus since the Reformation they spent a staggering £2,600. Inside there was a memorial to Elizabeth I "reigned in 1558-1603" but few recent ones.

The building was burnt down in the Great Fire with the parsonage and Strype suggests that it was rebuilt, although elsewhere it is stated that it then combined with nearby St. Andrew's (which generally seems the more likely outcome).

Carter Lane just to the north of St. Andrew's was once known as Shoemaker Row, and today there are various lanes and alleys leading off it. One of these, Church Entry was once a route into the priory between the nave and the chancel beneath the steeple, and here is a churchyard used by St. Anne's with a parish room. An information board notes the nave had seven bays, measuring 60' x 11', and a plaque in Carter Lane records the founding of the priory in 1278. Nearby is Ireland Yard pertaining to Shakespeare and here are located the only remains of the priory above the ground.

The other significant connection is to John Dowland who was born at Westminster in c.1563 and became a composer and lutenist for various noblemen. Initially he went to Paris under Sir Henry Cobham and for some years worked at the court of Christian IV of Denmark. Feted as the most famous musician of his age he published music in London including *A Pilgrim's Solace* and was lutenist to James I (see burial below).

Blackfriars Precincts - This was an area of castles and turrets perhaps like Whitehall from St. James's Park today. In fact, at the same time as the monastery was built, Edward I decreed the walls should be raised up with a large *Tower* made fit for a King's reception and for pleasure, and this remained until John Shaa mayor 1501 took it down.

Likewise, there was another *Castle* on the site of the Bridewell nearby but this fell into decay and its stone was used to rebuild the cathedral after an early fire. An adjacent house remained for some time and King John once held parliament there. Henry VIII built his palace to the east (see St. Bride's), and the west part was devolved to the Bishops of Salisbury. The priory was in fact located on prime land near to St. Paul's and a number of significant buildings were erected there after the Dissolution.

In the first instance there was a thespian connection and Blackfriars Theatre was built in the area of the modern Mermaid. James and Richard Burbage purchased rights from the Cawarden Estate in 1596 and set up what was mainly a private venue for the wealthy. After the Globe Theatre burnt down in 1613, Shakespeare moved to a house in Ireland Yard situated just off St. Andrew's Hill - primarily, due to its convenience.

The French Ambassador's House was also in the precincts below Ludgate, and on 26 October 1623 some 300 gathered for a Catholic sermon and rites given by Father Drury, a Jesuit and gentleman. However as the sermon taken from *Matthew* was started the floor collapsed and a number of people were lost, some only saved by escaping through a door into the main residence. The jury concluded the building was weak despite claims by the architect to the contrary and dismissed any suggestions of "a Popish plot."

After the Great Fire there was considerable restoration within the precincts. The King's Printing House was formerly situated there in Hunsdon House and Wren decreed that it should be rebuilt - therefore a new property was completed in Printing House Yard (later Playhouse Yard) by 1677. This was just west of St. Andrew's beside Water Lane and John Walter established a printing-shop there after a twelve year vacancy on 25 March 1784, then set up a logographic press and started *The Times* newspaper in 1788. [1]

Just to the north up Water Lane (Blackfriars La.) was Apothecaries Hall established by charter in 1617. The company purchased Cobham House a guesthouse of the friars from Lady Anne Howard sister-in-law of Lady Cobham for £1,800, and it was rebuilt after the fire by 1672. In the late 18th century the fine courtyard with its classical lines was much restored - but the entrance, staircase, hall and parlour date back to the 1670s.

M. 24 October 1626 Simonds D'Ewes married Anne Clopton licence (see St. Faith's)

B. Priory (by) 1243 Hubert de Burgh, 1st Earl of Kent
1336 John of Eltham, Duke of Cornwall brother to Edward III
1509 Sir Thomas Brandon knight of the garter; 1514 Lord Thomas Scrope
Margaret Queen of Scots, Countess of Arundel/Huntingdon, King James of Spain

Church 20 February 1625/26 John Dowland doctor of musick

---

[1] Charles Frederic Moberly Bell was born in Alexandria in 1847 his father Thomas a merchant. He was related to the Moberlys with links to St. Petersburg and Winchester College and also to the Carver family of Gibraltar. As Egypt correspondent for *The Times* from 1865 he wrote several books, but was called to London by John Walter (III) in 1890 as managing director. Bell worked on the *Times Atlas* and *Encyclopaedia Britannica* and died at Printing House Sq. in 1911.

St. Benet's, Paul's Wharf

"Eglwys Urdd Bened Sant"

A church has stood on the site since 1111 and the dedication comes from St. Benedict (420-80) founder of the monastic order. Nearby was a main landing stage since Roman times called Paul's Wharf and to the west was the watergate of Baynard's Castle. The mediaeval church had a different aspect to today and was on the north side of Thames Street which was the main thoroughfare - with St. Benet's Hill just to the east.

Paul's Wharf was owned by the Dean and Chapter and was used to unload materials for the building of St. Paul's, thus the church was also known as St. Benet Hithe. There were just a few ancient memorials viz. Sir William Cheney lord chief justice 1442, Sir Gilbert Dethick garter king at arms 1565 and David Smith embroiderer to Elizabeth I 1587; and Nicholas Barker a coppersmith bequeathed a tenement for the fabric (1524).

Henry Fielding (1707-54) published the bawdy tale of *Tom Jones* in 1749, two years after marrying his maid.

William Shakespeare (1564-1616) lived nearby at Ireland Yard. In *Twelfth Night*, Act V Scene 1, the clown having received two pieces of gold from Duke Orsino, adds, "The third pays for all, like the bells of St. Bennet one-two-three." But the duke replies, "You can fool no more money out of me at this throw!"

The church had little sign of repair or beauty bestowed upon it up until 1632, and like the College of Arms it was rebuilt in a greatly improved fashion after the fire.

There was then a complete change in status as Wren produced a Dutch-style church in 1677-83. It was built by the mason Thomas Strong and had red and blue brick with stone quoins and carved garlands over the windows. There was a hipped roof on the north side and the tower had 12 feet of the original, but was encased in brick and stone surmounted by a dome and cupola with ball and weathervane at 115 feet.

Some dispute exists as to who actually designed the church, but some favour Hooke since he mentioned it in his diary - and unlike Wren had visited the Netherlands.

The interior is no less impressive and this was one of the few to survive the blitz, thus some claim that it is Wren's *most authentic church*. Being of square design it retains its north and west galleries, its reredos, a Baroque Dutch altar, pulpit by Gibbons and font with cover. The carved door with Stuart coat of arms was given by Charles II.

There were two important connections to the church and it was a chapel to the College of Arms from 1555, whereas Doctors' Commons arranged many marriages there some of these being quite hasty in nature. These two institutions were situated on St. Benet's Hill just above and many lawyers were lodged there. In fact both had dedicated seats in the balcony with "College to the rear and Doctors to the front." Several officers of arms were buried in the churchyard and their banners were displayed there. [2]

Other buildings in the area were Le Neve Inn on Thames Street belonging to the Earl of Salisbury and Sir John Beauchamp, and Berkeley Inn at the south end of Adle Street by Puddle Wharf - built of stone and timber. The latter was a tenement by the late 16th century but the arms of Lord Berkeley still appeared in stonework on an arched gate. In addition there was a small toft of ground nearby where the parsonage once stood.

Regarding the church there were several later memorials including Inigo Jones architect 1652, Sir Robert Wiseman a dean of the Arches 1684 and Steven Price an advocate of Doctors' Commons 1688. Two of the more interesting ones are those to Gregory King (1648-1712) and to Delariviere Manley (1670-1724). The one to King is on the east wall by the balcony and states he was a skilful herald, a good accomptant surveyor, also skilled in mathematics and political arithmetic - "The Father of Statistics."

St. Benet's, Paul's Wharf - "The Welsh Church" with coat of arms, north balcony and chancel.

---

[2] Thomas Stanley, 1st Earl of Derby married Margaret Beaufort, Countess of Richmond mother of Henry VII and built Derby House situated in the parishes of St. Benet and St. Peter. Queen Mary and Phillip gave it to Gilbert Dethick the principal garter king of arms &c. on 18 Jul 1555 and it became Garter House (or the College of Arms) but was rebuilt after the fire.

The latter has a floor memorial in the main aisle. She was born in Jersey the daughter of Sir Roger Manley a Royalist officer, historian and Governor of Forts (her name from the wife of Sir Thomas Morgan his superior). At her father's decease in 1687 she went to live with her uncle John Manley a Tory M.P. and had a child by him in 1691.

She then resided with the Duchess of Cleveland a mistress of Charles II and wrote and travelled from 1694-96. Her play *The Lost Lover* was performed at Lincoln's Inn and she made incisive attacks on Whig politicians, while her *New Atalantis* in 1713 placed British politics on a Mediterranean island and libel cases ensued. Her saucy, energetic style was translated into German and she died at Old Fish Street on 11 July 1724.

An Act of Parliament was on the table to demolish the church as early as 1854 and it was redundant by the 1870s. However the Welsh Anglicans of St. Etheldreda petitioned Victoria and came there in July 1879 with services in the Welsh language every Sunday at 11.00 and 3.30 since. It became the official Welsh Church in London and united with St. Nicholas, whilst in earlier times Welsh embroiderers worked at Baynard's Castle.

Great changes took place with the arrival of Queen Victoria Street and there is plaque to Doctors' Commons demolished 1867 just to the west. Later realignment then left St. Benet's nestled in a spur of Upper Thames Street, on the remains of St. Benet's Hill. It became a guild church under the reorganisations of 1954 while a J.C. Bishop organ dated 1844 was rebuilt after a serious fire in 1973. There are just "two bells" today (dated 1663 and 1685) whereas the building retains a quaint, timeless quality inside.

M. 30 March 1706 Charles Young of St. Martin in the Fields and Elizabeth Nash of St. James's Clerkenwell ob. licence [organist and father of Cecilia]
22 May 1725 Theophilus Cibber of St. Paul's Covent Garden, Middlesex married Jane Johnson of St. Martin in the Fields [s. of Colley Cibber and relative of Arne]
4 June 1737 William Elliott of St. James's, Westminster Esq. bach and ye Right Hon. Lady Frances Nassau of St. George's Hanover Square spin - see St. Martin's
27 November 1747 Henry Fielding of ye Middle Temple wid. and Mary [Mc] Daniel of St. Clement Danes [maid to his first wife, Charlotte Cradock of Salisbury]
25 May 1751 John Rocque of St. Martin in ye Fields widower married Ann Bew of the same parish widow [mapmakers of some renown]

B. 26 June 1652 Mr. Inigo Jones was buried - with parents, copy inscription
3 September 1712 Gregory King Esq. Lancaster Herald at Arms in the chancel
14 July 1724 Delariviere Manley a widow in the church

St. Peter's, Paul's Wharf

The small parish church of St. Peter's (Parva or Little) first noted in 1170 was just east of St. Peter's Hill on Thames Street and had no monuments except to Queen Elizabeth. It was repaired in 1625 and there was a fair table of commandments at the upper end of the chancel (1619). A parsonage house was apparent in 1636 but not in 1693 and there were no gifts or legacies to the poor, thus it was not rebuilt and joined to St. Benet's in 1666 and to St. Andrew's in 1954. The Blacksmiths Hall was nearby in Lambeth Hill and there is a plaque today in Queen Victoria Street noting its presence (1668-1775).

Old Fish Street

Thus we leave Castle Baynard and move eastwards into the ward of Queenhithe which covered seven parishes including the three below, those listed in the next section and St. Peter's just treated. St. Mary Magdalen is also considered here due to its proximity to the other three churches - all located in Old Fish Street (& Hill) down to Labour in Vain Hill. Unlike many other wards the modern one covers a remarkably similar zone.

St. Mary Magdalen

Regarding churches this area was a bit of a backwater in mediaeval times and St. Mary's was described as, "A small parish church with few monuments." It was located where Knightrider Street met with Old Fish Street at the south of Old Change, the site today being in the area of Old Change Court which leads through to Distaff Lane.

The first record of the church came in 1181 and in mediaeval times it was designated as *by St. Paul's, at Elde Fish Strete*, or *at Lamberd's Hill*. To the west was Do Little Lane so designated for its lack of artificers or shopkeepers and Sermon Lane corrupted from the "shere moniers" who melted down silver for coinage. The College of Physicians was situated in Knightrider Street from 1518-1614, and within the same locality is a plaque to the Upholders Hall (or Upholsterers) destroyed in the fire.

Of the few memorials were ones to Barnard Randolph common sergeant d.1583 who paid for a conduit west of the church for water from the Thames, George Coleman who lost all his lands when the French took Calais d.1600, and Joan daughter of Alexander Serle procurator general and wife of Gilbert Dethick d.1607.

Thomas Berrie fishmonger and benefactor had a brass plate fixed near the font with the inscription, "How small soever the gift shall bee, thank God for him who gave it thee" (dated 1586) which is now at St. Martin's, Ludgate. In addition there were some repairs in 1630 and John Evelyn recorded his visit for Holy Communion in Easter 1653, when such Anglican services were banned by the Commonwealth.

The building was destroyed in the fire and according to Strype it was replaced by, "A fair lightsome church without pillars." Wren carried out the reconstruction in 1683-87 on Old Fish Street & Old Change in Portland stone including round-headed windows, balustrade and a tower capped by a small lantern on a dome.

Rev. R.H. Barham (1788-1845) - minister of **St. Mary Magdalen** (left) and the author of: *The Ingoldsby Legends.*

Few events of great moment happened here however this changed when Rev. Richard Harris Barham was appointed rector during 1824-42. Barham was educated at St. Paul's School and Oxford and first contributed to *Blackwood's Magazine* in 1826 then produced *The Ingoldsby Legends* of myths, ghost stories and poetry in serial form in 1837. These were very popular being published as books during his time at the church, and sported illustrations by John Leech and George Cruikshank.

However, there was a serious fire at the church in 1886 and this being a time when many were demolished it was not rebuilt, and was removed by 1893. The font with late 17th-century bowl went to All Hallows, London Wall, and the pews, stalls, pulpit and a painting passed to St. Martin's Ludgate. The parish combined with the latter.

B. 21 June 1845 Richard Harris Barham rector of St. Augustine and St. Faith aged 57

St. Mary Mounthaw

A short distance eastwards along Old Fish Street was St. Nicholas (see below) followed by a turning south into a hill of that name. The southern portion of the hill was called Labour in Vain with a courtyard reminding the inhabitants of the futility of their labours, and on the west side was the small church of St. Mary Mounthaw. [3]

Meanwhile to the east was one end of Five Foot Lane just above St. Mary Somerset and to the north of the church was the Bishop of Hereford's Inn or lodging an ancient house built of stone and timber. This sometimes belonged to the Mounthaunts of Norfolk but the Bishop of Hereford purchased it from them in about 1234.

The house was repaired by these ecclesiastics in c.1517 but it became ruined and was divided into tenements, the hall and principal rooms used for making sugar loaves &c. Adjacent to here was the parish church St. Mary *Monte Alto* or *Mounthaunt* which began as a family chapel and then had the Bishop of Hereford as its patron.

There were a few monuments including one to John Gloucester an alderman 1345 who bequeathed Salt Wharf for two chantries, and to John Skip the Bishop of Hereford 1539 (for twelve years) who died in London during a sitting of parliament. In the south aisle there was a picture of James I with *peace and plenty* on either side. However the church was destroyed in the fire and the parish joined to St. Mary Somerset in 1670.

St. Mary Somerset

At the south end of Labour in Vain up against Thames Street was the other church of St. Mary's sitting opposite the Broken Wharf. It was first recorded during 1150-70 and was possibly named after Ralph de Sumery owner of the ground i.e. Somer's Hithe - in the same way that there was Edred's or Queen's Hithe situated nearby.

The church had a number of memorials but at the time of Stow all were defaced, and he listed some he knew of regarding rectors: John Epus 1433, Thomas Cane also a notary 1444 and John Denham 1511 - other ones being to local fruiterers and salters.

---

[3] The site of St. Mary Mounthaw was just beyond the modern Lambeth Hill on Queen Victoria Street near the new pathway leading to the Millennium (Wobbly) Bridge.

In addition he recorded Benet Brocas a gentleman, servant to the Earl of Surrey and treasurer of England 1511 (with coats of arms), windows to pray for various citizens and an extant stone in the chancel to Richard Randall brewer, pewterer and the Governor of Christ's Hospital 1616. The church itself was repaired under the rector Thomas Burton in 1624 and during this vexatious work he applied the maxim, "The Lord is my rock and my fortress, my deliverer, my helper, I hope in him" (Psalm 18, Verse 2).

Like most others the church and its repairs were destroyed in the fire and Wren rebuilt it on a smaller, more regular site in 1685-94. This was an economical construction with a rectangular nave, no aisles, flat roof and round-headed windows plus western gallery on two pillars. The principal asset was its 120 foot tower at the southwest corner with eight Baroque pinnacles, which appears to have been added later by Hawksmoor. There were also two important "celebrities" connected with the church.

Gilbert Ironside was born at Winterborne Abbas in 1650 his father Gilbert being rector and he attended Wadham, Oxford where he was warden. Like his father he was made Bishop of Bristol and then also of the more lucrative Hereford, while as vice-chancellor of Oxford he backed the rights of fellows against the King. He died on 27 August 1701 and was buried at St. Mary's within the communion rails with a *Latin* inscription.

Secondly, Richard Steele was born in Dublin but was placed in the care of an aunt who was the widow of Sir Humphrey Mildmay and then married Henry Gascoigne private secretary to the Duke of Ormond. As a result he attended Charterhouse School where the latter was a governor. He then went to Merton, Oxford and joined the Life Guards going to Flanders but had left the army by 1705 to become a playwright.

Initially he was married to Margaret Stretch, but after she died he famously courted his "Dear Prue" and penned a reputed 400 love letters to her. In addition he was a Royal waiter to Prince George of Denmark and with Joseph Addison (whom he knew from school) published the first edition of *The Spectator* during 1711.

Steele was the M.P. for Stockbridge but expelled over the Hanoverian succession, then was reinstated under George I and was a governor of Drury Lane Theatre at a critical time. Afterwards he retired to Carmarthen with his wife who emanated from there.

St. Mary's had links to the Low Church and Malcolm in *Londinium Redivivum* recorded that Mr. Gunn the Methodist was once a preacher there, which association he believed explained, "Its trampled and dirty state." There was also a loss of the communion plate in the early 19th century and it was clearly not a wealthy church. [4]

Indeed, the Union of Benefices Act meant the last service took place in 1867 and the church was demolished four years later, but the tower was saved by Act of Parliament after an intervention by Ewan Christian the architect (who repaired Christchurch, Spitalfields). It now stands as a reminder of former times in a backwater on Thames Street and its underpass, just behind the Salvation Army International H.Q.

M. 9 September 1707 Richard Steele married Mary Scurlock [Prue] by Mr. Avignon

B. 1 September 1701 Guilbert Ironside, Lord Bishop of Hereford [younger, MA]

---

[4] James Peller Malcolm (1767-1815) was born in Philadelphia but studied at the R.A. and made engravings for the *Gentleman's Magazine*. He then published *Londinium Redivivum*, an ancient history and modern description of London, in 1802-05 and also other similar works.

St. Mary Somerset (left)

St. Nicholas Cole Abbey (right)

Both were products of the Wren "school of architecture."

St. Nicholas, Cole Abbey

Now we have a change of pace away from dedications to Mary and over to St. Nicholas a patron saint of fishermen, this area having included the pre-Billingsgate fish market. The church was just a kipper's throw away from St. Mary Magdalen on the south side of Old Fish Street, with a view up Little Distaff Lane to the Cordwainers Hall. Today its aspect has been opened up by Queen Victoria Street which went through its churchyard.

The mediaeval church was mentioned in 1144 and recorded as *Sci Nici retro Fishstrate* in 1272-73, while the annotation came from cold harbour or a lodging house for travellers. A large tower with south aisle were of later building in about 1378, and by the time of Stow it was quite ancient with the land raised up about it. This caused the parishioners to descend into the body of the church. There were plans to rebuild it during repairs, but this never took place as revealed by arching on the east side of the old steeple.

Various bequests left land and tenements to the church and there were memorials to numerous fishmongers with their coats of arms over several centuries, including Walter Turke fishmonger mayor 1349 and Richard Lacty the parson 1491.

Thomas Sowdley was appointed rector on 25 July 1547 and of St. Mary Mounthaw the following March but was deprived of both livings under Mary in 1554, and mass was held there immediately afterwards. Sowdley received the sobriquet "parson chicken" and was escorted through Cheapside in a cart followed by chamber pots and rotten eggs, but he was reinstated on the return of the Protestant faith (and d.1564).

On the north side of the church was a cistern to deliver water paid for by Mr. Randolph who donated £900 to the fishmongers for the purpose. Likewise, the building had new frames for its bells in 1626 and new battlements on the steeple in 1628.

However, it was destroyed in the Great Fire and was one of the first rebuilt by Wren at a cost of £5,042 in 1671-77 - being similar in design to his other churches built nearby. The nave was a simple rectangle without pillars or aisles creating a considerable space, and the exterior featured a balustrade plus an idiosyncratic leaded tower. The latter was somewhat "French" in composition, with flaming urns adorning each corner.

After some shops on Old Fish Street Hill were removed a new entrance and windows were built to the south in 1874, and a ship-vane on the spire came from St. Michael's, Queenhithe in 1876. District Line trains then rattled by underneath blackening it with smoke and it was dubbed "Cole Hole" thus attendances sank to an all time low.

However under the Rev. Henry Shuttleworth a Christian Socialist who was minister in 1883-1900 there were congregations of up to 450 people. This was the largest attendance in the City and could be compared to the efforts of modern day incumbents at churches such as St. Helen's, Bishopsgate and Holy Trinity, Brompton (see later).

Despite this the church was destroyed in 1941 and then featured among the bombsites in the escapades of *The Lavendar Hill Mob* ten years later. It was rebuilt by Arthur Bailey with the original pulpit, font, communion rail and reredos preserved in 1962 - but the steeple itself was just a facsimile, the Burne-Jones east window was by Keith New (who worked on Coventry) and the organ was by Noel Mandor.

The parish included St. Mary Mounthaw and Somerset and St. Peter but these were all transferred to St. Andrew's at this time, and the church became the H.Q. of the Diocesan Council. It was then leased to the Free Church of Scotland from 1982 to 2003 and there are now moves to convert the redundant building to a centre for religious education. For that purpose there have been promotional lectures at nearby St. Andrew's.

Painter Stainers Hall, Little Trinity Lane - The companies united and moved there in 1532 but the hall was rebuilt on three occasions: after the fire, in 1915 and again after the war.

St. Michael's, Queenhithe (1830s) - Despite the addition of a spire and pitched-roof, it was similar to St. Mary Magdalen and St. Nicholas - a standard design emanating from the Wren stable.

Queenhithe (ward)

Now we consider the three other churches in the ward which in ancient times included a large dock known as Edred's Hithe. This was capable of accommodating ships, barges and lighters and had various owners including King Stephen, William de Ypres and Holy Trinity Priory, Aldgate. It received its current eponym when owned by Queen Eleanor the wife of Henry III - then passed to the Earls of Cornwall by unknown means and at some time fell to the City and Sheriffs of London.

Holy Trinity the Less

A short distance past Bread Street was Trinity Lane and at the top end of Little Trinity Lane on the east side was a small parish church, perhaps annotated regarding the larger priory at Aldgate. John Brian alderman in the reign of Henry V was the main benefactor and the few memorials included one to John Mirfin auditor of the Exchequer 1471.

By the end of the 16th century it was very ancient and in danger of falling down. Some collections made for its repair were insufficient thus "it leaned upon props and stilts." It was completely rebuilt in 1607-08 with help from the Merchant Taylors and Vintners, and a list of contributions from City parishes hung in the south aisle. But due to such poverty it was not rebuilt after the fire and the parish passed to St. Michael's in 1670.

However this was not the end of the story. The site was then taken over by the Trinity or Hamburg Lutheran Church - the first Lutheran congregation in Britain. In 1666 there were many migrants from Germany and Scandinavia, also merchants of the Hanseatic League who were provided for in the embassies of Brandenburg and Sweden.

In 1668 they asked Sir John Barckman Leijonberg, Swedish Ambassador to appoint a pastor and Georg Martens took up the post at the ambassador's home in Covent Garden. Charles II was then petitioned and a delegation sent, thus the new church was dedicated in Trinity Lane on 21 December 1673 - with Rev. Martens as the minister.

The church was a small oblong building with an arched window and two circular ones on either side, whilst there was a simple square tower on the central roof. It served its purpose for many years but the land was bought by the railway in 1871 and the building was demolished - it is now modern offices near Mansion House underground.

In L. Trinity Lane on the west side was the Painter Stainers Hall although Stow noted that the workmanship of staining "was now departed out of use in England." There are parish markers dated 1824 in Gt. Trinity Lane and 1859 in Queen Victoria Street.

St. Michael's, Queenhithe

At the lower end of Little Trinity Lane on the west side where it met Thames Street was the church of St. Michael's. To the rear was a churchyard on Huggin Lane and opposite was the busy wharf of Queenhithe and the respite of Coffee House Lane. It was first recorded there as *St. Michael de Hutha Regina* in the 12th century and Stow described it atypically as "a convenient church," perhaps in easy reach for visiting pilgrims.

Again there were few monuments and most were defaced. However Stephen Spilman gent of Norfolk mercer, sheriff and chamberlain had no issue and left land to his family and money for bridges, the church and a chantry - buried in the choir in 1404.

The church was destroyed in the fire and rebuilt by Wren in 1676-86, with the main frontage opposite to Queenhithe having five round-headed windows and a sequence of circular windows at the clerestory. The principal features were a door and vestibule to the west on a different elevation, and a stepped ziggurat at the base of the spire.

Shortly after Wren senior completed the church his son, who also worked in his office as an architect, was married there. Philip Musard resided at 8 Buckingham Street in the Strand from 1676 (when it was built) until 1709 - and married Constantiae then had six children baptized at St. Martin in the Fields, including Mary on 12 September 1677. The father was in fact a high profile jeweller to the Royal family as detailed:

Calendar of Treasury Books

11 December 1677 - paid to Phillip Mussard for jewels for the King £720 [Charles II].
23 January 1687/88 - Sir C.W. surveyor reported that 4 acres were sufficient for a Royal mews and stables for 300 horses and 30 coach-houses with offices and lodgings.
24 January 1687/88 - £110 to Phillip Mussard for three bracelets and two rings delivered to the present Queen Dowager [Catharine of Braganza at Somerset House].

Sir James Thornhill father-in-law of Hogarth helped repair the altar-painting in 1721, but by the next century most occupants had moved away and the church was demolished in 1876. The parish, pulpit and woodwork went to St. James's, a ship weather-vane with barque for corn to St. Nicholas's, and G. England organ to Christchurch, Chelsea.

There is a parish marker at the bottom of L. Trinity Lane (see p. 123), and information by the inlet notes how King Alfred resettled London in 886. A garden was created in Huggin Lane while the remains of a Roman bath were found there in 1964. The site was mostly covered by Thames Street and later on by offices reaching across the road.

M. 14 May 1706 Christopher Wren Esq. [junior] married to Mrs. Mary Mussard of the same place by lycence by Mr. Richard Jenks curate [5]

St. Nicholas Olave

On the west side of Bread Street Hill was another convenient church among houses of cheesemongers, fishmongers and merchants. It was first mentioned in 1188 and the main memorials were to Henry Welles parson 1391, Thomas Lewen ironmonger, sheriff and benefactor 1555 and John Blitheman organist of the Chapel Royal 1591. The south aisle which was only roofed with rustic tiles was finally ceiled in 1628, which with repairs of the steeple cost £22. The parsonage was rebuilt after the fire but the parish went to Cole Abbey and the remaining churchyard appears on Rocque's map of 1746.

---

[5] Christopher Wren junior (1675-1747) was a member of the Commission for 50 Churches and helped survey many of their projects with his father and other architects (see Introduction). His wife Mary has a memorial in the Jesus Chapel at St. Paul's cathedral as do her parents, whilst he settled at Wroxall, Warwickshire and was buried there.

Garlickhythe

The final ward to consider in this section covered the four churches below and is roughly contiguous with the present ward; its name of Vintry being quite transparent and related to the large number of Bordeaux wine merchants trading beside the wharves. Other names of significance in the locality were Garlick Hill and Hythe, which recalled the sale and unloading of garlic from France beside the Thames in ancient times.

St. James, Garlickhythe

The church was first mentioned in 1170 and Richard Rothing and his son John who were both vintners completely rebuilt it from 1320. This was a church of some standing and Stow found a number of prominent memorials, and also noted several chantries which were served by priests who lived at St. James's Commons nearby. A fraternity of joiners was set up at the church in 1375 and this evolved into the guild of that name, their hall being a short distance east along Thames Street (opposite the Innholders).

A plaque on the north wall records six mayors buried there viz. John of Oxenford 1341 a vintner who gave a mill and 50 acres in Kentish Town to Holy Trinity priory, Sir John Wroth 1360 d.1407 fishmonger, William Venor 1389 grocer, William More 1395 vintner, Sir Robert Chicheley 1421 grocer and James Spencer 1527 vintner. In addition the church had memorials to Robert Gabeter mayor of Newcastle 1310, Lord Strange son of the Earl of Derby 1503, Lady Stanley and the Countess of Huntingdon.

Dr. William Boyce composer of *Heart of Oak* - "Come cheer up my lads 'tis to glory we steer…" also used by the Canadian Navy &c.

St. James, Garlickhythe "Wren's Lantern" with its south façade - once up against a row of shops, and replica clock.

The north aisle was repaired and the church replaced in 1624, but it succumbed in the fire and Wren came there and rebuilt it at a cost of £5,357 in 1676-82. At this point there was only a tower but no spire, and due to the height of the nave and its many windows it was known as *Wren's Lantern*. The east end had a large window in a projecting chancel with a barrel vault, and the main entrance was under the tower on Garlick Hill. However the south side was originally obscured by shops built up against the wall.

Richard Steele came there for a service in 1711 and after listening to the various highs and lows of Rev. Phillip Stubbs discourse, he provided a polemic on sermonising in an edition of *The Spectator*. Whether this included any debate about aspirations is unclear, but the steeple was belatedly added by Hawksmoor during 1714-17.

The latter consisted of an elaborate three stage Baroque spire, in stucco and Portland stone, whilst the belfry had louvered windows and a pierced parapet capped with urns. All of this sat above the original plain tower with its two small pediments.

William Boyce was born in the parish in 1711 and was a choirboy at St. Paul's then was appointed organist at the Oxford Chapel, Marylebone in 1734, eventually becoming the master of the King's musick and organist of the Chapel Royal by 1758. He composed a number of symphonies, anthems and sonatas, including the naval march *Heart of Oak* with inspiring lyrics by Garrick at the time of the Seven Years War.

Indeed, in the gallery above the double staircase of the church was a Bernard Schmidt organ although it was installed by Johann Knoppell in 1718. Other changes included the removal of the weak east window to be replaced by an Andrew Geddes painting of *The Ascension* in 1815 - the gift of Rev. Dr. Thomas Burnet the long term curate. In addition the chancel was enlarged in 1876 to take the pulpit of St. Michael's Queenhithe - other items from the latter including choir stalls, door-cases and a Stuart coat of arms. Another sojourner at the church was Charles Dickens who came there for a service and then mentioned it in his periodical work the *Uncommercial Traveller*.

Down the years there were a number of close calls for the building and it was possibly saved from the Union of Benefices by the fact ten livery companies were connected to it. There was considerable restoration in the Victorian era especially by Basil Champneys but a bomb from a Zeppelin caused superficial damage in 1917, another fell in the south aisle but failed to explode in 1941, and incendiaries damaged adjacent property and the exterior. Repairs after the war restored it as an authentic Wren church and a replica of the 1682 clock was installed on the tower. However a crane working on the Vintners Hall crashed through the roof in 1991 and the building was closed for two years.

Divine providence was undoubtedly at work since this remains a tribute to the design of Wren, and those who worked for its preservation. John Betjeman believed it was the best restoration in the City - despite its awkward location beside a dual-carriageway.

There is a tablet (& marker) in Great Trinity Lane stating the parish extends 10' 6" north dated 1889, and as one descends Garlick Hill the cobble stones evoke a different era. A small garden sits in front of the church and one enters under the west gallery, to see the richly carved woodwork and exquisite reredos with pilasters of Ionic gold.

The aisles have rose windows with Georgian and Stuart arms to the north and south, while there is a memorial to Robert Chicheley twice mayor d.1439 and a tablet to livery companies. The original woodwork includes the altar table, font cover and pews whereas the plate dating back to the 16th/17th centuries is from nearby churches. Just opposite is the Vintners Hall present from 1446 and behind were some old buildings including the house of the Earl of Worcester and the Fruiterers and Plumbers halls (before the fire). Its current façade was added after the widening of Upper Thames Street in 1910.

The parish now includes nearby St. Michael's Royal which came with All Hallows the Great; St. Martin Vintry, All Hallows the Less and Holy Trinity the Less (not rebuilt after the fire); and St. Michael's Queenhithe (demolished in the 19th century).

C. 11 September 1711 William Boyce son of John and Elizabeth [organist]

"The Music of the Spheres" brought harmonious design to **St. James's** church.

St. Martin Vintry

A short distance along Thames Street on the other side of New Queen Street was the fair parish church of St. Martin's. It was first recorded from the 12th century and annotated as in the Vintrie or de Beremand regarding a porter in the wine trade.

It was newly built in about 1399 by the executors of Mathew Columars a stranger and Bordeaux merchant whose arms appeared in the east window. There were memorials to two mayors: Sir John Gisors vintner 1311 who lived in the Vintry House (where Henry Picard entertained Edward III), and Sir Ralph Austrie fishmonger d.1494 who roofed and glazed the church. However there were no legacies or a parsonage attached.

There is a suggestion that the rood screen was dismantled in 1560 and thereafter used to provide wooden pews for St. James's. A number of repairs were carried out in 1605 and 1632, but the church was not rebuilt after the fire. The parish itself was joined to nearby St. Michael's and the site is now located underneath Thames Street. Despite the fact the church was long departed entries still appeared in its records, and it seems likely these were residents of the parish who had ceremonies at St. Michael's.

Christopher Magnay was a wholesale stationer at Upper Thames Street and College Hill with his sons from 1793-1830. For part of this time there was a partnership with William Pickering and they owned paper mills at Bledlow and Saunderton in Bucks. Magnay was master of the Stationers and mayor in 1821 and his son William was the mayor in 1843, at which time the Royal Exchange was opened. In fact, a deed showed that they owned part of St. Martin's churchyard with several adjacent warehouses.

C. 8 April 1794 Christopher James s. of Christopher and Jane Magnay b. 26 Dec
3 April 1795 William s. of Christopher and Jane Magnay b. 4 March

M. 16 October 1824 Christopher J. Magnay Esq. o.t.p. and Caroline Flower of Hendon licence by G.F.L. Nicolay rector present C. Magnay, W. Magnay &c. (see Aldgate)

St. Michael Paternoster Royal

The parish of St. Martin's encompassed land from Thames Street down to the river, while St. Michael's covered a smaller area sandwiched between St. Thomas the Apostle and St. John the Baptist (see later). This was indeed the church of Dick Whittington.

It was first mentioned in 1219 with the suffix coming from the sale of rosary beads at Paternoster Lane (later Elbow La. and College Street). An alternative was added perhaps from trading with La Reole near Bordeaux (from 1282), although more likely from Royal Street (College Hill) named for the Tower Royal. In Roman times the site was beside the riverbank and to the east was Walbrook stream and to the west Maiden Lane.

Sir Richard Whittington (1358-1423) Mayor and M.P.

A 19th century engraving copied from a painting at the "Mercers Hall." The long serving mayor was a great philanthropist, hence his name passed down into folklore and legend.

When considering Whittington it is often hard to separate fact from fiction or at least from pantomime. He was born in Gloucestershire in c.1358 and came to London to trade as a mercer dealing in high quality silks and velvets, which included selling of goods to Richard II. From this base he became an alderman for Broad and Lime Streets and was elected mayor in 1397-98, 1406 and 1419 as well as becoming an M.P.

He had a house next to St. Michael's and established an almshouse and hospital north of the church for 13 poor people (now in East Grinstead). In addition he established a college of St. Spirit and St. Mary for a master, four fellows, clerks and choristers to pray for his family and King Richard II &c. A licence was granted under Henry IV in 1409 and the mayor provided some vacant ground as confirmed by his will (d.1423).

Apart from the college he was a great benefactor and also rebuilt the church in 1397, and gave money to the Guildhall, St. Thomas's, St. Barts and Greyfriars Library. Any idea that he heard the sound of Bow Bells from Highgate was strictly a tale for the cats, and how he came to such prominence was probably a result of his philanthropy.

The collegiate church and its brothers were suppressed by Edward VI leaving only the almshouses, whilst early monuments included: Sir Richard Whittington and Dame Joan, Sir William Oldham speaker 1459, Sir John Yonge grocer mayor 1466, and Sir William Bayley draper mayor 1524. It was a peculiar of the Court of Arches but the upkeep was paid for by the Mercers (whose school came in 1808), and was a fair church with marble tomb to Whittington in the south aisle. This was reset at the time of Queen Mary when the parson dug it up looking for supposed riches - but was lost in the fire.

Edward Strong the mason rebuilt it to a Wren design in Portland stone from 1686-94, although the three stage spire with octagonal lantern at 128 feet was not constructed until 1713. The nave was then a simple rectangle with balustrade and it took over the parish of St. Martin's. Later memorials are to William Fellowes of Lincoln's Inn, his brother Sir John a merchant d.1724, and Sir Samuel Pennant mayor d.1750 (by Rysbrack).

The neighbouring church of All Hallows the Great was pulled down in 1894 and many of its fixtures came there viz. stone figures of Moses and Aaron, panels, screen, and the candelabra fittings (Brm. 1644). However, St. Michael's was hit by a flying bomb in 1944 and there was a recommendation to restore just the tower, but with backing from the City (perhaps due to its historical associations) it was rebuilt during 1964-68.

The original main entrance on College Hill became the Whittington Rooms housing the offices of the Mission to Seamen (established 1835), whereas the organ went above in the west gallery. The interior was simple in design with a pulpit attributed to Gibbons and the restoration included reredos, lectern and candelabra. A new window was added by John Hayward with its contemporary *Whittington*, *swag bag* and *enigmatic cat*; whilst the parish was transferred plus attachments to St. James Garlickhythe.

St. Michael Paternoster Royal

The church was originally built by Dick Whittington in 1397, then again by Sir Christopher Wren in 1694.

On the south side of the church is Whittington Gardens once covered by tenements and courtyards, whereas to the east is the Innholders Hall which occupied the site from 1521. Its elegant old court room, dining hall and façade date from 1670, and beneath the hall are secreted the ancient foundations of a Roman quayside.

B. 7 May 1601 Peter Blundell was bur. [clothier, founder of Blundell's School, Tiverton] 6 May 1658 Mr. John Cleveland was bur. in the church d. 29April [a cavalier opposed to Cromwell and a poet]

St. Thomas the Apostle

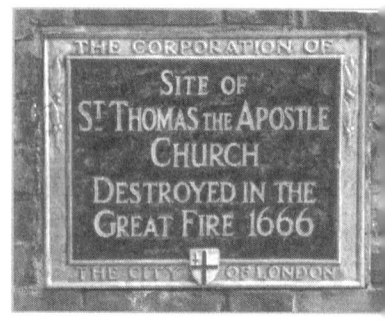

The church was to the east of Wringwen La. above the junction with St. Thomas Apostle. It had a similar antiquity to others but Stow observed no monuments except arms in the windows and stonework - perhaps of John Barnes mercer mayor 1370 a great builder thereof. In the past there were memorials to Thomas Romane mayor 1309 who gave one of several chantries; and to Sir William Littlesbury alias Horne (named as such by Edward IV for his musical prowess) salter mayor 1487.

Several significant buildings were located nearby and just to the east was Tower Royal situated above Cloak Lane. This was first used as a Royal residence by King Stephen and thereafter was the Queen's wardrobe, thus the mother of Richard II lodged there for safety at the time of Wat Tyler. It gave rise to Knightrider Street which ran west from St. Thomas's through to Creed Lane and Ludgate, and it was here that the knights of Tower Royal *rode armed and mounted* to be inspected by the King and others. It was lost in the fire and covered by courtyards, and recently there was a short street of that name.

West of the church was a great house Ipres Inn home to William of Ipres, which was built there to be near to Tower Royal. The said William was a favourite of Stephen and gave Queen's Hithe to Holy Trinity and established Boxley Abbey in Kent. The family retained the house after the Flemish left, and John of Gaunt made an escape from there as the property was surrounded during a feast in 1377. Adjacent was Ormond Place, a stone building once home to the Earls of Ormond but later tenements. [6]

The church was not rebuilt after the fire and New Queen Street was inserted through the site; whilst Georgian houses were built to the west and there is a plaque on their forecourt by a paved area (see above). Initially the parish passed to St. Mary Aldermary and later on there were Presbyterian and Catholic chapels just to the west.

---

[6] James Butler of Kilkenny was created Earl of Ormond in 1328 and married the granddaughter of Edward I. The family were very wealthy over several generations with senior positions.

City South

Moving on from such Royal assignations and their illicit alliterations we now arrive at the more humble market of the struggling peasant. This area had much of candles, grass, fish and wool about it with a wick to light the way, whilst education was at the forefront with several grammar schools - a sure remedy for Sir William Curtis and his mis-spelt three R's.

Walking in the footsteps of pioneering Victorians in bathing machines with seaside souvenirs we learn of "the Stocks Market that had no stocks." And on no less than two occasions, following in the Biblical steps of take up thy bed and walk, a church takes up its foundations and moves!

There is a delving into the deepest depths of history to uncover the story of an ancient stone, then again a hasty shake of the umbrella to ward off any rain resulting from St. Swithin. Finally we go to the future with smoky rail-arches of Doré beneath London and a spaceship in the vicinity.

The illustrious abound with Addison, Brontë, Dryden and Vanbrugh to pen but a few, while Mackonochie that namesake of McGonagall sermonises and may be remembered for a very long time. There is a gem of Hawksmoor, some musical organists, and also trench memories from those days.

St. Stephen's, Walbrook (in the entrance vestibule)

"This miraculous building by the talented Christopher Wren was restored to greatly protect his church - 1987."

Walbrook (ward)

Once upon a time in an imaginary land there were some swampy marshes by a great river where Mediterranean merchants plied their trade. Barques and dhows of all descriptions moored up in a little stream by the waterway, unloading their cargoes at the quayside, as merchants and barrow boys hastened about in the shadow of a church's cobbled-tower. A priest hurried by muttering Hail Mary's in the trenchant mud, while children and curs ran about, following women in dresses flouncing on the dirt. Colour and uproar was the order of the day throughout, garlic and spices perfuming the pungent air.

However, this was no historical fantasy. From the Roman era the Walbrook provided a safe haven for ships - like its larger neighbour the Fleet and this continued into mediaeval times. In fact, the tributary was still important in the days of Stow and he used it as a significant boundary to separate the City's eastern and western wards. Today, it is long gone having been concealed in culverts underground but has likewise formed a basis for dividing up the eastern and western sections.

Thus, we now look at the wards to the east of the Walbrook and strangely of the forty surviving churches twenty are on each side of this historic stream. The Walbrook ward included the four churches below which all sat close to the banks of the rivulet, as well as St. Swithin's situated on firmer ground away to the east.

St. John the Baptist, Walbrook

This was a church of little historical significance although once stood by the Walbrook with its western end up against the stream. On the south side of the church was a small street (now Cloak Lane) which came to Horseshoe Bridge which went over the brook, however at the time of Stow the latter was already vaulted across.

The church was first mentioned during the 12th century, and the parson obtained some land north of the quire to enlarge it in 1412. There were almost no monuments of note although there was one to William Combarton skinner who gave lands d.1410, and John Stone tailor and sheriff 1464. Further repairs were undertaken by Robert Peterson the rector in 1621 but there was no parsonage and it was not rebuilt after the fire.

The parish then passed to St. Antholin's in Budge Row just to the north in 1670 and the churchyard appeared on Rocque's map at the corner of Cloak Lane and Dowgate Hill. In addition it was transferred with the former to St. Mary Aldermary in 1873.

The arrival of the District Railway destroyed most of the remaining churchyard in 1884, but someone thought it was of some significance. A large memorial was erected to record its "four centuries of occupation" by Rev. Lewis Bobbett White D.D. rector of St. Mary Aldermary and his two churchwardens on the north side of Cloak Lane. It remains today with the tube trains just below and the parish is now with St. Mary le Bow.

St. John's may have had little impact itself but its parish being on Dowgate Hill was the location of numerous livery companies and their halls. In fact, if this were New York it would no doubt have been designated *The Livery District*. Just to the west on Cloak Lane were the Cutlers and Turners halls above Whittington College, while on the west side of

Dowgate Hill were the Tallow Chandlers, Skinners and Dyers in quick succession. Across Elbow Lane (College Street) were the Innholders and beyond Thames Street the Joiners whilst the Plumbers were opposite in Chequers Yard (from the fire to 1863).

Today, a promenade along Dowgate Hill beside Cannon Street station reveals that three of the remaining forty livery halls are still located there. On the corner of Cloak Lane the Tallow Chandlers have a small memorial garden recording their presence since 1476, and down an enticing little corridor is their hall built under the guidance of Hooke in the years 1672-77. In fact they were originally formed as a fraternity of St. John's.

St. John the Baptist at Walbrook

A memorial in Cloak Lane, and two parish markers in College Street - sited just behind the Dyers Hall.

Just to the south is the Skinners Hall with classical pediment façade fronting a cloister of ancient origin, the guild having occupied the site since the 1400s. Also known as the furriers there was a bitter dispute over precedence at the barge procession in 1484, thus mayor Robert Billesdon decreed they would alternate with the Merchants Taylors guild. And this dispute possibly gave rise to the phrase "at sixes and sevens."

The adjacent Dyers Company were in the locality from the 15th century and converted two houses on Dowgate Hill in 1731. A number of their halls have stood there but the present structure was built in 1840 to complete this triumvirate.

St. Mary Bothaw

Another small church, this was situated on Turnwheel Lane below Candlewick Street and just east of Dowgate Hill. In fact, it was not far from what Stow termed Walbrook Corner. There was a turnpike in the middle of the lane, and the annotation *Boat Haw* referred to the building of boats in a haw or yard at the Dowgate nearby.

A stone house on the north side belonged to the prior of Christchurch, Canterbury in 1167, while the church had a small cloister attached, its precincts the burying ground of several noblemen. The most significant memorial was to Henry Fitz Alwine draper and first mayor 1189-1212 - in office during the turbulent times of Richard I. [1]

---

[1] Strype records that Fitz Alwine had a dwelling house in the parish now three tenements whilst his memorial, window-arms and benefaction from the Drapers were all in the church. Yet, Stow against all this evidence claimed he was buried at Holy Trinity priory in Aldgate.

There were only three other monumental inscriptions that were legible including one to Lancelot Bathurst alderman and grocer died 1594, whilst that to Elizabeth I recorded she was vanquisher of the Spanish Navy and had enriched all of England.

There was no parsonage house and a few repairs in 1621, but after the fire the parish went to St. Swithin's and the churchyard remained between tenements on later maps. The site was covered by Cannon Street station designed by J. Hawkshaw, John W. and Edward M. Barry (sons of Sir Charles) in 1863-66 to relieve congestion on London Bridge.

St. Mary Woolchurch Haw

The Walbrook stream continued north past St. Stephen's to the site of Mansion House, and it was here that the church of St. Mary's once stood on the eastern side. During the mayoralty of Henry Walleis 1282 a number of buildings were erected to the maintenance of London Bridge, and one was sited next to the stocks in the middle of the City. Here the way was broad and large, and it was appointed as a market place for fish and meat. Any rents received for the bridge came under the jurisdiction of the mayor.

The Stocks Market, as it was known, sat on the north side of St. Mary (Wool Church) and was listed as one of five places permitted to sell fish and meat in 1322, whilst it was rebuilt in 1410. The church itself was so named for a beam placed in its churchyard for the weighing of wool in the days of Edward II. But this role was moved to the newly built Customs House at Wool Quay near to Billingsgate in 1383.

A fair and large church was built there under licence in the reign of Henry VI viz. 1442 but had to be fifteen feet from the market to allow sufficient light for the latter. There was a tithe received from the masters of Bridge House and several monuments pertaining to its precincts, including John Winger grocer mayor 1504 who helped rebuild it.

Before the Dissolution there were a number of chantries, and John Handford grocer provided the font and Richard Shore draper the porch. The church was richly repaired in 1629 but on the night of the fire burnt to the ground, and the parson was seen saving the church valuables whilst he let his own house fall. Indeed, the parsonage was not rebuilt after the fire and the site with the market was covered by the Mansion House designed by George Dance (the elder), in the Palladian style, in 1739-52. A plaque on the west side of the Mayor's residence marks the site of the church, whereas one to the north states, "Adjoining this spot stood the Stocks Market 1282-1737."

Mansion House (from Ackermann's *Microcosm of London* dated 1808)

The entrance portico had six Corinthian columns on a restricted site, while the Egyptian Hall was an uneasy compromise of classical architecture from Greece and Egypt. Compare the ceiling to that of St. Stephen's over the page.

St. Stephen's, Walbrook

The first church is believed to have existed from Saxon times, c.700 A.D. and the earliest reference was on the bank of the brook in 1096. The old church stood on the west side and nearby was Sernes Tower close to Bucklersbury. It was here that Edward III kept his "monies" and he donated the tower to the chapel of St. Stephen's in 1359.

The next development came in 1428 when Robert Chicheley the mayor gave ground on the east bank for a new edifice duly completed in 1439. This measured 125' x 67' and Chicheley also donated £100 to pay for the lead and timbers. Sir Robert Whittingham who laid one of the foundation stones purchased the patronage from John of Lancaster, Duke of Bedford (uncle to Henry VI & Edward IV) and presented it to the mayor.

Stow - "Then lower down in the street is one other fair church lately built on the east side thereof, for the old church stood on the west side. In place where standeth the parsonage house, and therefore so much nearer the brook, even on the bank."

There was a memorial to Thomas Southwell first parson of the new church in the choir whilst the most significant one was to John Dunstaple master of astronomy and musick d.1453. He is thought to have received patronage from the above Duke of Bedford and Duke of Gloucester and thus travelled to France. His grand epitaph "a secret knowledge of the stars" was later reinstated at the church (in 1904).

During the time of Queen Mary, Rev. John Feckenham, the Dean of St. Paul's and last Abbot of Westminster, came and preached Papal doctrine there; whilst the rector Dr. Pendleton forsook the religion of Edward VI although he denied this at a latter date. In addition there were memorials to three mayors: Sir Richard Lee 1460/69, John Cootes 1542 and Rowland Hill 1549 also Dr. George Owen physician to Henry VIII. [2]

Repairs were carried out on the chancel, aisles, pews and pulpit costing £126 in 1622-33 but the mediaeval church was perhaps fortuitously destroyed in the fire.

Wren's Church - Wren was made surveyor of works in 1669 and the building of twenty churches started in the next two years. Being a parishioner and living at 15 Walbrook the foundations of St. Stephen's were laid as early as 17 December 1672.

It was the only church started that year and those present included the mayor Sir Robert Hanson, six members of the Grocers who were patrons, and a member of the Chicheley family. Wren was occupied with providing the designs for St. Paul's at this time and in St. Stephen's we see his mind developing the cathedral blueprints. It was indeed a significant period in his career and the church was completed by 1679.

His inspired dome supported by arches sitting on columns was the first in the country, whilst the 16 Corinthian pillars part of a rectangle appeared as if - *the trees of a forest*. It was a true masterpiece of Classical design, and with Pevsner considering it one of the top ten in England, it should be viewed on a level with the Pantheon in Rome.

---

[2] Rev. Henry Pendleton appears on the list of rectors from 1556-57 and was given the epithet of *The Vicar of Bray*. This referred to the incumbent of Bray on Thames, Berks who "adapted his faith" over time from the late 18th century - being immortalised in song, opera and film.

On the west side were 13 steps leading up to the vestibule under the tower, these being adjacent to the site of the old east bank of the Walbrook. However the main church was located some distance away from here due to the restrictions of site. Internally there were high box pews installed in 1678 accommodated by the tall bases of the columns; while the font, pulpit, reredos and screen arrived by public subscription the next year.

To the north there was once a cloister and Wren planned to erect a portico here with colonnades leading out to the market, but this was never built. On the south side was "a forum" like that at St. Mary le Bow today - with a statue of Charles II mounted in the centre (moved to Newby Hall, Ripon). The north door was later blocked up due to the smell from the market, and there was a memorial to Dr. Nathaniel Hodges d.1688 who wrote of the plague which began in Bearbinder Street just to the rear.

However, the church was only completed when the steeple was added in 1714-17 and this resembled those of St. James's and St. Michael's nearby in Thames Street. Vanbrugh the famous architect of Blenheim Palace and Castle Howard lived in houses he designed at Blackheath and Whitehall. At this time he recommended underground drainage for London, wrote plays - one of them a sequel to Colley Cibber, and was a Commissioner with Hawksmoor and the Wrens on the Fifty Churches project from 1711. Due to the latter association he was buried at St. Stephen's after his death in 1726.

An organ was installed by G. England in 1765 but was moved to St. Bartholomew's in 1886 (except the case), and replaced with one by William Hill in 1906. A painting of the saint was given by Benjamin West, American artist and R.A. president, for an altar piece but was later on the north side. In fact, this was a valuable living and George S. Townley was the rector from 1784-1835 followed by George Croly L.L.D. in 1835-61.

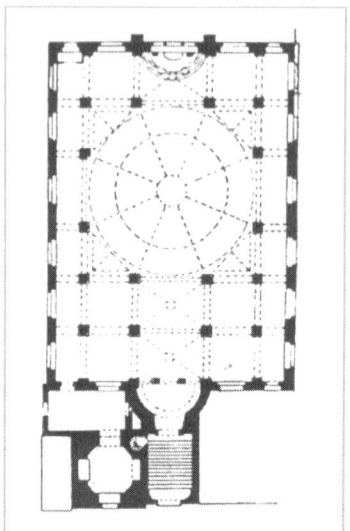

St. Stephen's, Walbrook showing the *perfect* dome and regular floor plan.

Opposite - "A jewel in a poor setting" revealing the problems of location.

There are memorials to Rev. Townley who d.1835 aged 88, and one to George Alfred Croly son of the rector - lieutenant in the Bengal L.I. who fought at Kabul but died at Ferozeshushur during an assault on the Sikhs' camp in 1845. Charlotte and Anne Brontë also visited with their publisher to hear a sermon by Rev. Croly in 1848. [3]

The next incumbent of note was the Rev. Robert Stuart de Courcy Laffan M.A. from 1899-1927 who played a significant role in the revival of the Olympic Games. After the efforts of Dr. William P. Brookes at Much Wenlock and Baron Coubertin to reinstate the Olympics, it was Rev. de Courcy Laffan hon. sec. of the British Olympic Association who wrote thousands of letters from the rectory to secure the games in 1908. [4]

After considerable war damage the church was restored in 1951-52, whilst the parish was extended thus it eventually included St. Benet Sherehog, St. Swithin's with St. Mary Bothaw, and St. Mary Abchurch with St. Laurence Poultney.

It was at this time that Dr. Chad Varah arrived at the church as rector having worked and done counselling in other City parishes, and established the Samaritans there in 1953. A poignant telephone in the church records this momentous event.

---

[3] In *The Wizards of Wight* by the author a clue states, "Enter the station of the saints and say a prayer for safe departure, walk into the wall where once a brook ran with force." The heroes learnt that St. Pancras was a red herring, but found a stream at Walbrook and entered the church with its two ghostly sisters. They also visited London Stone and the Mithras Temple portal.

[4] Rev. de Courcy Laffan was the principal of Cheltenham College in 1895-99 hence his interest in sports. Mount Vesuvius erupted during 1906 therefore the Italians declined to hold the Games in Rome, and they were transferred to London and the White City Stadium was built. One of the promoters of the association with de Courcy Laffan was Sir Frederick J. Wall fifth secretary of the F.A. - and Great Britain beat Denmark 2-0 to win the soccer gold medal.

"Modern Times" - The exterior of the church was not intended to match the interior since it was originally less visible, hidden among the market buildings and tenements of the area. Internally the walls were perfectly squared off, unlike most Wren churches, and the corners dipped down to meet the columns with classical reverence.

Despite such perfections it never quite worked in a strictly liturgical sense, even after the box pews were removed (in 1888) and choir stalls were introduced to the central space. This resulted in a more traditional nave and chancel - with the altar at the east end.

A major restoration took place funded by Lord Palumbo in 1987 (also see Poultry) and at this time Henry Moore designed a controversial stone altar which was positioned in the centre. On entering from the vestibule (with tablet) one is struck by its presence as much as by Wren's ornate columns and dome. The dome creates an illusion of "square space" but it is the geometrical lines emulating the Creator that are most impressive.

However one critic retorted, "Never was so rich a jewel, placed in so poor a setting." Predominantly this referred to its dull exterior with green copper dome but also alluded to location and environment. This problem was then exacerbated over time.

Originally it had suffered due to the noisome stench of Stocks Market, then it became concealed behind the Mansion House with its large attics (later removed), and finally was abutted by a building of soulless lines at its southern corner. The only partial relief being the classical white stone façade of Walbrook House situated to the south.

But alas this respite is no longer present. It is now replaced by *The Walbrook* designed by Foster & Partners for Minerva PLC, which makes the furore around No. 1 Poultry seem like a fleabite of inconvenience. The sharp lines of the former like the fins of some spacecraft jar on the Wren tower in most troublesome fashion, and one might ponder planning criteria regarding, "location next to listed historical buildings."

In addition Bucklersbury House just opposite was deemed by Pevsner to be one of the dullest structures in London. However Legal & General plan to replace it with Walbrook Square by Foster &c. which will *float like a dream*, with the Mithras Temple (discovered in 1954) re-housed near to its original location on Walbrook stream. Both of these herald a great change for the area with modernism being the leading prerogative.

B. 14 June 1688 was buryed Dr. Nathanoll Hodges in ye valte
31 March 1726 was buried Sir John Vanbrough in ye north d. 26 March

St. Stephen's (nave)

Wren's *"forest of columns"* produces a classical play of light, unlike the Baroque Gothic of Vanbrugh.

Also - The Henry Moore altar and Wren pulpit, a subtle combination.

Dowgate

The Dowgate ward beside the Thames encompassed some of the halls discussed under St. John the Baptist, but only covered the two parish churches listed below. A number of properties were located on Dowgate Hill among these halls, including Jesus Commons a college of priests with a great library but suppressed under Edward VI. At the corner of Elbow Lane (College Street) was a great stone house replaced by wooden tenements, and on the eastern side towards St. Mary Bothaw was "The Erber."

The latter had a complicated history but variously belonged to the Earl of Warwick, the Duke of Clarence, the Scrope family, Henry VII and the Drapers, also at one time being a lodging of Sir Francis Drake. Just to the west on Thames Street was the Joiners Hall then beside the river a number of wharfs including Dowgate, Steelyard a liberty of the merchants of Almaine (Germany) and Cold Harbour (named after a house).

Cannon Street Station

This was once the site of Dowgate and Steelyard wharves - where the foreign merchants held privileges. All Hallows Lane is just to the east and the Thames Path gives access under the station, with signs of modern commercial activity.

The surviving towers, built by J. Hawkshaw and J.W. Barry, are like church spires and form a foil to St. Paul's behind. Inside is a statue to the Plumbers' Apprentice whose hall was on the site.

One of the main watergates was situated at Dowgate or Downgate and a conduit was built there to supply the neighbouring hill in 1568. Regarding Steelyard Liberty this was agreed by Henry III in 1259 since his brother Richard Earl of Cornwall was the King of Almaine. However at the time of Edward I under the mayoralty of Henry Walleis in 1282 there was a serious dispute. In exchange for their rights, the merchants were meant to maintain Bishopsgate and its defences but had failed to carry out this duty.

The German and Dutch merchants operating in this location provided corn and other produce at reduced rates, such that in the time of Henry IV there were further disputes, and the liberty was confiscated into the King's hands in 1551. Despite this Elizabeth I was forced to buy from them - rather than her own subjects. As a result, she encouraged new merchant societies and further restricted foreign privileges there.

All Hallows the Great

On the east side of Cannon Street station where it passes above Thames Street is the location of All Hallows Lane, where once stood two parish churches.

The "Great" church was first mentioned in written records in 1235 and had a number of different annotations including *of the seamen*, *in the hay* regarding Hay Wharf and its trade, and *in the Ropery* (Corderie) since there were ropeyards nearby. In fact such yards were found in many locations beside the Thames on historic London maps.

All Hallows the Great or More was a fair church with a large cloister on the south side and served the members of the Hanseatic League in the neighbouring Steelyard Liberty. The fraternity also had a small chapel in the liberty, but used this for their parish church. However, by the time of Stow the cloister was a ruin and many memorials were defaced. Of these the most significant was to William Lichfield D.D. d.1447 a great student who wrote many books, both moral and divine, and some 3,083 sermons in writing. His most memorable work, however, was *The Complaint of God unto Sinful Man*.

Other memorials included one to John Brickles draper and benefactor who died 1451, and those to Nicholas Loven and William Paston who founded chantries there. At the east end of the church down Hay Wharf Lane was a brewhouse and several properties were built by the Earl of Shrewsbury. One resident was John Butler draper sheriff 1420 but his house was sold and the money donated to the poor [in Less]. In addition there was a grammar school attached to the church founded by Henry VI in 1447.

Some rebuilding took place in 1627-29 with a west gallery and new north door, whilst significantly as it appears much cost was bestowed upon the steeple. Then in 1632 all of the pews and chancel aisles were raised in height to better accommodate the parishioners. After the Commonwealth the parish raised a petition to retain Rev. Robert Bragge their Puritan minister who was "Sound in Doctrine and of Holy Conversation."

Most of the edifice was destroyed in the fire and like many other parishes a temporary structure was erected in the intervening period. A new church was then built with north and west façades at a cost of £5,641 in 1677-84, the likely designer being Robert Hooke who made a number of visits there. However, it only had a plain tower and despite many requests a cupola or spire of adornment was never added (as seen elsewhere).

Rev. William Cave vicar of Islington held the living in 1679-89; but the church suffered from its site and the tower/north aisle were demolished to widen Thames Street, which came very close, in 1876. A new tower and vestry were then added on the south side.

All of this was in vain since with falling numbers the nave was demolished in 1894 and only the tower remained, while the parish transferred to St. Michael Paternoster Royal with sculptures of Moses & Aaron, organ case (a replica of 1749), lectern (gone), panels and chandelier. Meanwhile the important rood screen of 1683-84 went to St. Margaret's, Lothbury and the Wren period pulpit to St. Paul's, Hammersmith.

All Hallows the Great - looking west to Queenhithe. The tower and north aisle were removed in 1876.

The arrival of Cannon Street station greatly changed the area and the church-site was covered by commercial buildings, while the £13,129 raised from the sale helped build All Hallows at Gospel Oak. The remaining tower was demolished after being bombed in the war, but a plaque at the site is no longer extant (east side of All Hallows Lane).

All Hallows the Less

A short distance along Thames Street across Campion Lane was the neighbouring church of *the Less* or *on the Cellars*, since it was erected on stone vaults. The most significant aspect was the fact the choir and steeple stood on the arch of a gateway, which was once the entrance to Cold Harborough an illustrious mediaeval mansion house. [5]

The house had several owners but was sold to Sir John Poultney son of Adam the four times mayor in 1335, and it thus became Poultney's Inn. The original church dated from the 13th century and he rebuilt it but died in 1349, and his widow married Sir Nicholas Lovel &c. In fact two messuages pertaining to Cold Harborough within the Ropery were given towards enlarging of the church in the 20th of Richard II (1397).

Later on the house passed to the Bishops of Durham and Earls of Shrewsbury but was pulled down for tenements. The choir being ancient fell down and was rebuilt in 1594 then Sir Thomas Glover paid for dormer windows to lighten it in 1613-16. In the years before the fire galleries were added on three sides but the church was not rebuilt, and the parish was joined to its neighbour - the site now offices and Dowgate fire station.

On Rocque's map, Cold Harbour was on the east side of the remaining churchyard and led down to the Thames and the Watermans Hall, while Dyers Hall was nearby. Just to the north was Suffolk Lane and here was the Merchant Taylors School established by Sir Thomas White mayor in 1561. The school occupied a manor house located in the parish of St. Laurence and remained there until 1875 (a plaque is to be erected).

The Merchant Taylors School

This was in the *Manor of the Rose* at Suffolk Lane. The first master Richard Mulcaster taught both Edmund Spenser (poet) and Lancelot Andrewes (churchman).

When Charterhouse moved out of London they took their site at Goswell Road in 1875, but moved to Northwood in 1933.

---

[5] There is a surviving example of such an arrangement regarding St. Swithin's upon Kingsgate, Winchester. The chapel stands over a gatehouse near Wolvesey Palace and the cathedral.

Candlewick (ward)

When considering Cannon Street there are three things that come to mind: cannons that demolish castle walls, canons sitting on pious thrones, and canons of mediaeval script to dictate doctrinal law. But none of them apply in this instance! Cannon Street was in fact a truncated form of Candlewick Street pertaining to the candlemakers of the area.

The ward boundary changed very little over the years and included five churches - four of them detailed below and St. Clement's which for convenience is in the next section. St. Swithin's is also included here being at the eastern border of Walbrook ward.

The original inhabitants were candle-wrights, chandlers and makers of wax and tallow candles in the wick or place - as with village names in the countryside. During the reign of Edward III numerous Flemish weavers came there and met at St. Laurence Poultney churchyard, whilst those from Brabant met at St. Mary Somerset. But the weavers did not remain long and were replaced by drapers selling rich woollen cloth.

One point of interest was the shape of the parishes in this ward viz. St. Laurence's, St. Martin's and St. Michael's whose churches were south of Cannon Street and Eastcheap. Unlike those of All Hallows to the west which were square in nature, they had elongated strips each of them leading down to the Thames. Presumably the reason was historic and was regarding access to the docks or tithes, like ribbon parishes with rich meadowland by a river or spring leading up to coarser moorland (as with the South Downs).

St. Laurence Poultney

Quite how the name became corrupted is unclear but the church of St. Laurence *by the Thames* or *next Candlewicke Strate* was first mentioned during the 12th century. It came to prominence when Sir John Poultney mayor (1330, 31, 33, 36) established a College of Jesus there, with a master and seven chaplains, under Edward III in 1334.

A number of buildings were connected to the institute including cottages, tenements, shops, cellars, solars, stables, courtyards &c. The College of Corpus Christi, as it was also known, obtained the manor of Catford, Kent in 1340 and owned the living of St. Mary Abchurch. Poultney's Inn was then exchanged for Napton, Warwickshire in 1385 and it was clearly very rich, but was dissolved under Edward VI - being valued at £79.

There were ancient memorials to Robert Radcliffe d.1542 and Henry Radcliffe d.1556 the Earls of Sussex, both prominent Tudor courtiers who resided at Cannon Row. Also one to Elizabeth Lucar d.1537, with a fine inscription erected by her husband Emanuel a member of the Merchant Taylors. This recorded that she could write, paint, sing and speak several languages and was the author of *Curious Calligraphy* (1525). [6]

The church was one of the grander mediaeval structures with a steeple-leaded and five new bells, whilst the aisles were levelled and all was repaired in 1631-32. However it was not rebuilt after the fire and the parish passed over to St. Mary Abchurch.

---

[6] The memorial inscription to Elizabeth Lucar was removed to St. Michael's, Crooked Lane after the fire, but was also recorded by Stow and Strype for posterity.

St. Laurence Poultney (left) - The vestry beside the churchyard and wall. A plaque is located there.

St. Martin Orgar (right) has a tower, rectory and a garden with plaque.

Both the church and college are commemorated on a plaque. The visitor is surprised to find two gardens in Laurence Pountney Hill, with the red-brick Vestry House built in 1900-01. There is a passageway running east-west which the rector once tried to close but he received a precept, stating - "It is a Common Way." Some ancient walls still remain whereas the church stood to the north and the churchyard to the south.

St. Martin Orgar

Walking east from Laurence Pountney one comes to the striking tower of St. Martin's, an unexpected survivor from earlier times. It was described as a small and insignificant church whilst the term Orgar indicated Danish origins. Two of the neighbouring tenements were part of Poultney's chantry in St. Paul's cathedral but were suppressed by Edward VI.

Despite its smallness the parish had several benefactions and a parsonage house, while William Crowmer mayor built a chapel on the south side and was buried in 1433. There were also memorials to three other mayors: John Matthew 1490, Sir William Huett 1559 and a fine monument in the chancel to Sir Allen Cotton of Allington near to Whitchurch, Salop d.1628. There were some major refurbishments in 1630 including the steeple, the east window and the three great south windows at a cost of £122; but much of this was destroyed in the fire and the parish passed to nearby St. Clement's.

It was decreed that the churchyard should be walled for use by the parishioners and the tower remained standing, however the French Protestants applied to Parliament to build a chapel adjacent. Upon hearing this the residents put up a disputation stating they did not object, "except that it should be built elsewhere." In the meantime the vestry agreed to the request and against their wishes the chapel was raised on the old ruins just behind the tower in the 1670s. The agreement included a fifty year renewable lease.

From that time the liturgy was said in French and this continued until they left in 1820. The church then fell into disrepair, and the tower was removed when Cannon Street was widened in 1847. A new bell tower and rectory were built on the site for St. Clement's in 1851-53, and remain today next to the ancient churchyard wall (with its plaque).

St. Mary Abchurch

There were seven lanes leading out of Cannon Street, four going to the north and three to the south. All of these were named after the churches that stood on them.

One of these, St. Mary's was situated on Abchurch Lane and the latter may have derived from Abe with reference to 'Up' or a hill, or perhaps from a founder or cleric Abbé. A deed records Robert a priest of *Habechirche* in the 12th century and the earliest named rector was Luke in 1323. The church initially belonged to St. Mary Overie but transferred to the College of Corpus Christi attached to St. Laurence Poultney in the 15th century. After the Dissolution the living was held by the Crown. However, Archbishop Matthew Parker arranged for the advowson to be transferred to Corpus Christi, Cambridge in the reign of Elizabeth I (he being the master). And it remains with them today.

Simon de Winchcombe founded a chantry and there were ancient memorials to two mayors: Sir James Hawes 1574 and Sir John Branch 1580. The latter's widow one Dame Helen left money to the Drapers and to the poor of Abchurch. The old building had a nave with aisles and a bell tower. But little survived the fire except for some church plate including a chalice dated 1581, the registers, and the crypt now under the yard.

St. Laurence was added to the parish in 1670 and a temporary structure was erected on the site in 1674. Wren then rebuilt the church one of the few with a dome for £4,922 in 1681-86. Like at St. Stephen's he was experimenting and the stress of the dome, which spanned 40 feet, was carried down into the four walls without the use of buttresses. The red brick exterior with white quoins was reminiscent of St. Benet's, and the tower in the northwest corner had a lead covered spire with a bell inside.

Archbishop Matthew Parker (1504-75)

He was appointed master of Corpus Christi in 1544 and Archbishop of Canterbury from 1559. His *De Antiquitate Ecclesiae* was just one of the works in the Parker Library at the college, and he was a patron of Stow who produced biographies of these ecclesiastical chroniclers.

In common with St. Stephen's the dome was one of its principal glories and was painted by William Snow a painter-stainer at a cost of £170 in 1708. The work was attributed to Sir James Thornhill in earlier times although this was later found to be erroneous.

Its other chief attribute was the reredos carved by Grinling Gibbons, this being the only authenticated example of his work in the City - the receipts at the Guildhall Library. Sir Patience Ward mayor 1680 had a memorial d.1696 and his wife was buried at the *Great Church* of Amsterdam, whereas Sir Thomas Gresham was a benefactor in 1725.

St. Mary Abchurch in Abchurch Lane - with a view of the church from the south, reredos by Grinling Gibbons and detail from the dome.

Like St. Benet's, Paul's Wharf the church claims to be the most authentic Wren building having experienced few changes down the years. The box pews were for the most part removed in the 19th century and replaced by choir stalls, while the western gallery was used by students from the nearby Merchant Taylors School until 1875.

There was serious damage to the dome in September 1940 and the reredos was literally blown to pieces. But the panels and its elements were collected and stored at St. Paul's. The church was then repaired, cleaned and the Gibbons' reredos completely renovated. In fact the *pelican emblem* on the latter and on the weather-vane above the door is that of Corpus Christi its patrons. This was a long process and it became a guild church in 1954 whereas it was finally rededicated by the Bishop of London in 1957.

The parish then became part of St. Stephen Walbrook and the incumbent was termed a priest. An organ-casing (dated 1717) from All Hallows, Bread Street demolished in 1877 still survived, but the organ itself was replaced by the firm of N.P. Mandor.

Today, the church is an unexpected gem hidden away from the hurrying traffic of the main highway, and only improves on entering the nave. It is square in design apart from the tower and gallery and reminds one of an estate chapel, with its monumental reredos of Corinthian columns, period pews and exquisite panelling. The ceiling depicts worship in Heaven with angels, cherubs, glorious rays, and the divine name in Hebrew.

C. These include foundlings such as Samuel and Jeremiah Abchurch

B. 22 July 1696 [Sir] Patience Ward alderman living in St. Laurence Pountney buried in the chancel d. 10 July [silk and cloth merchant, memorial south wall] [7]
1 October 1712 George Fellowes bur. in the chancel [haberdasher and mercer]

---

[7] Sir Nicholas Crisp purchased Westerham Manor, Kent in 1680 and built Squerryes Court. It was sold to John Ward in 1731, son of Sir John mayor 1718 and great-nephew of Patience.

St. Michael's, Crooked Lane

The church sat on the eastern side of St. Michael's Lane the latter being concurrent with Miles Lane - shown on present day maps. Crooked Lane which distinguished the edifice from others of that ilk was situated just south of the churchyard.

At one time the church was small and homely being made dirty by the refuse running down from Eastcheap Market away to the north. However a parsonage was built on the site and a new church was erected by John Loveken fishmonger thrice mayor 1348-66 who was buried in the quire. His one time assistant Sir William Walworth also fishmonger mayor 1374/80 added a new quire and some side chapels, and was involved in the arrest of Wat Tyler. He established a college there with a master and nine chaplains to say mass in the church, and was buried in the north chapel (d.1385).

St. Michael's was just to the rear of St. Martin's and had connections with the Plumbers to the west and the Fishmongers in Thames Street to the south. In the church there were further memorials to five mayors: Simon Morden 1368, John Pattesley 1440, John Olney 1446, Sir John Bridge 1520 (who endowed a college in Crooked Lane), and Sir Henry Amcots 1548 - as well as those of several stock fishmongers.

The Fishmongers Hall stood south of the church on Thames Street and was originally the residence of Loveken, Walworth and Askham three fishmonger mayors, then was secured for the company in 1444. Initially it had two branches: the stock fishmongers (wet traders) at Thames Street and the salt fishmongers (dry traders) in Old Fish Street. These differences were settled in 1536 and they joined at the former site while the grand hall contained a courtyard, offices and wharf. The Fishmongers were always prominent operating their own court and came fourth in the order of precedence. [8]

Meanwhile, the church received a new roof and east window at over £500 in 1621, but was destroyed in the fire and rebuilt by Hooke from 1684-98. It had a plain rectangular nave and a northwest spire with circular leaded-core and volutes was added in 1709-14, like at St. Nicholas Cole Abbey. To the south on Miles Lane was a small Presbyterian meeting house which later attracted Rev. Alexander Fletcher. However with the building of London Bridge and King William Street in 1831 the ancient church was demolished to accommodate the approaches. The parish then passed to nearby St. Magnus.

St. Swithin's, London Stone

This was situated on Cannon Street at the southwest corner of St. Swithin's Lane, with the churchyard being to the rear in Salters Hall Court. The first mention was in the 13th century although the location was recorded somewhat earlier (see below).

Sir John Hinde draper mayor was an especial benefactor with arms in the window and a memorial; hence it was he who rebuilt the church and steeple in 1405. Catrin Glyndwr the wife of Edmund Mortimer and daughter of Owain was taken at Harlech in 1409, and went to the Tower - although her burial was recorded at St. Swithin's in 1413.

---

[8] The current Fishmongers Hall was designed by Henry Roberts in the Greek Revival style in 1831-35. He worked for Robert Smirke who was building New London Bridge at the time, and a young George Gilbert Scott prepared drawings for the hall in Roberts' office.

But, what were the origins of the church's unusual name? From mediaeval times a large stone was fixed on the south side of the street like some ancient monolith of heathen worship. Stow noted that the London Stone was first chronicled in documents relating to Athelstane, King of the West Saxons and in records of a fire which raged from Paul's to Aldgate in 1135. In fact Henry son of "Eylwin de Londenstane" (recorded 1188) had a house in St. Mary Bothaw parish and was the inaugural mayor.

A number of conjectures were made as to the origin: It was a central point with regard to the river; debts were settled there prior to the Royal Exchange; it was named for John or Thomas Londonstone who lived nearby; it was erected for devotion to Christ he being the very stone the city was set on; it was a Roman mile-stone this once being the chief street; or pertained to heathen worship by Druids a custom coming from the Greeks.

John Dryden (1631-1700)

He was appointed *Poet Laureate* in 1668, during the "Age of Dryden."

There were also memorials to Ralph Jocelyn mayor 1464/76 a church benefactor; and a fine monument in the south chancel to Sir George Bolles mayor d.1621 by his wife Joan daughter of Sir John Hart mayor - both of them being grocers.

To the west of the church was a large house which was home to the Earls of Oxford then to Sir Ambrose Nicholas 1575, Sir John Hart 1589 and his son-in-law Humphrey Smith (later Oxford Court). On the far side was a garden and beyond two properties in Walbrook, the homes of Sir Richard Empson chancellor of the Duchy of Lancaster and Edmond Dudley Esq. privy councillor and speaker for Henry VII. The garden had an entrance gate from each house and here they met to discuss matters of state.

Above the church just west of St. Swithin's Lane was situated the Salters Hall with its courtyards and gardens. This livery company were established by Royal charter in 1394 and removed to the area from Bread Street in 1641. [9]

The church was repaired in 1607-08 and with events mounting soon witnessed a most significant marriage. John Dryden was born in Northants, a relation of Jonathan Swift, and after a good education worked for the Puritans and was acquainted with Marvell and Milton. He then transferred allegiances and was a leading critic and playwright, marrying Lady Elizabeth sister of Sir Robert Howard auditor of the Exchequer to Charles II - with whom he wrote. Later on he was a Catholic, and one of his best comedies was *Marriage à la Mode* and of his literary titles *The Works of Virgil* in 1697.

---

[9] There were three Salters Halls on the site from 1641-1941 the last being built in 1827. After this they spent 35 years without premises until moving to Fore Street in 1976.

St. Swithin's - the west side c.1810 and London Stone as denoted.

However the church (& hall) burnt down in 1666 and it was rebuilt by Wren at a cost of £4,687 in 1677-85. It was centrally planned (one of five such schemes) and had an octagonal dome in a square, like at nearby St. Mary's, combined with a fine fret ceiling and an absence of pillars. There were large central windows and an octagonal spire similar to St. Antholin's and St. Margaret Pattens, although here it was disproportionate to the nave.

The parsonage house was also burnt down and rebuilt by Henry Whisler of St. Mary Abchurch who received £4 rent per annum. Later memorials included one to Michael Godfrey a merchant who helped establish the Bank of England with William Paterson in 1694. However he died from cannon-shot whilst visiting King William for patronage in the trenches at Namur, Holland the following year!

Meanwhile, London Stone was moved to the north side of Cannon Street in 1742 and then to a spot in the church wall in 1798 where it stayed for many years. The church was destroyed in 1941 and little survived - the pulpit going to All Hallows Barking (1682), and the font cover to St. Ethelburga (1687). The parish was joined to St. Stephen's. For a time the church precincts were used as a garden, but it was demolished in 1962 and sold off for offices - the stone being incorporated into the drab new structure.

There was once a parish marker in Salters Hall Court whereas the churchyard remained at the rear of Cannon Street adjacent to Oxford Court. The future of the latter is unclear since it recently housed some portacabins for construction of *The Walbrook* (discussed earlier), but is designated as a preserved open space.

M. 1 December 1663 John Dryden and Elizabeth Howard married by ye licence

Lombard Street

A series of parallel streets ran north from Cannon Street but these were all bisected when King William Street was inserted up to Bank in the 1830s. The result was the separation in a geographical sense of the area above from that residing below.

This brings us to Langbourn ward which was quite idiosyncratic in nature and stretched from the central banking area almost to Fenchurch Street station, although an historical assessment explains this. In ancient times, a brook ran along Fenchurch and Lombard Streets then turned south at Sherborne Lane towards the Thames - just below St. Mary Woolnoth. This gave rise to the Long Bourne (ward) comprising a narrow band on each side, and only the width of the road where it crossed Gracechurch Street.

As a result of its extended nature on a main routeway it encompassed seven churches, including the four below and Dionis, Gabriel and Staining discussed later. St. Clement's in Candlewick ward is included here due to its location, while the modern ward is solely north of the two streets and in shape points to Bank (quite literally).

All Hallows, Lombard Street

The Lombard district was so named for goldsmiths from Italy who were granted rights to trade in the 13th century. From an early date they provided a role as moneylenders but were evicted by Elizabeth I, although this long remained a centre for banking.

In addition, the eastern end of the street intersected with Gracechurch Street and the junction was known as "The Four Corners." In this area was situated the very extensive Grass Market for hay and herbs which stretched along Lombard Street to St. Edmund's but was later reduced in size by several encroachments. One feature was the charging of a fee to any merchants bringing produce there by cart for peddling. [10]

All Hallows was originally of Saxon origin and sometimes annotated as Grasschurch but was recorded as being given to the Dean of Christchurch, Canterbury in 1053. As such it was a peculiar of the Deanery of the Arches. It was located on the northwest corner at the junction of Lombard and Gracechurch Streets, just south of Bell Yard.

The church was rebuilt in 1294, but John Warner a grocer built the south aisle in 1494 and his son Robert completed this in 1516. The Pewterers also contributed to the north aisle. A bell tower was added to the church in 1544, and at this time the porch and bell-frame came from the dissolved priory of St. John's at Clerkenwell. But the bells never arrived and as a result there was just one bell. The building was greatly concealed and hidden, being hemmed in with its churchyard by tenements on all four sides.

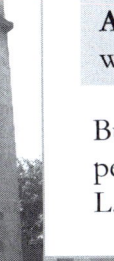

All Hallows, Lombard Street with tower and linking vestibule.

Built by Wren 1694, Rebuilt for the people of Twickenham 1940. "AH L. St. recreated A MCMXL D."

Parish marker of "1883" located in Lombard Street (south).

---

[10] Lombard Street, San Francisco is famous for its winding road sections, and was just north of Greenwich Street leading down to the docks and merchant warehouses. It was probably named after a similar one in New York (later renamed) - either Monroe Street or Trinity Place.

It was mostly destroyed in the fire although the tower remained and Wren rebuilt it in 1686-94 (one of his last). A Renatus Harris organ was also installed the next year. Strype noted some extensive wainscot (panelling) with a fine altar, the arms of the Queen, and a list of the benefactors including the rector Rev. Dr. John Aucher.

Wesley came and preached there in 1789; but after the Union of Benefices Act it was under considerable pressure, even though ten bells arrived from St. Dionis with further items in 1879. There was much debate about its survival after the First War, and being found in poor repair it was demolished for Barclays Bank in 1939.

It soon followed in the footsteps of St. Mary Aldermanbury and the tower and fittings were removed to North Twickenham the next year. A mission of St. Martin's was begun there in 1918 and this became All Hallows with the foundation laid on 11 July 1939. It was then dedicated to the people of Twickenham by Bishop Arthur Foley in 1940.

When driving through the suburb past the rugby stadium it is a considerable surprise to see the distinctive Wren tower rising above the highway. There is a modern nave but the adjoining passageway contains monuments from the old church and a doorframe, also some inscriptions regarding its rebuilding as well as an information plaque.

One of the memorials formerly on the north wall of St. Dionis is to Dr. Edward Tyson and is dated August MDCCVIII (1708). After being influenced by naturalist Robert Plot first professor of chemistry at Oxford and keeper of the Ashmolean, he went to London and was closely associated with Robert Hooke. He then founded comparative anatomy of animals and as a physician improved the Bethlem Hospital.

St. Clement's, Eastcheap

Just to the south below the modern Lombard Court was the diminutive St. Clement's concealed up a lane of that name above Eastcheap. However, the rather private location departed once King William Street was inserted directly past its western door.

A charter of Westminster Abbey dated 1067 mentioned the church and it was listed as of *Candlewick Strate* in the 13th century. William Chartney and William Overie founded a chantry and the living was with Westminster and the Bishop of London, while the few monuments included Francis Barnham d.1575 and son Benedict Barnham d.1598.

Both were drapers, sheriffs and aldermen, and the latter was an M.P. for Minehead and Yarmouth, I. of W. with land in West London. He married a daughter of Ambrose Smith a Cheapside mercer - supplier of silks and velvets to Elizabeth I, and his four daughters had good matches. Of these Alice was raised by her step-father Sir John Pakington, and at a young age married Sir Francis Bacon scientist, philosopher and statesman.

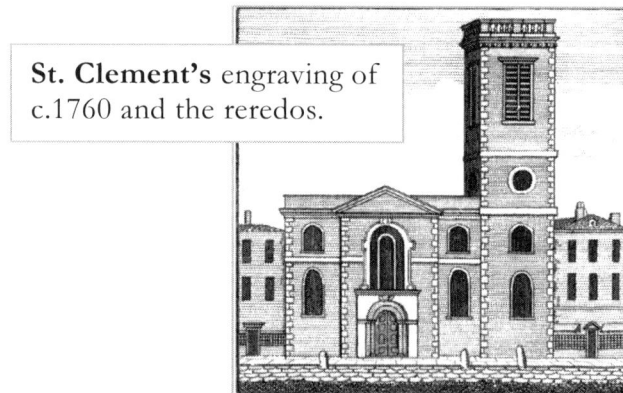

St. Clement's engraving of c.1760 and the reredos.

St. Clement's, Eastcheap - A brass on the north wall (of 1878); and Alice Barnham, Viscountess of St. Alban's (1592-1650), wife of Sir Francis Bacon and Sir John Underhill.

Other links included John Milton who married Mary Powell at Oxford in 1643 but she returned to her family in the Civil War, and they were reconciled in lodgings beside the church two years later. Likewise, Bishop John Pearson and Rev. Thomas Fuller scholars and historians lectured there in the 17th century, the latter writing *The Worthies of England* and *The Church History of Britain*. Brian Walton who was the rector of St. Martin's and the Bishop of Chester produced *The Polyglot Bible* (with nine languages) in 1652.

The church, meanwhile, was destroyed in the fire and despite its diminutive size was rebuilt to a similar scale by Wren in 1683-87. In fact, the tower was on a different plane to the main nave, none of the walls were regular, and the south aisle was very small. At this time it was joined with the defunct parish of St. Martin Orgar.

Later connections included Edward Purcell (1689-1740) and Jonathan Battishull (1738-1801) who were organists; whereas a tablet just north of the church records that Dositey Obradovich, traveller and pioneer of Serbian education, lived next door in 1784.

With the arrival of the Union of Benefices there was concern that the church would be demolished, especially given its size and awkward location. However, it was restored by William Butterfield in High Anglican style in 1872 - at which time the galleries were taken down, plain glass was inserted, the reredos was divided and the organ moved to the aisle. Then, in 1933, Sir Ninian Comper *repaired* some of this damage taking the organ back to the west gallery, and restored the reredos as before. [11]

C. 4 June 1592 Alice Barnham daughter of Mr. Benedict - other baptisms 1585-98

M. 28 April 1583 Benedict Barnham and Dorothy Smyth were married

B. 4 July 1740 Edw'd Purcell near ye organ gallery doer organist [son of Henry]
5 August 1765 Edward Henry Purcell by the organ galary [his grandson]

---

[11] The organ was probably by Renatus Harris in 1696 and the casing dates to that time, but the organ itself has been renewed and restored many times since.

St. Edmund King and Martyr

A short distance west of All Hallows was a church dedicated to St. Edmund who was the King of East Anglia. This grand edifice could be seen distinctly from St. Clement's Lane with the pinnacle tower of St. Michaels rising up as a silhouette behind it.

Significant Roman remains were found in Lombard Street but the first church dated back to Saxon times. Matilda wife of Henry I then bestowed the living on Holy Trinity priory in 1150 and it was recorded as the Grasschurch ref. the market in 1292.

There were a number of significant memorials to mayors namely Humphrey Heyford goldsmith 1477, Sir John Milborne draper 1521, Sir William Chester draper 1560 and Sir George Barne 1586. There were also several benefactions to the poor. To the west was Birchover or Birchin Lane which had some significant properties, including those of Sir Martin Bowes goldsmith and of William de la Pole merchant to Edward III.

The church was repaired at a cost of £248 in 1631-32 but was destroyed in the fire and Wren reconstructed the façade in 1670-79, while Hooke designed the interior which like St. Benet's had a Dutch influence. Unusually, it was aligned north-south partly due to the elevated value of the frontages on Lombard Street, and also because the old church was situated beside a road which travelled up past the Roman forum.

The entrance was of Portland stone, whilst the tower with its pineapples and urns had an octagonal lead steeple rising above the parapets - dated 1706. There were also some garlands and flaming urns that were removed by the 20th century. Internally there was a plain rectangle but no aisles and a rather awkward shallow dome just above the sanctuary. The reredos with paintings of Moses and Aaron on each side was attributed to William Etty, and the woodwork including the pulpit, stalls and lectern was 17th century.

However despite such creativity the *Illustrated London News* dubbed it as "Wren's worst church," then Butterfield carried out restorations in 1864 creating the atmosphere of a gentleman's living room. Some of the simplicity was gone, but it was badly damaged by a direct hit on 7 July 1917 and the remnants of the bomb remain in the altar frame.

There was further damage during the Second War but it continued as a parish church being combined with St. Nicholas, St. Benet (and St. Leonard) 1867, St. Dionis 1878 and All Hallows 1940, then finally was linked with St. Mary Woolnoth in 1988. Meanwhile, it was unused and neglected thus the Bishop of London made it a Centre for Spirituality and bookshop from September 2003.

Joseph Addison poet, essayist and M.P. (pictured right) married the Countess of Warwick a resident of Holland House - to whose son Edward Henry Rich, 7th Earl he was a tutor.

St. Edmund's - other celebrities at/near the church

Alexander Pope a Catholic born at Plough Court in 1688 (plaque)
Abiell Whicello was organist at the church from 1712-47
Edward Ironside a parishioner was the Lord Mayor in 1753
Mackonochie came and preached for harvest in October 1875
Rev. Joseph Leycester Lyne, Fr. Ignatius of Llanthony (1837-1908) gave a sermon and local apprentices pelted him with apples

St. Edmund the King

"An Italian Job"?

The buttress is used to solve the problem of a Gothic tower sitting on a Classical portico.

Externally it reminds one of an Italian church with large volutes supporting the tower, and inside the books certainly evince shades of "a gentlemen's club." The organ-casing came from St. Dionis and houses a John Compton organ of 1932, a fresco of a Dominican friar found at St. Nicholas is in the vestry, and there is a display of church plate. A plaque on the west wall commemorates Geoffrey Anketell Studdert-Kennedy famous during the First War as "Woodbine Willie," and the rector there from 1921-29.

M. 9 August 1716 Joseph Addison of Bilton, Warwick Esq. was married unto Charlott[e] Countess Dowager of Warwick and Holland of Kensington by Mr. Nathaniel Hough

St. Mary Woolnoth

The name may come from Wulfnoth the founder of the church, or the wool market across the road in mediaeval times. It was situated on the so-called 'High Street.' There is evidence that it dated back to the Saxon era and was replaced by a Norman structure in stone. However the first written reference is to *Winod Marie Cherche* in 1198.

Sir Hugh Brice goldsmith mayor rebuilt the edifice with a spire in 1485 and was the governor of the King's Mint, while Thomas Nocket draper founded a chantry there. Simon Eyre draper mayor d.1459 established a fraternity and was founder of Leadenhall grain market. The memorials included to Sir John Percival merchant taylor d.1504, Sir Martin Bowes goldsmith d.1566, Sir Thomas Ramsey 1577 (all mayors), William Hilton tailor to Henry VIII d.1519 and Robert Amades master of the King's jewels. [12]

The church had a number of significant ministers in the 17th century including: Josiah Shute (1611-43) chaplain to the H.E.I.C., a Royalist vexed by the rebels who produced manuscripts, then Ralph Robinson a Presbyterian (1643-55) - both being buried there. At the Restoration came Robert Owtram (1662-66) who wrote religious works with sermons on *Faith and Providence* and went to St. Margaret's, Westminster.

---

[12] Sir Martin Bowes (1496/97-1566) was mayor in 1545, butler at Elizabeth I's coronation and left the Goldsmiths his portrait and royal cup. John Lyon, Earl of Strathmore married heiress Mary Eleanor Bowes in 1767 (taking her name) - and were ancestors of the Queen Mother.

Unlike many of the churches the steeple and walls survived the fire and Wren did some remedial work rebuilding the north wall and the roof. At this time the church was mainly on Lombard Street with the west façade at the junction of St. Swithin's and Sherborne (or South Bourne) Lanes. The other two sides were still concealed by buildings, and the parish was combined with that of St. Mary Woolchurch Haw.

When Stow visited he stated that, "it was more necessary to look to the repairs which were to come than those that were already gone," and fortunately there was a wealthy benefactor nearby in the form of the influential Vyner family. Regarding this there was a white marble effigy inside to Sir Thomas Vyner goldsmith mayor d.1665.

His son Sir Robert Vyner mayor 1675 paid to restore the church, and built a large house to the east on the site of a tavern that year. Such was his contribution it was known as *Vyner's Church*, while his property with paved courtyard, stabling and convenient access housed the General Post Office from 1678-1829 and a tablet marks the site. [13]

According to Strype there was a memorial in the old church, "on the east wall near the little north door," to Sir William Phipps an adventurer who found off Hispaniola in 1687, a Spanish wreck with gold and silver worth £300,000. He also took forces to fight the French in Nova Scotia and Quebec, and was Governor of Massachusetts under its new charter in 1690 when he put a stop to the conflagration in Salem.

St. Mary Woolnoth (built 1716) was once hidden among narrow streets, but can now be found as Hawksmoor intended. Below is the Egyptian Hall on Piccadilly which stood from 1812-1905, a style that clearly inspired the architect.

---

[13] A plaque in Princes Street nearby notes the General Letter Office was located there in Post House Yard from 1653-66 and produced the first post marks in the world. The large property of Robert Vyner in Lombard Street appears as an extensive Post Office on Rocque's map and was located there until moving to St. Martin le Grand in 1829. Today, Post Office Court with its cafes is behind the church and seven wall tablets depict arms, emblems and naval motifs.

Meanwhile, the church was found to be unsafe and demolished in 1711. Funding for rebuilding came from the Commission for 50 Churches, although this money raised via the coal tax was predominantly for new parishes beyond the city limits. St. Mary's and St. Michael's were among the few that obtained such funds before this practice was stopped, whilst the outcome was a church quite different to any designed by Wren.

Hawksmoor was employed to rebuild it from 1716-24 and its imposing Baroque façade with striking inverted coursing at the lower level, surmounted by Corinthian columns and two flat turrets, is reminiscent of his churches in East London. Externally the focus was to the north and west (with niches) these faces being exposed at the time. But the interior was Roman comprising "a square within a square," and the central space had groups of three columns supporting the ceiling. Availability of funds was paramount and the nave, recalling the Egyptian Hall designs by Vitruvius, was extremely expensive.

Into this rather opulent setting came John Newton who was born at Wapping in 1725 and worked on a slave ship but after being flogged by the Navy, and left in West Africa by crewmates, had a conversion in 1748. He was ordained as a curate at Olney, Bucks in 1764 and through John Thornton was appointed to St. Mary's in 1779. As one of the few evangelicals in the City he was involved in abolition and Wilberforce worshipped there being inspired to continue, whereas Rev. Newton remained for 28 years.

He was followed by Samuel Birch (1807-48) father of the prominent Egyptologist who has a memorial in the north aisle, and William Josiah Irons (1872-83) also at Brompton and Newington a theological writer of the Tractarian viewpoint.

Some significant changes then took place firstly when the site was opened up by King William Street in the 1830s. Secondly, William Butterfield the Gothic architect arrived in 1875 and removed the box pews as revealed by the raised bases of the columns, and took down the galleries whose fronts were then surprisingly attached to the walls! In addition Victorian tiles were introduced into Hawksmoor's pure classical interior.

The church came under threat when the City & South London Railway were building Bank Station in 1897-1900 and it was to be demolished. But public protest saved it and instead they built below, removing the crypt and underpinning the building. It was joined to St. Edmund's in 1988 and the restored interior is one of the finest in the City.

The interior of **St. Mary's** with restoration work carried out by William Butterfield.

St. Mary Woolnoth - parish records

C. 6 November 1558 Thomas s. of Francis Kydd citizen, writer of the Courte letter [14]

M. 24 April 1614 Mr. Josiah Shute married Elizabeth Granville o.t.p. by lycence
10 February 1680/81 Thomas Arne of St. Paul's Covent Garden and Mary Thursfield of St. Martin in the Fields in ye county of Middx. marryed by ye licence [15]

B. 21 February 1694/95 Sir William Phipps d. 18th b. vault under the organ gallery
17 February 1712/13 Edward Loyd d.15th and buried mid-aisle - of Stocks Market [16]
31 December 1807 Rev. John Newton d. 21st (the service was by his friend Rev. Henry Foster minister of St. James's, Clerkenwell and Sunday sermon by Rev. Richard Cecil minister of St. John's Chapel, Bedford Row) - re. Josiah Pratt curate and lecturer
4 July 1848 Rev. Samuel Birch D.D. rector for 41 years and of Little Marlow, Bucks

Rev. John Newton (1725-1807) - Once an infidel and libertine, servant of slaves in Africa and 28 years rector of St. Mary's. He wrote the Olney Hymns with William Cowper including *Amazing Grace* in 1779.

---

[14] Thomas Kydd (1558-94) son of a scrivener attended the Merchant Taylors under Mulcaster and was educated there with Edmund Spenser. He was a famous dramatist and wrote the very popular *The Spanish Tragedie* in the 1580s.

[15] Thomas Arne was a box numberer at Drury Lane but had financial problems and moved to Islington then ended up in the Marshalsea. He died in 1713 and was buried at St. Paul's, Covent Garden however his son Thomas established a theatrical dynasty there.

[16] Edward Lloyd opened a coffee house at Tower Street in 1688 and merchants and ship-owners met there to discuss insurance &c. The shop moved to Lombard Street three years later and this practice continued after his decease, but a break away group formed a committee nearby in Popes Head Alley in 1769 and went to the Royal Exchange as the Society of Lloyd's in 1774. They had a brief period at South Sea House when the Exchange was rebuilt and moved to the Leadenhall area in 1926 - then had three buildings there - the latest a controversial modernist structure by Richard Rogers, incorporating part of the old façade, built in 1986.

Amazing Grace (by John Newton)

Amazing Grace! How sweet the sound that saved a wretch like me,
I once was lost but now am found, was blind but now I see.

Twas grace that taught my heart to fear, and grace my fears relieved;
How precious did that grace appear, the hour I first believed.

Through many dangers, toils and snares, we have already come,
Tis grace have brought me safe thus far, and grace will lead me home.

When we've been there ten thousand years, bright shining as the sun;
We've no less days to sing God's praise, than when we first begun.

St. Nicholas Acon

Just to the south of St. Edmund's was Nicholas Lane and on the west side was the parish church dating to Saxon times, also known as Hacon from an early benefactor. Sir John Bridge draper mayor 1520 repaired and embattled the building and was buried there.

William Lambarde was born in the parish on 18 October 1536 before the records were started, his father John a master of the Drapers. Lambarde entered the legal profession and as an antiquarian published his famous *Perambulation of Kent* in 1570, the first of its kind, and died on 19 August 1601. His memorial at St. Alphege's, Greenwich was later removed to Sevenoaks. St. Nicholas also had memorials to Francis Bowyer grocer sheriff d.1581, and John Hall a master of the Drapers and of London Bridge, who was father of twenty-seven children by three wives, and died in 1618 aged 93.

The church was repaired in 1615 but was destroyed in the fire and not rebuilt, while the churchyard remained on Rocque's map of 1746. But that was not the end of the story and Equitable Life the first scientific life assurance company was begun in the parsonage in 1762, and moved to Blackfriars in 1774 - *its policy holders* Coleridge, Wilberforce and Scott. A plaque records this event and there are three parish markers: St. N.A. 1852/53 with another 1836 by the adjacent passage. It was united with St. Edmund's and a fresco discovered during excavations in 1964 was removed there.

C. 1 April 1540 was chr. Anna daughter of John Lambarde [sister]

B. 20 September 1540 Julian the wife of John Lambart

St. Nicholas (plaque) was one of the churches lost in the fire; and the birthplace of **William Lambarde** first "perambulator of Kent."

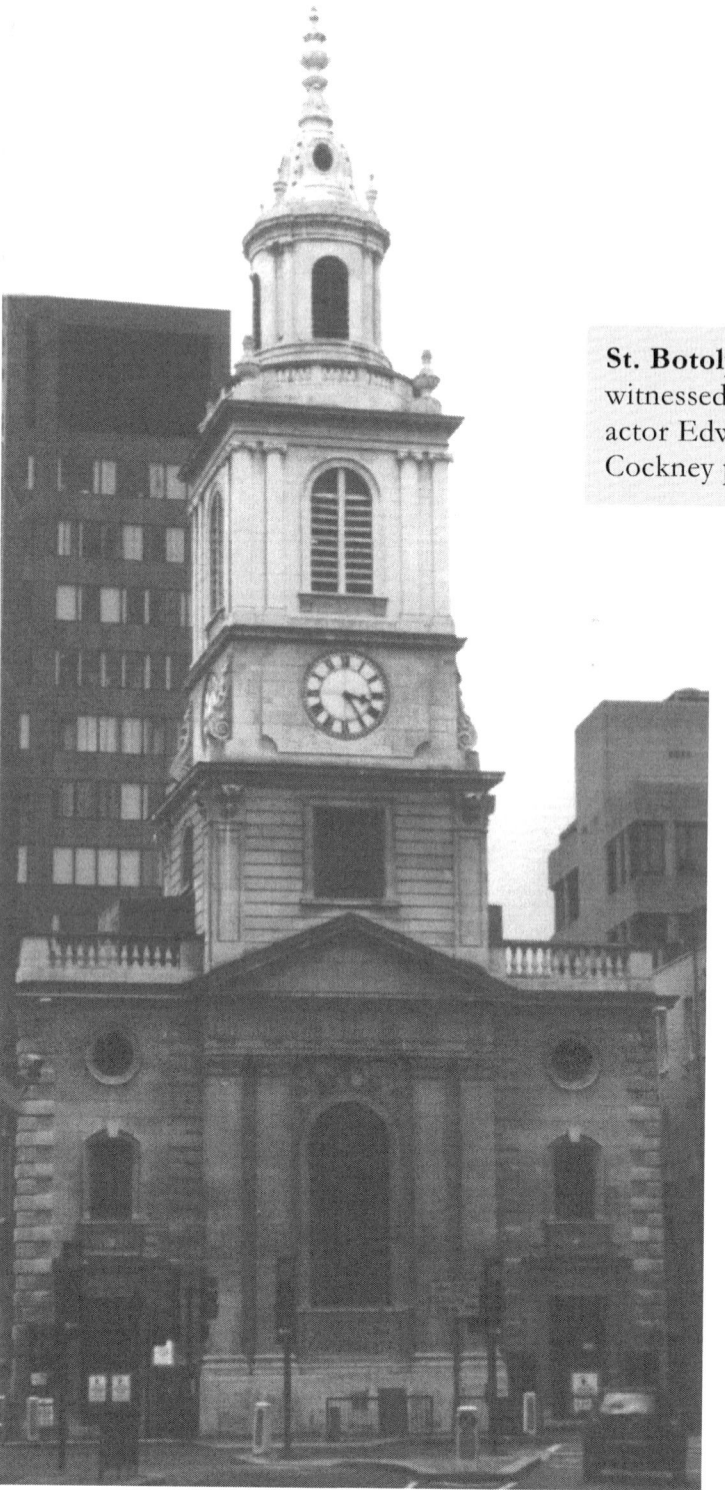

St. Botolph's, Bishopsgate witnessed the baptisms of the actor Edward Alleyn and the Cockney poet John Keats.

City North East

We now wend our way to some more northern climes beginning at Bank the financial hub and ending at the City gates. Within this space were gardens, monasteries, grand houses, churches and public buildings of note nestling in among the more lurid tenements and warehouses.

This was the domain of the Drapers and Merchant Taylors who sewed for precedence and clothed many a King, whilst close by was a college of the knightly Gresham and a bubble colonnaded - just waiting to burst!

Here were Augustinian, French and Jewish churches with Arabic translators into the mix, while to the east were Steamboat Willie (long before Disney) and the story of East Smithfield and "what Watt did there?"

Famous people abounded in the vicinity including the schemes of Poyntz, the colonies of Calvert and conversions of Newman. In addition Gould led us on a merry Dance, Stow penned the fabric of history and Docwra posted his claim - not forgetting the poetic flamboyance and artistry of those all time greats Alleyn, Bentham, Defoe and Keats.

St. Michael's, Cornhill

The main doorway below the tower unmistakably designed by Sir George Gilbert Scott, with *"The avenues and alleyways of the City"* beyond.

Parish Markers in Creechurch Street
St. James Duke's Place and St. Kath Cree

Cornhill

This area was generally considered the High Street and went through to Leadenhall, the whole of it being a market for corn and other produce from ancient times. Originally this was a small ward covering Cornhill, Birchin Lane, Finch Lane and some alleyways to the north and south, but today extends into what were Broad Street and Bishopsgate wards. There were just two churches in its precincts: St. Michael's and St. Peter's.

At the western end were some stone houses as decreed by Henry Fitz Alwine in 1189 against the risk of fire, but by Stow's time these had been made into four or five storey tenements. Two of these buildings in particular were of interest and formed part of the King's estate. One, the Pope's Head Tavern still displayed a coat of arms with *lions and fleur-de-lis*, and the other was originally "King John's lofty house" or palace.

These Royal connections were then confirmed in the 16th century. Richard Clough the representative of Thomas Gresham in Antwerp declared that - "London traders walked about in the rain more like peddlers than merchants!" As a result Gresham built a place for merchants to assemble on the north side of Cornhill in 1566-67, and Elizabeth I came there from Somerset House via Fleet Street and Cheapside on 23 January 1570/71. After dining with Sir Thomas she viewed the new bourse with her heralds and trumpets in attendance and it was thereafter known as the Royal Exchange.

Gresham made large sums renting out shops on the site at £751 per annum while after his decease in 1579, Lady Gresham claimed she should be entitled to 21-year leases. But the City and Mercers who formerly held the soil and made agreements (confirmed by his will) contested these rights, stating they were for the City and Communality.

The Exchange was rebuilt after the fire with Gresham's statue placed in an alcove, the total cost to the owners being £80,000. The new building had piazzas, galleries and vaults for the merchants while the façade of Portland stone "exceeded all others in Europe." It had many classical features with niches for the Royal statues, except those who had ill-used the City by revoking its charters, and opened in September 1669. [1]

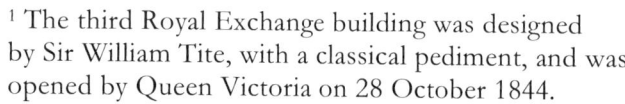
The Royal Exchange

The Exchange was built by Sir Thomas Gresham in 1566. The print shows the second building next to Cornhill, with a view of Cheapside and St. Paul's in the distance, in 1751. **Below:** A statue of George Peabody, philanthropist, behind today's building.

------

[1] The third Royal Exchange building was designed by Sir William Tite, with a classical pediment, and was opened by Queen Victoria on 28 October 1844.

To the rear of the Exchange were many coffee houses and at the junction with Birchin Lane high quality drapers selling India silks and muslins. At the centre of the street was a stone tun or prison for night walkers &c., which was illegally used to imprison clerics, and beside it a well which were both erected by Henry Wallis the mayor in 1282.

It was converted to a conduit or cistern using water from the Ty Bourne with cages and stocks above for bakers and millers of bad produce in 1401, whereas Sir Martin Bowes whose garden lay behind enlarged it in 1546. Peter Morris a Dutchman then raised water under pressure from the Thames to a high point at Leadenhall in 1582, and a new pump was erected by Nathaniel Wright in 1799 and remains today (with inscription).

St. Michael's, Cornhill

The church sat on one of the two hills (with Ludgate) which the Romans founded their capital on, and was a Saxon foundation given to the Abbot of Evesham in 1055. A new steeple was begun in 1421 and bells were added a few years later. The church benefactors included William Rous a goldsmith and sheriff and Robert Drope mayor d.1487 who left generous bequests to the poor and provided new pews. Elizabeth Peake a widow gave the living to the Drapers in 1503 (all three having monuments).

There were a plethora of memorials and benefactions in particular a grey marble on the north side to Robert Drope and Viscountess L'Isle, which despite their generosity to the parish was departed. The former represented Langbourn and Cornhill, became mayor in 1474 and left money for clothing, hospitals, prisons and Lazar houses. His widow Joan married Edward Grey, Viscount L'Isle and was mother of John Grey, 2nd Viscount and she died in 1505. Others were to Peter Houghton grocer 1596 who had prominent son-in-laws and John Vernon the master of the Merchant Taylors 1609. [2]

However, its main accolade was as "church of the chronicler." Robert Fabian, alderman and sheriff under Ralph Astry the mayor, published his *Chronicles of England and France*. This was a laborious work which was republished d.1513. Secondly, John Stow was born in the parish in c.1525, and his grandfather Thomas 1526 and father Thomas a tallow chandler 1559 were both buried there. The latter left money to the church and made his wife Elizabeth executrix, but left household goods to another son Thomas.

Historically, there was a fraternity of St. Anne present with various chapels but this was suppressed under Edward VI. An area to the north with cloisters was surrendered and four tenements built: "Whereby the church was greatly darkened and other ways annoyed." In fact, it still is today. There were major repairs at a cost of £644 in 1618-33 which included a new roof over the chancel, but it was mostly burnt down in the fire.

Wren rebuilt the church in rectangular form during 1670-77 and other furnishings were added in 1701, in particular the Tuscan columns forming the arcade and a noble altar. Likewise the mediaeval tower was dismantled and replaced by a Hawksmoor and James design in Gothic style in 1715-22 (similar to Westminster Abbey, St. Alban's and St. Mary Aldermary). In fact the funds for the steeple, like at St. Mary Woolnoth, came from the Commission for Fifty Churches - even though it was not one of them.

---

[2] Elizabeth Woodville married (1) Sir John Grey brother of Edward in c.1452 and (2) Edward IV in 1464. Henry VII of the House of Lancaster married their daughter Elizabeth of York.

Stephen Poyntz (1685-1750) - the Georgian courtier.

St. Michael's, Cornhill, as seen from Castle Court, with tower by Hawksmoor and interior re-designed by George Gilbert Scott.

Two prominent inhabitants were present in the parish during this period. In the first instance William Poyntz an upholsterer of Cornhill married Jane Monteage, who was the niece of Richard Deane a famous sea general. Their son Stephen was promoted through connections he made at Eton and Cambridge. Initially he was an envoy for the Duke of Devonshire and Lord Townshend then was tutor to the Duke of Cumberland, the second son of George II. He married Anna Maria Mordaunt maid-of-honour to Queen Caroline in 1733, and had a vital role at Court, but as Walpole noted, "He was not wealthy due to a number of cousins whom his wife married off at his own expenses."

Regarding this, his ambitious daughter Margaret Georgiana married John Spencer the Whig politician (Lord Althorp), and with further connections to the Duke of Devonshire his humble origins in Cornhill reached a new level of distinction. Poyntz also purchased an estate called Midgham near Thatcham, Berks and died there in 1750. [3]

Secondly, Phillip Gray an exchange broker and milliner with his wife Dorothy had ten children baptized at the church in 1712-25. A son Thomas attended Eton and Cambridge where he met Horace Walpole and they went on the Grand Tour together - promising a poetic future. In fact, he was Regius Chair of Modern History at the university in 1768. His most notable piece *Elegy Written in a Country Churchyard*, included the famous line "far from the madding crowd's ignoble strife" later utilized by Hardy.

The church tower, meanwhile, was damaged after a bad fire in Cornhill in 1748. But the greatest changes came with the renovations of Sir George Gilbert Scott in 1857-60 and

[3] Earl Spencer or Viscount Althorp and his wife Margaret (née Poyntz) owned Althorp and had three children George John, Georgiana and Henrietta Frances. The son was Lord of the Treasury and Admiralty also the Home Secretary under Grenville, while Georgiana married the 5th Duke of Devonshire and *Devonshire House* in Piccadilly was a centre for Whig politics. The third child married Frederick Ponsonby (Bessborough) and their daughter Caroline was raised by her aunt then married William Lamb and came to notoriety though Lord Byron, also a Whig politician. Lord Spencer the 1st Earl was in fact the ancestor of Princess Diana.

1867-68. The nave and aisles retained four bays in classical style with a plain groin vault, however most of the old furnishings were removed including the pews and reredos, and these were replaced by the work of William Gibbs Rogers. An incongruous porch was also added under the west tower and stained glass was inserted.

As a result the church is now mainly Victorian apart from a 17th century font, paintings of Moses and Aaron in the new reredos and panelling in the vestry. It is a strange mix of Gothic tower, Victorian Revival and interior reminiscent of a Catholic basilica.

The parishes of St. Benet Fink 1844 and St. Peter le Poer 1907 which both succumbed were added, and during the war there was little damage. Down the adjacent alley named after the church is the site of *the first coffee house in London* (dated 1657). This belonged to Pasque Rosée who established it with Daniel Edwards a trader in Turkish goods, while just to the rear are George Yard and St. Edmund's. The church exterior is little changed today, although only the tower itself is visible from Cornhill.

C. Circa 1525, John Stow son of Thomas and Elizabeth (prior to parish records)
-- November 1685 was baptized Stephen Poyntz son of William and Jane his wife
26 December 1716 Thomas son of Phillip Gray and Dorothy his wife was baptized

St. Peter's upon Cornhill

The parish of St. Michael's extended west to Stocks Market, while St. Peter's just to the east encompassed an area mainly across Bishopsgate into Leadenhall. There are claims for a very ancient heritage here, inter-twined and supportive of similar assertions regarding the arrival of Christianity, although their authenticity is generally questioned.

King Lucius a legendary *King of the Britons* is said to have written to Pope Eleuterus in Rome and asked to be converted, his story appearing in works by Bede and Geoffrey of Monmouth - but he may have been confused with a ruler of Britium in Turkey. This idea was copied onto a tablet at St. Peter's in the 14th century (recopied in the 18th) in some detail - stating that King Lucius founded a church there in A.D. 179. It then endured as the chief edifice for the next 400 years (purportedly), until the coming of St. Augustine in 597 when the premier role and See were removed to Canterbury. [4]

However, there is no archaeological evidence to support this although there may have been a Roman basilica nearby. Clearly there was an ecclesiastical centre in London, but Stow from his research states it was probably on Thorney Island, Westminster. [5]

The first documentary evidence of *St. Peter binnon London* was in 1040 and 1127, while a library was there from early times. Sir John Crosby (see St. Helen's) repaired it in the 15th century - his alms on the building. The next century John Leland "viewed its many books," but by Stow's time they were all gone leaving just a school teaching grammar (one of four established by Henry VI). There were several chantries including that of William Elliott in 1375, a number of bequests and a brotherhood of St. Peter.

---

[4] The rector of St. Peter's retained precedence over St. Paul's in the Whit Monday procession which used to start there - thus supporting its claim to be of great antiquity.

[5] The earliest churches in Britain include St. Peter's, Bradwell-on-Sea, Essex a chapel on the site of a Roman fort - and five others in and around Canterbury (all c.600 A.D.).

John Carpenter the town clerk under Henry V and VI resided in the parish and wrote the *Liber Albus*, one of the first books on common law, and by his will established the foundation of the City of London School. Early memorials included Sir William Bowyer 1543, Sir Henry Huberthorne merchant taylor 1546 both mayors, Sir Christopher Morice master gunner to Henry VIII and Edward Elrington chief butler to Edward VI.

Substantial repairs were carried out on the church body and spire at £1,400 in 1629-33 but after the fire only the base of the tower survived. It was rebuilt by Wren in Portland stone with a plain red-brick tower, belfry, small dome and octagonal spire in 1677-87. At the east end were five round-headed windows with a broken pediment above, embracing a sixth, and internally a tunnel-vaulted nave with narrow aisles. Its main feature, the chancel screen by Wren, is the only one to survive in its original setting.

Later connections there were Sir Benjamin Thorogood 1682 alderman who bequeathed three shops to provide for an organist, and Francis Breerewood Esq. 1707 a linen draper of Cornhill and treasurer of Christ's Hospital. In addition, Rev. William Jowett of the C.M.S. lectured in the 1830s and composer Mendelssohn played the organ in 1840-42. Another familiar with the edifice was Charles Dickens who noted its raised churchyard in *Our Mutual Friend*, using it as the setting for a failed marriage proposal.

The church was restored by James D. Wyatt in 1872 and was unique in being a parish on its own, whereas it was hemmed in by buildings on Cornhill and the churchyard was accessed via St. Peter's Alley (as it is today). However it ceased to hold regular services thus the pews went to Canewdon, Essex in 1989, and it was later used by the successful St. Helen's ministry for both Bible study and training (see later).

M. 22 November 1604, Thursday: Mr. George Calvert of St. Martin in the Fields a gent and Mrs. Anne Mynne [Mayne] of Bexley, Hertfordshire by licence [6]

St. Peter's, Cornhill

The church claims a heritage back to the time of King Lucius in A.D. 179. It was rebuilt by Wren after the fire, with an east façade on Gracechurch Street and main entrance in Cornhill.

---

[6] George Calvert (1579-1632) was born at Kiplin, Yorkshire then attended Oxford and Lincoln's Inn from 1593-1601. He held senior positions under James I being Secretary of State but his wife Anne died in 1622 and he was left with ten children including heir Cecilius. He stepped down due to his Catholic faith under Charles I and was made Baron Baltimore in 1625, then sailed to Avalon, Newfoundland in 1628. Finding the winter too harsh the colony removed to Chesapeake Bay and Maryland was established just after his death in 1632 (see St. Dunstan in the West).

Bank

The Broad Street ward was located north of Cornhill and covered an area around the street of that name, from Walbrook stream in the west up to London Wall. Within its precincts were six parish churches, three of which are discussed here as they were near to Bank and three in the next section - they being closer to Broad Street. In addition, there were St. Anthony's and the Augustine Friars religious institutions as well as the Drapers and Merchant Taylors halls, two of the most prominent liveries in the City. [7]

The most significant building in the ward was the Bank of England which moved from rented premises at the Grocers Hall to the current site on Threadneedle Street in 1734. The initial building was quite narrow with a colonnaded front and courtyard to the rear whilst there were alleys on all three sides (not the most secure of situations).

The architect Robert Taylor extended it eastwards in 1765, but after the Gordon Riots it was clearly vulnerable to the west and St. Christopher's was deconsecrated and demolished in 1782. The bank then occupied a more familiar position and John Soane their surveyor rebuilt it over time in 1788-1830, enclosing it with a windowless wall. However to some criticism it was enlarged and rebuilt again by Sir Herbert Baker in 1925-39.

The Bank (or Old Lady) in 1797, after the removal of St. Christopher le Stocks which stood on the left. It was later developed over many years by Sir J. Soane.

St. Anthony's (church and school)

On the north side of Threadneedle Street were many large houses, but at the corner with Broad Street was a hospital in the parish of St. Benet. The site was a synagogue for the Jews from 1231 but in Henry III's reign it was granted to the fraternity of *St. Anthony of Vienna* for a master, priest, schoolmaster and 12 poor men. Henry VI donated several manors to John Carpenter j. (bishop and chancellor) the master in 1442 to send students to Eton and Oxford, whilst it was annexed to St. George's Windsor in 1485.

Sir John Tate a mercer gave some adjacent land to enlarge the church, and the school and its almshouses were situated just to the west. Inside the edifice there were ancient memorials namely Sir John Tate d.1514, Walter Champion draper sheriff 1529 and John Taylor a master of the rolls d.1532. Regarding the Dissolution, the plate and ornament were transferred to Windsor and the almsmen "were put out of their houses."

---

[7] The modern ward boundary for Broad Street remains similar, but begins above Throgmorton Street and extends past London Wall to the east of Finsbury Circus.

Despite this the school had a good reputation like St. Paul's and its scholars walked in procession from Mile End to Aldgate and Bank with streamers and flags. In fact, Stow noted how Elizabeth I was most surprised on visiting the Earl of Leicester at Kenilworth Castle in 1575. He recounted to Her Majesty "of being quite bookish" and how he learnt of *Aesop's Fables* and Virgil during his time at Paul's and St. Anthony's.

However the church was much decayed by the time of the fire due to being plundered and was then replaced by a French or Walloon chapel. The Huguenot congregation had several buildings around London including at Wheler Street in Spitalfields, whereas this "French Church" opposite to Finch Lane was demolished in 1840. A plaque on the site recalls both the 13th century hospital and the Protestant church.

St. Bartholomew by the Exchange

This church was on the north side of Threadneedle Street east of Bartholomew Lane. It was first recorded in 1225 initially being known as *The Less* to distinguish it from the Abbey at Smithfield. However after the Dissolution when the adjacent hospital church adopted the same epithet it became *Little St. Bartholomew beside St. Anthony*, and once the Royal Exchange was built it received its more common appellation.

Thomas Pike an alderman and Nicholas Yeo sheriff built the church in 1438 and the memorials included: Sir W. Capell mayor 1510 who had a mansion nearby (Capel Court) and raised a chapel on the south side, George Barne(s) haberdasher mayor 1552, John Dent salter nominal sheriff of the Spanish and Muscovy trade d.1595, Richard Bowdler draper of the *Society of Merchant Adventurers* d.1603 and Richard Croshawe a master of the Goldsmiths d.1631 who helped the poor during the plague.

The most significant connection, however, was Miles Coverdale Bishop of Excester [sic] who had a stone tablet in the chancel d.1569. Coverdale produced the first English Bible on the Continent in 1535 where he spent much time during those turbulent years, and his work was synonymous with both Tyndale and the *Matthew Bible*. However, he came to favour again under Edward VI and was rector of St. Magnus from 1564-66.

The church was repaired in 1620 but it was destroyed in the fire and Hooke recorded the decision to pull down the steeple. It was then rebuilt by Wren's office in 1675-83 with a basic offset rectangular nave and stone-work tower at a cost of £5,077.

In addition the parsonage was replaced - but there were numerous encroachments: The timbers of The Cock alehouse were laid into the wall, a coal hole was placed east of the south aisle, a cistern and closets were set in the churchyard, and a large chimney was built into the steeple! In front of the church on Threadneedle Street were shops rented to the poor, but the minister seized these thus the poor received no further benefit.

A Plaque on the Royal Bank of Scotland. This replaced Sun Life by Cockerell - pulled down in 1970.

Parish Markers to 3 churches on the wall of the Bank of England.

This was not a good situation and after the Royal Exchange was destroyed by fire in 1838, it was decided to widen the street hence the church was demolished in 1840-41. A (new) memorial to Coverdale was moved to St. Magnus and an 18th century organ case passed to St. Vedast's, while the parish was combined with St. Margaret's. John Carlos of the *Gentleman's Magazine* decried the apathy with which this took place but added, "It was minor compared to the destruction of City churches likely to follow."

After its demolition Charles Robert Cockerell (1788-1863), the son of S.P. Cockerell, designed the Sun Life Assurance Building on the site, and "replica of the church" under the same name at Moor Lane, Cripplegate with many original furnishings and materials. This was also demolished in 1902 and a third church was erected at Stamford Hill. [8]

B. 19 February 1568/69 Rev. Miles Coverdell doctor of divinity bur. [d. 20 January]

St. Benet Fink

Just to the southeast was the parish of St. Benedict and Robert Finke the elder built the church, which was first recorded in 1216. His family occupied a house on the west side of Finch Lane and held tenements in that parish and at St. Martin's to the east.

It had just a few memorials or benefactions including John Wilcockes who left money for poor maidens to marry d.1561 and William Borrodaile merchant taylor d.1600 and Dame Anne (later the wife of Gideon Awnsham) who had a monument. The latter left a bequest for a new church-loft and to the poor. Richard Baxter, a great orator who had preached to soldiers in the Civil War near Coventry and Kidderminster, was married in the building after the Restoration - but was excluded from preaching.

Stow noted there were illegal gaming houses for cards and dice nearby which had to be closed down. The church itself was repaired in 1633 - the parish being centred at the junction of Broad and Threadneedle Streets and up as far as Throgmorton.

Wren rebuilt the edifice in 1670-75 and introduced a distinctive design perhaps based on St. Andrew Quirinal in Rome by Bernini whom the former had met in Paris. Here he adopted a central-plan utilizing an elongated decagon with an oval dome on six columns and lead lantern, whilst the two irregular aisles had barrel vaults. The exterior itself was faced in Portland stone and the western tower had a square bell cage with distinctive oval openings, lead dome, and ball and cross above. It was unique in having a small cloister on Swithin's Rents which had survived the fire, but was mostly surrounded by buildings except against Threadneedle Street on the northern side.

A list of benefactions was erected in particular to George Holman Esq. a Catholic who paid £1,000 towards rebuilding. In addition there were memorials to Nathaniel Castleton "a good Protestant," and Mrs. Sarah Gregory who left £400 for an organ and house to play it in and £100 to put parish boys to a trade - both died in 1714.

---

[8] The Muscovy and East India Company were the first to trade in shares in 1688, using two coffee shops Garraway's and Jonathan's in Exchange or Change Alley, between Cornhill and Lombard Street. This was the location of the South Sea Bubble in 1720 and a tablet marks the site. As a result the brokers were regulated as the Stock Exchange and moved to Threadneedle Street in 1748 and just east of St. Bartholomew's (Capel Court) in 1801. A new building was erected there in 1972 but after deregulation they removed to Paternoster Square in 2004.

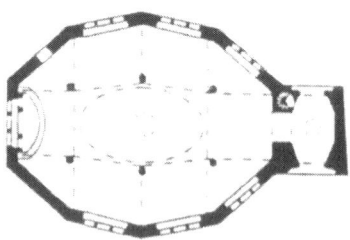

St. Benet Fink whose plan had Roman inspiration… and **Cardinal Newman (1801-90)** who turned to Rome through the Tractarians.

However regarding the most prominent resident, John Newman a banker perhaps of Jewish descent married Jemima Fourdrinier of Huguenot extraction at Lambeth in 1799. Their son John Henry Newman was born opposite the church in Threadneedle Street in 1801, and as the eldest of six he learnt a modified Calvinism from his mother. [9]

He was educated at Ealing and Oxford then after his father's bank failed was ordained in 1824, and appointed vicar of St. Clement and St. Mary's in that city. Rev. John Keble preached *National Apostasy* there in 1833 stating Christianity served a higher authority than Government; then Newman of Oriel and Pusey of Christchurch wrote the *Oxford Tracts* supporting a religion of the Apostles, with a move towards Catholicism.

The Tractarians or Oxford Movement continued until the conversion of Manning and Newman in 1845, while the latter published a biographical *Apologia* and was a cardinal by 1879. He also promoted Brompton Oratory built in 1884 and his statue is located in front, whilst he has a plaque recording his birth at 60 Threadneedle Street.

Despite the fact he had rallied the High Church with devotees like Fa. Mackonochie, St. Benet's was demolished in stages when the Exchange was rebuilt in 1842-44 and the parish went to St. Peter's. Carlos again registered disapproval, but the proceeds built a church of that name in Tottenham, and paintings of Moses and Aaron went to Emanuel School, Battersea. A plaque now marks the site beside Royal Exchange Buildings. [10]

Nearby are a statue to George Peabody (1795-1869) American housing philanthropist, a bust of Paul Julius Reuter founder of the *News Organisation* in 1851, and the Drapers and Merchant Taylors fountain of 1878. In Cornhill is a statue to James H. Greathead chief engineer on the City & South London Railway inventor of the travelling shield.

C. 9 April 1801 John Henry son of John Newman and Jemima his wife was born 21 February and baptized by Robert Watts curate

M. September ye 10th 1662 was married Richard Baxter a clerk and Margaret Charlton gentlewoman late of the parish of St. Leonard's, Shoreditch

---

[9] The other Newman children were born in 1804-11 but they were baptized elsewhere.

[10] Sir Richard Sackville of Chiddingly steward to the Ab. married Winifred d. of John Bridge mayor. Their daughter Lady Anne Dacre wife of Gregory Fiennes founded the school in 1594.

St. Christopher le Stocks

The church sat on the north side of Threadneedle Street between Princes Street and the early Bank of England, with tenements west of the Exchange just opposite. The first record was in 1282 and the epithet referred to its location near to Stocks Market. There were memorials to Richard Sherrington who gave lands (1392) and four mayors viz. John Gidney 1427 draper, William Hampton 1472 a benefactor, Sir William Martin 1492 and Roger Achley 1511 who rented a house in Cornhill owned by Cobham College.

Of these John Gidney married the widow of Robert Large (a former mayor) in 1444 but by doing so she broke a vow not to re-marry, and both were made to pay penance by the Church. Richard Shore a sheriff 1506 gave money toward the building of the steeple and after the Dissolution any bequests for prayers were transferred to the poor.

In addition John Kendrick Esq. a wealthy draper of the parish left a monumental will donating vast sums to the Drapers, to the needy poor, to release prisoners in debt, to support the church, and to benefit Newbury and Reading, Berks d.1624. The church was also repaired at great expense at this time but was burnt down in the fire.

Wren undertook the rebuilding in 1669-71 using much of the old material and this was one of the first completed, being one of five with a Gothic tower and corner pinnacles. But this was only a temporary measure and it was largely rebuilt by William Dickinson, who was also a Commissioner of the Fifty Churches, during 1711-14.

However its location with alley and yard behind posed a threat to the Bank and it was demolished in 1782 - making it the first Wren Church to depart. A painting of Moses and Aaron (1700) went to St. Margaret's Lothbury, the reredos and communion rails to St. Vedast's and the pulpit to Canewdon, Essex. Today, the only indications of its presence are two parish markers located on the Bank - one being at the front (see p.180).

Broad Street

Within Broad Street ward were two of the most senior livery companies, the Drapers coming third in precedence and the Merchant Taylors sixth/seventh (set in 1516).

The original fraternity of *Mary the Virgin of the Mystery of the Drapers* dated to the 13th century and some members were attached to St. Mary Bethlehem, Bishopsgate but for convenience transferred to Mary le Bow and then to St. Michael's, Cornhill (as today). Its members were shopkeepers and also wealthier merchants, while the first charter was laid out in 1364 and a hall was taken on St. Swithin's Lane in the 1420s.

Originally there were tenements just west of Austin Friars but Sir Thomas Cromwell a master of the King's Jewels and Rolls, Vicar General, Earl of Essex and High Chamberlain built a large house with lawns on Throgmorton Street. For that purpose he appropriated a portion of all the gardens to the north - marking out a line and building a large wall with no warning at all. Stow noted how his father owned one and that no man dared to argue, adding, "The sudden rise of some men causeth them to forget themselves."

However, at the demise of Cromwell in 1540 the house was forfeited to the King and he sold the estate to the Drapers for 1,800 marks in 1543. It became their hall and was rebuilt after the fire and in 1772 then had a new façade, courtyard and garden in the 1860s. In fact this remains today on Throgmorton Avenue (by Lyons) with impressive gates and figures, grand white hall, red brick walls, chandeliers, stained glass and ornate gardens.

Their nearby rivals the Merchant Taylors had even greater antiquity with a first charter in 1327, the fraternity linked to St. John the Baptist and known as the *Taylors and Linen Armourers*. They occupied a site south of Threadneedle Street from about 1347 and apart from some re-roofing in the 16th century the old structure remained until the fire.

A new building replaced this, but it was destroyed in September 1940 losing the main west entrance, grand staircase, hall, galleries, and drawing room - although the library, court room and kitchens survived. A restored hall and courtyard opened off Finch Lane in 1959 using the gutted foundations and walls, whilst part of the crypt of the east chapel and some of the old flooring dating to ancient times still remains.

The Austin Friars

At the junction of Broad and Throgmorton Streets was the entrance to the friary for the hermits of St. Augustine whose church was built in 1253 and enlarged in 1354. This had distinctive broad aisles each as wide as the nave and a fine steeple was erected soon after. The memorials included one to Humphrey de Bohun, Earl of Hereford and Essex, the builder who died in 1361 and many others to baronets, earls and esquires.

At the Dissolution the estate passed to Sir William Paulet and he built a great house on the north side towards London Wall in place of the Friars house, cloisters, and gardens. However he left the nave and aisles of the church and it was granted to *Germans and other strangers* in 1548. This gift was confirmed to the Dutch nation as their preaching place and was very spacious with a library and minister's house at the west end.

It was customary for the Dutch and Walloon Church to pay a deference of thanks for sanctuary to the Bishop of London and the Mayor on taking office, and occasionally the Lutherans were permitted to worship there from that time. Austin Friars stood in the parish of St. Peter's and in 1600 the parishioners sent a plea to the Marquis of Winchester who by then owned the land of the Paulets. The spire, an architectural wonder, was in a tottering condition and "in great risk of falling" - however their urgent request had no effect and like the east end it was removed and replaced by housing.

In addition, a footpath once went up to All Hallows on the west side but was blocked by the estate and people were forced to go past St. Peter's instead. Likewise its gardens were eventually covered by properties built on Winchester Street. Sadly, the remaining Austin Friars was destroyed in 1940 and rebuilt by Arthur Bailey in stark, perpendicular, modernist style but with an impressive hall-like interior in 1954.

A number of alleyways around Austin Friars Square demark the original hermitage, with the church at the centre, and on the north side is the Furniture Makers Co. This guild was not established until 1959 since the profession was carried out by upholders, turners, cabinet makers &c., while they moved to the hall (No. 12), already a listed building, in 2005.

Rev. Samuel John Stone (1839-1900) - the influential minister of All Hallows, London Wall and writer of *The Church's One Foundation.*

All Hallows - today and in 1730.

The church was designed by George Dance the younger. Note the blank-wall exterior and apse based on the Temple of Venus, Rome.

All Hallows, London Wall

At the far corner of Broad Street ward the north and west boundaries coincided with that of Coleman Street ward. Just above were the open wastelands of Moorfields which were delineated by Moorgate Arch (demolished in 1761) and Little Moorgate just west of the church. Coleman Street was the main routeway going north at this time and in between were numerous alleys and courtyards - including the Drapers' gardens.

The first church of All Hallows was built on a bastion of the Roman wall in the reign of Henry I (1100-35) being linked to Holy Trinity priory at Aldgate. It was probably rebuilt in the 15th century and Martin Allen leather-seller gave the rector his tenement nearby for prayers to be said in 1432. Early memorials recorded Mr. Stanley priest and steward to the Earl of Winchester the Lord Treasurer d.1560, and Edmond Hammond Esq. who left 150 legacies and was a benefactor d.1642 (in the south chancel).

Due to its location the church survived the fire however the mediaeval building was rebuilt by George Dance the younger in 1765-67, as the population increased. The plain brick walls of the exterior with their half-windows, and square tower with open rotunda, gave no indication of the beauty to be found inside. Dance had just returned from Italy and the barrel-vaulted nave with inset windows and stucco detail was crowned with an exquisite sanctuary. The latter included a half apse, Ionic columns, diamond-patterned ceiling and motifs based on the remains of the Temple of Venus &c. in Rome.

In addition there was a small gallery with an organ, coat of arms at the west end above the entrance, and exquisite covered font from St. Mary Magdalen, Old Fish Street. The walls had four classical half-columns on each side, and to the north was a raised wooden pulpit accessed through a first floor doorway. Of the few wall memorials there was one to Mrs. Joan Bence daughter of Sampson Cotton mercer d.1684 (north side).

There were also later memorials to some of the incumbents in the vestibule including Rev. William Beloe prebend of St. Paul's and Lincoln, twenty years the rector, d.1817 and Samuel John Stone for ten years rector (see below). Also in the north chancel were ones to Mr. Joseph Patience d.1797 and his son d.1825 both architects. There was a parsonage house west of the church and a semi-circular vestry on a bastion of the wall.

Regarding its rectors, William Beloe son of a Norwich tradesman was born in 1758 and attended Corpus Christi - then married Mary Anne Rix daughter of William town clerk of London in 1780. He was an assistant at Norwich and a master at Emanuel, Westminster whilst he received the living of Earlham in 1791, then established the *British Critic* and contributed to *Tooke's Biographical Dictionary*. After arriving at All Hallows in 1797, he was made under-librarian at the British Museum in 1803, but was dismissed three years later due to a robbery. At this time he translated Herodotus, wrote anecdotes of literature and scarce books, and published some recollections of city life.

Secondly, William Stone came from gentry of Kinsale, Ireland and attended Wadham then was vicar of St. Paul's, Haggerston (1858-74) and also of Alfriston, Sussex. His son Samuel John was born at Whitmore near to Newcastle under Lyme in 1839 and went to Charterhouse and Pembroke then was ordained by Samuel Wilberforce in 1862.

Initially he was a curate at New Windsor, Berks where he wrote a series of hymns for the poorer congregation to teach faith, including *The Church's One Foundation* with music by Samuel S. Wesley in 1866. He joined his father as curate at Haggerston in 1870 and became vicar four years later, then moved to All Hallows in 1890. By then it was in a poor state of repair and he spent the first two years living at the church, contributing his small income to the fabric while introducing a new dignity to worship.

After moving to 70 The Common, Upper Clapton he noticed how poor female workers came to the City on early trains to take advantage of reduced fares. They were then left to walk the streets until their work began, so he opened the church from 6-30 to 9-00 providing shelter, food, hymns, and prayers. At first just one or two came but as news spread the numbers increased to 160 women each day. However, after he died in 1900 (with a service by the Bishop of Stepney) the congregation declined.

Regarding the church, new rooms were built to the rear in 1902 then after war damage it was restored in 1952 and furnished by the Carpenters who had links for 600 years. This company had three halls to the west below London Wall the first in 1429, the second with banqueting hall by William Wilmer Pocock master costing £50,000 in 1876, and the third with classical façade in 1960 (above Austin Friars and the Drapers).

All Hallows became a guild church in 1954 the parish transferring to St. Botolph's, and it was utilized by the *Council for the Care of Churches* with occasional services until 1994. However under Rev. Garth Hewitt (once a singer with Tear Fund) it was revived and now houses five charities which include Art and Christ, the Amos Trust, Church Wallspace, Stamp out Poverty, and Greenbelt in the rooms behind.

B. 18 April 1817 Rev. William Beloe rector o.t.p. of Kensington Square, 59 by Thomas Rennell [junior] the vicar of Kensington - usually A.P. Poston

Albion Chapel, Moorfields - Rev. Alexander Fletcher (1787-1860) a Presbyterian came from Scotland to Miles Lane in 1811 and also attended Surrey Chapel. Larger premises were soon needed and William Jay son of a preacher and student of D.R. Roper built him a classical edifice with dome on the site of Bethlem Hospital by Moorgate in 1815. But after a dispute, Rev. Fletcher built the larger Finsbury (Cong.) Chapel east of Finsbury Circus near St. Mary Moorfields ten years later (see Vol. II). The Circus which replaced the hospital is one of the oldest open spaces in the capital, whilst Albion Chapel itself was demolished in 1875 and is demarked by Albion Place.

St. Martin Outwich as seen from Bishopsgate was designed by Samuel Pepys Cockerell in 1796-98. Behind is the silhouette of St. Michael's, Cornhill and a plaque now marks the church site.

St. Martin Outwich

This was a small church at the south corner of Threadneedle Street facing Bishopsgate and was dedicated to the Bishop of Tours. It was named after Martin, Nicholas, William and John Oteswich who were *the new builders* in mediaeval times, as shown by their many monuments. In fact John Churchman sheriff 1385 gave on their behalf the patronage of the church, four messuages, and seventeen shops to the Merchant Taylors, to provide funds for the building of almshouses at the west end of the building.

Other memorials were a brass to Nicholas Wotton rector d.1482, Matthew Pemberton merchant taylor who repaired the St. Lawrence's chapel at the church d.1514 and George Sotherton the master of that same guild who d.1599.

Stow recorded that the edifice was situated by a well with two buckets but lately turned into a pump. It was then repaired in about 1558 but "this repair and beauty were lost and much expense was needed." Due to the limited site its churchyard was to the northeast by the defunct St. Augustine Papey in Camomile Street (east of Outwich Street).

A fire burnt the mediaeval building in 1795 consequently it was rebuilt by Samuel Pepys Cockerell in 1796-98, with a French façade of grooved stone like St. Mary Woolnoth and a small cupola tower above. However, it was demolished for street widening and offices in 1874 and the monuments and parish were transferred to St. Helen's.

St. Peter le Poer

Just east of Austin Friars and south of Paulet House on Broad Street was St. Peter's. The annotation is uncertain and Stow suggests this was a poor parish that later had many fair houses. However this seems rather fanciful and the postscript more likely refers to one of several such saints who took vows of poverty in a mediaeval monastery.

There were several memorials including Richard Fitzwilliam merchant taylor 1520, Sir William Roche mayor 1540, John Lucas master of requests to Edward VI d.1556, Martin Calthorpe mayor 1588, and Sir William Garaway who extended the north aisle by placing pillars on the old wall at £400 d.1625. A number of other repairs took place soon after with a new chancel window, west gallery and steeple at £1,587.

These repairs took place under the ministry of Rev. Richard Holdsworth, a student of Cambridge, who became rector from 1625. He was divinity lecturer at Gresham College and president of Sion College being appointed master of Emmanuel, Cambridge in 1637, however lost the position due to his Royalist leanings. One of his students was Simonds D'Ewes and his large collection of books passed to the University Library. A memorial to him with Latin inscription was placed on the southeast wall (d.1649).

The church was rebuilt in the classical style by Jesse Gibson in 1788-92, although the ornate façade concealed a circular nave behind with skylight dome above. However with population decline it became surplus and was demolished in 1908 - the parish going to St. Michael's, Cornhill. The resulting funds provided a new edifice at Friern Barnet where there is an ongoing list of rectors dating back to the 14th century.

St. Peter le Poer, Old Broad Street was wealthy by design.

The (New) South Sea House was built by J. Gould with a quadrangle in the 1720s.

The South Sea Company was formed by Robert Harley, Earl of Oxford (Tory) to take on Government debt in 1711, but the infamous "Bubble" took place nine years later. Their "old house," an excise office on Broad Street, burnt down and was replaced by the Palladian *City Club* by Philip Hardwick in 1834 - its members Peel and Wellington. Their "new house" on Threadneedle Street, just opposite to St. Martin's, was used by them until the 1850s but was remodelled in 1900.

Bishopsgate

The extensive Bishopsgate ward included areas "within and without" the City gates and covered the three churches below. In the south it went down to Lombard Street but was wider to the north reaching to the liberties of Norton Folgate and Old Artillery Ground. In the west it went across to All Hallows and Moorfields while to the east it included the area of Spitalfields Market. Likewise it abutted with Spitalfields hamlet, part of Stepney, and the northern portion of Portsoken ward adjacent to Petticoat Lane.

Initially we shall consider the area outside the gates parallel to the road running north to Shoreditch and its theatres, most of which was covered by the parish of St. Botolph's. To the west there were market gardens then Finsbury Avenue (Long Alley) and to the north the parish boundary at Worship Street (Primrose Street and Hog Lane).

Stow recorded that the gateway was built by Hanseatic merchants in 1471 in exchange for privileges at Steelyard Wharf (as discussed), being situated just below the church and located near to the junction of Camomile and Wormwood Streets. This was replaced as late as 1735 however was demolished for road widening in 1760.

On the west side above the church was the *Hospital of St. Mary of Bethlehem* which was founded by Simon Fitz Mary a sheriff in 1246 and was certainly of great longevity. This was originally set up for a priory of canons, brethren and sisters, but by the next century it was being "used for distracted people." Following the Dissolution the City purchased the patronage in 1546 and combined it with the adjacent parish in 1551.

Sir Thomas Rowe merchant taylor mayor enclosed land near the ditch by Moorfields for their burial ground in 1569, and over the gate was his name, sermons being held on Whit Sunday. But under Elizabeth the old chapel was pulled down, houses were erected, and patients charged for their care. Stow noted how properties to the north were *built up* with alleyways and "pestered with people" - perhaps prospective patients. [11]

Meanwhile, the area above the wall to the east had some grand houses, the residences of wealthy and influential courtiers or merchants. The first building past the gate was a large inn called The Dolphin which was situated for the receipt of travellers, followed by an extensive property the residence of Lord John Paulet. Just beyond was the abode of Jasper Fisher a goldsmith who had little real wealth or calling but erected a mansion with some pleasure gardens and bowling alleys. It was known as *Fisher's Folly* and then passed down to the Earls of Devonshire and Oxford. [12]

Beyond this locality were the Lollesworth marshes beside Ermine Street and Roman urns and burials were later found nearby. Walter and Rosia Brune established St. Mary's priory hospital there in 1197, in the area of Spital Square up to the edge of Shoreditch, and it was renamed "Spittle Fields." The last prior donated land to Henry VIII for the Old Artillery Ground and nearby were some grand houses, one home to Sir Horatio Pallavicini ambassador to Elizabeth I and to the Archduke of Austria during his envoy to James I.

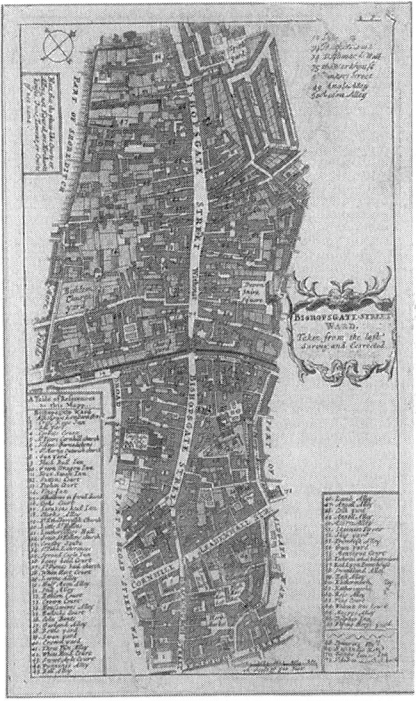

Bishopsgate Ward from a map by Richard Blome in 1720 (after a survey by Stow) showing the old city walls. Also the ancient gate engraved by W. Hollar in 1650.

---

[11] The Bethlem Hospital had a courtyard, chapel and gardens but care was poor and it became tenements in 1675. A new building 540 feet long was erected by R. Hooke below Moorfields on London Wall and inmates included playwright Nathaniel Lee from St. Clement Danes. Many believed the problem was a moral weakness and Hogarth depicted it in *A Rake's Progress*, whilst it moved to St. George's Fields, Southwark in 1815-1930 (then Beckenham). The Imperial War Museum took over six years later having been at the Crystal Palace and South Kensington.

[12] On this site was built Devonshire Street with its Square behind, whereas the Coopers whose hall was at Basinghall Street from 1522-1940 moved to this location in 1957.

The churchyard of the hospital remained with a large cross like at St. Paul's and Royal processions started there, but Huguenots occupied the area in the 18th century which had alleys, courts, tenements, a market and the East India Co. warehouses (now offices with a plaque). Bishopsgate Station *the worst in London* was built on Commercial Street in 1840 and replaced by Liverpool Street in 1874, while St. Mary Spital church built on the priory ruins became a parish from 1845-1911 (see Vol. II).

St. Botolph's, Bishopsgate

This was one of four dedicated to the patron saint of travellers and was first recorded in 1212, but there were only a few memorials including to the rectors John Picking d.1490 and John Redman d.1523. It was situated in a fair churchyard by the town ditch and was anciently enclosed with a comely wall of brick. The church and wall were then repaired by Sir William Allen mayor 1571 - who was born and buried in the parish.

Of its residents, his namesake the Elizabethan actor Edward Alleyn was baptized there in 1566, the son of a local innkeeper. He took on major roles with the Admiral's Men and went into business with Henslowe, then utilising the proceeds purchased the Manor of Dulwich in 1605 and established a college there by 1619. [13]

The other notable resident at this time was Sir Paul Pindar who had a large property just above the church and was ambassador to the Ottoman Empire under James I. On the north side of the chancel was a tablet recording this role, he being a resident of Turkey for nine years from 1611 and also a great benefactor of the parish d.1650. [14]

On the south side was an area known as Petty France due to the former nationality of its inhabitants, but part was given over to the churchyard by 1615, and on the wall was a Latin inscription with the name Stephen Gosson rector and his churchwardens. One of the early burials beyond the walls was that of Coya Shawsware, merchant and secretary to the Persian ambassador d.1626 - who was buried using the rites of that country.

Due to having such wealthy neighbours the church became prominent and its various benefactors included: Humphrey Swan embroiderer who gave the pulpit cloth in thanks for surviving the pestilence of 1625, Mr. William Hobby a brewer who donated the tenor bell bearing his name "Hobby," and William Earl of Devonshire d.1628 who gave £100 to the poor (forever) which was distributed as bread.

The church was repaired in 1617-20 under Rev. Stephen Gosson who was a satirist, and prior to his appointment published *The School of Abuse*. This was a skilful invective aimed against the immoral aspects of playwrights and poets d.1624.

---

[13] Edward Alleyn spent his early life on the stage at the Rose, Fortune and Paris Garden theatres but in later life used the proceeds to establish three almshouses at Bishopsgate, St. Luke's and Southwark also the *College of God's Gift*, Dulwich as a worthy penance. The latter started as a charity with almshouses and chapel (where he was buried), whilst a grammar school was built just opposite in 1842 and Dulwich College by Charles Barry junior in 1866-70. The Lower School then became a separate entity as Alleyn's at Townley Road, East Dulwich in 1882.

[14] The location of Sir Paul Pindar's house was later part of a tavern, and then became the ground for Liverpool Street station in the 19th century. Its original façade was moved to the Victoria and Albert Museum whereas Skinner Street was then renamed as Pindar Street.

There was also a memorial to Thomas Worrall D.D. incumbent and prebend of St. Paul's d.1639. The church survived the fire, but it was rebuilt by James Gould with his son-in-law George Dance in 1724-28. The building in the Palladian style had pilasters and pediment at the eastern end, although the tower above was perhaps out of proportion. The latter was unique in the City rising above the chancel, while the interior had a barrel vaulted roof, galleries over the aisles, and separate choir (unlike Wren). It was completely different to St. Botolph's, Aldgate built by the same architect twenty years later.

One of the most significant events was the baptism of John Keats in 1795 (see insert), whereas two ministers had a prominent role in the 19th century. Charles James Blomfield (1786-1857) was appointed to the rich living of St. Botolph's in 1819 and was Bishop of London from 1828. In this post he mediated with the Tractarians and spoke in the House of Lord's, whilst he was a writer and contributed to various magazines. [15]

Likewise William Rogers (1819) was made perpetual curate of St. Thomas Charterhouse by Bishop Blomfield in 1845 and was a great social reformer creating local schools. He was a chaplain in ordinary to Victoria, prebend of St. Paul's, and the long term rector of St. Botolph's from 1863. His work included restructuring the Alleyn Charity on a public basis leading to a separate lower school in 1882, and founding of the *Bishopsgate Institute* designed by C.H. Townsend. He died nearby at Devonshire Square in 1896.

This was a large district considered for a chapel by the Fifty Churches, but All Saints, Skinner Street was built in the Gothic style by Michael Meredith in 1828-30. However it was demolished and re-joined the parish due to the building of the railway in 1869.

St. Botoph's, Bishopsgate with nave/chancel and its hall once home to the Fan-makers.

<hr>

[15] His son Sir Arthur William Blomfield (1829-99) trained as an architect under Philip Charles Hardwick then worked on the Bank of England, Law Courts and Southwark Cathedral.

The churchyard was one of the first turned into a public garden in 1863 and the church had the first memorial to the Great War reference the Battle of Jutland. There was little damage in the next war, and the Company of Fan Makers (established 1709) came from Redcross Street, Barbican to use the church hall from 1952-92. Today, the interior is little changed and has tablets to Paul Pindar and the Hon. Artillery Company, also windows by the Bowyers Company - but the exterior is now dominated by the Heron Tower.

C. 1 of September 1566 Edward Allen [sic] baptized of Edward and Margaret
16 August 1668 William Docrowa s. of William and Rebecka was baptized (see p.197)
20 May 1759 Mary Wollstonecraft da. of Edward John and Elizth (see St. Pancras)
18 December 1795 John Keats son of Thomas and Frances born 31 October

M. 8 September 1763 Francis Perigal [jun.] of the Liberty of Norton Folgate and Mary Ogier o.t. same a minor with consent by lic witness Thom. A. Ogier, Fran. Perigal [16]
13 May 1850 William Wall servant of 12 Bishopsgate Street s. John grocer and Elizabeth Mansfield d. of William shoemaker banns by J. Jones M.A. curate [17]

B. 3 September 1650 Sir Paule Pindar d. 22 August, a worthie benefactor to the poore
7 April 1801 Henry Jowett [his son John was a founder of the C.M.S.]
28 July 1840 Benjamin Mayson of 11 Milk Street, Cheapside [father of Mrs. Beeton]

John Keats (1795-1821) - one of the Romantic poets with Byron and Shelley was born in the Moorgate district, his father being a publican. He trained at Guy's Hospital, but through his poetry came into a circle with Leigh Hunt and John Hamilton Reynolds, and despite a lack of money moved to Hampstead - with rooms at Well Walk and *Wentworth* (now in Keats Place). Inspired by Hazlitt, and romantically involved with Fanny Brawne his neighbour, he wrote *Endymion, Hyperion, Ode to a Grecian Urn* and *a Nightingale*. As a member of the Cockney School he was much criticised by Croker and died of consumption in Rome.

On Chapman's Homer - "Much have I travelled in the realms of gold, and many goodly states and kingdoms seen; round many western islands have I been..." (He went to the Lake District and Scotland in 1818)

---

[16] Francis Perigal was a master of the Clockmakers at the Royal Exchange and his first children were baptized at St. Peter le Poer and St. Bartholomew. A child Marianne was born at Queen Square, Bloomsbury in 1780 and married Anthony Brady storekeeper of the Royal William Yard, Plymouth at Berry Pomeroy near Totnes in 1810. He then removed to the Victualling Yard at Deptford and son (Sir) Antonio was born there the next year (one of eight) - The latter became a senior Admiralty official, wrote on church reform and did work on natural history d.1881.

[17] William and Elizabeth Wall were parents of Sir Frederick Joseph Wall (1858-1944) who was born at Battersea and educated at St. Mark's College, Chelsea then became a solicitor's clerk. He rose up the soccer hierarchy to become F.A. Secretary after Charles Alcock in 1895 and resided at Lancaster Gate meeting both Hitler and Mussolini (and retired in 1934).

St. Ethelburga is on Bishopsgate Within and has a memorial garden for peace to the rear.

St. Ethelburga

This ancient church was dedicated to the Abbess of Barking, daughter of Ethelbert of Kent and sister of St. Erkenwalde who was Bishop of London in the 7th century.

Its first reference came in 1250 but the Early English-style church was pulled down, and the resulting rubble was probably used to build the current edifice in c.1411. The living passed to the Convent of St. Helen's in 1366 then after the Dissolution was granted to the Bishop of London by Queen Elizabeth I in 1569 (and remains so today). One of the early memorials was to Mr. Williams who attended on 42 mayors and died 1583.

Henry Hudson an explorer with the Muscovy Co. is reputed to have taken communion before sailing to find the North-West Passage in 1607, and later helped settle New York with the Dutch E.I.C. Of the rectors William Bedwell (1563-1632) worked on the Arabic *New Testament* but then transferred his efforts to the *King James Bible* instead.

The church was repaired in 1612 and the steeple (being greatly decayed) in 1620, then a gallery was built in the south aisle at the cost of Owen Saint-Peere in 1630. There was also a parsonage house nearby and some benefactions but few other memorials, while a small bell turret was attached in 1775. However, it was always diminutive and there was "standing room only" when John Wesley preached in 1785. Likewise John M. Rodwell the rector from 1860-1900 translated the Qur'an into English in 1861.

There were shops immediately adjacent on both sides until they were removed in 1932 and it survived the Great Fire and Second War, but was seriously damaged by an I.R.A. bomb in 1993. St. Botolph's had its windows blown out and the vestry papers went all over the street, but St. Ethelburga which had stood for 600 years was reduced to a pile of rubble. It was finally restored after a public outcry and is now a centre for reconciliation with events examining the relationship between faith and conflict.

Today, there are memorials in the south arcade to Thomas Pestill d.1799 who resided in the parish *in the house where he was born* for 60 years; and Rev. William Parker d.1843 the rector of 36 years. A 19th-century font survived all the devastation and includes a Greek palindrome which translates as, "Cleanse my transgressions, not only my face."

St. Helen's, Bishopsgate

The third church on Bishopsgate was quite an oddity and was built below St. Ethelburga on land originally granted to St. Mary Overie priory at Southwark in 1161. This passed to the Dean and Chapter of St. Paul's and, according to Stow, William Basing dean gave permission for a Benedictine nunnery there in about 1212. Another William Basing, a sheriff, was a benefactor to the establishment in the time of Edward II. [18]

The original church was only a small thing reaching to the south door; however the priory of the black nuns was built on the north side and the whole was extended west. This resulted in an unusual double nave with partition - one part for the nunnery and the other part for the parish; with a chancel and chapel to the south. Whereas the church and appurtenances were part of two large courtyards: Little and Great St. Helen's.

This situation pertained for three centuries and the south nave/arcade was rebuilt in the 15th century, whereas a number of benefactors were connected as revealed by the early monuments: Thomas Langton chaplain d.1350, Adam Francis mercer mayor 1352 (south chapel) and Sir John Crosby d.1478 - built Crosby House nearby (see below).

However, the nunnery was suppressed at the Dissolution and the church and monastic buildings were sold to the Leathersellers Co. in 1543. At this time they converted the old dormitories &c. into their hall (on the north side), whereas the partition between the two naves was removed - resulting in a substantial parish church. The Leathersellers remained in these buildings for the next 250 years and built seven almshouses adjacent. [19]

St. Helen's with its double nave, and doorway designed by Inigo Jones dated 1633.

---

[18] A reprint by Clarendon Press, Oxford in 1908 confirms there was no Dean Basing, and it was Dean Alard de Burnham who made the grant to William Goldsmith at that time.

[19] The Leathersellers Co. were initially at London Wall in 1476-1543 then moved to the monastic surrounds of St. Helen's, but these became expensive to maintain and were cleared in 1799. St. Helen's Place was laid out on the site and for a time they occupied a merchant's house then had a new hall designed by William Fuller Pocock in 1822. There were further halls built in 1879 and in the Adam-style after war damage in 1960, whilst a portrait is displayed of John Locker clerk of forty one years and fellow of the Royal Society who translated Voltaire.

Meanwhile, the status of this large church was assured and it had numerous significant connections, although a steeple promised by Sir Thomas Gresham in recompense for the room taken up by his monument - *never materialised* and there was just a small bell turret. On the west side of Bishopsgate were inns for travellers, and the abode of two mayors who were buried at the church: Sir William Hollis 1539 and Sir Andrew Judd 1550 who built six almshouses and was the founder of Tonbridge School.

Other memorials were to Robert Rochester Esq. sergeant of the pantry (comptroller) to Henry VIII d.1557 and Sir William Pickering ambassador to Spain d.1574 who has a large monument between the two naves. Shakespeare occupied a property in the parish from 1597-98, although being in default he removed to Southwark soon afterwards.

The parsonage was rented out at the Queen's expense to Captain Nicholas Osseley of the Armada and the church was repaired at £1,300 in 1631-33. This included the current font and south door-case by Inigo Jones with fluted Corinthian columns at the charges of the livery company (dubbed *The Tardis*). Later memorials were to: Sir Julius Caesar Adelmare d.1636 who married the daughter of Sir Richard Martin and was a lawyer at Temple, of the Admiralty, M.P., P.C., chancellor, master of the rolls and St. Katharine's; and to John Standish D.D. d.1686 chaplain to Charles II and James II.

St. Helen's with its ancient naves remained steadfast down the years and was one of only five with St. Andrew's and St. Ethelburga's to survive both fire and war. Indeed, as other city churches closed their doors Rev. Dick Lucas became rector from 1961-98, and transformed it from a small congregation to a thriving evangelical ministry. In particular he introduced training courses for clergy and today there are regular services, mid-week groups, and many activities extending to both St. Andrew's and St. Peter's.

However, the building was badly damaged by two I.R.A. bombs in 1992/93 and was restored by the Palladian architect Quinlan Terry. Today, the main features are the 12th century nave, a Jacobean pulpit and monuments to John de Oteswich (from St. Martin), Sir John Spencer 1609 south door, Sir William Pickering canopy, Sir Thomas Gresham north-east, Sir John Crosby and Sir Andrew Judd east end, William Bond alderman and merchant adventurer 1576 and Captain Martin Bond 1643 north wall, and in the gallery John Robinson merchant of the staple 1599 (from St. Martin).

B. XIth day of December 1579 Sir Thomas Gresham knight d. 21 November
6 March 1702/03 Dr. [Robert] Hooke in ye midle of the south isle
(There is no trace of a memorial or of any picture of him)

"Westminster Abbey of the East" showing the nave of the nunnery with memorials to Sir John Crosby (1478) and Sir Andrew Judd (1558).

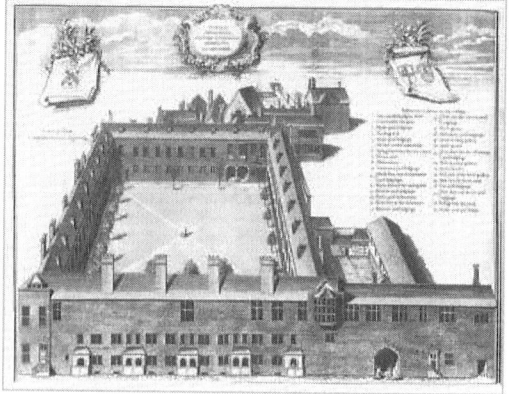

Sir Thomas Gresham (1519-79) and the college he established in c.1740. Later it was the site of the Nat West Tower.

Crosby House - This was built by Sir John Crosby alderman grocer d.1478 south of the church on tenements of Alice Ashfield prioress in 1466. Of stone and timber it was the tallest in London and rented to Richard (III) Duke of Gloucester prior to him becoming king. Henry VIII bestowed it on Anthonio Bonvici an Italian merchant in 1542.

William Bond the famous merchant adventurer and sheriff d.1576 added a turret to the roof, whilst of his sons Sir George was master of the haberdashers and mayor 1587 and Martin established a literary and scientific institute (their memorials on the north wall). This was a residence for many visiting ambassadors including those from Denmark and France, whereas Sir John Spencer mayor 1594 also resided in the property.

The building became part of a square with a Presbyterian meeting house founded in 1672, but was later converted into a warehouse and the façade was restored in 1836-42. Eventually there were plans to move the building during redevelopment and the grand hall with hammer beam ceiling went to Cheney Walk, Chelsea, in 1908-10. The new site was on land once owned by Sir Thomas More who also resided at Crosby House.

Gresham College - Thomas Gresham (1519-79) was born in London however came to prominence as a mercer in Antwerp, advising Edward VI and Mary on financial matters and setting up the Royal Exchange in 1565. He built a mansion of brick and timber on Bishopsgate with eight almshouses but his main legacy was his remunerative will.

His only son Richard had already died, and he left the rents from the Exchange for the establishment of a college in his property after his wife Anne's decease. This was to have seven chairs: divinity, music, astronomy, geometry, physic (medicine), law and rhetoric and it came into being in 1597. The estate then passed to the City and Mercers Co. and after the fire it was rebuilt on a site nearer to Broad Street. It was an important centre for learning and housed the Royal Society from 1663-1710.

Of its associates, Wren lectured on astronomy, Hooke was professor of geometry and meetings were held with the likes of Boyle. It remained there until 1768 then took new premises in Gresham Street and later moved to Barnard's Inn at High Holborn - part of Gray's Inn. A memorial window to Hooke at the church was lost in 1993.

Shipbrokers - Bishopsgate St. (Within) was home to shipping/steamship agents, shipowners, naval architects, merchants, marine surveyors and insurers in the 19th century. Charles Alcock a shipbuilder in Sunderland removed to Chingford and was a ship and insurance broker at *Ethelburga House*, 70-71 Bishopsgate Street. He worked there with his sons John Forster and Charles who helped form the Football Association in 1863, the latter secretary of the F.A. and of Surrey C.C.C. and founder of the Cup. After his death in 1881, his son John F. was a shipbroker and ice merchant at 21 Great St. Helen's with supply interests in Norway from 1895-1910 and lived at Northchurch, Herts.

Leadenhall

Aldgate ward covered the area inside the walls from Bishopsgate across to Aldgate and then down past Fenchurch Street to Crutched Friars in the east. Within its bounds were situated Holy Trinity priory, the three churches listed below and St. Katharine Coleman which is treated later. The modern ward is similar but does not go as far south.

At the southwest corner were Lime Street and its small ward which in ancient times had a narrow strip of land reaching up past St. Andrew's right to the city walls. Today the latter ward also incorporates the area adjacent to St. Helen's church.

To the north there were the houses of merchants and the Fletchers Hall (see below), while to the south was Lime Street which Stow *supposed* came from the making or selling of lime. Here were the abodes of Edward I, Sir Simon Burley, the Merchant Taylors and mayors William Bowyer and Henry Huberthorne, also the Pewterers Hall.

The ancient Manor of Leadenhall was held by Sir Hugh Nevill and Sir Humphrey de Bohun Earl of Hereford in the 14th century, but passed to Sir Richard Whittington and he donated it to the City in 1411. As a result Simon Eyre draper mayor built a granary there at his own expense in about 1444 and this became Leadenhall Market with a chapel for priests and a school. One feature was the delivery of bread carts from Stratford le Bow but this practice was stopped due to "short-measures" in 1568.

Stow recorded the presence of scales for weighing wool and other produce, whilst part of the site was reserved for entertainments and pageants. In the 18th century there were a number of buildings including the green and hide markets, whereas East India House once the property of Sir William Craven was located on the eastern side. [20]

On the west side of Lime Street is a plaque to William Dockwra who founded the penny post at his mansion there in 1680. Dockwra was baptized at St. Olave Jewry in 1635 and apprenticed as an armourer, then entered the Customs House and married Rebeckah Dukeson at St. Clement Danes in 1661. He was agent for the Grosvenors and his wife's niece Mary Davies married Sir Thomas, her dowry a fortune in land.

In addition he operated copper mines and developed the postal service with receiving houses, six sorting offices, and delivery to the Exchange 6-8 times a day, plus suburbs rated at two pence per item. He became comptroller of the post in 1697-1700 but was dismissed after irregularities and petitioned Queen Anne for relief d.1716.

Lime Street ward had no parish churches since two went before the fire: **(1)** St. Mary Pelliper with its links to the skinners was above St. Andrew, and joined the latter in 1562 then became a school and warehouse. **(2)** Further up St. Mary Street as Stow called it was Camomile Street and here was St. Augustine Papey in the wall near the inn of the Earl of Oxford. It was a poor house of priests but was suppressed and the parishioners went to All Hallows and it became an apothecary's stable/dwelling. The churchyard was used by St. Martin Outwich, and part of its wall is in a garden of modern offices.

---

[20] Sir Horace Jones the architect of Billingsgate and Smithfield designed the current building in 1881, with its canopied green ironwork and arcades; whilst it has appeared in a number of films including *Harry Potter & the Philosopher's Stone*. East India House which remained until the 19th century is now the site of the idiosyncratic Lloyd's Building by R. Rogers built in 1978-86.

Bevis Marks Synagogue

The area north of Leadenhall was originally an estate of the Bassets but passed over to the Bishops of Bury and was their inn from c.1156. From this were derived the names of *Buries Marks* and *Berry Street* to the south and west. At the Dissolution this transferred to Sir Thomas Heneage a friend of Henry VIII and member of privy chamber including a large house, court and gardens - with Bevers Marks being situated nearby.

The Jews were originally expelled from England by Edward I in 1291. However they re-established themselves in this locality in the 17th century, and a blue plaque at the corner of Creechurch and Bury Street records, "Site of the First Synagogue after Resettlement 1657-1701." This refers to the meeting place of the Sephardic branch with origins in the Iberian Peninsula. In addition a Great Synagogue was erected above Duke's Place by the Ashkenazi or Central Europeans in 1690. George Dance the elder then built an enlarged one there in 1766 but a third synagogue was destroyed in the war.

David Nieto became the chief rabbi of the Sephardic synagogue in 1698 however the premises were too small, and they moved to a new building on what is now Bevis Marks between Bury and Heneage Streets. The interior was based upon the great synagogue in Amsterdam and is little changed today, being the oldest still in use in England.

Sir Moses Montefiore (1784-1885) was a member of Bevis Marks and a stockbroker for his brother-in-law Nathan Mayer Rothschild. He was a banker, philanthropist and sheriff whilst he went on missions to the Sultan of the Ottoman Empire to secure Jewish rights. There were several disputes about modernising the faith, and Isaac Disraeli the son of Benjamin a merchant took his sons to the Church of England. The families of Mocatta, Montefiore, Henriques and Goldsmid then led the way in establishing the West London Reform Synagogue at Oxford Street in 1840, with Sir Moses an outspoken critic.

M. 31 March 1756 **or** 29 Adar II 5516 Biniamin D'Israeli & Ribca Mendes Furtado
24 May 1765 **or** 4 Sivan 5525 Binjamin D'Israeli and Sara Shiprut de Gabay [Villareal]
1 February 1802 **or** 29 Shevat 5562 Isaac de Benjamin Israeli (D'Israeli) and Miryam [Maria] de Naphtali Basevi [parents of the PM]

Left: Bevis Marks and Sir Moses Montefiore. **Below: St. Andrew's** with the mediaeval west entrance.

St. Andrew's with interior in the perpendicular style dates to 1532.

Hans Holbein was an artist and parishioner.

St. Andrew Undershaft

The church was recorded as St. Andrew *juxta Alegate* in the 12th century but was rebuilt in the early 14th century, and by that time had the epithet *Undershaft*. Chaucer talked of the great shaft of Cornhill which was erected near to the church door on May Day for use as a maypole. This practice continued until it was abolished in 1517 after apprentices and other youths rioted against aliens, whilst the maypole was stored under the eaves of nearby houses until 1550. The minister of St. Katherine's then preached at Paul's Cross, stating it was being used as an idol hence with Puritan zeal it was disposed of.

As stated the church survived both the fire and the war thus the exterior is that built in Tudor times from 1520-32, except for the lower tower which is older. This was designed in the perpendicular style with tall nave and aisles, plus striking east and west windows, and there was little distinction between the nave and chancel. Clearly such architecture was well suited to the demands of the burgeoning Protestant faith.

Four main people paid for the rebuilding and Stephen Jennings merchant taylor mayor, founder of Wolverhampton Grammar, funded the north nave and quire but was buried at the Greyfriars d.1524. John Kirby and John Garland merchant taylors and Nicholas Levison mercer then took on his philanthropic mantle to complete the project.

The church was dedicated to Andrew the Apostle, and was on the southeast corner of St. Mary Street where it met Leadenhall (or High Street), just inside the ward of Aldgate. Its main features were the attractive stone tower, the great east window depicting Kings and Queens, and a fair library of books within the nave - some pertaining to its history. It was united with nearby St. Mary's by Elizabeth I in 1562 and the latter building was then a parish school - its parsonage and rents being used towards church repairs.

Of the many memorials to sheriffs, aldermen &c. the most significant were to Bishop Henry Man D.D. d.1550 and John Stow chronicler died 5 April 1605 in the north aisle erected by his wife Elizabeth. In addition there were those to four mayors: Sir Thomas Offley merchant taylor 1556, Sir William Craven 1610 benefactor to the poor, Sir Hugh Hamersley d.1636 (north wall) and Sir Christopher Clitherow d.1642.

To the north of the church were some grand houses belonging to merchants, including one owned by Sir William Pickering and then Sir Edward Wotton of Kent. Just beyond them near to Bevis Marks was the Fletchers Hall (now transferred to Cloth Fair).

The top of the tower was replaced in the 19th century, whilst a later route-way termed Undershaft was built after the war and replaced parts of Crosby Street and its square. In fact in modern times the location was opened up and today the church is notable for its position between the "Gherkin," erected on the site of the Baltic Exchange, and Lloyd's Insurance building. Internally, the edifice's main features are its perpendicular lines and high clerestory windows while some of its many memorials are as follows: [21]

North Side - John Stow 1605 northeast corner, Hugh Hamersley merchant adventurer governor of Christ's Hospital 1636, William Ramsay secretary of the E.I.C. 1813, Rev. Robert C. Billing rector 1888-98 Bishop of Bedford, and Charles H. Turner rector of St. George in the East 1882-97 and this church 1898-1912 also Bishop of Islington.

South Side - In the southwest corner is a tablet, "To the glory of God and in memory of John alias Hans Holbein painter to H.M. King Henry VIII sometime resident in this parish b.1497 d.1543." Others are to Edward Warner citizen and merchant d.1628 and Mr. Mathias Datchelor d.1686 and family (above that to Holbein).

However the most significant link is to the chronicler Stow, he being a member of the Merchant Taylors and parishioner from the 1570s. Indeed, *The Changing of the Quill* ceremony takes place on 5 April each year. The church is used by St. Helen's for counselling, meetings and refreshments but on Stow's *Special Day* the mayor and his guild arrive, then, with much ceremonial aplomb, a quill is placed in the hand on his monument.

C. 24 March 1680/81 William Dockwra son of Mr. William was baptized
12 June 1682 Peter Dockwra son of Mr. William was baptized

B. Mr. John Stoe was buried ye 8th day of April 1605 **(see picture)**

St. Katherine Cree

The next two churches were connected and have an interesting history being related to the Augustinian priory founded north of Leadenhall by Maud wife of Henry I in 1108. The land for the foundation was just inside Aldgate and took up four ancient parishes viz. St. Mary Magdalen, St. Michael's, St. Katherine's and the Blessed Trinity.

It was arranged that the new priory of Holy Trinity would replace them as one parish and there was a separate area for the townsfolk, but, "By the noise of several celebrating mass together, a great confusion and disturbance was occasioned." The residents of St. Katherine's then petitioned for a separate chapel, which was built in the churchyard to the south in 1280, and the prior gave them a canon for divine services.

---

[21] The Baltic Exchange with its distinctive marble columns and Portland stone façade was built in the shipping district in 1903 but destroyed by an I.R.A bomb in 1992 - this also saw the demise of stained glass windows in the church dating from the 16th century. Initially, English Heritage wanted the Exchange façade restored, but this proved impractical and the salvage was purchased in 2006 to be rebuilt in the centre of Tallinn, Estonia - an historic trading port.

St. Kath Cree built in Jacobean times in 1628-31 with memorial to Sir Nicholas Throckmorton.

They were required to visit the main priory church for christenings, marriages and all important holidays, but much discord arose over their failure to do this and restraint was put on them regarding chapel use. As a result at the time of William Haradon prior and Bishop Richard Clifford in 1414 it was decreed that St. Katherine's would be a separate parish, although it was still to show deference and repair for certain holidays.

Thus the monks and the laity were separated to their mutual tranquillity and the new church was denoted as, "next to the priory of Christ or Cree Church at Aldgate." Initially it was rebuilt at the end of the 15th century whilst Sir John Percival also added a new bell tower in 1504. Henry VIII then offered the prior a preferment hence it was surrendered and the canons dispersed elsewhere in 1531 (before the Dissolution).

Sir Thomas Audley who greatly assisted the King was given the estate and offered Holy Trinity to anyone who would pull it down! Of its bells four went to Stepney in 1544 and five lesser ones were offered to St. Katherine's to move their church nearer the road, but they refused. Eventually the priory was pulled down by workmen but little was salvaged and Audley then built a fair house there. This passed to the Duke of Norfolk through his daughter's marriage and in this way became Duke's Place. [22]

At the time of Stow, St. Katherine's was antiquated as revealed by the raised pavement beside it, and was rebuilt with Corinthian arcade, a tall nave with Gothic roof and rose window in 1628-31. The mediaeval tower was retained and William Laud the Bishop of London then consecrated the building. Features dating from that time are the font and stained glass; whilst a gateway dated 1631 in the church garden on Mitre Street once gave access to Leadenhall Street. There are parish markers in Creechurch Street and another (with All Hallows) was previously in Billiter Street (1817). [23]

---

[22] A number of esquires, ladies, baronets and children to King Stephen were buried at Holy Trinity; while Stow made a case for Henry Fitz Alwine mayor d.1213 but Strype disputed this.

[23] A memorial by the gate records James Fitch (1762-1828) cheesemonger of the parish and his nephew George Fitch (1780-1842) &c. The family were citizens and freemen of the City up until the 20th century and were also principals of the firm Fitch Lovell Ltd.

The church is the only one of Jacobean origin and one of a handful to survive the fire. Of its memorials these included Thomas Fleming, Lord Rowles of Essex d.1464 and Sir Nicholas Throckmorton chamberlain to Queen Elizabeth I who married Anne Carew then had 10 sons and 3 daughters d.1570-71 (south aisle). The latter was Ambassador to France and a Royal adviser while daughter "Bess" married Sir Walter Raleigh.

The organ was installed in 1686 and Henry Purcell played it soon after while Handel who was born at this time played it at a latter date. A new top was added to the tower in the 18th century and items came from St. James's church when it was demolished viz. the reredos and five memorial tablets dating to the early 1800s (N.W. corner).

Little war damage occurred and it became a guild church in 1954 with the parish going to St. Andrew's. However, the walls were in danger of falling down and major repairs were undertaken in 1962 - concealing the west window and restoring the ceiling.

The Bells of St. Katherine first rang out in 1552 but they were recast by Thomas Lester and Thomas Pack at the Whitechapel Bell Foundry in 1754, followed by the tenor by Thomas Mears in 1842. Due to problems of weight they went out of use in 1880 and an attempt to re-hang them on the old timbers in 1911 did not help. They were first tried again in 2007, and H.S.B.C. and Lloyd's Insurers then pledged money to renovate them. As a result the bells and old timbers were briefly left on display in the nave.

B. 29 November 1543 Hans Holbein was buried [the younger]

St. James's, Duke's Place

The inhabitants of Duke's Place were destitute of a parish and initially used Holy Trinity and then St. Katherine's. But, this was all somewhat of a burden (well borne) and with the support of Sir Edward Barkham the mayor they petitioned the King for some land, and a new parish church was built on the ruins of the chapter house as late as 1622. This was of red brick with a square tower, three roof gables and round-headed windows - the mayor's name being engraved on the chancel ceiling to his memory.

This took place despite local opposition and it was consecrated after New Year's Day with many patrons present including Sir Peter Proby the mayor. Barkham left money by his will to the parson in 1632 and the church was rebuilt in 1727. But much of the area was occupied by Jews with the Great Synagogue nearby and it was demolished in 1874, and the parish and reredos went to St. Katherine's. The church site was located below St. James's Passage east of Mitre Square and adjacent to Sir John Cass School.

B. 8 Apr 1667 John Booker [astronomer] - memorial by Ashmole who inherited his work

"The Bells of St. Katherine" cast in 1754 and player of the organ, **Handel (1685-1759)**.

Aldgate

The area without the city walls was delineated on two levels - the Portsoken ward and parish of St. Botolph's, which were not wholly contiguous. The boundary of the old ward went up to Bishopsgate then along Petticoat Lane towards Whitechapel, and south by the Minories to Goodman's Yard and on to Tower Hill. Today's ward is more restricted than before both to the north and south.

However, the parish of St. Botolph's also extended into East Smithfield and went past the liberties of the Tower and St. Katharine's Hospital (of 1148) down to the river. The small parish of Holy Trinity was created out of its bounds on the eastern side.

During the time of King Edgar or possibly Canute there were thirteen knights of favour who were given properties and land east of Aldgate, the land having been deserted as of too much servitude. This was confirmed after they performed certain tasks of combat in East Smithfield and they were thereafter known as the Knighten Guild.

Such liberties were retained by William I and the knights gathered at Holy Trinity priory in the time of Henry I. They gave the area outside the walls down to the river (with St. Botolph's on its land) to Prior Norman in 1125, and this was confirmed in a bull by Pope Innocent II twelve years later - as required. The prior then seized the lands without the walls "part" of the City suburbs in the "soke" of the Knighten Guild. [24]

In fact Holy Trinity was very wealthy owning all of the land from Aldgate across to St. Kath Cree and up to the walls, the livings of All Hallows and St. Augustine on the Wall, and St. Edmund's given by Queen Maud. But Nicholas Hancock the prior surrendered it to Henry VIII in 1531 for harbouring a thief - and the ward then fell to the City.

Aldgate itself had two towers in Roman times and was one of four principle gateways whilst it was rebuilt after 1108 and again in 1215. The presence of the priory just inside secured its prominence and Chaucer, a customs officer at the Port of London, lived in rooms above it from 1374. But it was rebuilt in 1607-09 and pulled down in 1761.

The last item of interest in the area was a Cistercian abbey built at East Smithfield by Edward III, in thanks for God's grace, in 1352. This was a former burying ground of the priory and was known as East Minster or the Abbey of St. Mary Graces. Its wealth was extensive with lands in Gravesend, Woolwich, Poplar and western England.

After being valued at £546 in 1539, it was pulled down by Sir Arthur Darcy and others then became a storehouse for victuals and its ovens baked "bisket" for the King's ships. The Royal Mint came there and occupied a building designed by Robert Smirke in 1809 (and was present until 1975) while the gatehouse, structure and walls remain today.

A fair was held near the site of the abbey at East Smithfield from the time of Henry III, but there was a degree of contention concerning City rights in this area. In general, the land held by Holy Trinity beyond the ward boundary, including St. Katharine's and East Smithfield, was a liberty outside the trading restrictions operated by the city guilds. As a result it was occupied by tenements, workshops and divided land parcels from the earliest of times. However, as shall be shown it was a place of considerable industry.

---

[24] Part of the ward was given up to form St. Katharine's Hospital (see Volume II).

Holy Trinity, Minories

The Franciscans or Friars Minor had a second order for women called the Poor Clares who were established in 1212. Meanwhile, a small street ran down from Aldgate beside the town ditch outside the walls, and it was here that Edmund Earl of Lancaster, brother of Edward I, established St. Clare's Abbey in 1293. His wife Blanche Queen of Navarre brought the first nuns over and these Minoresses owned several properties in the City, whilst to the east and south was a large farm pertaining to the nunnery.

There were few records of its memorials other than the Duchess of Norfolk c.1506, while after the Dissolution it passed to John Clark Bishop of Bath and Wells and then to Henry Duke of Suffolk, including the *Minory House*, in 1552. The property was soon put to a number of sundry uses and the precincts were a workhouse and store for armour. The land beyond was farmed by one Trollope and then by Mr. Goodman who lived like a gentleman - and in his youth Stow collected milk from the farm.

However, the wall and town ditch were covered over and replaced by yards, alleys and gardens by the 1600s. The farm itself was taken by Leman, Mansell and Prescot Streets and a tenter field for clothworkers was located on Goodman's Fields. To the south was Goodman's Yard and the main thoroughfare was designated as the Minories.

A small parish church called St. Trinity or Holy Trinity was established in the nunnery church in 1539, with Trinity Court to the north and Heydon Square to the south. It was repaired with a fine steeple in 1618-20 and a new entrance and wall were erected in 1623, the memorials including ones to Sir John Pelham d.1580 and his son Oliver d.1584. The former resided at Laughton in Sussex and was M.P. for that county, whilst he married Judith daughter of Oliver St. John, 1st Baron Bletsowe. [25]

Due to its location the church survived the fire and was rebuilt in the classical style by an unknown architect in 1706. Goodman's Railway Depot was then built immediately to the north in the mid-19th century (the spur can be seen from the DLR). The church was closed in 1899 and the font (of 1620) went to St. Lawrence Jewry and the parish to St. Botolph's Aldgate. However any remains were destroyed in the war and St. Clare Street and a small garden now demarcate the site.

St. Botolph's, Aldgate

The original church is likely to have been Saxon 10th century, but the first reference is in 1125 when the prominent Holy Trinity priory took possession of it with the surrounding lands. It was situated just beyond the "Old Gate" on the north side of the road, which continued east through Whitechapel and on to Mile End and Stepney.

Robert Burford a wealthy bell-founder left money to enlarge the building in 1418 at which time it had a new chapel to St. Mary, aisle to St. Katherine and lofty steeple. There were also various fraternities and chantries, whereas the prior paid for repairs hence the arms of Holy Trinity were engraven on the building. The main highway itself had some grand properties and numerous inns for travellers from Essex.

---

[25] A fine memorial to the Pelhams with kneeling figures and coat of arms was erected at Holy Trinity, but after it closed this was removed to Stanmer church near to Brighton.

St. Botolph's was built by George Dance the elder in 1739-44. The interior was restored by J.F. Bentley in the late 19th century and has exquisite ceiling detail.

However, the adjacent area was greatly built up in the 16th century having previously been covered by fields. To the north was Hog Lane later known as Artillery and Petticoat Lanes and here were hedge rows of elm trees with bridges and stiles leading to pleasant fields: "Very commodious for the inhabitants therein to walk, shoot and otherwise to recreate and refresh their dull spirits in the sweet and wholesome air." Stow noted that in the previous five years this area, some land to the south, and Houndsditch was entirely built up with houses, tenements, gardens, tenter yards and bowling alleys.

As a result the parish was greatly increased in number and the church was *pestered* with lofts and seats to accommodate the inhabitants. Edmund Spenser poet was born nearby in 1552 however there were only a few memorials. These included Thomas Lord Darcy, Sir Nicholas Carew and other family (now in the baptistry) who contested Henry VIII over the monasteries, John Clark the Bishop of Bath and Wells d.1540 of the nunnery and ambassador to the Duke of Cleve, and Robert Dow a merchant taylor d.1612 who left many endowments to the church, hospitals and prisons.

The mediaeval building was repaired in 1621 and adjacent land levelled in 1633, whilst there was a churchyard by a victualling yard to the east, from the days of the abbey. One unusual feature was it north-south orientation (there being only three others) and it survived the fire but was rebuilt by George Dance the elder in 1739-44. The new church was of red brick with a fine tower and spire delineated by quoins, the interior comprising a rectangle with slanting long galleries - but no separate sanctuary.

J.F. Bentley architect of Westminster Cathedral then remodelled it during the late 19th century. He added side screens to create a chancel, removed the box pews, replaced the gallery fronts with a balustrade and introduced a carved plasterwork ceiling.

A bomb pierced the roof in 1941 but did not explode, while the vicar slept in the crypt coming out onto the roof during air raids. There was a fire in 1965 and it was renovated by Rodney Tatchell and J.S. Comper, who created a new baptistry within the vestibule. The bright reredos panels were designed by Thetis Blacker in 1982 - based on St. John's colourful account of the Holy City observed through the gates of Heaven. [26]

---

[26] Rev. John Comper was born Pulborough, Sussex but took the Oxford Movement to Scotland and his son John Ninian was born at Aberdeen in 1864. The latter was one of the last Gothic Revival architects and married Grace Bucknall sister of his partner in 1890. They had four sons including J.S. Comper architect and Nicholas an aircraft designer; whilst they lived at The Priory, Beulah Hill (designed by Decimus Burton) and entertained John Betjeman there.

Other features today include the busts of Robert Dow (1552-1612) and Sir John Cass (1661-1718) in the baptistry - the latter with schools opposite and in Stepney Way, also a list of rectors from Prior Norman in 1108 and the aldermen of Portsoken. The organ by Renatus Harris in the south gallery was reinstalled in 1744 and is the oldest playable in London, whilst there are eight 18th century bells from Whitechapel Bell Foundry and the north window is a copy of Rubens *descent from the cross* of 1857. Today the population is mainly Jewish and Muslim and the congregation consists of business people.

C. 28 February 1660/61 John Cass son to Thomas carpenter and Martha his wife
2 October 1719 Henry Jowet[t] son to Henry and Elizabeth of East Smithfield
14 February 1747/48 Jeremy Bentham son of Jeremia and Alicia of Church Lane
3 March 1763 Charles Flower son of Stephen and Mary, the Minories born 18 Feb
26 July 1791 Elizabeth Flower d. of Charles and Ann, 3 Crescent born 30 June
14 March 1820 Alfred George Goodwyn son of Thomas Wildman and Elizabeth of the brewery, Lower East Smithfield by Dr. Hollingworth born 17 August 1819

M. 1 January 1683/84 Danill Ffoe bach and Mary Tufflie spin by Mr. Hollingworth

B. 23 October 1741 Elizabeth Jowett wife of Henery, East Smithfield
18 April 1747 Henry Jewett of East Smithfield
10 February 1773 Stephen Flower of the Minories
25 March 1831 William Symington of Buzz Street age 68
22 September 1834 Sir Charles Flower of Bolton House, Russell Square age 72

Notable Residents - There were several links and Isaac Newton lived opposite when he was warden of the Royal Mint in 1696, and John Cass was treasurer of the Bethlem and Bridewell and his foundation was joined to St. Botolph's. Thomas Bray was rector in 1706-30 having initiated the *Society for Propagation of the Gospel* (in North America) and *of Christian Knowledge* just prior to his arrival. He was a writer and philanthropist at the church and a tablet to him was unveiled there by the Queen (in 1980).

Daniel Ffoe was born in London in c.1659 and was a general merchant but seldom out of debt, whilst his political pamphlets took him to the pillory and Newgate. Despite this he was married to a lady with a dowry of £3,700 and had eight children possibly residing at Cripplegate, then changed his name to the more aristocratic Defoe. He was employed by the spymaster Robert Harley Earl of Oxford and produced Government pamphlets at the time of the union, then did his most famous work *Robinson Crusoe* in 1719 and *Moll Flanders* in 1722. He died in 1731 and his memorial is at Bunhill Fields.

Other parishioners were Henry Jowett head of a dynasty of evangelists who was born at East Smithfield in 1719, and strangely went to live at Smithfield (see St. Sepulchre), and Jeremy Bentham who was born north of the church in 1748. He attended Westminster and Oxford then became a philosopher, legal adviser and social reformer, his designs for the *Panopticon* being highly influential in prison building around the world.

However one of the most interesting links was Sir Charles Flower whose family lived in the parish for at least three generations. His father Stephen was a cheesemonger in the Minories but had little ambition, whereas the son began in the same profession and soon outstripped the competition, being a merchant at 75 Minories by 1788. He married Anne

Squire and had eight children baptized at the church, then moved to 3 The Crescent at the south end of the Minories and was a sheriff, alderman of Cornhill and master of the Framework Knitters. His wife Anne died in 1803 but he took a new address at Finsbury Square and was appointed mayor in 1808-09 - being knighted the next year.

Daniel Defoe (1659-1731) *shipwrecked* but not alone;

And **William Symington (1764-1831)** leading pioneer of steamboats and a rival of engineer James Watt.

Despite a lack of education and literacy he was a skilled merchant who persuaded those in business he had *their* interests solely at heart, and on losing a Government contract exclaimed, "Damn it Sir, I missed it only by fourpence in three pigs!" and the accounts proved this to be completely correct. However, he seldom missed out and on another occasion he manipulated victuals for the Peninsular War to his great benefit.

On moving to Finsbury Square he entertained the Duke of York through lavish feasts, and brought many senior people there by inviting the Bishop to meet the Archbishop, the Lord Chief Justice to meet the Chancellor, and the Lord of the Admiralty to meet the Lord of the Treasury - all this on a pretence without having been introduced to any of them himself! He was a resolute turtle-eater who enjoyed his success via culinary delights, and he was often seen to thrust wasted food into his pockets when dining.

He had many prominent connections and of his daughters: Elizabeth Flower married Thomas Wildman Goodwyn in 1809 (see inset), Ann Mary married the Hon. Michael H. Percival on the Legislative Council of Quebec and was an amateur botanist, and Caroline married Christopher James Magnay whose father and brother were mayors.

Meanwhile, Sir Charles with his son Sir James of Belmont House, Mill Hill (later part of the school) entered into a partnership with Harvey Combe, Joseph Delafield &c. of the Combe & Co. brewery at Long Acre, Covent Garden in 1818. In addition the father was a director of the Thames & Medway Canal Co. who were involved in building the Strood Tunnel at the time, although this later became part of a railway line.

Sir Charles resided at 67 Russell Square from 1829 although he still owned property at the Crescent, Minories and when he died in 1834 he left £551,000 - most of which went to his son, with several bequests to his daughters and their husbands. His son retained an interest in Combe & Co. and was an M.P. for Thetford under Sir Robert Peel.

Continuing such industrial links, William Symington was born at Leadhills, Lanarkshire in 1764 and was encouraged by Gilbert Meason a mine owner to develop steam engines with his brother, after the latter fell out with Boulton and Watt. As a result he developed the ideas of Newcomen &c. to produce his patented atmospheric engine in 1787.

Over several years he developed a steamboat and was engineer at the Carron Works after Smeaton, being hampered by opposing patents. His most notable creation was the *Charlotte Dundas* for Lord Dundas, the first practical steamboat, in 1801 but the Duke of Bridgwater's order was cancelled. Having little financial success he was overshadowed by Watt, and due to mounting debts went to live with his daughter in London in 1829. His bust can be seen in Edinburgh and there is a plaque on the south wall of the nave.

There is also a tablet on the east wall to the R.H. Sir Marcus Samuel, an alderman of Portsoken from 1891-1921 and mayor in 1902, who founded the Shell Company after a visit to the Black Sea. He purchased Mote Park, Maidstone from the Marshams in 1895 (sold in 1929) and was 1st Viscount Bearstead, whilst he was involved with Kent C.C.C. who played there and won four championships at that time.

"James Watt" comes to Aldgate

The Red Lion Brewery by the river at Lower East Smithfield was started in 1492, whilst the owners included Robert Earl of Leicester, Sir John and Humphrey Parsons who were both mayors, Sir John Hynde Cotton and Marshe Dickinson another mayor.

Henry Goodwyn and his son (also Henry) lived at Deptford and became owners in the 1760s, while the latter had seven children baptized at St. Botolph's in 1779-90 - his address the Brewhouse at Lower East Smithfield. Despite learning his trade in a long established concern the father wished to modernize and visited Boulton and Watt at the Soho Works in Handsworth. He sent a firm proposal for a rotative engine in 1784 noting, "The great trust and confidence we place in you respecting this business."

He then added, "It will be a great disappointment to me if this engine is not fixed by you before any other brewing trade, should it not, I acknowledge my pride and vanity will be much hurt." The first 4-h.p. engine was erected there in May 1784 to do both pumping and malting, however it was the 10-h.p. engine supplied to Whitbread's shortly after that attracted universal acclaim and a visit from the King and Queen.

Henry Goodwyn senior resided at Maze Hill, Greenwich but died in 1805 and by then the Hoare family of bankers had joined the business. His son Henry continued the link until 1823 whilst grandson Thomas and his brother Charles became soap & starch makers at Goodman's Yard. The brewery remained with the Hoares and was worth £1.6 million in 1894 but passed to Charringtons in 1934 - the site next to St. Katharine's dock.

The next generation inherited money from both the brewery and Sir Charles and were much involved in India. Mary Goodwyn daughter of Henry married Samuel Enderby the explorer and whaler and their grandson was General C.G. Gordon (see Greenwich), while Alfred G. Goodwyn his 'cousin' was a major general R.E. and had medals for the Afghan and Sikh Wars, taking part in the siege of Lucknow under Lord Clyde. He retired to Bath and his son of the same name played in the first Cup Final for the Royal Engineers.

City East

The final section of the City encapsulates three wards leading from London Bridge to the Tower, although long term development of the waterfront in general obscures this connection. In deed, the begrimed noisome highway of Thames Street breaks up all integrity of the environs.

However, there is still much of interest weaved amongst the alleyways and passages "at hill" above the river - with a monument to Wren's aspirations, a prominent fish market, some ancient customs and a Royalist castle.

Despite this there have been numerous changes and just five churches and a folly-ruin survive the ravages of time. The arrival of Rennie's bridge brought a whole new dimension to the street pattern, and relegated New Fish Street to the background while a memorial to oppression was secreted.

Of the rich and famous there was a Bible translator, some poetic parents, multiple American connections, a man of letters with Arthurian name and a writer who saved the area from both fire and brimstone.

A Tale of Two Pews

St. Olave's, Hart Street was mentioned by Dickens and the Admiralty were based nearby.

ENTRANCE TO THE SOUTH GALLERY AND THE NAVY OFFICE PEW OFTEN MENTIONED IN THE DIARY OF SAMUEL PEPYS.

THIS TABLET ERECTED A.D.1891

St. Margaret Patten displays the only example of canopied pews (for churchwardens) in the City.

Fenchurch Street

Initially we must consider one of the outstanding wards namely that of Langbourn which ran from Bank right across to Fenchurch Street station. Four of its churches have been discussed under Lombard Street and below are Dionis and Gabriel - whilst Staining due to its location is discussed later. In addition to these edifices we include St. Benet's which was immediately adjacent sitting at the north end of Bridge ward.

St. Benet Gracechurch

The first of the *fallen churches* was at the southeast of Fenchurch and Gracechurch Streets, diagonally opposite to All Hallows, with a small church-yard behind. It initially belonged to Christchurch, Canterbury in 1053 and was by the herb/hay market which ran east to west. The market's tariffs were listed under Edward III: every foreign cart with corn or malt ½d, for cheese or a combination 2d, from the Temple or St. Martin le Grand a farthing, but St. John of Jerusalem hospital was free of any charges.

Such protectionism secured the local traders and they were able to spend £700 on the church repairs in 1630. Three years later a new turret was placed on the tower and also a clock with chimes. However, there were few monuments except those to John Harding salter 1576, John Sturgeon a haberdasher and chamberlain of London, Philip Cushen a Florentine and famous merchant 1600, and James Bunce a burgess d.1631.

The edifice was destroyed in the fire and rebuilt by Wren in 1681-87, while the parish took over St. Leonard's nearby. There was a basic rectangle, groin vaults, and five round-headed windows with round ones above to the north. However its spire at the northwest corner was the main feature with broken cornice, clock, vented belfry, domed cupola, and obelisk at 149 feet. It was like St. Michael's, Queenhithe built at the same time.

For nearly two centuries it sat on the main thoroughfare leading south into (New) Fish Street Hill with the Monument, St. Magnus and London Bridge beyond. In the chancel there was a tablet to Rev. James Townley A.M. rector for 28 years d.1778. [1]

Dr. George Gaskin came as minister in 1791 and was also a prebend of Ely then took up the living at Stoke Newington in 1797 (whilst retaining St. Benet's). He was secretary of the *Society for Promoting Christian Knowledge* for 37 years, being well known in this role and distributed numerous Bibles then died at Stoke Newington in 1829.

However, the church was demolished for the site value and to widen the street which curved to meet the new London Bridge in 1868. A sum of £24,000 was realised and this helped build St. Benet's, Mile End Road while the parish passed to All Hallows opposite. Other items such as the pulpit (1685) went to St. Olave's, Hart Street and the font to St. George in the East. Just to the south was St. Benet's Place which now has a plaque.

---

[1] Rev. James Townley (1715-78) published *High Life Below Stairs* a farce in two acts in 1759 viz. Act II Scene I - KITTY "Shikspur, Shikspur, who wrote it, no I never read Shikspur!" LADY BAB "Then you have an immense pleasure to come." - Quoted by James O'Donnell Bennett in *Much Loved Books* (1928) when discussing *Hamlet*. Rev. Townley also published *False Concord* in 1764 performed once at Covent Garden, but his son in law J.P. Roberdeau claimed this was plagiarised by George Colman and David Garrick in *The Clandestine Marriage* of 1767.

St. Dionis Backchurch

A short distance to the east at the corner with Lime Street was a church named for St. Denis patron saint of France, but unlike the famous basilica north of Paris with its flying buttresses and perpendicular ambulatory, this was rather small. Regarding the epithet of backchurch this referred to its location down Lime Street behind a row of shops.

The mediaeval structure was rebuilt in the reign of Henry VI the main benefactor John Bugge whose arms appeared in the quire, whereas the south chapel or aisle dedicated to St. John was added soon after by John Darby an alderman in 1466.

There were a number of memorials including those to several mayors viz. Hugh Witch 1461, Sir Thomas Curtes pewterer fishmonger 1557, Sir James Harvie ironmonger 1581 and Sir Edward Osborne clothworker 1583. There were further repairs in 1629-32 when the middle aisle was re-laid and the steeple received a turret and bell frame, while Peter a man of Indian ancestry was baptized there under James I in 1616.

However, the church burnt down and was rebuilt as an irregular quadrilateral by Wren in 1670-86 with the aid of many benefactors. An alley between the shops led to a stone tower at the southwest corner with balustrades and small turret, and the aisles had low flat ceilings. Another feature was the east façade on Lime Street with pediment, pilasters and round arch window - as at St. Lawrence Jewry and St. Michael's Wood Street.

The interior received many adornments including a communion table from Sir Anthony Ingram, marble font from Sir Henry Tulse, commandments and woodwork from Philip Jackson and a velvet carpet and prayer book from Sir Robert Jeffreys.

Dr. Nathaniel Hardy preached there from 1643 and initially supported the Presbyterian faith, thus he attended the Treaty of Uxbridge an attempt to end the Civil War. But after being convinced by Henry Hammond &c. he went to The Hague to meet Charles II and became Royal chaplain, the Dean of Rochester and rector of St. Dionis in 1661. After he died in 1670 his widow Dame Elizabeth married Sir Francis Clark of Ulcombe, Kent and they donated £30 and £50 apiece towards the reading desk, pulpit and "Clark's pew" in the rebuilt church (also see St. Martin in the Fields).

Later memorials included those to Sir Robert Jeffreys mayor d.1703/04 president of the Bethlem and Bridewell with almshouses in Shoreditch; and Dr. Edward Tyson d.1708 a physician at the Bethlem, comparative anatomist and fellow and curator of the Royal Society. A Renatus Harris organ was installed at the building in 1724 and Dr. Charles Burney father of Fanny, Madame d'Arblay was organist in 1749-51.

However, the church then became redundant and was demolished in 1878, and the parish passed to All Hallows Gracechurch. A plaque marks the site and there is a parish marker in Philpot Lane dated 1888, next to one for St. Andrew Hubbard. Other significant items were dispersed as follows:

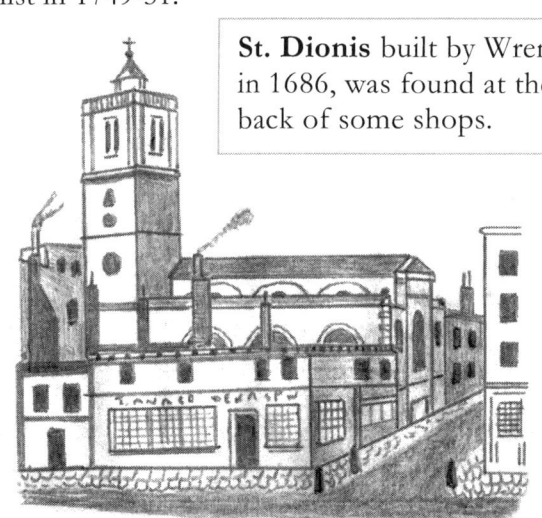

St. Dionis built by Wren in 1686, was found at the back of some shops.

All Hallows - bells, fittings and memorials
St. Edmund, Lombard Street - organ casing and the 17th century Royal coat of arms
St. Mary Aldermanbury - vestry door pediment
St. Dionis, Parsons Green (1884) - font with a cover in shape of the church, and the pulpit

St. Gabriel's, Fenchurch Street

But what of the watery surrounds of Fenchurch? Stow believed that the name derived from some fenny or moorish ground pertaining to the long brook which once ran across to Lombard Street. However, other opinion suggests it came from *fœnum* in reference to the hay, herbs and grasses sold there. Rocque's map recorded St. Dionis with the epithet of "back" by the Pewterers Hall with a small herb market behind - however St. Gabriel's was located right in the middle of the street like at St. Mary le Strand. [2]

This was a small church and Helming Legget gave his house and garden to the rector Sir John Hariot for a churchyard and parsonage at the end of Edward III's reign in 1476. It received some new bells in 1552 but had no memorials of note, and was extended in length and repaired at a cost of £537 in 1631-32. Nearby was Denmark House where the Russian Ambassador was lodging at the time of Queen Mary I.

However it was not rebuilt after the fire and according to Stow "whereby the street is made the fairer." The parish was united to St. Margaret Pattens in 1670 and then passed to St. Edmund's in 1954 and St. Mary Woolnoth, while the churchyard in Fen Court was retained with some of its old memorials. More recently it received some *modern art* due to its links with the latter, and a plaque marks the site in Fenchurch Street.

Fen Court (St. Gabriel's)

A bicentennial sculpture, regarding the abolition of the slave trade, was unveiled by Archbishop Desmond Tutu in September 2008. It records the role of Rev. John Newton and sermons at St. Mary Woolnoth. The plaque is nearby on the main road.

Bridge Ward

The ward commonly known as Bridge (Within) was centred on London Bridge and went north on either side of Fish Street Hill, up as far as Lombard Street. Within its bounds were four churches including the three detailed below and St. Benet's situated at the far north end, which was already discussed in the previous section.

A short distance up Fish Street Hill on the west side was Crooked Lane, so named for its windings, and just above here was a great stone house once the residence of Edward the Black Prince, son of Edward III. In the time of Stow this was a hostelry with a sign

---

[2] The Pewterers owned the site in Lime Street from 1484 and halls were built in 1496 and 1670 but it fell out of use and was demolished in 1932. They moved to Oat Lane near the Guildhall although the company still owns the old site and retains some of the oak panelling.

The Monument
by Wren located on
the east side of Fish
Street Hill, and…

London Bridge
from St. Saviour's,
Southwark in 1616.

the Black Bell and nearby was Bell Yard. This was immediately opposite the Monument and is now partially covered by the underground station, while the area to the east in the vicinity of Pudding Lane still contains a number of alleyways and courtyards.

Regarding the antiquity of the bridge there is evidence of a crossing in Roman times and a wood construction at the time of Ethelred in the later 10th century, whereas Peter de Colechurch built the first stone bridge with arches and a chapel in 1176. The Archbishop gave 1,000 marks towards this and it was completed in 1209, however there was regular rebuilding and numerous houses were added to the solitary chapel over time.

The maintenance of the bridge was regulated by the Bridge House Estate situated at the south end near to St. Olave's church, and John Reinwell mayor built a stone tower and drawbridge at the north end in 1246. This was for defence and access to Queenhithe. In fact a similar structure was later inserted at the Southwark end.

Eventually the bridge and its twenty arches was covered with large houses, one of these virtually a palace known as Nonsuch House, and this was how it remained until the late 16th century. However, there was a fire at the north end in 1632 due to some coals left carelessly by a maid, and this section remained empty until it was rebuilt with some fine properties in 1645. It was likewise repaired and re-inhabited after the Great Fire with two mills at the northern end - which did not affect the flow of water. [3]

Then, in commemoration of this event, one of the landmarks of the City was built in Fish Street Hill. The Monument was erected by Wren near to the King's bakers on the site of St. Margaret's in 1671-77, and was 202 feet high surmounted by a flaming urn as suggested by Hooke. The plinth had a *bas relief* by Caius Gabriel Cibber showing *liberty, architecture* and *science* directing Charles II and his brother James in the rebuilding. In fact the Doric column of Portland stone also had astronomical and scientific aims.

---

[3] The bridge like the gates into the city caused serious congestion over many years and all the houses were removed in 1758-62, while the two central arches were replaced by a single span. A new bridge was designed by John Rennie to the west with five arches and new approach roads in 1831, this being replaced by the modern bridge of Mowlems in 1967-72. The old bridge now a tourist attraction sits proudly at Lake Havasu City, Arizona (a new town of 1964).

St. Leonard's, Eastcheap

This church was on the east side of Fish Street Hill by Talbot Court at the junction with Gracechurch Street while Great and Little Eastcheap went across the top. It was known as Eastcheap Corner being near to an important meat market and St. Leonard's was also called *Milk Church* after William Melker who was its mediaeval builder.

There were few extant monuments except those to Walter Dogget vinter sheriff 1380 and John Dogget d.1456 who donated lands to the church and various coats of arms. In the past there was a memorial to Thomas Riggeley rector d.1432 and several to grocers, ironmongers and butchers whose hall was nearby after the fire. Despite such a lack of memorials, the rectors were studious in their writings and one of these efficient scribes inserted a note in the parish records dated 17th December 1599:

In this booke are registered all and singular suche mariages, christnings and burialls which have been donwth in the parishe churche of St. Leonard's neere East Cheape in London sithence the XXVth daye of October Ano. Dni. 1538 made in parchment as decreed by a canon of the Archbishop of Canterbury, the bishops of both provinces and parliament at Westminster, in the reign of Elizabeth copied from the original - signed Mr. John Hearde B.D. parson, John Wallington turner, Jno. Symson grocer

Of these the most significant was the baptism of Thomas Hood, son of a merchant taylor, in 1556 - although not to be confused with the poet. After training as a physician at Trinity College, Cambridge he was appointed mathematical lecturer for the City at the Staplers Chapel, Leadenhall (by the market) in 1588-92. During this period he developed astronomical charts and helped to promote Copernicus, whereas he lived at Abchurch Lane and the Minories then moved to Shrawley, Worcester d.1620.

The church was destroyed in the fire and the parish was joined to St. Benet's, although the churchyard remained squeezed in between Fish Street Hill and Pudding Lane (which has a parish marker). Today, a blue plaque in Eastcheap denotes the original site.

C. 23 June 1556 Thomas Hood sonne of Thomas Hood

St. Magnus the Martyr

This grand edifice stood sentinel east of the bridge from time immemorial hence their stories were intricately entwined. It dated to the 11th century but was dedicated to an earl and saint of the Orkneys from the next. Local traders included merchants, mercers and haberdashers on the Bridge, and fishmongers and grocers in New Fish Street, while the church once had numerous ancient monuments but most were utterly defaced.

These included Henry Yevele freemason to Edward III, Richard II and Henry IV who worked on Westminster Palace, St. Paul's, The Tower, sundry castles, Canterbury and St. Alban's cathedrals and St. Thomas's Chapel on London Bridge d.1400.

Other memorials were to John French baker and yeoman to Henry VII d.1510, Maurice Griffith Bishop of Rochester d.1559, Robert Harding salter sheriff d.1568 and mayors: John Blund 1301-07, John Michell 1436, Sir William Gerrard 1555 and Sir John Gerrard 1601. The father was born there but went to St. Christopher's, and he was a haberdasher and merchant adventurer in Africa and Russia "equal to the best of that time."

The church was initially held under charter by Westminster Abbey but then passed to Bermondsey, and the parish was compensated by the *Chapel on the Bridge* for loss of alms re travellers from the south. There was a series of senior rectors: Miles Coverdale (1564) author of the *English Bible*, John Young (1566) later Bishop of Rochester who employed Edmund Spenser, Theophilus Aylmer (1592) the Archdeacon of London and Cornelius Burges (1626-41) whose patron was Robert Rich, 2nd Earl of Warwick.

One of the most notable links was Ben Jonson (1572-1637), who attended St. Martin's and Westminster under William Camden then was a tradesman and soldier in Flanders. He returned in 1594 and married at the church (ref. Mark Eccles *1936*), whilst his wife possibly lived on London Bridge. Initially he acted with Henslowe in the Admiral's Men and wrote *Every Man in his Humour* in 1598, but fell out with Dekker over his satires and did masques for James I - receiving a pension and position of Poet Laureate.

Regarding the church it was lost in the fire and Wren rebuilt the nave on the remains of the walls during 1671-87, this being one of his major compositions. The style owed something to Alberti who restyled San Francesco, Rimini as the Temple Malatesta in the 1450s - although unlike the latter *prototype* St. Magnus was eventually completed.

The exterior was simple in design with plain side walls, round-arched windows and a clerestory level above with some oval apertures. The west tower was of Portland stone and had Corinthian pilasters, a pediment and balustrade at the top. Internally there were two rows of distinctive Ionic columns supporting a barrel vaulted ceiling, adjacent to the side aisles, a grand reredos and even grander pulpit to the south.

In general the church combined both Classical and Gothic elements whilst the steeple was added in 1703-06, comprising an octagonal bell turret surmounted by lead-covered dome with a cupola and short spire. The composition was clearly based on St. Charles Borromeo, Antwerp and was its principal feature when seen from London Bridge which was adjacent. A ring of ten bells was also inserted there in 1714.

Meanwhile, regarding punctuality Charles Duncombe was tardy for an appointment due to not knowing the time and lost his job as a result. He later became both a Knight and Mayor and resolved to rectify the matter for future apprentices. Thus he paid £184 for a clock with chimes on the tower in 1709, and also contributed an organ three years later.

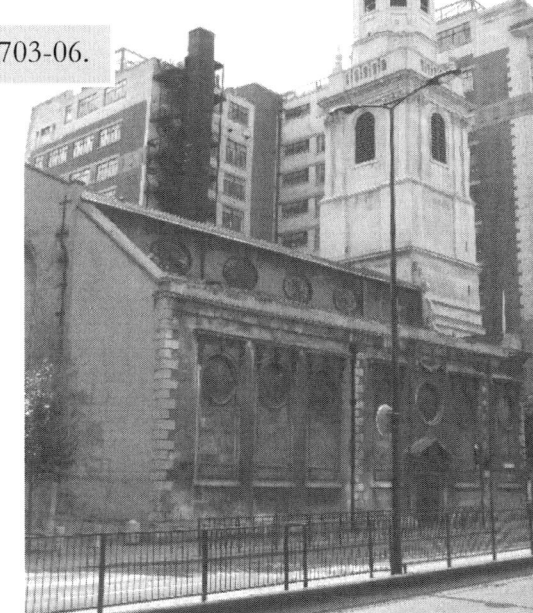

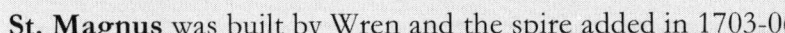

St. Magnus was built by Wren and the spire added in 1703-06.

216

St. Magnus - the footpath to the bridge and clock dated 1709.

The church then underwent a series of changes. The widening of the bridge in 1759-60 meant two end bays of the aisles were deleted (leaving one window instead of three), the north doorway was removed, and a footpath was inserted under the tower to the bridge. The north windows were made smaller due to traffic in 1782, whereas Thomas Rennell came as minister and was also of Sion College, Temple and Dean of Winchester.

At this point the church still had a commanding position then the bridge was moved west and the parish joined to St. Michael's, Crooked Lane (demolished) in 1831. But the greatest change came in the 20th century, a change from which the church architecturally never recovered. T.S. Eliot who worked nearby as a bank clerk mentioned the building in *The Waste Land* in 1922, recording "Its inexplicable splendour of Ionic white and gold," however he did not document the transition taking place outside.

Adelaide House, which thereafter dominated the west façade in unsightly fashion, was designed by Sir John Burnet during 1920-25. The latter partly owes its style to a trip he made to Egypt at the time, although its influence appears to be more Art Deco with its stark lineal façade, star shapes, and grand cornice. Little damage befell the church during the war but in reality the damage was already done by the developers.

In addition, shortly after T.S. Eliot's sojourn there was a major change to the interior as Martin Travers re-designed it in the neo-Baroque style in 1924. This was clearly with the Anglo-Catholic congregation in mind - with side-chapels and numerous ornaments.

Virtual Tour - At the entrance the main features are timbers from a Roman wharf found in Fish Street Hill in 1931 (dated A.D. 75), stones from the original London Bridge, and five parish markers on the tower ref. St. Magnus 1787/1847 and its two related churches. Inside there is a wooden vestibule with two 17th-century chests, while this is the livery church of the Coopers, Fishmongers and Plumbers (once of St. Michael's). Indeed, one of the ancient windows from the latter's hall was moved there in 1863.

The Catholic link is confirmed by an icon on the north wall painted in Moscow in 1908 and the Lady Chapel at the east end with its statue of *Our Lady of Walsingham*, built by Travers and associated with Father Fynes-Clinton rector in 1921-59. Moving across there are 17th century altar rails and a fine reredos by Grinling Gibbons - although the upper storey was added in the 19th century when the east window was bricked up.

The adjacent pulpit by William Grey dates from Wren's time; and behind are memorials to Miles Coverdale rector and Bishop of Exeter transferred from St. Bartholomew at the request of the Rev. Thomas Leigh in 1840. In the southeast corner is a font and cover donated by grateful benefactors in 1683, whilst the organ sits under an arch at the west end and was built by Abraham Jordan at the expense of Mayor Duncombe.

M. 14 November 1594 Beniamine Johnson and Anne Lewis maryed [Ben Jonson]

St. Margaret's, New Fish Street

The thoroughfare above the bridge was also annotated as Bridge Street, and the church was situated on its eastern side. Another street to the south (opposite to Crooked Lane) went through to what was termed as Pudding or Rother Lane.

However, there was little money spent on it and there were literally no monuments. As a result the parson Rev. Wood sent his clerk to request the presence of Mr. Stow, and there he was shown the figure of a man with the inscription Joannes de Coggeshal, citizen of Bridge Street, d.1384 - by St. Peter's altar on the north side. There were a few charities pertaining to the parish plus a parsonage house and Stow believed "it would be worthily trimmed and beautified," but it was not rebuilt after the fire and went to St. Magnus.

The land then passed to the City and the Monument was built on the site while a plaque just to the north records the church. For many years all the streets traversed the hill in a line including Fish Street Hill, Pudding, Botolph and Love Lanes, but Monument Street was built across them at an angle from the Square to Salutation Court after 1883.

Billingsgate

To the east of St. Magnus were a series of alleys (or quays) reaching from Thames Street to the river including Botolph's Wharf followed by Lyons, Somers and Smarts Quays. In addition there were several watergates giving free access to the city, and in this location was Botolph's Gate and just beyond Billingsgate Dock with its gateway and stairs.

The area comprised its own ward with the boundary passing north up Pudding Lane, then across just beyond Eastcheap, and south again in the location of Idol Lane. Within its bounds were the five churches listed below, whilst St. Dunstan in the East situated in the Tower ward is also covered here due to its close proximity.

There was an increased trade in fish, fruit and grain through the dock and generally it supplanted Queenhithe which was restricted by the drawbridge. A toll was charged for such goods entering from the time of Edward III, and an Act of Parliament made it a free market for the sale of fish in 1699. However after a violation of these rights where fish were resold thereby raising the price, Sir Robert Bedingfield (mayor 1706) stated that such actions were illegal and it could only be retailed elsewhere.

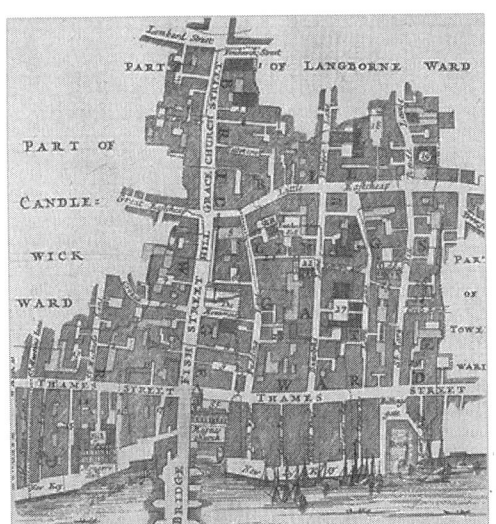

Billingsgate Market itself was erected on the dock by Thames Street in 1849, while Sir Horace Jones designed a new arcaded hall built by Mowlems in 1875. However the *market* relocated to Canary Wharf in 1982 and the property was refurbished as offices by (Lord) Richard Rogers.

Bridge and Billingsgate (Wards)
A map by Richard Blome dated 1720 after the earlier survey by Stow.

St. Andrew Hubbard

The church of St. Andrew's was on Little Eastcheap between Botolph and Lovat Lanes, its name derived from one from Hubbert a mediaeval benefactor. In a similar fashion the latter was originally Lucas Lane after its owner and corrupted to Love Lane.

Of its three minor benefactions the main ones were from the ironmongers and vintners, whilst it was repaired at a cost of £600 in 1630, but not a single memorial of note was recorded. Consequently it was one of the over thirty churches not rebuilt after the fire, and the site (which is to have a plaque) was soon put to optimal use.

The parish was transferred to St. Mary at Hill and some funds were used to pew that church, although Mr. Thomas White the incumbent of the latter gave £75 p.a. back from the coal money. The parsonage which was also burnt was seconded to the City, and the church ground was disposed of to public use with part being laid into the street.

On the remaining land a new King's Weigh House was built with an ante-room, piazza and stocks, whereas at the east end a parish vestry was added in 1693. At this location *merchant strangers* had their goods weighed to determine tariffs, and soon after this date they established an Independent or Congregational chapel in rooms above the building. The chapel was known as the King's Weigh House and its most famous minister was the Rev. Thomas Binney who was active in the area during 1829-69. [4]

After spending a brief time in Bedford and on the Isle of Wight he moved to London where he became known as the *Archbishop of Nonconformity*. He became prominent for his sermons and had a leading role in the British and Foreign Anti-Slavery Society.

London Bridge and its approaches were developed in 1831 and the Weigh House was demolished for road widening soon after, hence a new chapel for 1,000 people was built on the west side of Fish Street Hill in 1833-34. From there Binney was a leading reformer and the congregation included Samuel Morley a manufacturer, philanthropist and owner of the *Daily News* a radical paper. The latter started the Y.M.C.A. with George Williams in 1844, and became an M.P. under Gladstone and founder of Morley College. [5]

The south side of Eastcheap was demolished during the building of the Metropolitan Railway in 1882, and the site was then occupied by notable Victorian premises. Regarding this a year later Peek Brothers, tea and coffee importers, built extravagant new offices at No. 20 on the east side of Lovat Lane - just opposite the church site.

---

[4] A small beam to weigh corn was located at Aldgate from 1357 and Richard II appointed John Churchman of Wool Wharf, Tower Ward operator of "the great beam" in 1383. But such rights devolved to the Grocers and a new weigh house was built on the north side of Cornhill, east of Finch Lane, by Sir Thomas Lovell in c.1532. A dispute occurred between the City and Grocers over who owned these rights whereas the latter building was burnt down in 1666.

[5] On maps they were denoted as *Presbyterian Chapel* at Eastcheap in 1746 and the *Weigh House Chapel* at Fish Street Hill in 1862. The latter was compulsorily purchased by the Metropolitan Railway in 1882 and became Monument Station. Hugh Grosvenor, Duke of Westminster, then offered the site of a small chapel at Duke Street below Oxford Street, and a red brick Gothic auditorium with tower was built by Alfred Waterhouse in 1891. It transferred to the Catholics in 1967 retaining the cognomen of the King's Weigh House, then became the Ukrainian Catholic Cathedral. The adjacent roads were designated as Binney and Weighhouse Streets.

Billingsgate with open air market and inlet in the early 19th century... **St. Botolph's churchyard** now strangely referred to as One Tree Park.

The main feature was a circular tower at the corner with a relief by William Theed who produced the African group on the Albert Memorial. It depicted three camels travelling across the desert, led by a Bedouin, with a cargo of the finest coffee beans and remains today. An equally impressive structure (now Citibank) occupies the original church site whereas just opposite is Hill & Evan's vinegar warehouse at No. 33-35.

This was a notable red-white Gothic building by Robert Lewis Roumieu of 1868 and included a relief alluding to the Boar's Head Tavern. However the actual hostelry was at the top of St. Michael's Lane, Great Eastcheap - removed for King William Street. The latter featured in Henry IV, Part II pertaining to Prince Hal and John Falstaff and was visited by Washington Irving who wrote a sketch about it in 1819-20.

St. Botolph's, Billingsgate

Two other edifices were situated in the immediate vicinity of Botolph Lane leading down to the river from Eastcheap, and at the southern end by Thames Street was the church of St. Botolph's. The name arose from its location near a watergate or entrance to the city and was first mentioned as early as 1181.

Thomas Snodland the parson gave lands and tenements by his will for a chaplain and brethren confirmed in 1370. In addition there were a number of bequests and memorials of note (now gone) viz. John Rainwell fishmonger mayor 1426 d.1445 who gave a stone house to the church, Stephen Forster also a fishmonger mayor in 1454, several sheriffs and Christopher Langton a doctor of physic d.1578.

Much of the parish was inhabited by "strangers" including those from the Netherlands reducing the income received by the City, and in general the most expensive properties were near to the river. In fact another Boar's Head on Thames Street paid for a chantry and was sold by William Sanderson in the time of Edward VI for £2,668.

The church was repaired in 1624 but was destroyed with the parsonage in the fire, and despite plans to rebuild it the land went to Sir Josiah Child. He then laid the chancel into the ground to improve Thames Street and access to Botolph's Wharf. A house was built on the site and rents received, whilst the parish passed to St. George's. The churchyard above was enclosed and remains at the junction by 31-35 Monument Street.

B. October 1602 Thomas Morley [a secular composer and organist of St. Paul's]

St. Dunstan in the East

The mediaeval church was built in about 1100 and was situated at the junction of Idol Lane and St. Dunstan's Hill. This was a large parish stretching from Fenchurch Street to the river, a peculiar of the Deanery of the Arches with many rich merchants, including ironmongers and salters. It was noted that "the church was of ancient building" and its status was revealed by a large number of extravagant monuments.

These included general ones (both extant and defaced) pertaining to John Kennington parson d.1374, William Islip parson d.1382, Alice Brome wife of John Coventry mayor d.1433, John Rycroft sergeant to the larder of Henry VII/VIII d.1532, Edward Waters the sergeant at arms d.1558, Sir John Hawkins the treasurer of the Navy d.1595 and the family of Sir Henry Billingsley haberdasher and mayor 1596.

In addition this might have been termed the *Mayors Church* there being a large number of such worthies recorded: Sir Bartholomew James 1479 a generous benefactor south of the chancel, William Hariot 1481 d.1517, Sir Richard Champion 1565 all of them drapers; Sir Christopher Draper ironmonger 1566 d.1580 with alabaster memorial, Sir Wolstane Dixie skinner 1585 and Sir William Webbe salter 1591 d.1599.

Not surprisingly the building was richly repaired with walls of Portland stone in a large churchyard in 1632, and for the most part survived the fire being patched up in 1668-71. However Wren rebuilt the tower in Gothic style with a spire of flying buttresses to match the old church in 1697, and Lady Dionys Williamson of Hales Hall, Norfolk paid £4,000 towards the repairs. Her grandfather Richard Hale d.1620 had a memorial there as did Sir John Moore the mayor and president of Christ's Hospital d.1702.

Due to this composite nature it was in a poor state by the 19th century and was rebuilt (except for the tower) by David Laing and William Tite in the Georgian perpendicular style from 1817-21. Severely damaged in the war it was left as a ruin, but the walls were repaired and part was a private chapel within the parish of All Hallows, latterly housing a charitable foundation. The gardens were laid out as open space with "folly ruin" in 1971 and this exotic location became a prime site for avant-garde filming.

Local Buildings - Just east of the church was the Bakers Hall on Hart or Harp Lane, the livery company dating to 1155 and claiming to be the second oldest. Initially they had a tenement at Dowgate but moved to a mansion, once owned by John Chicheley the Chamberlain of London, in 1506. This had a banqueting hall, minstrels' gallery and fine gardens with vines leading down to the river but was replaced three times after the fire. The modern hall occupies the original freehold site in Bakers Hall Court. [6]

Immediately behind the hall sat Trinity House amongst the tenements between Harp and Water Lanes. This was established by Capt. Thomas Spert at Deptford in 1514, its primary aim to regulate pilots and protect the coastal waters. The main office was moved to Water Lane in 1660 - but rebuilt after the fire and in 1714. A new building was then designed by Samuel Wyatt on Trinity Square in 1796. In fact, Great Tower Street and Thames Street were only joined together at the end of the 19th century.

---

[6] John Chicheley was the son of William a grocer alderman. His uncles were Robert Chicheley mayor in 1411/21 and Henry Chicheley (1364-1443) the Archbishop of Canterbury.

St. Dunstan in the East (ruins) by lane and hill, and parish marker of **St. George's** in Botolph Alley.

To the south of Water Lane was the Customs House established in 1275 but replaced in 1378/59. Wren rebuilt it in commodious fashion after Charles II paid £10,000 in 1671, but it was destroyed by fire in 1715 and Thomas Ripley provided the "Long Room." A much larger structure by architect David Laing then replaced this, immediately to the east of Billingsgate, in 1813-17.

St. George's, Botolph Lane

An explorer walking up the modern Botolph Lane arrives at a paved alleyway passing over it, whilst to the left is St. George's Lane and on the north side stood St. George's. Nearby is Pudding Lane with a plaque recording the shop of Thomas Farynor, the King's baker, where the fire started in September 1666. This was erected by the Bakers Company on the 500th anniversary of their charter (which was first granted in 1486).

The mediaeval church of *St. George's in Estchep* was first mentioned in the 12th century and restored in 1360, then again beautified in 1627. There was a parsonage house, some minor benefactions and chantries. Despite being small there were also well-preserved memorials: Adam Bamme mayor 1396, William Combe stock fishmonger sheriff d.1452 a church benefactor, Richard Dryland steward to the Duke of Gloucester d.1487, William Forman mayor 1538 and James Mountford surgeon to Henry VIII d.1544.

After the fire it was rebuilt by Wren using stone from its defunct neighbour St. Botolph's during 1671-76. It had a barrel-vaulted nave, plain exterior, three round-headed windows and square tower surmounted by urns at each corner. The cost was £4,466 but the lanes and alleyways nearby were often dirty and slippery due to the fish trade &c.

The most significant later connection was William Beckford who was born in Jamaica in 1709 and made a large fortune from plantations. However he was educated at Westminster and as an ironmonger was an alderman for Billingsgate ward in 1752, then M.P. for the City two years later. From his residence at Soho Square he represented the Whig interest in particular sugar in the West Indies, whilst he backed Pitt the elder and John Wilkes. He was mayor in 1762/69 but died at the latter date and on the south side of the church was an ironwork scroll "to that real patriot" with his coat of arms. [7]

However, the last service took place in 1890 and the parish passed to St. Mary at Hill (with 17th century Royal arms) and the unstable church was demolished in 1904.

---

[7] William Beckford married Maria d. of George Hamilton M.P. and their son William Thomas (1760-1844) was M.P. for Wells, a novelist, art collector and builder of Fonthill Abbey.

St. Margaret Pattens

The church was dedicated to Margaret of Antioch and the first wooden building was erected by 1067, whilst there was also an annotation *Near the Tower*. The name of St. Margaret de Patins first appeared in 1275, and referred to pattens or wooden shoes sold nearby to raise the wearer above the muddy streets. The building was on the east side at the junction of Eastcheap and Rood Lane and just beyond was Idol Street beside Little Tower Street. The latter intersection was straightened in the late 19th century.

For a brief time Richard Whittington held the patronage, then it passed to the Mayor and Communality in 1411. However, the mediaeval building fell into disrepair and was rebuilt from 1530-38. A rood or cross was erected in a tabernacle for devotion and gifts were left, but this idol was broken up by persons unknown on the night of 23 May 1538. In addition several treasures were lost in the Reformation, although the name survived as Rood Lane, and the church was repaired at £275 during 1614-32.

There were only a few memorials including those to Mr. Reginald West B.D. parson in the chancel d.1563, Richard Glover pewterer twice the master of that company d.1615 and Mr. Giles Vandeput a merchant of Antwerp d.1646.

However, the old church and parsonage burnt down in the fire and the churchwardens visited Wren, "to put him in mind of the building of the church." Suitably chastened he carried this out at just under £5,000 from 1684-87. The west façade sat up against Rood Lane and there was a high rectangular nave, north and west galleries, and arched/round windows to the south. At each end there were larger windows with pediments.

Two lead water-heads on the north wall have the date "1685," and an impressive steeple was added at the northwest corner using coal tax money from 1699-1703. It is the only surviving example of a lead-covered timber spire by Wren being similar to St. Antholin's. The land of St. Gabriel's was added in 1670, and Sir Peter Vandeput gave £100 gift to the poor of the parish. There was an ornate memorial on the south wall of the chancel in memory of Peter Delmé who was mayor in 1723.

Of the rectors, Thomas Birch was born into a family of Quakers and coffee dealers at Clerkenwell, but married Hannah Cox daughter of the curate of St. Botolph's, Bishopsgate. As a result he was baptized at St. James's, Clerkenwell in 1730 and was a priest the next year, whilst as a friend of Sir Philip Yorke was tutor to his son. He was rector of Epsom and held the living of St. Margaret's from 1746, then as a member of the Royal Society and secretary of the Antiquarians wrote biographies and court histories. After his death in 1766 his library and manuscripts were donated to the British Museum. [8]

The church was damaged during the war and was restored in 1955-56 at which time the north gallery was converted to lecture rooms. However it is basically a Wren building and has a light old-fashioned atmosphere, much original woodwork, gallery steps and ancient memorials. Upon re-opening it was designated as a guild church, being associated with both the Basketmakers and Pattenmakers who have windows there.

---

[8] The list of rectors notes Robert Drew M.A. 1727, Thomas Birch D.D. FRS 1746 and Peter Whalley D.D. 1766. A memorial on the west wall records Ms. Penelope Birch d.1828 relative of Thomas, also Ann Birch descendant of Willhelmus de Birches who obtained arms by taking the standard of France at the Battle of Poitiers (1356) d. MDCCI.

The main access is through the south door where there is a vestibule and inside are original canopied pews reserved for the churchwardens - the only such examples. Above the door are the Royal arms of James II and in the west gallery is an 18th century organ case. The reredos displays a painting by Carlo Maratta (1625-1731) depicting Christ with two angels, and a fine pulpit and "eagle" lectern are located on the south side.

Outside, there is a row of 18th-century houses which obscure the south façade, while the spire reaching 200 feet matches those seen at St. Bride's and St. Mary le Bow. A road bollard by the main doorway displays the inscription "1817 St. M.P."

B. 14 Jan'y 1766 Rev. Dr. Thomas Birch under the Rev. Mr. Browne's stone, chancel

St. Margaret Pattens with Georgian shop-fronts and Wren interior... however the environs are much changed. A tea and rubber market (of 1935) is now Plantation Place (2004), while the first sky-scraper built at 20 Fenchurch Street in the 1960s will become the incremental "Walkie Talkie."

St. Mary at Hill

A number of churches claim to be *The Most Authentic Wren* including St. Margaret's, St. Benet's and St. Mary Abchurch, but none claim the most historic location. However, if an award were given for this particular class then the gold would surely go to St. Mary's secreted down a cobbled alley, reclining beside a hidden courtyard, with an idiosyncratic façade - as if trying to squeeze itself out from the surrounding buildings.

This was located on an ascent just above Billingsgate with the main entrance in Love Lane and a small private passage on the south side. It was first recorded as *Sanctee Mariae Hupenhulle* in 1177 being adjoined to the town house of the Abbots of Waltham Abbey thus the abbot's kitchen was to the south. The edifice was enlarged at the end of the 15th century with aisles on each side and a spire, the work paid for by the wills of John Phillip a priest of the church and Robert Revell one of the sheriffs (1490).

Sir William Leman donated £40 for a divinity lecture, and Thomas Tallis was organist from 1538-39 when there was a fine choir. There were also memorials to several mayors: Nicholas Exton fishmonger 1386, William Cantbridge 1420, William Remington 1500, Sir Thomas Blanke 1582 (and Dame Margaret), and Sir Cuthbert Buckle 1593.

Other commemorations were to Anne wife of Thomas Wilson master of St. Katharine's d.1574 and William Holstocke Esq. comptroller of the Queen's ships (at the time of the Armada). There was also a chapel to St. Katharine and in the parish a chantry entitled the *Septum Cameræ* with a priest to pray, but suppressed under Edward VI. The old church was much decayed and repaired in 1616 then again once every four years.

Not all of the building was destroyed in the fire and Wren built a new one in 1672-77 but retained the mediaeval tower and the side walls. This work was probably supervised by his colleague Robert Hooke who definitely designed the western rooms beneath the tower. In fact, due to its variegated nature the total cost came to just £3,980.

The interior, similar in design to St. Anne and St. Martin Ludgate, was exquisite in its execution with a shallow partitioned dome and entablatures on four Corinthian columns, the latter notable for their fluted slender scale. The west gallery stood on pillars and the organ went above, while the windows were round-headed and a blank wall took the altar at the east end. In general, there was a Greek cross plan with barrel vaults around the dome, except for the west end and tower which were quite separate.

One of the most famous connections was Edward Young who was born at Upham in 1681, his father later the Dean of Salisbury. He was educated at Winchester and Oxford and was nominated to the law at All Souls by Archbishop Tenison. As a poet his works included *On Lyrick Poetry, An Apology for Punch, Epistles to Mr. Pope* and *Night Thoughts* whereas he dedicated them to patrons and also produced plays. By 1728 he was a Royal chaplain with a college living at Welwyn and married Lady Elizabeth Lee, but spent much of his remaining life in quiet retirement d.1765. He was in fact portrayed in a letter sent from his curate John Jones to Dr. Thomas Birch (of St. Margaret's). [9]

Edward Young (1681-1765) was a poet and dramatist of high renown.

St. Mary's has "one of the least spoilt interiors" according to John Betjeman.

[9] Elizabeth Lee was the daughter of the 1st Earl of Lichfield and initially married her cousin Col. Francis Lee. A daughter Elizabeth married Hon. Henry Temple son of 1st Viscount Palmerston and grandson of Abraham Houblon, Governor of the Bank of England, in 1735. Henry was married secondly to Jane daughter of Sir John Barnard M.P. mayor and their son Henry (1739) became the 2nd Viscount and was an M.P. and fellow of the Royal Society, whilst their grandson was Lord Palmerston (P.M.). Elizabeth the wife of Edward Young died in 1740.

St. Mary at Hill - showing the east façade, tower on Lovat Lane and enclosed courtyard.

However, the church required a number of renovations and a spire was added in 1695 but George Gwilt the elder carried out major repairs in 1787 including a new brick tower, west façade, south wall, vault, and ceilings. The walls were restored in 1827 and after a fire James Savage did further repairs replacing the woodwork and box pews in 1848. It also survived a threat to be demolished for the railway in the later 19th century.

The church had been filled with the music of Tallis and Mundy in earlier years and had a resurgence under Wilson Carlile, the rector from 1892-1926. He was born at Brixton in 1846 and became successful in business attending the Plymouth Brethren at Blackfriars, then became influenced by the American evangelist Dwight L. Moody in south London. As a result he was ordained in 1880 and appointed curate at St. Mary Abbots. He tried to make the church accessible to the poor and left to do mission work in the slums (with parish permission), consequently he started the Church Army in 1882.

This grew to become the largest mission society within the Church of England and St. Mary's was its base. Rev. Carlile played the trombone and led a band around the nearby streets on a Sunday - filling them up with music. Likewise, fish porters and shop girls came there to eat and watch lantern shows (according to their shifts). On occasion, the latter visits caused some people in the church considerable displeasure.

There was little damage to the building in the war and the parish then covered a large area including St. Andrew Hubbard (1666), St. George's and St. Botolph's (1904), and St. Margaret's and St. Gabriel's (1954). A serious fire took place in 1988 and much today is from a restoration, while its William Hill organ of 1848 is the largest in existence.

A stone carving from the gateway of St. Giles in the Fields (c.1600) is by the south door and nearby is the rectory dated 1834 with a Wren vestry. However, the church bells are retained at Whitechapel due to the prohibitive cost of restoring them. Further down St. Mary at Hill is the hall of the Watermen and Lightermen of 1780, the only Georgian survivor in the City. In fact Thomas Doggett an actor and owner of Drury Lane funded a race for watermen with Wilks and Cibber from 1715.

M. 6 January 1709/10 Phillip Gray married Dorothy Antrobus [parents of Thomas poet]
4 August 1730 Edward Young chaplain and ye honourable Elizabeth Lee (see text)

Tower Ward

The precincts of the Tower of London were extra-parochial, and the open expanse of Tower Hill, mostly to the north, was a liberty - all outside the jurisdictions of the City. In latter years there was some encroachment around Coopers Row and the Minories, and three wards reached to the boundary viz. Aldgate, Portsoken and Tower Street.

Regarding the latter ward this started at Billingsgate, travelled along the south side of Fenchurch Street then came down to the area of Trinity Square and past All Hallows to the Thames. In fact the modern ward has given up some land in the west and taken in parts of Aldgate and Portsoken. Three churches lay within its boundaries: namely All Hallows and St. Olave's plus St. Dunstan's (already discussed), while those of Coleman and Staining are included here due to their proximity.

Between Billingsgate and the Tower there were a large number of wharves however the Queen was defrauded of her customs. As a result it was newly decreed *where goods could be landed* in 1559, including Billingsgate for fish, Three Cranes (Dowgate) for wines and oils, the Bridge House for corn and *sundry other wharves* for general merchandise.

In addition "strangers" could only be based at the Steelyard and no other landing places were to be used from Gravesend up to London Bridge. The maritime nature of the ward was secured by the presence of the Customs and Trinity Houses in its bounds; however the main feature of the environs was clearly the imposing Tower of London.

The original White Tower at the centre was begun by William the Conqueror in 1078 and today stands defiant as an ambivalent monument to times of conflict. In one sense it represents pageantry, history and Royal achievement but in another Norman oppression, Governmental power struggles and an instrument of subjugation down the ages. In fact one person's traitor would become a hero and martyr under the next regime.

Stow summarised the role of this great fortress in lucid terms: "This Tower is a citadel to defend or command the city; a royal palace, a prison, the only place of coinage, an armoury, a treasury of ornaments and jewels, and the conserver of ancient records of the law from Westminster." It was also a regal menagerie from the time of Henry III.

The Tower - A 15th century print with London Bridge just behind. Also a map dated 1597 which omits the City housing but shows All Hallows and the town ditch.

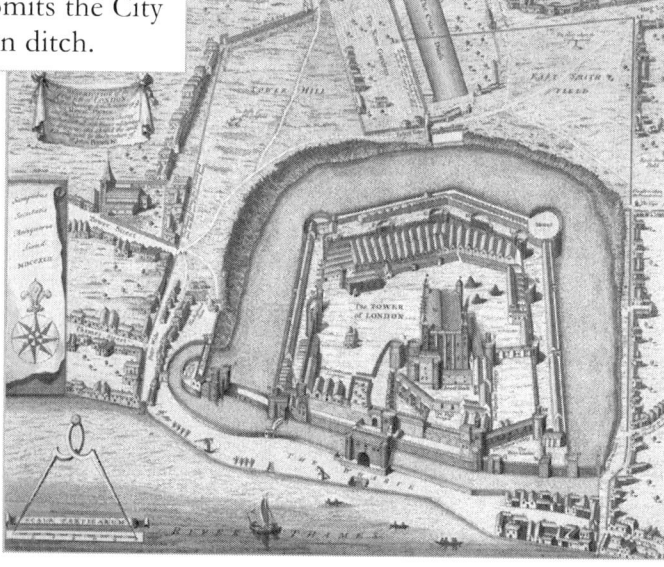

Regarding its religious institutions the White Tower contained the Chapel of St. John built in c.1080 with its Romanesque ambulatory reminiscent of St. Bartholomew's; while the church of St. Peter ad Vincula (or in chains) was situated to the northwest. The latter chapel was built just before the *Magna Carta* in c.1210 and provided "a parish" for those within the precincts and in areas of encroachment on Little Tower Hill.

At the time of Henry III it was quite spacious with chancels to St. Mary and St. Peter and Royal persons retired there for devotions. It was then restored at the start of the 14th century. However, it was burnt down in 1512 and rebuilt by Sir Richard Cholmondeley the lieutenant of the Tower in 1519-20. The new chapel was a small flint building with brick tower and lantern, while the nave and aisles were supported on slim columns and inside were several memorials. These included the builder d.1521, Sir Richard Blount also a lieutenant d.1564 and Captain Valentine Pyne master gunner of all England d.1677 as well as those to Royal and religious persons who suffered there.

St. Peter ad Vincula was a most appropriate saint for "**the chapel in the tower.**"

The chapel sits just left of the *Beauchamp Tower* - named for Thomas the Earl of Warwick who was imprisoned there by Richard II from 1397-99. He was restored to his lands and title under Henry IV.

Strype in his survey recorded only the later memorials - including those above, whilst he noted that the Chapel of St. John was ascended by a great number of steps. Inside it was found to be most *darksome* with venerable pillars of a plain order, "but now only used as a repository for old records, where they lye in dust and confusion."

Much of its darker history is well documented but the Tower also had several prisoners whose sojourn is far less obvious. In fact, the Knights Templar were imprisoned there in 1308 followed by those dissident notaries William Penn (1669), Samuel Pepys (1679) and that "great defender of freedom" John Wilkes (1764).

Other significant events to be recorded were the melting of the Crown Jewels during the Commonwealth, the imprisonment of those *involved* in the Popish Plot, repairs by Wren in 1694, movement of the Royal Mint to East Smithfield in 1810, imprisonment of the Cato Street gang, the closure of the menagerie in 1834, the draining of the moat in 1843, and restoration of the chapels: St. John's in 1857 and St. Peter's in 1876.

All Hallows Barking

Erkenwalde Bishop of London founded an abbey for his sister Ethelburga at Barking, Essex in 666, and the church was established on abbey-land beside the Tower in 675. It was one of the first churches in the City, being on the east side of Seething Lane with Tower Street below. There was a large churchyard beyond the chancel, and its extensive parish for the tenants of the abbey stretched right down to the river. [10]

Richard I established a chapel on the north side in the 12th century, then Edward IV licensed the Earl of Worcester to promote a fraternity which held lands at Streatham, Totingbroke and Okeborne. Richard III rebuilt this chapel in the mid-15th century with a college of priests and Robert Tate mayor 1488 was buried there, but this was suppressed by Edward VI and demolished - being replaced by a garden then a storehouse.

The edifice also had a chapel to St. Mary and was repaired with new furnishings in 1613 and a gallery was installed in the south aisle in 1627. However the church and tower were nearly destroyed when gunpowder exploded at a ship chandler's shop on the south side in 1649. Ten years later the spire was reconstructed in brick with new tiles, a dial over the street, and a sixth bell - the roof being a v-shape timbered construction. Pepys climbed the tower to observe the fire and the church itself was only saved when Admiral Penn demolished nearby housing to create a firebreak.

The memorials included those to Nicholas Bremisgrave 1416 and Thomas Vyrby 1453 early vicars, Humphrey Monmouth draper sheriff 1535 a promoter of the *English Bible* who harboured Tyndale and left money for Bishop Latimer &c. to preach there, William Thynne master of the household to Henry VIII 1546 and other Tudor servants, several merchants of the staple (of Callis), various knights and earls, and the initial resting place of Archbishop Laud before he was removed to Oxford.

On the west side of the church was Sydon or Sything Lane [sic] and here were located some prominent households. Sir John Allen mayor, privy councillor to Henry VIII, built a house which went to Sir Francis Walsingham, the Earl of Essex and Sir Nicholas Salter, and nearby was the residence of Sir Edward Sharington forfeited to the Earl of Arundel. In addition there were a number of charities and the church held tenements in the parish, at St. Martin Vintry, and thirdly at Bermondsey Street, Southwark.

After surviving the fire the church was little changed down the years and a free school was established there by Alderman Hickson in 1692. Dr. John Gaskarth and others then paid for it to be paved with Portland stone and for two new portals during 1701.

Charles Young the famous composer was organist there from 1713-58 and his daughter Cecilia a top soprano married another composer Thomas Arne (see Covent Garden) - his other daughters Hester and Isabella were also singers and on the stage. Afterwards came his grandson Charles J.F. Lampe son of Isabella who was organist from 1758-67.

The building was restored by J.L. Pearson in 1894-95 and a two-storey perpendicular porch was added on the north side - to face the newly created Byward Street. The latter joined Thames Street to Tower Street and went immediately north of the church.

---

[10] Barking Abbey was dissolved in 1541 and the site was then used as a quarry and a farm; while today the curfew tower remains beside the parish church of St. Margaret's, and the foundations of the abbey are situated next to an industrial estate.

All Hallows - the east end with uneven aisles, arcade detail and Gibbons' font cover.

The mediaeval church had survived the fire and ravages of time but was destroyed by a bomb in 1940 with only the 15th-century outer walls still remaining. These were retained when it was rebuilt by Lord Mottistone in 1949-57, and a new perpendicular nave with an arcade and clerestory windows was inserted between the broad aisles. The ancient tower at an angle to the church had survived, but the original cupola was replaced by a Baroque copper-clad ogee-topped spire (of Wren style) in 1959. It was probably the worst part of the restoration. The parish of St. Dunstan in the East was also added after the war.

In more recent times the main associations were with Albert Schweitzer who did organ recordings there, and Rev. Phillip T.B. Clayton ("Tubby") vicar from 1922-62 who has a memorial. With Rev. Neville Talbot he started a rest home for soldiers called Talbot House behind the lines at Poperinge, Belgium in 1915. This was affectionately known as "Toc H" after its call sign and had no social or denominational distinctions, then was continued at Kensington and around the country from 1919.

The Church Today - All Hallows by the Tower remains a striking building steeped in history. Indeed, its copper-clad spire, Gothic perpendicular windows, and rustic brick are a prominent landmark when observed from Tower Hill.

Inside there are seventeen brasses dating from 1389-1651 and there is a brass rubbing centre, while the copious windows illuminate the high nave and its ancient walls beyond. Just south of the entrance is the baptistry with an exquisite Grinling Gibbons font cover dated 1682 - which originally cost just £12. Meanwhile, its initial wooden base went to Christchurch, Philadelphia in 1697 to commemorate the links with William Penn.

In the south aisle are stained glass coats of arms to the Drake family, and a memorial to Charles de Beauvoir 1702 of Seething Lane and the Customs House. The vestry itself was restored in memory of Walter Clifford Northcote and his family.

However, the most significant attributes are found in the crypt and undercroft which were repaired after the bombing. There is a 2nd century Roman pavement, a Saxon-arch of Roman bricks and a Norman pillar also some pre-Conquest art, and at the far end an altar from Athlet, Israel brought to London by the Knights Templar. There is likewise a memorial to William Penn erected by the *Pennsylvania Preservation Society* in 1911.

All Hallows Barking parish registers

C. 1555 Lancelot Andrewes - s. of Thomas master of Trinity House, Thames Street
25 October 1644 William the sonn of William Pen and Margaret his wife (tablet outside)

M. 26 July 1797 John Quincy Adams Esq. of Boston in the U.S. North America and Louisa Catherine Johnson o.t.p. by licence by John Hewlett B.D. in presence of James Brooks, Joshua Johnson, Joseph Wall, Thomas Beldain and Catherine Johnson

William Penn (1644-1718) - Admiral Sir William Penn came from Bristol and was appointed commissioner of the Navy Board in 1660 and thus worked there with Pepys his neighbour. His son William was born at Tower Hill and educated at Oxford then spent time in Paris and Ireland, looking after the family estates, becoming a Quaker at the latter place in 1666. He produced a number of pamphlets against the Church but under increasing persecution he suggested a colony for Quakers, thus Pennsylvania (Penn's Forest) was established by charter under Charles II in 1681. He invested much money and travelled there to help establish the colony, having territorial conflicts with Lord Baltimore, but died penniless and was buried at a Quaker meeting house near to Chalfont St. Giles, Bucks.

John Quincy Adams (1767-1848) - John Adams came from Braintree, Massachusetts and after going to Harvard was a member of the Continental Congress signing the Declaration of Independence in 1776. He was an envoy to Europe from 1788-82 and was the 2nd president after George Washington. His son was born at Braintree (now Quincy) and accompanied his father overseas, then was minister to the Netherlands and Portugal in 1794-96 and to Prussia in 1797-1801 - being married at All Hallows in 1797. His bride was the daughter of Joshua Johnson an American businessman who promoted Maryland mercantile interests in Europe from 1771 (and first U.S. Consul in London) and Catherine Nuth an Englishwoman. Adams was elected to the Senate in 1802 and became the 6th President in 1825-29, while his wife Louisa was the only first lady to be born outside the United States.

William Penn

John Quincy Adams

All Hallows Staining

Just to the north of Tower Street were Mincing and Mark Lanes, and at the top of the latter on the west side was another All Hallows. This was at the far end of Langbourn ward and had a churchyard with the Clothworkers Hall behind. The Ironmongers were a short distance to the north between Fenchurch Street and Billiter Square. [11]

The church was first mentioned in the late 12th century and according to Stow its name derived from the use of stone, when other ecclesiastical buildings were mainly of timber. One of the first benefactors was John Costin girdler d.1244 whose name was etched in the roof and left tenements and charcoals to the poor. There were a number of early memorials in this small edifice including Sir Robert Test and Dame Joan 1487, Sir John Steward and Dame Alice, Sir Richard Tate ambassador for Henry VIII d.1554 and Sir John Wriothesley principal king at arms and several members of his family.

Despite surviving the fire it was in a weakened condition and almost fell down on the sexton, thus it was rebuilt using mediaeval foundations and materials from 1674-75. The vestry was paid for by Sir John Fleet an alderman and the font by John Ince an attorney, whilst the east window was given by the Grocers who were its patrons.

However, the main church was demolished in 1870 and the parish transferred to nearby St. Olave's, whereas the Clothworkers restored the tower in 1873 and removed the 12th century crypt from Lamb's Chapel to the site. The surviving tower has a two-light west window with cinquefoil (14th century), although the lower parts may be earlier. In fact, the northwest stair turret of the same date once led up to a higher storey.

Regarding the more recent history, Fenchurch Street station was opened just opposite on London Street in 1841, and its current façade was added in 1858. St. Olave's operated a temporary church on the site during repairs in 1948-54, and the Clothworkers built a hall for the parish beside the ancient tower in 1957.

B. 31 October 1656 Steeven Batchiller minister in new ch'yard [of New England] [12]

---

[11] The Clothworkers owned the site at Dunster Court on Mincing Lane from the 15th century and were formed by the joining of two smaller companies in 1528. They had some prominent masters viz. William Huett 1543 mayor, Adam Winthrop 1551 grandfather of John Winthrop first governor of Massachusetts, William Lamb(e) 1569 founder of Sutton Valence school and builder of a conduit across the fields, and Samuel Pepys 1677 who recorded the halls destruction in the fire. There were also new buildings in 1856 and in classical style after the war.

The Ironmongers had a charter in 1463 and bought a property in Fenchurch Street, their third hall being built there in 1745. However, this was damaged in the First War and was demolished thus the company moved to a new site at Shaftesbury Place, Aldersgate Street in 1922.

[12] Stephen Bachiler attended St. John's, Oxford, then was vicar of Wherwell, Hants in 1587-1605 but was deposed for Puritan leanings and resided at Newton Stacey. He married Helena Mason the widow of the incumbent of Odiham, whose daughter Mary married Richard Dummer of Bishopstoke, and was a member of the Company of Husbandmen in 1630. The two established the Plough Company to send settlers to the New World and purchased land in Maine. But only Dummer made any money, and Bachiler arrived in Boston in 1632 then established Hampton in New Hampshire in 1638-39. He was also a missionary and returned to England in c.1651 while his descendants included presidents Richard Nixon and Gerald Ford.

St. Katharine's depicted in the 1800s and gates/plaque.

All Hallows, Staining
(Mediaeval Tower).

St. Katharine Coleman

The church was at the east end of Fenchurch Street on the south side down Magpie Lane with the churchyard in between - just below the parish of St. Kath Cree. It came under the Aldgate ward and at one time there was a Jewish synagogue nearby, whilst there was a dedication to All Saints although this was changed at an early date.

One Coleman had a large haw or garden in the precincts of Holy Trinity priory and was the likely mediaeval builder. Nearby was Blanche Appleton manor on Mark Lane where the basket-makers worked, and Northumberland House home to Earl Henry Percy at the time of Henry VI - later converted to tenements and used for bowling and dice.

There were only a few monuments but Mr. Wright "the learned parson" showed Stow a window in the south aisle to William White mayor 1489, and they both concluded he was "the builder of the aisle." Others were to Henry Webbe Esq. usher to Henry VIII d.1552, Sir Henry Billingsley mayor d.1606 who left money to the poor and had a dwelling there, and David Doeringk with connections to the Elector of Saxony.

The church was improved with a new vestry and gallery for the poor in 1620-24, then after escaping the fire was repaired in 1703 under Thomas Harper the rector. However this was replaced with a new structure in the Georgian style by James Horne in 1739-40. It was built in the Wren tradition and manner of Gibbs but was plain with a square brick tower, thus it was demolished in 1925. The memorials and vestry-panelling went to St. Olave's, although the churchyard and its 18th century gates remain (with plaque).

C. 20 April 1720 John son of Hannah and Robert Thornton [13]

---

[13] Robert Thornton merchant banker married Hannah Swyncocke on 18 September 1716 and had children baptized at St. Andrew's Holborn and St. Nicholas Cole Abbey. Their son John a merchant lived in Clapham and was involved in gospel ministry through anonymous donations and buying of hymn books - with links to Whitefield and the Countess of Huntingdon.

St Olave's, Hart Street

At the northwest corner of Hart Street and Seething Lane was a church dedicated to Olaf the King of Norway, who had helped Ethelred the Unready stop the Danes in 1014. But today it is more rightly remembered as *The Church of Samuel Pepys*.

The building was first mentioned in 1222 but has a well of an earlier date and a groin-vaulted crypt from its rebuilding in 1250. However the current edifice generally dates to 1450. Richard Cely a wool merchant d.1482 held the advowson at this time and was the principal builder leaving money for the tower and altar, his arms in the roof. It was built in the perpendicular style with an arcade of three bays by the aisles, columns of Purbeck limestone, a large east window, wooden-beamed roof and small stone tower.

Despite being of restricted size there were several prominent connections as revealed by its memorials which included: John Clarentiaulx the king at arms d.1427, Sir Richard Haddon a mercer mayor d.1524 brass (*north aisle*), Phillip van Wylender musician of the privy chamber to Henry VIII and Edward VI d.1553, Thomas Beckingham merchant of the staple of Callis d.1565, Sir John Radcliffe knight in armour *fragment* d.1568 and Dame Anne his wife, Sir "Jacobus" Deane of Hackney a benefactor d.1608 (*south chancel*) and Paul Bayning Esq. a relative of Viscount Sudbury d.1616.

Another significant monument was to William Turner physician, church reformer, and natural historian on the southeast wall d.1568. He studied at Pembroke Hall, Cambridge coming under the influence of Latimer and Ridley then was made doctor of physic to the Duke of Somerset, protector to Edward VI. After writing books against Rome he went into exile travelling in Germany and Italy but was restored to the Deanery of Wells - then wrote an early book on birds and his famous *Herbal* in the 1550s.

The church itself was greatly decayed and there were significant repairs costing £437 in 1631-32. These included a new middle-aisle roof, windows and frames, and two galleries at the lower end on each side. In addition there was a dial erected over the street.

Admiral Penn and Samuel Pepys helped to save the church from the fire by blowing up adjacent houses, thus the building has remained little changed since mediaeval times. The later memorials included Elizabeth Pepys d. Nov. 1669 (*north chancel*) above Bayning, Sir Andrew Riccard eminent Levant merchant and E.I.C. chairman d.1672 a statue of white marble (*north aisle*) both by John Bushnell, Sir John Mennes of Sandwich comptroller of the Navy Office under three Stuart Kings d.1670/71 (*south chancel*), and Rev. Daniel Mills the rector of thirty-two years at the time of Pepys d.1689.

A brick top was added to the tower in 1731-32, and other features are a 15th century door-case, low-pitched roof (1632), old vestry (1662) and Grinling Gibbons pulpit from St. Benet Gracechurch. In addition the 17th century gateway inspired the name of "St. Ghastly Grim" in the *Uncommercial Traveller* by Dickens, whilst a clock was received from All Hallows in 1870 and some panelling from St. Katharine Coleman in 1921.

However the building was gutted by fire in 1941 and much of the interior, which had little division between the nave and chancel, dates from the renovations. The church was re-dedicated in the presence of King Haakon VII of Norway on 15 June 1951, since he had worshipped there during the war - and a tablet in the nave records this fact. Finally a new organ was installed in the western gallery by the John Compton Co. and a modern rectory was inserted just north of the tower.

Samuel Pepys - The diarist was born at Fleet Street in 1603 the son of John a tailor, and attended St. Paul's and Magdalene, Cambridge his relative Dr. John Pepys being a fellow. He had links to Huntingdon and his future was secured through Richard Pepys M.P. of the Exchequer and Sir Edward Montagu 1st Earl of Sandwich both cousins.

Initially he joined Montagu's household and married the young Elizabeth de St. Michel of a Huguenot family at Westminster in 1655, then worked as a teller in the Exchequer at Whitehall under George Downing (the street being laid out in the 1680s).

Regarding his diary it was started after the death of Cromwell as Gen. Monck marched from Edinburgh to London, and Charles II returned to England from the Netherlands. The Restoration occurred on 29 May 1660 and Montagu became an admiral and an earl, whilst Pepys was appointed secretary to the Navy Board on 13 July at a beneficial salary of £350. He also moved to official accommodation in Seething Lane.

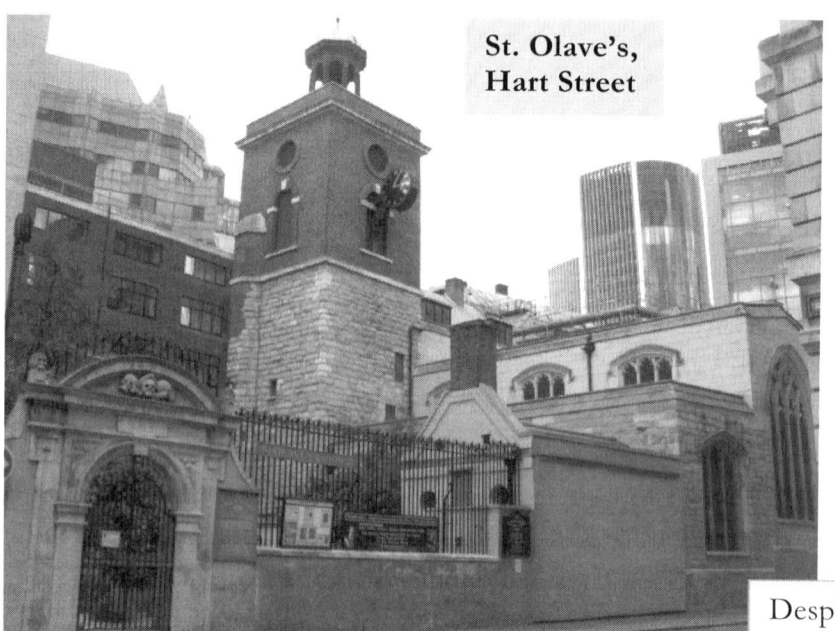

St. Olave's, Hart Street

Despite the city location John Betjeman deemed it to be "a country church."

In general he was more able than some of his senior colleagues Penn, Carteret and Batten and played an important role being involved, through Montagu, in the short-lived colony at Tangier. These were turbulent times thus his diary chronicled major events in particular the Anglo-Dutch war which placed much pressure on him, the plague in 1665 when his wife was evacuated to Woolwich, and the Great Fire of London.

However it also considered the more minute details of domestic life and talked of his genuine relations with his wife, bawdiness with a servant and companion Deborah Willet, and contrition and remorse over this and drinking of wine. Being cultured he became a fellow of the Royal Society and entered into correspondence with Newton, whilst he was an accomplished musician and composer who taught his wife to sing.

Meanwhile, the Navy Office was a considerable distance from the Admiralty and his diaries recorded how he travelled to Whitehall on a regular basis. His wife Elizabeth died after the fire in 1669 but he improved his position and was secretary to the Admiralty, an M.P. for Harwich, master of Trinity House, a benefactor to Christ's Hospital school, and president of the Royal Society in 1684-86. He had an island named after him in the South Atlantic in error (later found to be part of the Falklands), and after his imprisonment as a Jacobite he retired to Clapham where he died in 1703. [14]

Samuel Pepys (1633-1703)

.... **Memorial** by Sir A. Blomfield c.1883 - his exhaustive diary was evocative of the Stuart era.

John Watts - He was born in New York in 1715 and became a wealthy landowner and benefactor to the hospital and library sitting on the Council from 1757. His brother-in law and partner Oliver Delancey was also a Loyalist and joined the militia, but Watts left for England during the revolutionary war in 1775. His memorial is located on the south wall of St. Olave's and states that, "He was president of the Council of New York and North America when that country was subject to British Government d.1789."

His son, also John Watts (1749-1836), remained overseas as a lawyer in opposition to his father's beliefs, and was a member of the New York State Assembly in 1791-93 and of Congress from 1793-95. He was involved in a commission to build Newgate Prison in that city and was buried at the Anglican Trinity Church on Lower Broadway.

The Crutched Friars - Ralph Hosier and William Sabernes established the crouched or crossed friars in three tenements owned by Stephen tenth prior of Holy Trinity at 13s 8d p.a. in 1298. They were recorded as *Fratres Sancta Crucis* and took a permanent building south of Hart Street opposite the church from Richard Wimbush twelfth prior in 1319, and they also held land at Aketon [Acton] and Waldingfield in Suffolk.

There were several memorials at the friary including to Sir Thomas de Mollinton 1408, Sir Thomas Asseldey clerk of the Crown, sub-marshall of England and J.P. for Middlesex

---

[14] Henry Benjamin Wheatley (1838-1917) DCL CSA was the editor of the first complete edition of *Pepys Diary*, and through his efforts a memorial to Pepys with his portrait in a garland was erected on the south wall in 1883. The entrance to the Navy Office Pew in the south gallery was mentioned in his diary and has a memorial tablet dated 1891 outside (see p.209).

and John Rest grocer mayor 1516. In addition Sir John Milborne draper mayor 1521 was a benefactor and asked for 13 bed-men of the adjacent almshouses to pray for his soul at mass and was buried there, then at St. Edmund's, Lombard Street.

Early in the reign of Henry VIII, the Common Council granted *the prior & convent* land to enlarge their church in return for prayers, but there were serious problems at a latter date. During a visit by Barthelot, a representative of Cromwell - the Vicar General, the prior was found not at his devotions but in bed with a whore at 11.00 in the morning! To compound matters he gave the said Barthelot a sum of £30 and promised a like sum, such events no doubt hastening the dissolution of the monasteries.

Consequently the order was suppressed by the King in 1539 and no ruins of the friary remained, except for a street name. In its place were built the noble Navy Office, some other fine residences, a carpenter's yard and several tennis courts.

The Navy Office - This was located opposite the church in Seething Lane and was built on land occupied by the Crutched Friars, and latterly by Lumley House, in 1656. In this respect the Admiralty's role was to take strategic decisions, while the Navy Office carried out the day to day running of ships, provisioning, and employment of seamen.

When Pepys arrived at Seething Lane the building was new however it was rebuilt after a fire in 1674-75, and was demolished when they removed to Somerset House in 1788. The land was then taken by the extensive warehouses of the East and West India Dock Company, with a Corn Exchange on Mark Lane. A new Trinity House with a green in front was also built just to the east by Samuel Wyatt during 1796.

The Port of London Authority who controlled the docks replaced the warehouses with a monumental structure by Mowlems in 1919. The area to the rear then became a garden and Pepys Street was inserted behind Trinity House, and a plaque there records, "Site of the Navy Office in which Pepys lived and worked destroyed by fire 1673."

C. XVI th November 1585 Elizabeth the d. of Sir Phillip Sidney knight bapt.
XXII th Januarie 1590/91 Robert Lord Deveraux sonne and heir of Robert Earl of Essex in the Walsingham house ... Doctor Andrewes preached and baptized the child [15]
8 March 1669/70 John son of Mr. William Docwra and Miss Rebecka his wife bapt. (also five other children from 1670-77)

B. 9 June 1703 Samuel Peapis Esq. in a vault under communion table
21 August 1789 John Watts Esq. in the middle chancel vault

---

[15] Sir Philip Sidney (1554-86) courtier and poet of Penshurst married Frances Walsingham the daughter of Francis "the spymaster" of Elizabeth I in 1583. Their child Elizabeth was born at Walsingham House and the Queen was her Godmother at the baptism, while the father died at Zutphen, Netherlands and Frances married Robert Devereux in 1590. Dr. L. Andrewes had the patronage of Walsingham and was elevated to senior positions (see St. Giles).

Renaissance by Comparison

When discussing church architecture in London it would be remiss to consider it as a separate entity, or to analyze its attributes in isolation, since from the earliest of times there was a strong influence from the Continent. In the first millennium masons and builders were limited by the knowledge available - thus churches were often of wood or had a single nave with solid walls and meagre openings.

The central problem was how to create a significant span but at the same time provide an enclosed space for the protection of those inside. Much of the building expertise from the ancient world was unavailable and without superior techniques was literally useless, since open temples were unsuited to the inclement weather of northern Europe! Another factor was the mandates of the Christian religion, whose style of worship would dictate building forms down through the centuries.

When considering Saxon architecture there are few cases in London due to the great changes which took place there, thus the best examples are found in the provinces such as Sompting with its impressive tower, Bradford on Avon once preserved as a barn, and that outlying cell of Bradwell-on-Sea in Essex. Regarding architectural style in religious buildings one might simplify matters into six distinct phases:

1. Norman or Romanesque introduced after the invasion of 1066
2. The Gothic style with its three forms brought to England in c.1180
3. Italian Renaissance of the 15th century first seen in Elizabethan times
4. Baroque classical style used by Vanbrugh, Wren and Hawksmoor
5. 18th century Neo-Classicism   6. Victorian Gothic Revival

At the outset Norman design was connected to expansionist aims, hence robust castles with their motte and bailey were built to subjugate the residents. As an expression of the permanence of this new relationship, old wooden churches were swept away and stone edifices erected in their place. This period witnessed evolution from an austere single cell to walls and towers with round-arched arcades and intricate ornamentation.

Good examples can be seen at the Chapel of St. John in the White Tower and the nave of St. Bartholomew the Great, once part of an extensive monastery. In these - solid stone piers, an ambulatory behind, dark spaces amongst the arches, combined with grooved and toothed ornament - provided a suitable mediaeval ambience.

However, in a similar fashion to the wheel the major breakthrough was the development of *the pointed arch*, which took a greater load and allowed increased spans and more light. It was an innovation that altered the course of church architecture, and was adopted by the monasteries and priories whose buildings reached ever nearer to God.

Parish churches and grand cathedrals around the country display all three Gothic styles of *Early English* with its simple groin vaults, *Decorated* with its ribs and bosses, and the more prevalent *Perpendicular* with its soaring lines and fan-vaulting. These were brought to England by the Plantagenet rulers as seen at Westminster Abbey; then introduced to priories and parish churches in the capital by its abbots, priors and priests. The result was a series of majestic edifices - although few survived the vicissitudes of time.

The next developments came in Italy during the 15th century as architects employed the techniques of those great empires Greece and Rome. Here they combined functionality with a desire to create perfect forms - reflecting spiritual ideals and aspirations. Various City States vied for prominence in trade and artistic grandeur, thus Milan led the way in terms of the Romanesque and Siena was instigator of the Gothic.

However, some of the most significant buildings were in Florence and Santa Maria del Fiore "the Duomo" was begun in Gothic style in 1296, but its dome the crowning glory was completed by Brunelleschi during 1420-36. Its bell tower by Giotto and extravagant marble exterior was then duplicated in basilicas of monastic orders viz. San Lorenzo with Corinthian arcade by Brunelleschi (1419), Santa Croce by di Cambio (1294-1442) with a 19th century façade, and Santa Maria Novella with entrance by Alberti (1456).

Apart from these four great churches there were other buildings of significance such as the Pitti Palace in Romanesque style, the Palazzo Vecchio begun by di Cambio, Palazzos Strozzi and Medici Riccardi, and *Hospital of the Innocents* at the Piazza St. Annunziata by Brunelleschi - although parts of this square were built at different times.

This witnessed the birth of the Renaissance with its arcades and classical columns; but the greatest influence was Andrea Palladio (1508-80), a native of Padua, who studied in Vicenza and Rome. His talent was recognized at a young age and wealthy benefactors promoted his work in the Republic of Venice, while he rediscovered classical principles of Vitruvius who laid down five orders and dimensions in the 1st century B.C.

Palladio then wrote *I Quattro Libri dell' Architettura* (Four Books of Architecture) with descriptions and diagrams that inspired generations of classical architects. However, his real monument was his basilicas in Venice, palazzos in Vicenza, and impressive villas in the countryside nearby. The most significant of these was undoubtedly the Villa Rotunda designed for Canon Paolo Americo in 1566-71, but completed under Vincenzo Scamozzi his protégé from 1580 - then owned by O. and M. Capra from 1591.

Villa Capra or **"Villa Rotunda"** located near to Vicenza, Italy.

Designed by A. Palladio for a local canon, this country house combined with his other works to provide inspiration for many British architects. One example was the Earl of Burlington who built Chiswick Villa.

The Roman Baroque

St. Susanna by C. Maderno and nearby St. Carlo by F. Borromini with their distinctive *Two Tiers* pre-empted designs in London during the late 17th century.

Often known as the Villa Capra it embodied Vitruvian ideals bringing architecture into harmony with the natural surroundings through the use of columns, pediments, domes, refined scale and Roman adornments. However, this was just the beginning and several palazzos were built in Vicenza including the Barbaran and Thienne by Palladio, whilst his influence was transferred to the wealthy trading city of Venice.

Here was the Doge's Palace in the Gothic style and San Marco cathedral in Byzantine form, supplemented by a large number of churches with classical facades - including San Giorgio Maggiore and Il Redentore by Palladio and Santa Maria della Salute by his pupil Longhena. The latter three were built in thanks for deliverance from the ravages of the plague and created an arc of churches at the mouth of the Grand Canal.

Following on from Florence and its Tuscan leadership, and Venice, Vicenza and the work of Palladio, came the architectural sponsorship and religious authority of the popes in Rome. Not only was this the City of Caesar Augustus and the Roman Empire but it was the centre of Western Christianity - with many heathen sites transmuted into basilicas and churches. It was clearly a major rival to London. Within its bounds on the banks of the Tiber were some 120 churches, mostly built in the Renaissance, their classical façades literally growing from the crumbling ruins of the decadent empire.

Structures such as the Roman Pantheon *For Every God* became Santa Maria Rotonda, and the Baths of Diocletian became Santa Maria degli Angeli. This assimilation of the old order was seen around the city and another example was San Nicola in Carcere with its façade by della Porta - the very columns incorporated in its walls. Other churches were simply erected within the Forum, and the twinned Santa Maria di Loreto and Santissimo Nome di Maria created a dramatic backdrop to Trajan's Column.

For many centuries the pope resided in the Lateran Palace by the cathedral of St. John Lateran to the east, whilst a second great basilica Santa Maria Maggiore was nearby. But Pope Gregory VIII commissioned the Quirinal Palace on a central hill in 1583 and it was a main residence and base for the Papal States until 1870. From here these mightiest of benefactors employed leading architects to design churches in the latest of styles.

Of these, one of the smallest but most significant was the Tempietto part of San Pietro in Montorio west of the Tiber, designed by Bramante for the Spanish monarchs in 1502. Despite its small size it symbolised the Renaissance with its pure Doric columns, dome and perfect proportions. But by comparison, St. Peter's basilica was an ancient Christian site and its rebuilding was initiated by Donato Bramante in 1506.

This was indeed a cause célèbre and a number of papal architects continued the work down the years, unlike St. Paul's mainly designed by Wren, an arrangement that took its toll. Raphael and Michelangelo then worked on the project after Bramante. The dome of concrete and pumice was completed by della Porta in 1590, the elongated façade by Maderno in 1612, and the sweeping grand piazza by Bernini in 1656-67.

However the Roman idealism and purity of the Palladian style gave way to something far more expressive and individualistic by the early 17th century. In fact it was during the Baroque era that the Renaissance could be said to have come of age. Good examples of this being St. Susanna on the Piazza San Bernardo with its façade by Maderno 1603, the nearby St. Carlo alle Quatro Fontane with its four fountains by Borromini begun 1634, and another of his works St. Ivo Alla Sapienza a chapel of the university 1638. The latter had a distinctive spiral tower which was later reproduced in Copenhagen.

Italian Influences on London Churches

After the Restoration there was a period of stability with a renewed interest in cultural affairs therefore many artisans and gentlemen embarked on the Grand Tour. One of the high points of this experience was to visit Florence, Rome and Venice thereby receiving inspiration and instruction through their architecture and antiquities.

The Romans with their Greek influence had already made an impact in Londinium and St. Peter's, Cornhill claimed to date back to that era. Indeed, the city's division into wards reflected the twenty *Municipi* around the Palatine Hill in Rome. Other links were the Lombard goldsmiths from northern Italy who helped establish the banking industry, and the Gregorian calendar which was assimilated into British time.

There was a long list of prominent travellers and Inigo Jones who went there in the late 16th century was the first to bring Renaissance architecture back to Britain - his works including the Queen's House, Greenwich and St. Paul's, Covent Garden with its Italian piazza. Many leading architects studied in Italy and Rome down the years including the Earl of Burlington, George Dance the younger, James Gibbs, Thomas Archer, Thomas and Philip Hardwick, Henry W. Inwood and Ambrose Poynter.

In fact, these visits were not transitory in nature. After spending several years learning their art under famous teachers and armed with portfolios of classical design, they came to London and touted for business. Although, Wren who went no further than Paris, and Vanbrugh and Hawksmoor who trained at home, were not inhibited in any way since they looked to the published designs of Palladio and others for inspiration.

The Renaissance was not just about architecture since it affected every aspect of design and artists, writers, sculptors and antiquarians followed in their wake; then embellished the churches that the former had created. Regarding such categories these included Anthony Munday, John Talman, F. Nollekens, L. Roubiliac (inspired by Bernini), Flaxman, Byron, Keats, Shelley, Charles Burney, Ld. Leighton, James Haliburton, William Hazlitt and the writer E.M. Forster who immortalised Florence with its roomy view forever.

Such obsession with *all things classical* was typified by Edward Gibbon who after a time in the militia travelled to Rome in 1763, then declared, "I can neither forget nor express the strong emotions which agitated my mind as I first approached and entered the eternal city, and after a sleepless night I trod, with a lofty step, the ruins of the Forum." After descending from several days of intoxication he embarked on minute and sober studies, and it was amidst the ruins of the Capitol, as vespers were sung in the Temple of Jupiter, that he formulated plans for *The Decline & Fall of the Roman Empire*. It was then published in six volumes from 1776-78 and like the empire itself was an epic work.

Such examination and scrutiny were then turned into reality and the tierceron and lierne of the Gothic were replaced by the entablature and triglyph of the Classical. However the decorative marble of Florence with its transitional architecture and the purity of Palladio with its orderly lines, were not in vogue when London was rebuilt. At this time Wren was the City Surveyor and the style he adopted was the Baroque, which he implemented to rebuild the great cathedral and many of its one hundred churches.

Vanbrugh and Hawksmoor supported him in this with similar schemes, and adopted a *theatrical approach* to architecture, the style being retained by the Commission for Fifty Churches in the 18th century. However, there were several differences between London and Rome, differences that set them apart. The former had Gothic towers and spires in their designs but seldom used two-tier façades, while steeples were nearly always absent in Rome. This was a disparity that clearly made comparisons quite difficult.

Secondly - London churches with their arcades, shallow chancels, box pews and pulpits were meant for preaching, a style emanating from the Reformation and its Puritan zeal. A style exemplified by the great churches of East London but still in the classical tradition. However, growth of the Tractarians and conversions of Manning and Newman wrought great changes - out went the pulpit and pew - and in came Catholic forms of worship combined with Ritualistic chancels, reredoses, and lavish ornamentation.

In tandem with this the new churches of West London abandoned any pretence towards the classical and took on the form of mediaeval edifices - good examples being found at Chelsea, Paddington and Kensington. In fact, Salviati of Venice worked on the latter thus bringing three hundred years of development full circle. The influence of the Tractarians and the Oxford Movement in church design must not be under-estimated.

Florence Duomo (1296-1436)

The skills used to build the Pantheon and Hagia Sofia had been lost in time thus models helped in the design.

St. Peter's, Rome (1505-90)

A multitude of architects worked on the basilica for the Papal Office but the façade added by Maderno conceals the dome.

The Pantheon (126) and **Temple of Venus (135-41)**

These famous antiquities of Rome inspired designs for St. Stephen's Walbrook and All Hallows, London Wall.

However, returning to the inspiration of the Renaissance we are drawn to that ultimate expression of classical style, first seen in the Pantheon two thousand years earlier. Namely St. Paul's Cathedral and its dome - a true masterpiece. Like the churches in Rome it has a two-level façade, whilst its dome improves on Florence with its brick and support rings and on St. Peter's with its archaic concrete and pumice. Wren's inspiration was to use a cone to brace the outer skin and cupola - with a false ceiling inside.

Regarding the interior, both premier cathedrals have an arcade of Romanesque arches with grand crossing and transepts. But St. Peter's remains less satisfactory. After the time of Michelangelo and della Porta their successor Carlo Maderno extended the nave and added a Baroque façade - its "attic" reminiscent of a stately home with dome subjugated behind. However, Wren, with his overriding control in one period, developed St. Paul's into a more satisfactory exemplification of the Baroque aspiration.

Following on from this we consider his City churches and St. Stephen's Walbrook with its own dome can be seen as a practice run for the cathedral. Exquisite in the extreme, it was one of his finest creations and the resemblance to the interior of the Pantheon, built some 1,500 years earlier, soon becomes apparent on examination.

In similar fashion, St Benet Fink beside the Royal Exchange was based on St. Andrew Quirinal near the palace of that name in Rome. This was built by Gian Lorenzo Bernini from 1661-70, its façade returning to the simplicity of Palladio with Corinthian pilasters, a grand pediment and semi-circular porch. Such simplistic lines contrasted with the more extreme Baroque of St. Carlo and St. Susanna, just a short distance away down the Via Quirinal. St. Benet's was begun immediately the former was completed, and followed its basic plan - in particular, by replicating the oval layout used for the nave.

Meanwhile, the most extreme incorporation of classical architecture in modern design came at the hands of George Dance the younger. He travelled to Italy to study at various academies in 1758 and his first commission was to redesign All Hallows, London Wall, whilst he succeeded his father as surveyor for the City Of London in 1768.

All Hallows was in a small space between the Roman walls and main road, and had a plain idiosyncratic façade, but inside was its true glory which was a real gem. The Temple of Venus in the Forum by the Colosseum was designed by Hadrian in 135-41, and was attached to a basilica with tower - but its columns disappeared and only the temple back remained. It was a replica of this design that he used for the chancel of All Hallows, and a similar scheme was implemented at St. Botolph's, Aldersgate in 1788-91.

Such copying of style took place in London and across Europe thus the church of St. Magnus, a prominent edifice dominating London Bridge, used patterns from two other significant buildings. The Franciscan church of San Francesco in Rimini dated back to the 13th century, but its transformation was planned by Alberti after 1450. His patron S. Malatesta, a nobleman, wanted it for his personal church, but after conflicts regarding territory with the Pope only the lower façade was ever completed.

This became known as the Temple Malatesta and its single level, round-arched features and squat pediment over three bays was repeated at St. Magnus. However, that was not all since the steeple of the latter was inspired by that of St. Charles Borromeo in Antwerp (or Sint Carolus Borromeus). The Belgian churches of that period often looked back to their roots and so there was a double link discernible in this instance.

Pieter Huyssens had worked for the Jesuits in Maastricht and also studied in Rome thus he built St. Charles for the order in 1615-23. The main feature was a notable decorated façade on three levels next to a square, this being similar to Il Gesu, Rome by Vignola and della Porta finished in 1551 - the latter a model for Jesuit churches around the world. In fact Rubens contributed to the paintings and the incongruous tower at the west end, and it was this soaring element that was replicated at St. Magnus in London.

St. Andrew Quirinal, Rome (right) - Wren travelled to Paris in 1665 and met G. Bernini architect of the church. It thus provided the blueprint for St. Benet Fink.

St. Charles Borromeo, Antwerp (above and left) designed by Huyssens and Rubens gave inspiration for the impressive steeple of St. Magnus in London.

The Commission for Fifty Churches

When considering architects who studied in Italy none are more significant than James Gibbs (1682-1754) who was born in Aberdeen to a Catholic family. Initially he attended the Marischal College but transferred to Scots College in Rome, to train as a priest, in 1703. Perhaps inspired by its great heritage of architecture he gave up this line of work after a year and entered the studio of Carlo Fontana, remaining until 1709.

His mentor was one of the great Baroque architects of the day designing several of the major churches in the city, and provided Gibbs with grounding in the style of Wren and Hawksmoor, which he then brought back to London. Gibbs soon did his most notable work, St. Mary le Strand which emulated the Baroque of Rome, and its neighbour St. Martin in the Fields developed from the grand neo-Classical school of Palladio.

St. Mary's was built by the Commissioners with input by Gibbs during 1714-23 and the final design betrayed a number of influences. The architect was dismayed by changes he had to implement, since it was meant to be Italianate with a basic campanile at the west end. However, due to problems of costing and site, it eventually had the standard steeple rising above a two-tier façade - with semi-circular porch and niche statues.

San Marcello al Corso with its façade by architect Carlo Fontana who was the teacher of Gibbs. The latter studied the genre and used it in his design for St. Mary le Strand.

Trajan's Column in the Forum with S. Nome di Maria (1736-41) behind. A replica is in the V & A, whilst it is similar to the Monument by Wren.

Regarding the exterior, Gibbs studied San Marcello al Corso near to the Piazza Venezia with its façade by Fontana, and for the porch looked to Santa Maria della Pace situated in a warren of alleys behind the Pantheon. The portico of the latter was re-designed by Pietro da Cortona in 1656-67 and was a significant building with prominent semi-circular porch at the lower level - supporting a series of pilasters and pediment above.

However, the two bear no resemblance in terms of their location. Santa Maria is among the back streets with its cafés and Roman ambience, whereas St. Mary's sits on a traffic island between the ceaseless streams of vehicles in the Strand. Despite such iniquities the latter has a most impressive hidden secret. Gibbs' interior, with its lavish ceiling and pure Italian sanctuary, was inspired by Santi Apostoli near the Piazza Venezia (Fontana) and Santi Luca e Martina in the Forum beside the Capitol Hill (Cortona).

Santa Maria della Pace (1656-67) with cloisters
The façade by Pietro da Cortona inspired St. Paul's, Deptford and other London churches.

In addition to these professionals there were several "gentleman architects" and with regards to the Commission the most prominent was Thomas Archer. After attending Trinity, Oxford he received training on the Continent in 1691-93, and in particular was influenced by Baroque designers Gian Bernini and Francesco Borromini from earlier that century. Upon returning home, his position as an M.P. and Tory courtier benefited him and he initially worked on Chatsworth House begun by William Talman in 1687.

He then collaborated with the Duke of Devonshire to design the north and west fronts in 1705, and in this respect was inspired by the façades of the Villa Farnese by Vignola, the Villa Aldobrandini by della Porta and the Villa Torlonia (Frascati) with its dramatic fountains by Carlo Maderno. All of these were situated within a short distance of Rome and were transitional from the Mannerist phase into the full blown Baroque.

Following on from this experience, Archer designed the blueprints for St. John's, Smith Square and St. Paul's, Deptford, even though Gibbs was one of the chief surveyors. At the latter he produced a Baroque masterpiece in complete contrast with the mediaeval church of St. Nicholas. However, at both of these edifices he crowned the composition with spires and towers - an architectural feature rarely observed in Rome.

With regard to St. Paul's the shape and scale of the interior was reminiscent of Palladio's Il Redentore opposite to the Grand Canal in Venice, whereas the semi-circular porch had for its model Santa Maria della Pace by Cortona - located near the Piazza Navona en route to the Vatican. In fact, the two settings were totally contrary. St. Paul's was in a spacious churchyard but Santa Maria backed onto a cloister designed by Bramante.

The London church was a great architectural success for Archer who described it as, "A theatre for the Anglican liturgy." Such schemes were re-created in a neo-Classical form by John Nash at All Souls and Robert Smirke at Bryanston Square, whilst at the same time Richard Boyle, 3rd Earl of Burlington earned a reputation as *The Architect Earl*.

Boyle spent an extended period on the Continent in 1714-19 and never made notes or sketches, but relied on the writings of Palladio, Scamozzi and drawings from John Webb a student of Inigo Jones. He became inspired by the purer forms of this earlier style and while working on the courtyard of Burlington House, Piccadilly, he dismissed James Gibbs and instead employed Colen Campbell and William Kent. Likewise his main assistant was Henry Flitctoft. As a result he ushered in a Palladian revival designing Chiswick House Villa and Horace Walpole dubbed him - *The Apollo of the Arts.*

However, the Baroque was not dead and Nicholas Hawksmoor took the work of both Vanbrugh and Wren to a new level, both in terms of sheer parish scale and the limits of the style. His grand edifices St. Anne's, Limehouse and St. George in the East were unforgettable additions to the East End landscape, with monumental towers and façades, and St. Mary Woolnoth in the City was quite different to any designed by Wren. But it was his other creations that gave the greatest insight into the ancient world.

Collaborating with John James at St. Luke's, Old Street and St. John's Horsleydown he introduced soaring obelisks, a most distinctive feature standing in for the Anglican spire. Clearly these looked back to ancient Egypt and several adorned the squares of Rome, brought there by various emperors viz. Piazza di San Giovanni in Laterano 15th century B.C., the Piazza Montecitorio 6th century B.C., and the Piazza del Popolo an obelisk of Rameses II which initially stood in the Circus Maximus. [1]

Regarding his other creations - St. George's, Bloomsbury had a classical portico based on the Temple of Jupiter at Baalbek, Lebanon and a tower similar to the Mausoleum at Halicarnassus; whereas Christchurch, Spitalfields with its emphatic and almost top heavy spire was a clear replica of Diocletian's Palace at Spalatro (Split). In the latter example he was most inventive since he copied an internal element for his exterior, while the palace itself only came to general knowledge under Robert Adam in 1764.

Il Redentore, Venice

This regal composition was designed by Andrea Palladio in 1577-92 and had a single grand nave. The drama of its location and the scale were then re-created at St. Paul's, Deptford in London.

---

[1] Such a trend continued and the ruler of Egypt donated one of Rameses II from Luxor for the Place de la Concorde, Paris, in 1833. Another from Heliopolis was presented in honour of the Battle of the Nile, but remained in Alexandria and only came to the Embankment in 1877-78. In addition a second obelisk from Heliopolis was obtained for Central Park at this time.

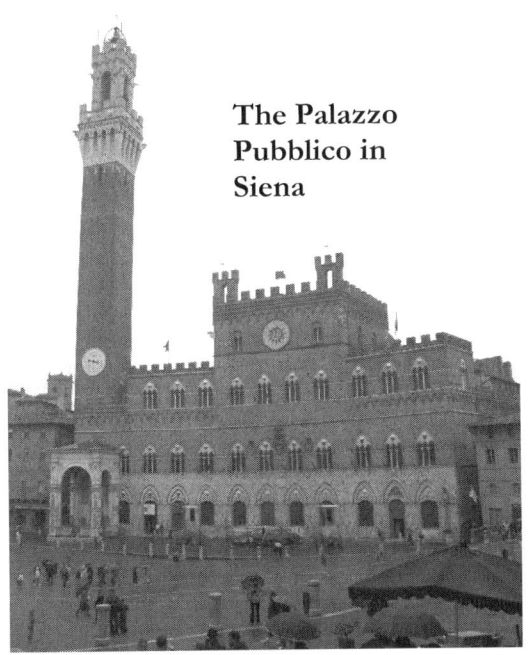

The Palazzo Pubblico in Siena

San Marco, Venice which gave inspiration with the tower at Siena for Westminster Cathedral.

The Earl of Burlington (1694-1753) re-introduced the Palladian style to London.

Once the commissioners had drawn up their purse strings there was no diminution in the desire to replicate the Classical genre. Although in the Georgian period, the dominant aesthetic moved away from the Baroque to the more simplistic neo-Classical style. One of the principal exponents was Thomas Hardwick who studied under William Chambers at the Royal Academy Schools. He then journeyed to Europe in 1776 and spent two years living in Naples and Rome, whilst he travelled around with his old classmate John Soane and then designed several churches - in particular St. Marylebone.

However, tastes were changing by the 19th century and the last flourish of 300 years of Renaissance style involved the Greek Revival, with some of the best examples done by William Inwood and his son Henry. The latter explored Italy and Greece in 1818-19, but unlike his predecessors was drawn towards the ancient architecture of Athens, and wrote essays about the remains and methodologies he observed there.

This was then transferred into solid form at St. Pancras, Euston Road where they built a parish church with a grand Ionic portico, and steeple based on the Tower of the Winds in the Roman agora. In particular the side porches, although differing in scale, were fine representations of the Temple of the Erectheum next to the Parthenon. Such inspiration was also used for All Saints, Camden Town but with a semi-circular portico.

There was a long relationship between the modern architect and classical world starting with Covent Garden similar to the Piazza San Marco, the Baroque of the Wren churches, the Monument based on Trajan's Column, right down to the revivals of the 18th century. Another example was the Marble Arch by Nash a replica of the Arch of Constantine by the Forum, but there was soon to be a decided change in fashion.

Horace Walpole who so admired the Earl of Burlington was a forerunner of a return to the Gothic with Strawberry Hill, Twickenham and James Wyatt used it for country houses, then it was introduced to churches in the 1820s. James Savage built St. Luke's, Chelsea with flying buttresses and soaring arcades, but was equally ok with the classical lines of St. James's, Bermondsey; whereas Ambrose Poynter designed St. Katharine's, Regent's Park in the *Tudor Gothic* style but with a Palladian composition.

There was a desire to produce cathedrals and parish churches with traditional values through design, and Augustus Pugin led the way with his works *Contrasts* and *Principles of Pointed Architecture* which promoted the style. This was combined with a return to ritual in worship and a number of architects embraced the High Church movement.

The Catholic Church also provided good examples and Brompton Oratory was like the titular churches of Rome with a two-tier façade, while St. George's, Southwark by Pugin was a superb tribute to the Gothic masons of old. However, the apex was Westminster Cathedral with its vast Byzantine space reminiscent of Hagia Sophia and San Marco, and tower that compared to the Palazzo Pubblico in the Piazza del Campo, Siena.

These designs be they Palladian, Baroque, neo-Classical or Gothic Revival were proved and tested yet are less common in the modern era of Foster and Piano. But on occasion old and new are combined to good effect such as the *Great Court* at the British Museum, Temple Bar in Paternoster Square, the *Millennium Project* at Southwark Cathedral and a scheme for Budge Row incorporating the Temple of Mithras.

Attempts to surpass the ancient styles, which many believed were harmonious with the aims of God, may ultimately prove unsatisfactory and ephemeral. Indeed they have been repeated many times over at St. Paul's, the Wren churches, in the East and West Ends and the suburbs beyond. The Classical with its perfect dimensions combined with soaring Gothic architecture in London as nowhere else, ensuring the capital maintained a stature equal to the Seven Hills of Rome right up to the present day.

The Arch of Constantine

Next to the Colosseum in Rome this was the model for Nash's Marble Arch in London. But it was built some 1,500 years earlier.

Bibliography, Sources

GENERAL RESEARCH

The Metropolitan Archives, Northampton Road, Clerkenwell
Guildhall Library and Map Room, Aldermanbury, London
(The City parish registers are now at the Metropolitan Archives)

London's Churches, Hibbert, Christopher (Queen Anne Press 1988)
A Guide to London Churches, Blatch M. (Constable 1995)
London: The City Churches, Bradley S. & Pevsner N. (Penguin 1998)
"Wren" by Whinney, Margaret (Thames & Hudson 1971/87)
London River, Weightman, Gavin (Collins & Brown 1990)
City of London Book, Tames R. (Historical Publications 2006)

Burke's Gentry Baronetcy & Peerage; Butterworth's Business Biography; Crockford's
Clerical Directory; Hart's Army Lists; Law Society Records; National Biography; Navy
Lists; Oxford and Cambridge Alumni; Who's Who

I.G.I., Free B.M.D., G.R.O. online (cert.), P.R.O. census-wills
Street Directories (various), Wikipedia, church websites

SPECIFIC RESEARCH

A Survey of London in 1598, Stow, John (Sutton Publishing Ltd. 2005)

John Strype Survey of London & Westminster 1708
(The book uses material taken from the earlier survey of John Stow)
Ref. the Stuart London Project, University of Sheffield (online)

John Rocque, Map of London 1746 (online ref. MOTCO)
Historical Map of London by Stanford 1862 (ref. mappalondon)

The Diary of Samuel Pepys 1660, Latham R. & Matthews W. (G. Bell 1974)
Commission for 50 new churches, Minute Books 1711-27 - British History Online
reference the London Record Society compiled by M.H. Port (1986)

Individual Churches from Stow, Strype, church pamphlets/sites, Wikipedia
"Hogarth," Paulson R. (Lutterworth Press 1991) ref. his baptism
The Short Life & Long Times of Mrs. Beeton, Hughes K. (Harper's 2006)

Research in the field: Florence, Rome, Venice, Vicenza and Antwerp

PHOTOGRAPHS

All church drawings and photographs are by J.B. Smart, whilst any other pictures are out of copyright and fall in the public domain due to their age and description as such. The images of city gates were made available by the University of Toronto.

Drawings - St. Mary Aldermanbury, St. Mildred's Poultry, All Hallows & St. Mildred's (interior) Bread Street, St. Gregory's, Christchurch (interior), St. Mary Magdalen Old Fish Street., St. Michael's Queenhithe, All Hallows Great, St. Swithin's London Stone, St Benet Fink, All Hallows by London Wall, St. Martin Outwich, St. Peter le Poer, St. Dionis Backchurch and St. Katharine Coleman.

Source: St. Mildred int. by E.J. Farmer, St. Gregory ruin T. Wyck ref. Bodleian and Christchurch Comm. Historical Monuments from "Wren;" All Hallows "London City Churches" and St. Katharine re. Nat. Monuments "Guide to London Churches."

Churches Index

CHURCHES FOREIGN

General Index

Blythe Smart Publications